THIS NATION UNDER GOD

Church, State and Schools in America

JOSEPH F. COSTANZO S.J.

HERDER AND HERDER

1964
HERDER AND HERDER   NEW YORK
232 Madison Avenue, New York 16, N.Y.

Imprimi potest: John J. McGinty S.J.
                  Praep. Prov. Neo Eboracensis
Nihil obstat: Brendan Lawlor
                  Censor Deputatus
Imprimatur: †Robert F. Joyce
                  Bishop of Burlington
                  December 13, 1963

Library of Congress Catalog Card Number: 64–13685
© 1964 by Herder and Herder, Incorporated
Printed in the United States of America

IN MEMORY OF MY
MOTHER AND FATHER

CONTENTS

Foreword 9
Introduction 17

Part One   Religious Liberty in Education 23
1   The Religious Heritage of American
    Democracy 24
2   Thomas Jefferson, Religious Education and
    Public Law 49
3   Religion in Public School Education 88
4   Prayer in Public Schools 117

Part Two   Federal Aid to Education 157
5   Federal Aid to Education and Religious
    Liberty 158
6   The Administration's Memorandum on Aid
    to Education 223
7   Religious Schools and Secular Subjects 285
8   This Nation Under God 369

Appendixes 401
    Note 402
1   Academic Freedom and the Catholic
    Intellectual 407
2   The Divided Allegiance of the Catholic 426

Table of Legal Cases 445
Index 447

FOREWORD

On Dec. 16, 1963 the President of the United States signed the College Academic Facilities Act. The preamble of this statute could well serve as an introduction to Father Costanzo's book:

The Congress hereby finds that the security and welfare of the United States require that this and future generations of American youth be assured ample opportunity for the fullest development of their intellectual capacities, and that this opportunity will be jeopardized unless the Nation's colleges and universities are encouraged and assisted in their efforts to accommodate rapidly growing numbers of youth who aspire to a higher education. The Congress further finds and declares that this need is so great that it is incumbent upon the Nation to take positive and immediate action to meet it through assistance to institutions of higher education. . . .

By this legislation Congress provides grants to institutions of higher education, public and private, church connected or not, for the construction of academic facilities to be used "for instruction or research in the natural or physical sciences or engineering or for use as a library;" . . . "to assist institutions of higher education to improve existing graduate schools and cooperative graduate centers, and to assist in the establishment of graduate schools and cooperative graduate centers of excellence." Congress also makes provision for loans to "institutions of higher education or to higher education building agencies" church connected or

9

not, for the construction of academic facilities, excluding "any facility used or to be used for sectarian instruction or as a place for religious worship. . . ."

Congress and the President of the United States, constitutionally bound by oath of office to make no law "respecting an establishment of religion," have thus, in providing important federal aid—available alike to qualified public and to church controlled colleges and universities—given a demonstration that they did not consider this action violative of the First Amendment. The College Academic Facilities Act of 1963 became a law after Father Costanzo's book was already in type. The new act points up the constitutional questions of wide importance which form the subject of his new work.

Anyone who studies the operation of our federal Constitution must be struck by the continual necessity of reconciling antithetical urges in our government. We are deeply committed at once to majoritarianism and to justice in government; yet we acknowledge that justice is not necessarily determined by the most numerous or the loudest voices. We place scrupulous limitations on the power of the government to impose criminal sanctions on the citizen; at the same time we recognize that a society without order would be one with "no Knowledge of the fact of the Earth; no account of Time; no Arts; no Letters; no Society; and which is worst of all, continuall feare, and danger of violent death; And the life of man, solitary, poore, nasty, brutish, and short."

In our constitutional text we delegate to our central government control over only a limited category of subjects; yet we perceive that our national society has become so closely knit that federal control must extend to some aspects of almost all governmental activities. In the presence of

10

each of these pairs of opposing aspirations, some reconciliation, some mutual accommodation has been necessary.

So too in the relation of religion to nation and state there are inconsistent aspirations. The First Amendment and, as the Supreme Court has told us, its analogue implicit in the Fourteenth, undertake a dissociation of government and any "establishment of religion;" yet as the preambles of our state constitutions suggest, and as the Supreme Court of the United States, speaking through Justice Douglas in 1952, wrote:

> We are a religious people whose institutions presuppose a Supreme Being. We guarantee the freedom to worship as one chooses. We make room for as wide a variety of beliefs and creeds as the spiritual needs of man deem necessary. We sponsor an attitude on the part of government that shows no partiality to any one group and that lets each flourish according to the zeal of its adherents and the appeal of its dogma. When the state encourages religious instruction or cooperates with religious authorities by adjusting the schedule of public events to sectarian needs, it follows the best of our traditions. For it then respects the religious nature of our people and accommodates the public service to their spiritual needs. To hold that it may not would be to find in the Constitution a requirement that the government show a callous indifference to religious groups. That would be preferring those who believe in no religion over those who do believe.

The reconciling of these two has not produced, and probably could not produce a clear, consistent, logical line of demarcation. We have long since been shown that the life of the law is not logic but experience.

Father Costanzo in the first part of his book explores the decisions of the Supreme Court of the United States, in which that tribunal has held religious instruction, prayer and Bible reading as classroom exercises to be forbidden in the public schools of the several states. But, as he points

11

out, our commitment to education for all still contemplates utilization of private education agencies, many of which are associated with churches and include religious exercises as part of their daily programs. Nation and the states give various sorts of aid to church connected education. Such aid is not immediately religious in motivation; nevertheless by aid to the church connected school or college in lay matters, indirectly the public gives some support to religious orientation. Thus the national School Lunch Act nourishes small children in parochial and public schools alike; states may protect children from harm in street traffic by transporting them at public expense to both public and parochial schools; the Supreme Court has held that a state may, within the bounds of the Fourteenth Amendment, distribute lay textbooks to students equally in public and parochial schools.

There remains unresolved by the Supreme Court the question, frequently asked in discussion, as to the point at which such nonreligious public subventions become so closely knit with religious activity that the First Amendment forbids Congress, and the Fourteenth forbids the states, to grant them to church connected schools and colleges. Father Costanzo points out that Thomas Jefferson, ardent champion of religious freedom, advocated that professors of divinity, not maintained at state expense, still have access to the facilities for instruction at the University of Virginia. The author has analyzed with care memoranda of the Department of Health, Education and Welfare dated March 1961, which marshaled the arguments tending to demonstrate that some aid to church connected schools below the college grade is constitutionally proscribed, whereas the same aid on the college level is permissible. Father Costanzo does not hesitate to make evident the

12

tendency of his own views, which incline toward a comparatively broader power of federal and state aid; but a reader, not of his church, will nevertheless admire the fairness with which Father Costanzo discusses the views of those in government and out who do not agree with him. And indeed one such reader finds difficulty in perceiving a clear line of constitutional cleavage between governmental aid to, say, first year instruction in a junior college and similar aid to, say, fourth year instruction in a high school. Perhaps nowhere in the literature of constitutional controversy is the distinction between constitutionality and congressional policy so often confused. Father Costanzo clearly makes this differentiation. He would put the responsibility for broad choice in policy on the elected representatives of the people in nation and state, rather than relying on the judiciary to make distinctions, based on historic experience though they be, but not explicit in the words of the Constitution.

Rational continuance of a democratic society can only thrive in an atmosphere of good humored and mutual self-respect, despite differing points of view. Father Costanzo's book is an admirable example. He writes calmly of matters which evoke much emotion; he presents his thesis with dignity, restraint and a courtesy not always evident in the literature of tense differences. For this all readers of good will can be justly indebted.

ARTHUR E. SUTHERLAND

Cambridge, Massachusetts

THIS NATION UNDER GOD

Which Way Neutrality: Abstention or Impartiality?

In the last few decades two religio-educational controversies have firmly occupied the forum of national debate and are not to be obscured by other momentous domestic and international issues. They are the place and role of religion in public schools and the inclusion of parochial schools in a general federal aid program to education. Both of these problematics pose difficulties which are unique to each.

For example, the greater part of the American community would seem to want a place for religion in our public schools. It is the precise function and the manner of incorporating religion in public education that raise the many questions. Obviously the right to an inviolable religious conscience in public schooling ought not to be contested. On the other hand, there is an equally strong claim of religious liberty in education which parents who send their children to state schools insist on exercising for the educational benefit of their youngsters. How to satisfy both the consentients and the dissidents constitutes a most challenging enterprise for educators, jurists, public officials and the parents. It simply will not do to reduce all religions to a common denominator and it is even less acceptable

17

to intermingle some religion of sorts with education for the construction of a sociological-cultural-what-you-will science of enlightened civics. To teach about religion in precollegiate schooling may raise more difficulties than solutions to the problem. As for formal religious instructions and exercises, Supreme Court rulings are in the process of fashioning a principle of neutrality which at the present seems to travel the road of abstention for the sake of the complainant rather than the road of impartiality which offered more positive prospects of solution in the Zorach decision.

I have addressed myself to both problems of public schooling, the place and precise function of religion in tax supported education and to what I still think is constitutionally permissible on certain forms of religious exercises. My reflections are guided for the most part by two controlling perspectives. One, I am firm in the belief that our public schools have the task and responsibility of transmitting to each generation of school children the religious heritage of our country, as that heritage is authentically embodied in our basic national documents. This is not to be mistaken or confused for an elementary historical study of religious life and events in America. The religious heritage I speak of is the official and authoritative affirmation of the relevance of belief and dependence upon divine providence for the well being of our Republic which first found its classic expression in the Declaration of Independence and which has been repeatedly reaffirmed as the American proposition in countless ways in official state documents and proclamations by every branch of government. What Lincoln epitomized by his immortal words, "this nation under God," the sovereignty of God over civil corporate societies as well as over persons, the United States Supreme Court reaffirmed with a more precise sense of dependence:

18

"We are a religious people whose institutions presuppose a Supreme Being."

Here in the solemnity of the highest judicial review on the constitutionality of official actions and laws, the high tribunal was not simply observing that as a broad, undeniable historical fact the American people have been traditionally religious, God-fearing and God-loving men. Rather, it said with calculated particularity that the public institutions of the American Republic rested on religious belief in God. In 1961 the state of West Virginia adopted the following preamble to its Constitution:

Since through Divine Providence we enjoy the blessings of civil, political and religious liberty, we, the people of West Virginia, in and through the provisions of this constitution, reaffirm our faith in and constant reliance upon God and seek diligently to promote, preserve and perpetuate good government in the State of West Virginia for the common welfare, freedom and security of ourselves and our posterity (See 3 W. Va. Code 1, 1961).

The adoption of this preamble by the state of West Virginia brings to fifty the number of states who make the dependence of free public institutions and the security of liberties dependent upon belief in God. It is within the context of this theology of American polity that I attempt to define the place and function of religion in public schools (and, of course, *a fortiori*, in church-related schools). The second perspective within which I approach this problem is the religious liberty in education which I am persuaded parents of students at public schools have a right to exercise (as do the parents of parochial school children) but with full regard and careful consideration for the conditions that provide for the integrity of free choice in the midst of conflicting claims of conscience. If the right of parents to choose a school for their children is guaranteed by the

19

Constitution, then should not the lesser right to guide the education of one's children in a public school also be guaranteed?

When I turn to the question of federal aid to parochial schools I am confronted with an array of suppositions and presuppositions. I have found in current literature that where the argument of alleged unconstitutionality cannot withstand the reasoned judgments of eminent jurists, there is a retreat to a consideration of public policy. And there is precisely where the argument really belongs. I hold for the ultimate validity of the private school in our democracy and even more so of church-related schools. These parochial schools, I have every reason to believe, prepare their students for an active and dedicated exercise of their citizenship in our Republic. Further, they provide the moral and spiritual motivations for the exercise of the civic virtues which our free society requires for its preservation and enjoyment. They are and ought on every account to be acknowledged as a constituent part of our national education. Since the full impact of the debate on federal aid to parochial schools falls mainly upon Catholics who count the largest number of church-related schools it is less than fair that Catholics should have to bear the full burden for justifying in intelligible terms the vital role these schools play in our democratic society.

I had for sometime been puzzled by the way Thomas Jefferson was quoted aptly for opposing positions. Patient search and study of this voluminous correspondence disclosed that Jefferson was considerably far more interested and critical of other people's beliefs and religious practices than he himself disclaimed on occasion to be. I found that Jefferson was very much of a dogmatist in regard to the theological and philosophical propositions to which he adhered and the propositions which he rejected. I con-

20

cluded to a very remarkable facet of Jefferson's intellectual greatness. In his role of a public servant, he was uncompromising in his insistence upon the exercise of religious liberty—let us note—in tax-supported education for the very creeds for which in his private letters he expressed ridicule and aversion. This is one of the many spiritual qualities that mark out the grandeur of Jefferson as a statesman. He, too, like the members of the present Court, strove to mark out a road of neutrality but the more he thought of it the more it took on the aspects of impartiality, of positive accommodations, of the necessary place of religious beliefs in an education from which the civil community must derive benefit. This Jeffersonian attitude of mind on state, religion and schools might perhaps on repeated reflection suggest ways of concrete implementation of separation of church and state, of which he was equally an uncompromising advocate, that would tend to construct a formula of neutrality in terms of impartiality and equal protection of laws rather than a governmental position of abstention. When does neutrality, a perfectly acceptable word but unfortunately capable of ambiguous content, not infringe upon the religious rights of consentients? When the dissident nonbeliever demands from the courts that the educational process be so insulated from religious values and references so as to accord fully with his conscience, does he not bring about an establishment of his ultimates or relativities or absolutes which the believers in God find offensive to their consciences?

It seems paradoxical that the absence of the complex difficulties inherent in the religious pluralism of public schools should be turned upside down against church-related schools for being singularly free of conflicting and contending claims of conscience, and constructing in turn an ominous argument of establishment that threatens all

21

sorts of dangers to our Republic. The time has come for the United States Congress to make a full and complete evaluation of the parochial schools and ascertain to its satisfaction whether or not they are part of national education and beneficial to our democratic institutions.

I have spoken of the array of suppositions and presuppositions with which a Catholic must contend when he engages in a discussion about parochial schools. Somewhere along the lines of many arguments, seemingly endless and repetitious, is the hard core that endures when other objections are met, namely, that potentially, Catholics, by reason of their faith and obedience to the papacy, remain a divisive force and may even someday pose a real threat to our constitutional form of government. Or, in other words, intellectually and spiritually, Catholics by faith and education are authoritarian in their make-up. Here the parochial schools, so necessary, as any Catholic ecclesiastical superior will insist, to the preservation of the faith and Catholic way of life, are latched on to the direction of the argument. Parochial schools, for all their evident dedication to America, are not really the same instrumentalities as the public schools for preparing the future citizens of a democracy. The argument is an old and tired one but it is not easily downed. For this reason I have thought it not inappropriate to include in this volume two essays on the allegiances and intellectual life of the Catholic.

One last note of explanation. The reader will find references to certain historical data, constitutional history, court decisions and legislative practices repeated throughout the book. The fullness of the argument seemed to require that this procedure be adopted in certain instances. Court opinions on state, religion and schools have found similar exercise of repetition appropriate and at times inevitable.

22

PART ONE
RELIGIOUS LIBERTY IN EDUCATION

1

The Religious Heritage of American Democracy

American political democracy was conceived and established within terms of a theology of politics. Throughout our national history this relevance has been consistently and authoritatively affirmed in numerous corporate and individual official acts of the three branches of our government. Further, this nexus has been predicated not only about the origins of our Republic but also for its survival and prosperity. To ignore or deny this relation is to separate in effect the superstructure from the foundation which sustains it and confers upon it its unique spiritual meaning.

Some prefatory remarks on the manner of conceiving the relationship of religion and polity in pagan and Christian societies will draw our perspective into focus. The Greek philosophers believed that the ideals and values of the City derived their validity from Platonic vision of the Exemplary Good, the heavenly *paradeigma* of the due order of being and truth. With Aristotle, the City was the embodiment of ethical purposes, the *politeia* a way of life, *ti biou*. But for want of an adequate metaphysics (there was the embarrassing impediment of a confounding array of mythological gods) pagan theology was at best the philosophers' order of suprasensibles, of first principles and of ulti-

24

mate origins of all that is as it is meant to be. Graeco-Roman statecraft was the constant endeavor to reconstruct in human affairs an abiding order of peace and justice in obedience to eternal laws.

With the advent of Christianity, man was supernaturally revealed as an image of divine personality endowed with authentic and transcendent purposes and accordingly invested with original responsibilities and connatural rights. As a consequence the prerogatives of the pagan state as the supreme moralizing force were radically undermined and the identity of the Ultimate Good with the common good of the City was canceled. The acknowledgment of a higher law, of which the State was no longer the oracle, and the revelation of the divine guarantee of eternal beatitude, liberated man from the self-enclosed system of nature of which he was wholly a part and the City his fulfillment. Man was freed from the Promethean struggle between the spiritual aspiration for liberty and the pagan cosmological necessitarianism.[1] The Christian martyrs, the Fathers of the Church and the Church apologetes brought the divine inheritance of man to bear upon the absolute Roman *imperium,* rendering it ministerial of justice in obedience to the fiduciary function of authority. It is to the credit of St. Augustine that he expressed in theological terms the metaphysical necessity for the consent of the governed, and to have brought out its new significance as a delimiting principle upon law and authority.

Consent as a practical source of power was recognized since the days of Solon. But the idea of proper and due relationship between government and governed necessarily presupposes the prior consideration of the specific equality of men in terms not only of the constitution and exigencies of man's nature but also in light of his transcendental

25

destiny. This more enlarged and definite view of man's essential nature is the metaphysical basis of the doctrine of inherent and inalienable rights which, because they are a divine investiture, render man inviolable (the connatural right of immunity from the arbitrary) and condition him to the use of consent. The basis of government derives not from consent alone, however, but from consent involving reservations of the law of human nature. By conjoining the doctrine of the divine origin and descent of authority to the doctrine of the equality of men, St. Augustine provided the initial premise for the development of constitutional limitation in medieval times—a limitation not merely of wrongdoing but as a limitation inherent in the power itself.

Christian doctrine fomented the transformation of political ideas and practices to the gradual evolution of a constitutionalism of medieval provenance. As the eminent Carlyle brothers abundantly documented in their monumental *History of Political Theory in the West,* this Christian tradition of law and government maintained that the immediate source of political authority is the community; that law and authority are both purposively ordained to the advantage of the governed conceived as justice and commonweal; that the contractual relation between ruler and ruled is reciprocally binding and its conditions mutually inviolable; and that the supremacy of law rests juridically, as Hincmar of Rheims pointed out, upon the consent of the governed.

The central truths which energized this historic process were the inviolability of human personality and its indestructible rights,[2] the equality of men in the divine adoption and the correlative doctrine of consent to governance, and the transtemporal value of human affairs. It was within

26

the context of this Christian tradition of the influence of religious truths upon law and government that the birth of the American Republic took place.

Religion is understood here as man's total ontological and moral dependency upon God, his Creator, and the divine-creature relations as the proper objects of intellection and assent, either through motivation of divine revelation or through the compelling persuasion of reason. To the Hebrew of the Old Testament, religion was God, the decalogue and the messianic promise. To the Christian religion is the fulfillment of the divinely inspired scriptural prophecies in the Incarnation. There is, in addition, a natural theology constructed by a rational analysis of the universe. Generally these believers are called theists rather than deists, for theists consent to the immortality of the soul and eternal reward by divine judgment, to God's special providence for man and to the efficacy of intercessory prayer.

Although our national history is rich in evidence that our political democracy was conceived in theological terms, not every American has posited religious beliefs as the spiritual wellspring of our democracy. Since the time of Washington there has been clear evidence of a secularist concept of our national experiment.[3] But this secular tradition is not the only American tradition. On the contrary, the religious tradition is the original and prevailing one; it is authentic in the very fiber of our body politic and as such constitutes the genuine American consensus. Such an admission must be made with as much compelling force as that with which a sojourner in the Soviet State, wholly unsympathetic to it, must allow that the Red State was conceived and founded on the dialectical materialism of Karl Marx. Nonbelievers were not the controlling promoters of American independence, nor were they the leading and responsible architects of the New Republic.

The historical record of our Colonial and Revolutionary periods—the Acts of the Continental Congress, the Declaration of Independence, the Northwest Ordinance, the Constitution, the *Federalist Papers*, the Bill of Rights, the long course of presidential utterances, Congressional acts, and declarations of our supreme judicature—constantly affirms that our American political democracy was conceived in and must survive on moral and religious foundations.

An inquiry into the original American consensus will indicate that during the "seedtime" of the Republic (1765–1776) the prevailing practice of the colonists was resort to a "higher law" in justification of their campaign of protest, resistance and revolt.

Clinton Rossiter writes[4] of the "habit, in which most colonists indulged to excess, of recurring to first principles." Rarely was a specific issue argued, he says:

. . . without first calling upon rules of justice that were considered to apply to all men everywhere. These rules, of course, were the ancient body of political assumptions known as natural law and natural rights. The great political philosophy of the Western world enjoyed one of its proudest seasons in this time of resistance and revolution . . . few people have made such effective use of recourse to first principles.

The Declaration of Independence was written, the Constitution adopted, and the Republic launched in an age when most men, whether subtle or simple, believed unequivocally in higher law, generally called the law of nature.

Exemplary illustrations of the polemic use of the natural law doctrine are James Otis' *Rights of the Colonists Asserted* (1764); John Dickinson's fourth *Letter to the Inhabitants of the British Colonies in America* (1774); and

28

James Wilson's *Considerations on the Nature and Extent of the Legislative Authority of the British Parliament* (1774). Whatever the variant versions of the ultimate source of natural law then extant—either the divine natural law or the secularized natural law of an indifferent deism, or the non-metaphysical, utilitarian, historically inductive law said to be "higher" because of a value proved constant by experience—the language of the theist prevailed in the Declaration of Independence.

The more we study the Declaration of Independence, the more we appreciate its profound theological and philosophical presuppositions. The Preamble is a public official confession of the all-inclusive comprehension of the divine moral order over the consciences and affairs of men and nations. Such a profession rests on truths declared to be self-evident, not because they are immediately or intuitively known, but because of the clarity of their evidential intelligibility. Realism engenders the certitude for the cause of freedom. Since realism was the source of personal liberty for the Founding Fathers, it was by the same token the only guaranty of social and political liberty. Political freedom does not ensue from doubts, conjectures or empirical hypotheses, but from philosophical certitude. "We hold these truths to be self-evident" will equate by the conclusion of the argument "the truth has made us free."

The Declaration then pronounces the theological major in justification of the revolutionary cause. It neither vaguely asserts that "all men are equal" nor affirms the equality of men by the mere fact of birth. Rather, it specifies the equality of men which is ensured unfailingly and immutably by divine creative action. Men are equal by reason of their relationship to God. Human nature is divinely endowed with rights which, because of their connatural inherence, fore-

29

close all alienability whatsoever to any superior temporal force or power. Those persons who read any utilitarian ideas into the phrase, "life, liberty, and the pursuit of happiness," should carefully regard James Madison's reflections on this very point. Writing to James Monroe, he observed:

> There is no maxim, in my opinion, which is more liable to be misapplied, and which, therefore, more needs elucidation, than the current one, that the interest of the majority is the political standard of right and wrong. Taking the word "interest" as synonymous with "ultimate happiness," in which sense it is qualified with every necessary moral ingredient, the proposition is no doubt true. But taking it in the popular sense as referring to immediate augmentation of property and wealth nothing could be more false. In the latter, it would be the interest of the majority in every community to despoil and enslave the minority of individuals.[5]

It was precisely on this basis of interest as "qualified with every necessary moral ingredient" that, two years before the Declaration, John Dickinson and James Wilson understood "ultimate happiness" to be the principle of reconciliation between English rule and colonial claims. Because of his inherent obligation in natural law to pursue his ultimate happiness, man has an inalienable right to all necessary means of attaining this end. Hence the profound significance in the illation "that to secure these rights, governments are instituted among men." The origin of politics is situated four-square in the theology of man. Governments are established primarily to secure, not grant such divinely endowed rights which protect the inviolability of the human personality and accordingly define the purposive direction of public authority.

The all-comprehensive divine moral order completes its arch in the Declaration when it asserts that the powers that derive from the consent of the governed must be just. As indicated above, consent as a practical source of power was recognized as far back as the days of Solon. But the subjection of popular consent to a higher law dates with the Christian revelation that "all power is from God." Unjust laws are not properly laws, arbitrary government is tyranny, unconstitutional exercise of power is usurpation. The unrestricted sovereignty which the colonials rejected in the British rule they would also reject for themselves in the guise of popular sovereignty. *Vox populi, vox Dei*—the absolutizing of popular sovereignty—was not part of the early American consensus. The people were collectively as well as individually dependent upon God and therefore considered themselves only as a second cause, never as the ultimate original source of all power. Even in the limited sphere of their own sovereignty they were sovereign only in a derivative, secondary sense. Man was never absolutely sovereign.

As a minor to the theological-moral premise, the Declaration catalogues repeated abuses and usurpations by reason of which both the natural law and the law of Englishmen justify in conscience not only the right but also the duty—such as obtains whenever any form of government becomes destructive of its proper ends—to institute a new government.

The revolutionary argument implicitly states that from the rights of God over men shall man better understand his own rights. There is Jefferson's own testimony that the Declaration is the embodiment of the original American consensus. Fifty years after the event, in a letter to Henry Lee, he wrote:

With respect to our rights, and the acts of the British government contravening those rights, there was but one opinion on this side of the water. All American Whigs thought alike on these subjects.

31

When forced, therefore, to resort to arms for redress, an appeal to the tribunal of the world was deemed proper for our justification. This was the object of the Declaration of Independence. Not to find out new principles, or new arguments, never before thought of, not merely to say things which had never been said before; but to place before mankind the common sense of the subject, in terms so plain and firm as to command their assent, and to justify ourselves in the independent stand we are compelled to take. Neither aiming at originality of principle or sentiment, nor yet copied from any particular or previous writing, it was intended to be the expression of the American mind, and to give to that expression the proper tone and spirit called for it by the occasion. All its authority rests then on the harmonizing sentiments of the day, whether expressed in conversation, in letters, in printed essays, or in the elementary books of public right, as Aristotle, Cicero, Locke, Sidney, etc.[6]

The historical explanation for popular concordance on the theological-moral presuppositions of the birth of the American nation lies in the fact that the experiment took place wholly within the broad Christian tradition of the divine natural law doctrine which had coursed its way from medieval Christendom through English Common Law and Whiggism to the new land.

Unlike the artificial theories of the eighteenth century and the French Enlightenment which deformed rather than illustrated the natural law, the Declaration conceived natural law as being wholly operative in human affairs because it ensues from the Divine Author whose sovereignty is complete over nations as well as individuals. There is no secularized substitute for the God-centered authority for law and government—hence the correct distinction and necessary relation in the Declaration between the law of nature and human positive law. In the events leading up to the Revolution and in the theological preamble of the Declaration, the appeal is made first to the rights of Englishmen and,

32

this failing, then to God's law, since in divine natural law the colonists had a right to their positive legal claims. This polarity of natural and human law was the very point made by Edmund Burke as he espoused the American cause, much to the dismay of the New Whigs who a decade-and-a-half later accused him of inconsistency. They failed to appreciate the radical difference between the American and French revolutions, between real and abstract rights. In his speech, *Conciliation,* Burke summed up the colonists' rightful claim to separation when he said that they were "not only devoted to liberty, but to liberty according to English ideas, and English principles. Abstract liberty like other mere abstractions is not to be found. Liberty inheres in some sensible object."[7]

The Declaration is hardly the instant creation of idealistic revolutionary leaders. But it is the most remarkable epitome of the theology of politics ever proclaimed within the concrete context of American history, and the most fruitful application of the theological convictions of the prevailing colonial mind to its cause. The year before the Declaration was written, the Continental Congress, fully aware of the choice it had to make between peace and war, made a public confession of total dependence upon divine providence, of the necessity of adoration, of intercessory prayer, of the confession and forgiveness of sins, and appointed July 20, 1775, as a "day of public humiliation, fasting, and prayer for preserving the union and securing just rights and privileges of the Colonies, that virtue and true religion may revive and flourish throughout our land; and that America may soon behold the gracious interposition of heaven for the redress of her many grievances, for the restoration of her invaded rights, for a reconciliation with the Parent State on terms constitutional and honorable to

33

both; and that her civil and religious privileges may be secured to the latest posterity."[8]

The proclamation of June 12, 1775, one of four fast-day proclamations of the Continental Congress prior to its first thanksgiving, had as its purpose the strengthening of the religious foundations of the colonial union as it was being molded into a nation. It coupled, with marked significance, a number of civil and religious privileges. The Northwest Ordinance of 1787 enacted by the last Congress of the Confederation reaffirms that "religion, morality, and knowledge, being necessary to good government and the happiness of mankind, schools and the means of education shall forever be encouraged."

The language of the offical corporate proclamations of the Founding Fathers is unmistakably that of traditional Christianity. Of the Thanksgiving Day proclamations, the 1777 enactment of the Continental Congress is strikingly unusual for its Trinitarian confession. In later federal and state proclamations, this confession was generally omitted with the obvious intention of pertaining equally to all believers. Such a deliberate change was in line with the consensus to band together all theists in spiritual support of American polity.

Wholly in accord with this original corporate and official profession of the religious foundations of American democracy are the individual official pronouncements of the highest government officers from the very beginnings of the Republic. To discount the long tradition of presidential utterances, especially the presidential Thanksgiving Day proclamations, as expedient and pious exhortations is to testify to the strength of the American consensus that the nation's religious foundations must be officially acknowledged and promoted.

34

The inaugural addresses, messages to Congress, the proc-lamations on Thanksgiving Days by the chief executives—from the first president to our own day—have all set an incontrovertible historical record of the religious presup-positions of our national existence and endurance. In his memorable Farewell Address, Washington pointedly warned against the deceptive insufficiency of a laic morality: "Of all the dispositions and habits which lead to political pros-perity, religion and morality are indispensable supports . . . And let us with caution indulge the supposition that morality can be maintained without religion."[9]

In his First Inaugural Address on March 4, 1797, John Adams gave similar vigorous expression when he listed the qualifications for the executive office:

> . . . a love of science and letters and a wish to patronize every rational effort to encourage schools, colleges, universities, academies, and every institution for propagating knowledge, virtue, and religion among all classes of people, not only for their benign influence on the happiness of life in all its stages and classes, and society in all its forms, *but as the only means of preserving our Constitution from its natural enemies* . . .[10]

Perhaps the most characteristically Christian and strik-ingly supernatural presidential utterance is John Adams' first Proclamation of Thanksgiving Day on March 23, 1798:

> As the safety and prosperity of nations ultimately and essentially depend on the protection and the blessing of Almighty God, and the national acknowledgement of this truth is not only an indispen-sable duty which the people owe to Him, but a duty whose natural influence is favorable to the promotion of that morality and piety without which social happiness cannot exist nor the blessings of a free government be enjoyed; and as this duty, at all times incumbent, is so especially in seasons of difficulty or of danger . . . I do hereby recommend that . . . 9 day of May . . . be observed throughout the United States as a day of solemn humiliation, fasting, and

35

prayer; . . . to the Father of Mercies . . . that all religious con-
gregations do . . . acknowledge before God the manifold sins and
transgressions with which we are justly chargeable as individuals and
as a nation, beseeching Him . . . through the Redeemer of the
World, freely to remit all our offenses, and to incline us by His Holy
Spirit so that sincere repentence and reformation . . . that our *civil
and religious* privileges may be preserved inviolate and perpetuated
to the latest generations . . . that the principles of genuine piety and
sound morality may influence the minds and govern the lives of
every description of our citizens, and that the blessings of peace,
freedom and pure religion may be speedily extended to all nations
of the earth.[11]

This presidential expression clearly authenticates the
original American consensus that the social happiness and
civil and religious liberties of free government are derived
from divine natural law. Both Washington and Adams
sharply rejected the alien importation of Jacobin atheism
in the guise either of French revolutionary totalitarian democracy or of Napoleonic supreme sovereignty. On March
6, 1799, President Adams warned of the subversive dangers
of religious neutrality and repeated his earlier insistence on
the nation's acknowledgment that it is a society dependent
upon God:

. . . the most precious interests of the people of the United States
are still held in jeopardy by the hostile designs and insidious acts of
a foreign nation, as well as by the dissemination among them of
those principles, subversive of the foundations of all religious, moral
and social obligations, that have produced incalculable mischief and
misery in other countries.[12]

Clearly in our earliest history as a new republic secularism
was officially declared alien to the American religious affirmation and inimical to it. Lincoln's phrase, "this nation
under God," gives focal point to the prevailing American
tradition. In recent times, Presidents Roosevelt, Truman

36

and Eisenhower have voiced this tradition as the authentic American affirmation. An illustration of President Roosevelt's witness occurred Jan. 4, 1939, when he personally gave his Annual Message to Congress. He identified the "ancient" American faith with the one prevailing "now as always:"

Storms from abroad directly challenge three institutions indispensable to Americans, now as always. The first is religion. It is the source of the other two—democracy and international good faith. Religion, by teaching man his relationship to God, gives the individual a sense of his own dignity and teaches him to respect himself by respecting his neighbors . . .

In a modern civilization, all three—religion, democracy, and international good faith—complement and support each other. Where freedom of religion has been attacked, the attack has come from sources opposed to democracy. Where democracy has been overthrown, the spirit of free worship has disappeared. And where religion and democracy have vanished, good faith and reason in international affairs have given way to strident ambition and brute force.

An ordering society which relegates religion, democracy and good faith among nations to the background can find no place within it for the ideals of the Prince of Peace. The United States rejects such an ordering, and retains its ancient faith.[13]

The protestations of the secularist, or neutralist, through the course of our national history have never been an authentic part of America's religious and political heritage. The secularist is not giving witness to the original and prevailing American affirmation. In a distinctly nonprophetic sense, his is the voice crying in the wilderness. It is the voice of dissent, a protest against our "ancient faith" prevailing "now as always."

That our nation was conceived under God, with a religious view of human rights and the purpose of government, is abundantly evident in our early national history and in the vigorous tradition carried on by every incumbent of the presidential office. But in what manner did the religious conception of government enter into the very fabric of our federal government, that is to say, into the Federal Constitution? By presupposing the sound doctrine of the distinction between and necessary relation of human positive law and divine natural law as expressed in the declaration, the Founding Fathers drew up the Constitution, as a juridical document, as a superstructure built upon this dual foundation and, as such, did not need to affirm it explicitly.

It is noteworthy that the very men who guided the colonists to independence within the Christian tradition of natural law doctrine were generally those same men who either participated in the momentous discussions of the Federal Convention or helped advance the ratification of the Constitution in their several states.

First of all, the procedure adopted for the ratification of the Constitution conformed to every ethical requirement of the natural law. In *McCulloch v. Maryland* Chief Justice John Marshall took judicial notice of the regard due the "consent of the governed" in the construction of a new federal government directly binding upon individuals as well as states. Among other things he recounted the mode of procedure adopted by the convention which framed the Constitution and by the Congress which submitted it, upon recommendation of the Federal Convention, to the states for acceptance. The conventions in each state were chosen by the people thereof. Chief Justice Marshall also noted the juridical binding effect of popular determination upon the state sovereignties as well as upon the people of the new United States. The federal government truly proceeds directly from the people, deriving its powers from them. And only rarely in history has the principle of the "consent of the governed" been observed with such scrupulous care as in the ratification of the Constitution.

Secondly, American sovereignty is not that of totalitarian democracy, nor the unrestricted sovereignty espoused in Rousseau's *Contrat Social* which, instead of presupposing natural law, holds itself to be the original source of morality. The right of the people to choose their own form of government must necessarily presuppose the major premise in natural law that civil government is requisite to "life, liberty and the pursuit of happiness." A government of limited powers specified in a written constitution is wholly in accord with the sovereignty of God over states as well as over individual persons. Plenary but not absolute, derivative and not original, American popular sovereignty is under God, from whom all power descends. It does not, as with Rousseau, reside ultimately and inalienably in the people.

Thirdly, in the institutional structure of the Constitution—e.g., the distribution and balance of empowerments in the delegation of limited and enumerated powers—there are provisions for the security and restraint of the supremacy of the rule of law over the rule of men. The supreme judicature is also prepared to arrest ventures beyond the prescribed limits. Tyrannical exercise of power or the usurpation of power itself is therefore doubly restricted both by supremacy of law and adequate institutional safeguards.

Fourthly, American supremacy of law is neither legal autocracy nor mere legal process; it is medial for the prosecution of substantive civil goods. American political democracy has a substantive content as well as a procedural course. The Preamble proclaims the purpose of the founding of the federal government to be the "establishment of justice, the promotion of the General Welfare, and the

39

blessings of Liberty." Substantive ethical goods are those rights and purposes of the law of human nature which have been historically and juridically secured even beyond human disowning. For the medievalist Bracton's dictum, *sub Deo et lege,* operated to the gradual realization of *homo liber et legalis.* Herein lies the radical significance of the American Bill of Rights. It juridically secures by the most endurable precedents of history those freedoms which the divinely endowed spiritual nature of man demands. The moral order enters concretely into human law and asserts that by no majoritarian or authoritarian determination will an American citizen be deprived of free exercise of religious conscience and worship; that before the bar of justice laws will be fairly and equally applied; that free speech and free press, the right to assemble peaceably and to petition the government are rational exigencies not only of the spiritual nature of man but also of the moral imperatives of society itself. What are preferred rights, due process and equal protection touching upon life, liberty and property if not the acknowledgment by law and the will of the people of that immunity from the arbitrary to which the spiritual nature of man is entitled?

American political democracy is more than a species of governance; it is a content as well as a process. But in the American context it is more so because of its unique historical genesis and successes as well as its purposive prerogative claims as a democratic *politeia.* The advantages of the democratic form of government rest with the political maturity of its citizens, who are called upon to participate responsibly in the direction and ultimate control of governmental policies; its broad purpose is the greater diffusion of opportunities for moral and material benefits. Both these ethical objectives and rational procedures are consequent

40

to a philosophy of man or, as Aristotle said, "a way of life." Democratic collaboration is self-defeating without commonly accepted principles, without a fundamental creed, without a common denominator of beliefs, without certain imperishable values which are beyond question. Surely there are sound and unsound democracies, but the former depends on its accordance with the ultimates of man's nature. A totalitarian democracy can be just as brutal and arbitrary as a totalitarian dictatorship. The dictum, "nothing above the state, nothing outside the state, nothing against the state," applies equally to both. But American political democracy admits to many realities beyond the competence and the dominance of the state: the church, the family, the countless number of free associations of human endeavor in art and science and in numerous cultural and recreational pursuits. It admits to many delimitations upon the state, such as the prior rights and prerogatives of individuals and of associations which arise from the law of man's nature and of societies. To the preservation and prospering growth of these substantial moral values and to the guarantee of immunity of these human properties, American democracy as a process is wholly medial. In the American historical context, a substantive deposit, the American heritage, has been continuously asserted and reaffirmed politically, juridically and socially.

Without a philosophy of freedom and order there can be neither free order nor ordered freedom. The argument that American democracy is procedural and that there are no human values that cannot be changed by majoritarian vote affirms that there are no political truths or wrongs to which men and societies are committed or if they exist they are not humanly cognizable. But with unquestionable certitude Americans have held certain truths

41

as self-evident and in this faith and conviction a new nation was conceived and has endured under God.

When the Federal Constitution affirms the equality of all men before the law, it recognizes that there are some equal rights given not by law, but by the Creator of men and societies; and that these rights must be secured with the full efficacy of human law and civil power. Legal expedients which proved historically efficacious for the security of fundamental rights were retained from our English heritage. The substantive and procedural rights of the American Bill of Rights and of the Fourteenth Amendment are historical reassertions and juridical securities of man's personal dignity and allow for the fuller expression of his capactiy for freedom. Anglo-American constitutional history is the continuous record of the development of the secondary nature of man (to borrow from Burke) in accordance with his first nature.

The writ of *habeas corpus,* for example, has a theological presupposition. The writ asserts the right of an individual, but a right presupposes a value that no power can cancel. And although the theology of man does not demand a writ of *habeas corpus,* it does say that law must provide proper and adequate means of securing that immunity from the arbitrary which accords with the personal dignity of man. Due process means that persons, rights and possessions must be treated with reverence even when they are charged with crime. The Constitution does not state explicitly that man is a child of God. But those lands and governments which explicitly or in effect deny that man is a child of God also fail to provide adequate securities for man's immunity from governmental arbitrary action. In such countries there is no writ of *habeas corpus.* A comparison between the trial of Cardinal Jozef Mindszenty and the trial of Communist leaders under Judge Harold Medina shows the vast advantages derived from a government with ultimate theological roots. Due process in reverse is a legal restraint upon the presumption that the alleged criminal can be mobbed and lynched by popular demand.

There is throughout the whole of American constitutional history the underlying affirmation of a "higher law" of which the state is not the oracle. The First Amendment declares the inherent incompetence of legislative power in matters of mind and soul and in so doing confesses to the independence and supremacy of the spiritual nature of man. The American state neither originates nor concedes the right of freedom of religion; it recognizes that this right descends from a source superior to itself and is thereby inviolable, and that consequently it is obligated to protect it. The freedoms of speech and press, of peaceable assembly and petition are not Voltairean absolutes after all, but rights fully in accord with man's participation in society. Moreever, they provide the means for a larger scope of democratic responsibilities contributory to the national welfare. There is no more striking feature of the American system than its expressed recognition that the government is one of limited powers, not because power corrupts but because power by reason of its divine descent is limited to the very purposes of the divine grant. Lastly, the Constitution is remarkably viable in accord with the dictates of sound reason. Providing the method of peaceable change, of identity through growth, it remains analogous to the natural law, so immutable in its fundamental principles and so progressive in its effects. Amendments to the Constitution preserve its substance for posterity. They do not annul or subvert it, least of all by the very provision inherent in the Constitution that makes possible the adaptations to the

43

growth of our nation. The goal, "to form a more perfect union," is ever toward a more indissoluble survival.

A word about the *Federalist Papers* is relevant to our discussion. Besides being a profound compendium of political wisdom on the basic problems of government, it enjoys the unique distinction of being frequently cited by the Supreme Court concerning the genuine meaning of disputed provisions in the Constitution. The argument of the eighty-five papers is that the Constitution is apt and necessary for the proper coherence of liberties and authority, of stability and energy in government (no. 1 and no. 37). But more relevant here is the admission that the superstructure of government must rest on ultimates which precede and should determine human choice and contrivance. According to Hamilton:

> In disquisitions of every kind, there are certain primary truths, or first principles, upon which all subsequent reasonings must depend. These contain an internal evidence which, antecedent to all reflections or combination, commands the assent of the mind (no. 31).

The American judiciary has repeatedly recognized that the nation's religious character bears upon American law and government. State and federal courts have declared that "Christianity is part of the law of the land," that "We are a Christian people,"[14] that "This is a Christian nation."[15] These judicial notices obviously are not intended to contradict the First Amendment (as Justice Joseph Storey observed[16]), much less to intrude upon and embarrass non-Christians. They simply acknowledge the Christian genesis and quality of American law. There is scarcely anything offensive to Christianity in our legal system and there is much in accordance with its moral standards. American law incorporates the sociological exigencies of the religious life of the nation. When the eminent scholar, the late Dr. Edward Corwin, sharply criticized the McCollum decision on historical and constitutional grounds, he pointed to the testimonial evidence of American history:

Is the decision favorable to democracy? Primarily democracy is a system of ethical values, and that this system of values so far as the American people are concerned is grounded in religion will not be denied by anyone who knows the historical record.[17]

As if in response are the concurring decisions of the New York State Court of Appeals[18] and the federal Supreme Court[19] in *Zorach v. Clauson.*

We are a religious people whose institutions presuppose a Supreme Being. We guarantee the freedom of worship as one chooses . . . When the state encourages religious instruction or cooperates with religious authorities by adjusting the schedule of public events to sectarian needs, it follows the best of our tradition. For then it respects the religious nature of our people and accommodates the public service to their spiritual needs . . . We cannot read into the Bill of Rights (such) a philosophy of hostility to religion.

In conclusion we affirm again that the American consensus on the religious foundations of our political democracy is substantially and abundantly evidenced in the testimony of the Founding Fathers in the Continental Congress; in the drafting of the Declaration of Independence; in the construction of the federal Constitution; in the long tradition of presidential statements; and in the judicial recognition of the religious experience of the nation. The long history of legislative acts favoring cooperation with religious life is a vast and consoling study in itself and presupposes the theological convictions underlying American democracy. Although there is a secularistic stream in the nation's history, it is not the only American tradition. Moreover, it is not the original American tradition, much less the prevailing one, and it is certainly not the genuine and authentic one. In light of the historical record, the secularist claim is wholly alien to the American mind and as such constitutes a dissent and a protestation.

Certain practical considerations can be drawn from this affirmation. Since the days of the Northwest Ordinance the nation's moral, educational and political issues have been conceived as necessarily intertwined. The question now is whether American democracy can survive without its original theological and moral foundations. Will it endure on secularistic substitutes for God-centered values? Educators and political scientists who abide by their own intellectual prepossessions and who attempt to rewrite American history falsify the record. The charge that American political democracy is essentially a process, wholly a method whereby any change may be effected provided it is done peaceably and according to the rules in the contest of ideas and by the majoritarian determination of the suffrage,[20] is a case in point. In answer to this question the problems of national security and the many issues[21] concerning loyalty and subversion must also be faced.

Other grave and complex questions will be seriously affected by the admission or denial of a political substance of American democracy which is resonant with religious and spiritual verities and values. Should public education, for example, be religiously neutral? What should be the nature and extent of cooperation in church-state relations? Is the religious neutrality of public education contrary to the official and authoritative admissions to the religious foundations of American democracy? Can patriotic loyalty survive without adherence to the religious orientation of American democracy?

In 1954 Congress reaffirmed that patriotic duty and national allegiance are not religiously neutral, and accordingly inserted the phrase "under God" (always taken for granted) into the official formula of salute to the national flag. On March 28, 1955,[22] the New York State Board of Regents spoke out in unequivocal terms against the secularism which has crept into the public schools under guise of religious neutrality. In a statement titled "Fundamental Beliefs, Liberty Under God, Respect of Dignity and Rights of Each Individual, Devotion to Freedom, the Brotherhood of Man under the Fatherhood of God," the Board urged that schools devote frequent periods to the teaching of the country's moral and spiritual heritage. To this purpose it recommended intensive study of American documents and pronouncements by presidents and other national leaders which provide "an understanding and appreciation of the student's role as an individual endowed by his Creator with inalienable rights and as a member of a group similarly endowed, of respect for others, particularly parents and teachers, of devotion to freedom and reverence for Almighty God."

Concerning the Declaration of Independence the Regents noted:

"All men are created equal" is the basic principle of the brotherhood of man and "endowment by their Creator with life, liberty, and the pursuit of happiness" is recognition of the fatherhood of God and that these most precious rights come from the Creator and not from kings, princes, or other men.

And to leave no doubt as to the relevance of religious beliefs in American political democracy the Regents cited as the traditional presidential affirmation of the original, authentic and prevailing consensus the words of President Eisenhower:

47

Without God there could be no American form of government, nor an American way of life . . . Thus the Founding Fathers saw it: and thus, with God's help, it will continue to be . . . Each day we must ask that Almighty God will set and keep His protecting hand over us so that we may pass on to those who come after us the heritage of a free people, secure in their God-given rights and in full control of a government dedicated to the preservation of those rights.

The freedom of man has come with divine revelation; it was not conceived in philosophical agnosticism, nor in religious indifference, nor in rational skepticism, least of all in scientific empiricism. Doubts, uncertainties and ignorance have never offered effective barriers in the minds of men nor provided the inspiration to fight usurpations of power. The threat to liberties comes from those who deny the sovereignty of God over nations as well as over persons. This is the meaning of "the Truth shall make you free," for God is truth.

The survival of American political democracy will not rest solely on a prosperous economy and military preparedness; it requires the religious perception that the insidious crime against the spiritual content of political liberty is indifference. There is no religious neutral ground between God and man for society.

2

Thomas Jefferson, Religious Education and Public Law

The majority opinion delivered by Justice William O. Douglas in the Zorach case of 1952[23] made no mention of the Jeffersonian metaphor, "wall of separation," which other members of the Court cited in their several opinions in the earlier Everson[24] and McCollum[25] cases of 1947 and 1948 respectively. Rather, the Court strove sedulously to contrive a formula of separation of church and state without resorting to the metaphor on masonry. Perhaps Justice Black's caustic remark about the "serpentine wall" stung some members of the high tribunal to less confidence about the masonic symbolism.

The three Court rulings were the occasions of widespread national controversies[26] and so thoroughly were the complex issues debated that a contestant today could anticipate the opposing argument. There is, however, one aspect remaining which has not been adequately explored, namely, the bearing of Jefferson's personal religious convictions, which he freely expressed in his private correspondence, on public law provisions for religious liberty, especially in the area of religious education. The contrast is, paradoxical as it may seem, an illuminating revelation of Jef-

49

ferson's conception of the scope and function of public law. With high-minded restraint motivated by principles of great statesmanship, he did not allow his prejudices and animosities or his personal convictions on religious matters to color his actions either as statesman or educator.

On Aug. 6, 1816, the sage of Monticello wrote to Mrs. Samuel Harrison Smith[27] that he had been variously charged with being "atheist, deist, or devil" and he countered these accusations by declaring that it was nobody's business what he was, religion being "a concern purely between our God and our consciences, for which we are accountable to Him." Notwithstanding Jefferson's frequent insistence on the privacy of religious beliefs he wrote openly about his own convictions to a number of correspondents. There is no evidence that he was being coaxed to do so; on the contrary, he would on occasion urge upon his confidants his own canons for the discernment of religious truths. What is more, Jefferson was far from inhibited in passing judgment upon the creeds of others. That he was taunted as atheist, devil or infidel can be attributed to the animosity which flamed with evident mutual relish between the federalist-clerical hierarchies of New England and himself.

The disclosures in Jefferson's letters about his personal religious convictions really allow only two questions: was he is a deist or a theist? Was he a Christian? The answers to these questions rest on certain presuppositions. Deism can be described as a rationalistic naturalism which discounts the supernatural, or whatever is not discernible by reason alone. Characterized by a spirit of criticism directed against the nature and content of traditional religious dogmas, deism arose and flourished among the individualistic free-thinkers of seventeenth and eighteenth century England.

In France, under the impact of the Voltairean age of Enlightenment, deism dispensed with the personal deity and survived only as a rationalistic moralism of an enthroned self-sufficient reason. Denunciations of the superstitions and corruptions of "priestcraft" abound in the writings of deists and they leave no doubt as to the alleged source of the various forms of Christianity and their practices.

Theism broadly includes all those persons who by natural or positive theology or both admit to a special as well as a general divine providence, the efficacy of intercessory prayer, immortality, and eternal life according to divine judgment. Thumb rules for distinguishing theists from deists are the doctrines of special providence and the efficacy of intercessory prayer. Obviously, the denial of the first renders the other useless. Theists who are not also supernaturalists are generally favorably disposed toward organized religion for its beneficial effects upon society. Theists may be adherents of a particular Christian church or they may simply profess latitudinarian Christianity.

In ascertaining whether Jefferson was a theist or a deist, it is necessary to acknowledge the difference between an individual's avowal of a religious tenet and his attempts to think as a theologian or philosopher about his religious professions. A believer's incompetence to think congruously and convincingly as a philosopher or theologian should not discredit the sincerity of his beliefs especially if his conduct conforms with the virtues of his faith. In this wise we will spare Jefferson, who was never embarrassed or hesitant to expound on theological matters with an extraordinary sense of competence well beyond his learning.

The central marks of theism are contained in Jefferson's second inaugural address of 1805:

51

I shall need, too, the favor of that Being in whose hands we are, who led our forefathers, as Israel of old, from their native land, and planted them in a country flowing with all the necessaries and comforts of life; who has covered our infancy with his providence, and our riper years with his wisdom and power; and to whose goodness I ask you to join with me in supplications, that he will so enlighten the minds of your servants, guide their councils and prosper their measures, that whatsoever they do, shall result in your good, and shall secure to you the peace, friendship, and approbation of all nations.[28]

In the report of the Commissioners for the University of Virginia to the state legislature, Jefferson wrote of "God, the creator, preserver, and supreme ruler of the universe, the author of all the relations of morality, and the laws and obligations these infer."[29] These moral precepts, he added, the Creator indelibly impressed in men's hearts.[30] From his earliest writings to his declining years, Jefferson repeatedly affirmed the self-sufficiency of reason alone to know truth, including the existence of God.[31] When Jefferson insisted on the independence of inquiry and freedom of thought, he meant freedom from external constraints in order that reason may have unimpeded access to evidence. His argument for disestablishment in Virginia in 1779 is introduced with the statement, "Well aware that the opinions and belief of men depend on their own will, but follow involuntarily the evidence proposed to their minds . . ."[32]

Nor was there doubt in his mind about the intelligibility and demonstrability of the existence of God[33] and though this would allow the possibilities for the science of natural theology, Jefferson did not elaborate on or for that matter examine and weigh the various arguments for the existence of God and his divine attributes. Perhaps he was conscious of his shortcomings as a philosopher, but his acknowledgement of God as a transcendent being appears from his frequent references to God as Creator. However, Jefferson did not seem to allow the possibility that such a God may choose to make direct revelations of truths otherwise inaccessible to human intelligence; for him reason and reason alone was the only avenue to truth. With this he foreclosed all possibilities of divine revelation and the various expressions of supernaturalism therein contained. In 1820, he wrote to John Adams that God was "an ethereal gas"[34] and that same year to W. Short: "I am a Materialist."[35] But here we must recall the difference between Jefferson's religious professions and his inept and clumsy efforts at philosophizing. Metaphysics was decidedly not Jefferson's forte; on the contrary, he had a deep-grained aversion for speculative philosophy except in moral studies, and even then to a very limited extent. His constant appeal to simple doctrines and fundamentalist residues of common agreement and acceptance reveals his impatience with complex and intricate thinking. The theological incongruity between God as creator, the author of all morality and God as a gaseous substance escaped him entirely. His unembarrassed statement of crude materialism may be traced to the stoic physics which he very likely imbibed without much reflection during his sojourn in France, where Voltairean discourse dominated.

Jefferson ought not to be taken with more seriousness than he did himself.[36] He believed in the immortality of the soul, man's accountability to God for his conduct on earth, and a future state of rewards and punishments. He conceived the work of salvation wholly as an individual and private endeavor: "If I could not go to heaven but with a party, I would not go there at all."[37] Despite his intense dislike of organized religion and his opposition to the support of the clergy through public funds, he is known to have contributed liberally in support of most clergy, and was a frequent attendant and participant at church services.[38]

For himself and others, Jefferson set the processes of reason alone as the exclusive and sufficient avenue to religious as well as other truths. Yet we find no elaborate argument, or a developed system of reasoning, establishing with demonstrative force any of his religious confessions— the existence of God and his attributes, as "creator, preserver, and supreme ruler of the universe, the author of all relations of morality, and of the laws and obligations these infer," the spirituality and immortality of the soul, etc. Thus he may oddly enough be termed a believer in what are objectively rational truths. Perhaps Jefferson sensed the inadequacy of his *fideism* and consequently made personal conduct the credentials of a faith; but this too involves certain rational discomfortures, for while true belief should issue into good works, goodness itself is no surrogate for truth. A believer of the true faith may fail to live according to his faith, and the believer of a false faith or a nonbeliever may live a good life out of generous impulses and unselfish qualities of character. Be that as it may, Jefferson does write of a moral law which is imprinted in our hearts by the author of our being. But here too his repugnance for absolutes and dogmas carried over from his theological creed, such as it was, so that he held to a morality whose highest commendation was its utility conditioned by geographic and environmental factors even to the point of contrariety.

Some men are born without the organs of sight, or of hearing, or without hands. Yet it would be wrong to say that man is born without these faculties, and sight, hearing and hands may with truth enter into the general definition of man. The want or imperfection of the moral sense in some men, like the want or imperfection of

54

the sense of sight and hearing in others, is no proof that it is a general characteristic of the species. When it is wanting, we endeavor to supply the defect by education, by appeals to reason and calculation, by presenting to the being so unhappily conformed, other motives to do good and to eschew evil, such as the love, or the hatred, or rejection of those among whom he lives, and whose society is necessary to his happiness and even existence; demonstrations by sound calculation that honesty promotes interest in the long run; the rewards and penalties established by the laws; and ultimately the prospects of a future state of retribution for the evil as the good done while here. These are the correctives which are supplied by education, and which exercise the functions of the moralist, the preacher, and legislator . . . Some have argued against the existence of a moral sense, by saying that if nature had given us such a sense . . . then nature would also have designated, by some particular ear-marks, the two sets of actions which are, in themselves, the one virtuous and the other vicious. Whereas, we find, in fact, that the same actions are deemed virtuous in one country and vicious in another. The answer is that nature has constituted utility to man, the standard and test of virtue. Men living in different countries, under different circumstances, different habits and regimens, may have different utilities; the same act, therefore, may be useful, and consequently virtuous in one country which is injurious and vicious in another differently circumstanced. I sincerely, then, believe in the general existence of a moral instinct. I think it the brightest gem with which the human character is studded, and the want of it as more degrading than the most hideous of the bodily deformities.[39]

Apart from the misleading parallel and inferences drawn by Jefferson between the physical complement of the human body and the totality of spiritual faculties in man, inclusive of a moral sense, the appeal to the efficacy of education and the weighing of practical motivations may serve in some instances as apt instruments for the awakening and development of a moral conscience in those persons in whom it is seriously deficient. But Jefferson capitulates completely to utilitarianism and moral relativism when he constitutes

55

utility as the norm of virtue and virtue itself and evil as interchangeable according to geographic location. There is not even a suspicion of the malice of sin as an offense against God, and of virtue as a conformity of human will with the divine out of love of God to whom we creatures owe adoration and obedience. There is no higher motive put forth for useful moral conduct than consequents, advantages, correctives. Jefferson scarcely advocates a universal and uniform utility, a very discouraging premise for international relations! For all his vaunted rationalism he turns out to be a moral sensist:

He who made us would have been a pitiful bungler, if he had made the rules of our moral conduct a matter of science. For one man of science there are thousands who are not. What would become of them? Man was destined for society. His morality, therefore, was to be formed to this object. He was endowed with a sense of right and wrong, merely relative to this. This sense is as much a part of his nature, as the sense of hearing, seeing, feeling; it is the true foundation of morality, and not the tokalon, truth, etc., as fanciful writers have imagined . . . This sense is submitted, indeed, in some degree, to the guidance of reason; but it is a small stock which is required for this: even a less one than what we call common sense.[40]

Far are we from denying that the author of our being meant the moral law to be useful and enjoyable to man, for otherwise human life would be extremely uncomfortable and well-nigh impossible. But we do deny that law or action is good only because it is useful; utility is merely one of the several positive social consequences of morality. Men may be called upon by the divine laws to sacrifice their properties and even their lives rather than violate them grievously, a sacrifice hardly useful in this life. Nor for that matter can moral law be said to be a utility ordained to

56

eternal happiness since beatitude is a companionable enjoyment of God, not a use of God. This misconception has led utilitarians to include religious life within the narrow principle of self-interest.

Jefferson finds the answer to the hazards of moral relativism in a general and prevailing consensus among the dogmatically differing faiths. This effect is inexorably guaranteed by the divine action which has destined man to live in a well-ordered society and has impressed indelibly on human hearts those moral precepts whose observance is foreordained to this end. The inevitable emergence of this general consensus is categorically affirmed by Jefferson in the interests of society despite the fact that "(t)he varieties in structure and action of the human mind as in those of the body, are the work of our Creator, against which it cannot be a religious duty to erect the standard of uniformity."[41]

Jefferson should not be wholly to blame for elliptical and incoherent reasoning. He is exercising the independence of the freethinker whose mind had been not only emancipated by the age of Enlightenment from the assumption of supernaturalism, the "personal inspiration" in the Reformer's "private judgment," but also cut from its ontological moorings by the discredit which eighteenth century empiricism visited upon speculative philosophy. Such a mind was content to acknowledge perforce the inexorable laws of physics and mathematics because nature was thereby made to yield its secrets to human calculation and to the utility of mankind.

In his first inaugural address, Jefferson in listing "the essential principles of our government" made vigorous affirmation of what he called the "vital principle of republics" —"absolute acquiescence in the decisions of the majority." But what are the other "essential principles" of his enumera-

57

tion but a bill of exceptions to this "vital principle?" They were, in fact, a catalogue of rights placed out of the reach of the majority, for fear that the majority might destroy them. In the same address, Jefferson even declared explicitly that the will of the majority was "in all cases" to prevail, that the will "to be rightful must be reasonable." "The minority possess their equal rights . . . and to violate (them) would be oppression." If the will of the majority was entitled to "absolute acquiescence," if it was "in all cases" to prevail, what safeguard was there for the rights of the minorities? Yet if minorities were indulged in their claims, how was the maintenance of their "equal rights" to be restrained from leading to minority rule? This basic ambiguity was to stir Jefferson from his earliest years in public service, and his inability to resolve it may be explained partly by the fact that he was the heir of a tradition from whose charm he could not escape. It was the problem of depositing in the right place the freedom of the mind and its perfection in "following" involuntarily the evidence proposed to it. And the eventuality of the uniformity among minds conforming to the same evidences—another word for absolutes, dogmas—ultimately arose from the congenital capacity in all men to attain alone or, usually, with the enlightening assistance of others the necessary truths of life.

While, therefore, Jefferson would not allow that God created man capable of arriving at the same speculative truths—such an intellectual agreement might conduce to that dreadful spectre of uniformity—he would nonetheless hold fast that God imprinted indelibly in our hearts moral precepts which even the "varieties in structure and action of the human mind" could not keep us from sensing. The content of this sensist moralism coincides with the moral precepts of Jesus and the obligation for observance it derives

58

from has no higher motive than the interests of society. The reasonableness of the law is in its utility.

WAS JEFFERSON A CHRISTIAN?

In 1816 Jefferson wrote to Charles Thomson:

> I am a *real Christian,* that is to say, a disciple of the doctrines of Jesus, very different from the Platonists, who call *me* infidel and *themselves* Christians and preachers of the gospel, while they draw all their characteristic dogmas from what its author never said nor saw. They have compounded from the heathen mysteries a system beyond the comprehension of man, of which the great reformer of the vicious ethics of deism of the Jews, were he to return on earth, would not recognize one feature.[42]

Since Jefferson distinguishes himself as a real *Christian*— the italics are in the original—presumably from the putative ones, in what sense was he a Christian or, in other words, what did he think of Christ? He always insists that he is a Christian in the only sense in which Christ wished anyone to be. With this, he then denies that Christ ever claimed divinity though "ascribing to himself every human excellence."[43] With the rejection of the dogma of the Incarnation, Jefferson also discounts the trinitarian dogma which he describes as the confection of platonizing priests.[44] Jefferson's enthusiasm and admiration for the man Jesus is unbounded[45] even with the admission of certain limitations, excusable, Jefferson thinks, in him. Christ, reared within the Jewish tradition of divine favors and gifted with an "eloquence which had not been taught him . . . might readily mistake the coruscations of his own fine genius for inspirations of an higher order."[46] Jefferson further allows that Jesus, in order to escape the snares of the "priests of . . . superstition . . . was justifiable, therefore, in avoiding these

59

by evasions, by sophisms, by misconstructions and mis-applications of scraps of the prophets, and in defending himself with these their own weapons, as sufficient, *ad homines*, at least."[47] Of course, he has his differences with Christ:

> It is not to be understood that I am with him (Jesus) in all his doctrines. I am a Materialist; he takes the side of Spiritualism; he preaches the efficacy of repentance towards forgiveness of sin; I require a counterpoise of good works to redeem it, etc.[48]

Jefferson exults in the purity, sublimity, benevolence of Christ's moral teaching, the "purest system of morals ever preached to man." All his references to it are in the superlative. Christ's moral teaching was a necessary corrective of the inferior ethics of the Jews,[49] superior to any taught by the pagan philosophers, and not excelled by anyone since. But his sublime and simple doctrines were "adulterated and sophisticated by artificial constructions" of the clergy "into a mere contrivance to filch wealth and power to themselves." Whereupon Jefferson urges several of his correspondents to join him in "extracting the pure principles" of Christ from the distortions and accretions that have been visited upon it since the days of Paul. It is a scissor and paste job, "cutting verse from verse out of the printed book, and arranging the matter which is evidently his (Christ's)."[50] Others take to his suggestion before he does and when Jefferson does complete his own compilation, news of it stirs speculation that there is a "change" in his religious life.

One is amazed at the degree of self-assurance with which Jefferson holds forth authoritatively as a textual critic of the New Testament. The original manuscripts had long since decayed and the fragments still extant were dispersed in distant European libraries. Countless translations of the original Aramaic and Hellenic Greek differed in the choice of idiom as to establish variant dogmatic interpretations. Yet Jefferson never doubts his own competence to penetrate to the original teachings of Christ. His canon for selectivity is remarkably uncomplicated: moral simplicity; everything else is disregarded. The most profound religious dogmas were registered in the words of Christ. Nonetheless Jefferson can, without any qualms, counsel John Adams to "select, even from them (the evangelists), the very words of Jesus" and arrange "the matter which is evidently his (Christ's)."[51] Jefferson's real purpose was to expurgate all record of the supernatural in the New Testament and abbreviate it to a summary compilation of the "morals of Jesus" as he called it, but what is now more properly known as the *Thomas Jefferson Bible*.[52] It is not unlikely that Jefferson saw his own role similar to Christ's. Just as Jesus was the great reformer of the ethics of the Jews so too would he undertake the restoration of Christ's original teaching.

Despite his repeated protestation that religion is a private concern between man and his Maker and his occasional avowal that he does not scrutinize the beliefs of others, Jefferson in his private correspondence discloses a facile inclination to do just that. He was far from reticent about his own religious convictions and not at all indifferent to the beliefs of others. On the contrary, he judged and at times even ridiculed the religious tenets of other creeds.

He was unrestrained in his contempt for the clergy, who were motivated by self-interest and power; worse, they had adulterated the simple teachings of Christ; worse still, they had judged Jefferson not to be a Christian, but an infidel, and even an atheist. In his denunciations his language is uninhibited and unsparing. He is unalterably opposed to all expressions of the supernatural. He never seems to have entertained the thought that a truth may be divisive of those who accept it as well as of those who reject it, just as, for

61

example, on a lower plane, the justice of a revolutionary cause which he himself helped to embody in the Declaration of Independence was divisive. Nor did he examine the possibility that God, the Creator, might favor mankind with truths which could not otherwise be known by reason alone.

In particular, Jefferson vented his spleen against St. Paul, no less, "the great Coryphaeus, and the first corruptor of the doctrines of Jesus,"[53] and Athanasius whom he brackets with Calvin as "impious dogmatists."[54] He was scornful of metaphysicians of the stature of Plato and Aristotle, but quite partial to Epicurus.[55]

Of his criticisms of particular creeds, we observe that his judgments are caustic rather than critical, temerarious rather than judicious.[56] His strongest strictures are directed against the Jews and the Calvinists. Jefferson's brusque evaluation of Judaic beliefs and moral code may have derived in no small measure from the Voltairean derision current in the France of his sojourn as well as from his aversion to the rigidity of Old Testament Calvinist theocracy which took early rootage in the northern colonies. He misses completely the profound significance of the divine insertion into human history, the prophecies, the messianic promise, the decalogue, the beauty and sublimity of the psalms and the many divine revelations and commissions to the patriarchs and prophets of the Old Testament. One must carefully guard against any suspicion that Jefferson was anti-Semitic, however. On the contrary he had a genuine and sensitive concern for the extension of social and civil rights to the Jews,[57] and for the suffering they had everywhere endured from religious persecution and oppression.[58] By far his sharpest darts are directed against Calvinism.

I can never join Calvin in addressing his God. He was indeed an atheist, which I can never be; or rather his religion was daemon-ism. If ever a man worshipped a false God, he did. The being described in his five points, is not the God whom you and I acknowledge and adore, the creator and benevolent governor of the world; but a daemon of malignant spirit. It would be more pardonable to believe in no God at all, than to blaspheme him by the atrocious attributes of Calvin.[59]

His sentiments toward the Presbyterians are in the same vein.[60]

It would seem that no purpose would be served in registering Jefferson's judgments upon the religious beliefs of others except to weigh how critical and judicious a theologian he was. Actually our intention points to a remarkable and, for all Americans, a highly profitable paradox. Jefferson rejects all forms and expressions of supernaturalism, either as dogmas or ministries. His language is sharp, caustic and many times without the tempered restraint that accords with scientific and specialized learning and scholarly canons of criticism. Truly amazing is the confidence of his own competence to review before the bar of his personal judgment the Old and the New Testament, the Greek philosophers Plato and Aristotle, among the Fathers no less a person than Athanasius, the faith of his contemporaries, and above all his confidence to pierce to the original teachings of Christ. Yet he could write as late as 1816: "I have never told my own religion nor scrutinized that of another." The remarkable paradox is that Jefferson is dogmatically intolerant—he is very sure he is right and his critics wrong, just as wrong as they think he is and more so. He has no doubt that he is the real Christian and they the infidels and atheists. Jefferson's own religious dogmatism seemingly is in contrast with his equally uncompromising public political tolerance of all religious creeds and consciences, but this apparent contrast is fundamentally sound and harmonious. Whoever holds to religious truths does so by an unshaken

63

belief in their veracity. No one willingly would hold to error. Even scepticism is not a denial of truth but rather a doubt that truth, if it exists, is available to human intelligence. Jefferson's aversion to dogma is not to dogma as such, but to dogma harnessed to the physical compulsions and coercions which interfere with free inquiry.

> That if there be one (religion) right, and ours that one, we should wish to see the nine hundred and ninety-nine wandering sects gathered into the fold of truth. But against such a majority we cannot effect this by force. Reason and persuasion are the only practical instruments. To make way for these, free inquiry must be indulged; and how can we wish others to indulge it while we refuse it ourselves.[61]

Here we have the key to Jefferson's thought. He is not an agnostic and he does not subscribe to religious indifferentism. The *Notes on the State of Virginia* were written shortly after his bill for disestablishment in Virginia had been submitted. Jefferson felt no incongruity between personal religious dogmatism and the corresponding need for public law tolerance which for him serves a double purpose: to secure by law the rights of religious conscience and to provide the suitable, free circumstance for making possible rational persuasion to the claimed true religion. This Jeffersonian conviction contrasts sharply with many persons today who deny the compatibility of religious dogmatism and public religious liberty for all. This is the underlying premise of his bill of 1779.

> (T)ruth is great and will prevail if left to herself; and that she is the proper and sufficient antagonist to error, and has nothing to fear from the conflict unless by human interposition disarmed of her natural weapons, free argument and debate; errors ceasing to be dangerous when it is permitted freely to contradict them.[62]

Throughout his whole life he never abandoned this fundamental position. Religious liberty meant for Jefferson not only the guarantee of the rights of religious conscience but also the rationally suitable provision for the freedom to search for religious truths as well as the best circumstances to propagate them by persuasion. This is what he meant when he stated the necessity of "fixing every essential right on a legal basis." Therefore it should not be surprising that in his program for education in Virginia, he was meticulous to guard against any "surprise" encroachments upon the religious consciences of students. At the same time he would provide by state financial support facilities for the teaching and worship in the various religious creeds by their own ministries and doctors of divinity on state university grounds and in state university rooms—creeds and ministries whose dogmas of supernaturalism and authoritative ministry he castigated and ridiculed in his private correspondence. These letters are dated contemporarily with his universal provisions for sectarian religious teaching and worship in the Virginia educational system. Yet some scholars have seen as a change of principle what was in fact a reasoned disposition to bring his provisions more in line with his unwavering conception of religious liberty.

RELIGION, EDUCATION AND PUBLIC LAW

The unalterable principle of religious liberty which underlies Jefferson's educational programs in Virginia was a conviction which he possessed from the earliest year of his public life. The clarity of the principle never dimmed in his mind. The application of it to the conditions of state education may stir unforeseen difficulties but this does not induce him either to compromise the principle or to shirk the responsibility of working out an equitable application wholly within the terms of that principle. The frequency with which he attends to the problem (which may be broadly described as public law and religious life) attests to his constant concern not to seek easy subterfuge or escape in a "neutral" position with all its concealed prejudices and discriminations.

A. Notes on Religion (c. October, 1776)

In a manuscript[63] which is a compound of "notes" to be used by Jefferson in speeches and petitions in the Virginia House of Delegates, particularly in connection with the disestablishment of the Episcopal Church, the young patriot of 1776 goes directly to the heart of the matter when he inquires what is a heretic. Since he does not allow the possibility of a divinely established church as guardian and teacher of the true faith, he is firmly convinced that the numerous Christian sects are all equally of human origin and invention. He finds the source of religious liberty in the "right of chusing and the necessity of deliberating to which we will conform"—but, he continues, "if we chuse for ourselves, we must allow others to chuse also, and to reciprocally (sic)."[64] Jefferson's extreme religious individualism is just as emphatically egalitarian. What we claim for ourselves we must vindicate for others too. Once within an ecclesiastical communion, how far does the duty of toleration extend? Jefferson answers: "No church is bound by duty of toleration to retain within her bosom obstinate offenders against her laws,"[65] and she has the right to exercise her proper power of expulsion or excommunication. However, "we have no right to prejudice another in his civil enjoyments because he is of another church."[66] Jefferson holds fast to the individual right of religious conscience to choose its religious communion and to the corporate right and freedom of action of the communion to exercise proper jurisdiction over its adherents. Jefferson then guards the freedom of the churches from interference from one another, by denying to any church the coercive arm of the civil magistrate. This denial is based on the dictates of reason. Force is ineffective for the salvation of souls because "God himself will not save men against their wills."[67]

Compulsion in religion is distinguished peculiarly from compulsion in every other thing. I may grow rich by art I am compelled to follow, I may recover health by medicines I am compelled to take against my own judgment, but I cannot be saved by a worship I disbelieve or abhor.[68]

Further, the civil magistrate is incompetent in the ways of salvation and therefore cannot have jurisdiction therein; nor can the people confer such jurisdiction upon the magistrate. The magistrate's jurisdictions extend only to civil rights. The compulsions of the secular arm are ineffective and incompetent in the ways of salvation. Besides, such presumptions usually entail incidents of civil inequality, religious favoritism, civil incapacitations, exclusion from office, denial of franchise, the exaction of a tax contrary to religious conscience. Therefore "all partial distinctions, exclusions and incapacitations (are to be) removed."[69]

B. A Bill for Establishing Religious Freedom (1779)

On June 13, 1779, when Jefferson introduced into the Virginia Assembly his bill for the disestablishment of the Episcopal Church, it aroused much opposition. Its passage

67

was delayed until 1786 when Madison, encouraged by his own success against Patrick Henry's bill for the state support of the teachers of the Christian religion, reintroduced Jefferson's original bill. It was adopted with certain changes.

Summarily, Jefferson states: God has created the mind free, subject only to the compulsion of evidence. Its freedom consists in unimpeded access to evidence. Governmental coercions beget hypocrisy and presume to do what God himself will not do. It is the "impious presumption" of fallible men to set up as infallible their own opinions and impose them upon others. Such imposition has perpetuated false religions. Compulsions may take the form of a fiscal exaction for the support of a religious teacher of a faith other than the one of personal choice. "(O)ur civil rights have no dependence on our religious opinions . . . (I)t is time enough for the rightful purposes of civil government for its officers to interfere when principles break out into overt acts against peace and good order."[70]

Jefferson safeguards religious liberty simply by denying that the civil power has any competence and jurisdiction to dictate in religious matters. He is equally insistent that the cause of religion is best served by religious liberty, and the most appropriate avenue to the true religion is free inquiry.

A telling commentary on Jefferson's bill of 1779 is Madison's *Memorial and Remonstrance* of 1785: "Who does not see that the same authority which can establish Christianity in exclusion of all other religions, may establish with the same ease any particular sect of Christians, in exclusion of all other sects? That the same authority which can force a citizen to contribute three pence only of his property for the support of any one establishment, may force him to conform to any other establishment in all other cases whatsoever?" Madison like Jefferson fought against the discriminatory, exclusive support of one religion in preference to others. Despite the clarity of Madison's text, Justice Rutledge in his dissenting opinion in the Everson case construed Madison's thought (apart from its irrelevance to the First Amendment, ratified six years later) as forbidding financial support of religion as such (*Everson v. Board of Education,* 330 U.S. 1, 28 (1947).

C. *Notes on Religion (1780–1785)*

The following year Jefferson, as governor of his home state, repeats his arguments against governmental compulsion in religion in his answers to the questionnaire which Francois Marbois of the French legation in Philadelphia had addressed to the several American states. On the limits and limitation of civil power he wrote: "The legitimate powers of government extend only to such acts only as are injurious to others." On the harm that coercion works upon religion itself: "Constraint may make him worse by making him a hypocrite . . . It may fix him obstinately in his errors." Besides, the use of force is by men who are themselves fallible and who may thereby perpetuate falsehood rather than truth. Jefferson never tires of stressing both the theoretical fallacy and historical failure of governmental coercion to achieve religious uniformity; The appropriate avenues to truth are reason and free inquiry; and the logical inference of egalitarian individualism (so characteristic of Jefferson's natural rights doctrine): "(H)ow can we wish others to indulge it (free inquiry) while we refuse it ourselves." Hence the necessity of "fixing every essential right on a legal basis."[71]

Underlying these repeated and ever enlarging affirmations

69

of the proper objectives of civil power and of the appropriate conditions for religious life is a gradually emerging concept of the scope and function of public law which will attain its maturity when Jefferson in later life copes with the problems of education in the state of Virginia. There is, however, discernible at this early stage Jefferson's profound insight that the social order and political allegiance are not contingent upon religious conformity. At the same time he affirms in explicit words the theological basis of human liberties.

D. Jefferson's Metaphor and Historic Commentaries

On Jan. 1, 1802, Jefferson wrote his celebrated letter containing the most quoted metaphor in American legal debate. A committee of the Danbury Baptist Association, in the state of Connecticut, had sent him a letter of high esteem and good wishes. If we bear in mind his fight for disestablishment in Virginia, his recurring arguments against all the discriminatory incidents of establishment in favor of one faith to the disadvantage of the nonconformists, that the Baptists to whom he addressed his answer were in such a disadvantageous status within the terms of the Congregationalist establishment in Connecticut, a situation that would endure until 1818, then his letter, while clearly obvious in its intention and explicit meaning, should not suffer the slightest misconstruction.[72] That same day Jefferson penned a note to Attorney General Levi Lincoln and referred to his letter. "The Baptist address, now enclosed, admits of a condemnation of the *alliance* between Church and State, under the authority of the constitution . . . I know it will give great offense to the New England clergy; but the advocate of religious freedom is to expect neither peace nor forgiveness from them."[73]

The meaning of a figure of speech is not self-contained; it is derivative. It loses its meaning if it is excised from its historical context and from its literal composition. Much less then should we ignore the author's consistent conduct and thinking. The meaning of a figure of speech is wholly in its referral to related thinking on a subject. Seven years later Jefferson had a similar occasion to respond to a letter of approbation and good wishes from the Society of the Methodist Episcopal Church in New London, Conn., in close vicinity to the Danbury Baptists.

No provision in our constitution ought to be dearer to man than that which protects the rights of conscience against the enterprises of the civil authority. It has not left the religion of its citizens under the power of its public functionaries, were it possible that any of these should consider a conquest over the consciences of men either attainable or applicable to any desirable purpose. To me no information would be more welcome than that the minutes of the several religious societies should prove, of late, larger additions than have been usual, to their several associations, and I trust that the whole course of my life has proved me a sincere friend to religious as well as civil liberty.[74]

Years before all the states would cancel their church establishments and decades before the Supreme Court would make the First Amendment on religious liberty operative upon the states through the Fourteenth Amendment, Jefferson was looking forward to the day when state governments would follow the example of the federal Constitution and guarantee by law equality of religious freedom. But a more immediate commentary upon the Jefferson

71

metaphor of the "wall of separation" is the treaty with the Kaskaskia Indians which he sent to the Senate on Oct. 31, 1803, scarcely two years after his letter to the Danbury Baptists.

> And whereas the greater part of the said tribe have been baptized and received into the Catholic church, to which they are much attached, the United States will give annually, for seven years one hundred dollars toward the support of a priest of that religion, who will engage to perform for said tribe the duties of his office, and also to instruct as many of their children as possible, in the rudiments of literature. And the United States will further give the sum of three hundred dollars, to assist the said tribe in the erection of a church.[75]

This action of Jefferson's during his presidency of the United States is remarkably significant and highlights with a precision that leaves no doubt his interpretation of the First Amendment religious clauses. Before the federal union came in existence, Jefferson had fought for equality of religious freedom by removing church establishment in Virginia. In his correspondence with the Danbury Baptists and with the Methodist Episcopal Church of New London, he hoped for the same in Connecticut. As President of the United States he refrained from proclamations of national days of fasting and prayer because, as he saw it, he would be prescribing religious exercise and discipline beyond the constitutional empowerments of his office. Yet in his second year as chief executive of the national government, he signs a treaty which provides federal financial subvention of a Catholic priest and three hundred dollars for the construction of a church of worship in order that the priest might instruct his faithful in their religious life as well as in literature. A more intimate involvement of the federal government with a particular faith could scarcely be contrived without violation of the no establishment clause of the First Amendment.

The primary and paramount purpose of Jefferson is obvious—the provision of conditions favorable to the Indians' free exercise of their faith and under federal jurisdiction. Washington had also made similar provision.[76] The striking significance of this presidential act cannot be minimized. It took place in the midst of a flurry of private correspondence wherein Jefferson never tired to inveigh against various expressions of supernaturalism. Here he pens his signature to the financial subvention of a cleric whose faith claimed to be no less than divinely revealed and divinely commissioned. Nor is there any record of doubts or pauses in Jefferson's mind as to its constitutionality. The gradual emergence of Jefferson's conception of public law on the equality of religious freedom has been marked with two characteristics, uniformity and universality, both secured by the proscription of establishment and the constitutional guarantee of free exercise of religious beliefs and worship. The essential ingredient of universality is impartiality and this is in no wise compromised when in certain circumstances the federal government assists a particular faith. Jefferson, on the contrary, saw this action as an application of governmental action to render actual the free exercise of religion. Nor did Jefferson construe his own action as an act of favoritism or discrimination, since in fact there were no other missionaries in similar circumstances with identical needs—surely none came to his consideration. Jefferson's sense of the universality of religious liberty and its impartiality, even when governmental support is directed by reason of circumstances to a particular faith, is remarkably premature in American history and marks him as a farseeing statesman of great stature.

73

E. Public Law, Education and Religion

From the year that Jefferson left the presidential office in 1809 to his death in 1826, two preoccupations seem paramount among his many varied interests. First, he wished to establish that he is the real Christian and his clerical critics the infidels. He has obviously been nettled by their charges that he is either devil, infidel or atheist. In order to vindicate himself as the real Christian and to establish their heresy, he urges in private correspondence that several of his friends join him in extracting the "simple," "unadulterated" and "genuine" moral teachings of Jesus from the "travesties," "sophistications" and "artificial constructions" which the clergy in their greed for power and wealth grafted to the "pure" teachings of Jesus. Concurrent with this personal concernment, there is another interest which preoccupies Jefferson's major efforts—the planning of state educational systems in Virginia. Inevitably the two became intertwined. From his own deep conviction of the theological basis of society, he insists on religious instructions at least in higher education. His own conception of the "complete circle of the useful sciences" includes sectarian teaching (and worship). The necessary involvement of sectarian religious learning in state educational institutions raises a knotty problem, the resolution of which he applies himself with great discretion and discernment. As we review Jefferson's educational proposals of 1814, 1817, 1818, 1822 and 1824, we observe that despite his own dogmatic intolerance of creeds of supernaturalism, which he repeatedly ridicules in his private correspondence, he preserves inviolate the equal and impartial protection and provision by public law of freedom for all faiths in institutions of learning. Just as he

74

would not allow a man's faith to suffer "civil incapacitations" neither would he allow a man's faith to incur inequality of circumstances and benefits in state schools.

On Sept. 7, 1814, Jefferson wrote to his nephew, Peter Carr, outlining a comprehensive plan of education for "our native state" to be supported by state funds.[77] He provides for three specified types of schools—the elementary, general and professional. Among the provisions for the last, he stipulates a department for "Theology and Ecclesiastical History" to which the "ecclesiastic" will repair as will the lawyer, physician, soldier or agricultor repair to their own appropriate studies. In this plan there is no mention of religious instruction in the curriculum of the elementary school. Jefferson is silent here on this question perhaps because he felt that the provision for theology and ecclesiastical history was safer for the professional grades than a similar provision for youngsters who would be no match for any "surprise" indoctrination by a teacher of a faith other than theirs. This conjecture is confirmed by the terms of his draft of an "Act of Establishing Elementary Schools" which he submitted to the General Assembly of Virginia on Sept. 9. 1817.[78]

(N)o religious reading, instruction, or exercise, shall be prescribed or practices inconsistent with the tenets of any religious sect or denomination.[79]

Evidently Jefferson thought of this particular problem during the intervening three years. He is careful to guard the religious conscience of all minors against the more learned persuasion of adult instructors. In the light of his insistence in private letters on the teaching of religious truths acceptable to all, it would seem that Jefferson proscribes only what is inconsistent with the tenets of any

75

religious denomination and not all religious reference and inculcation.

The following year the commissioners for the University of Virginia convened in Rockfish Cap, on the Blue Ridge, to draw up a report which Jefferson wrote for submission to the legislature of the state.[80] In the tentative outline of 1814 Jefferson had provided for a department of theology and ecclesiastical history to which the ecclesiastic could repair as would other professionals to their studies. In 1818, in the formal planning of the curriculum for the University of Virginia, he abandons this earlier provision and explains the change in terms of principles to which he has constantly referred for the rational justification of any concrete implementation. Now he argues against the provision of sectarian teaching by the state itself.

In conformity with the principles of our Constitution, which places all sects of religion on an equal footing, with the jealousies of the different sects in guarding that equality from encroachment and surprise and with the sentiments of the Legislature in favor of freedom of religion, manifested on former occasions, we have proposed no professor of divinity . . . rather as the proofs of . . . God, the creator, preserver, and supreme ruler of the universe, the author of all the relations of morality, and of the laws and obligations these infer, will be within the province of the professor of ethics; to which adding the developments of these moral obligations, of those in which all sects agree, with a knowledge of the languages, Hebrew, Greek, and Latin, a basis will be formed common to all sects. Proceeding thus far without offense to the Constitution, we have thought it proper at this point to leave every sect to provide, as they think fittest, the means of further instruction in their own particular tenets.[81]

This passage is undoubtedly the end result of much reasoned deliberation among the commissioners and Jefferson is anxious to make clear that the causes for the change of his own proposal of 1814 are reasons of principle. Referring first to the state constitution which abandoned church establishment by the Act of 1786, he argues that a professor of divinity of a particular sect would be offensive to religious equality. The implied argument points to the immense practical financial difficulty in providing professors of divinity of every denomination that a concrete implementation in accord with religious equality would entail. This forbidding prospect has the alternative: let each sect provide the instruction in its own peculiar tenets. However, the teaching of the proofs of God and his moral law by a professor of ethics whose appeal is not to revealed theology but to the construction of natural theology and ethics on the unitive basis of reason, wherein all sects can agree, is presented as the proper and sufficient surrogate.

But the abandonment in 1818 of the provision for a professor of divinity in the tentative outline of 1814, however painstakingly explained and justified in the cause of equality of religious liberty in education, was misconstrued as a disparagement of the place of religion in state education, much to the annoyance of Jefferson.

Four years later, Jefferson in his report to the legislature[82] re-examines the position of 1818 to make clear that, on the contrary, despite misrepresentation, a totally nonreligious education is a defective one, and he goes on to describe in greater detail than in 1818 the close cooperation that should obtain between the University of Virginia and the sectarian religions. In the 1818 report, the occasion for possible intrusion upon religious conscience and the danger of religious favoritism are eliminated. In the 1822 report a positive plan in favor of religious education is put forth in detail with sensitive concern for impartiality. In effect, what Jefferson establishes is that neutrality, total abstention, is not the only

77

universal, impartial disposition by law to avoid inequities; rather, a positive construction impartially and universally applied may be the more desirable alternative. What should determine the choice is the value involved, the rights of the religious conscience in all areas of human conduct regulated by law. It is obvious that Jefferson is annoyed with the misrepresentation of the 1818 report.

He quotes verbatim, with the necessary variation in tense and pronouns, from the Report of 1818, "in conformity with the principles of constitution," etc., to the conclusion of that passage wherein "they had left, at this point, to every sect to take into their own hands the office of further instruction in the peculiar tenet of each."[83] Obviously, Jefferson had before him a copy of the earlier report and may well have wondered how it could have been misunderstood. And then he adds immediately, as if to foreclose any further misconstruction:

It was not, however, to be understood that instruction in religious opinion and duties was meant to be precluded by the public authorities, as indifferent to the interests of society. On the contrary, the relations which exist between man and his Maker, and the duties resulting from those relations, are the most interesting and important to every human being, and the most incumbent on his study and investigation. The want of instruction in the various creeds of religious faith existing among our citizens presents, therefore, a chasm in a general institution of the useful sciences. But it was thought that this want, and the entrustment to each society of instruction in its own doctrine, were evils of less danger than a permission to the public authorities to dictate modes or principles of religious instruction, or than opportunities furnished them by giving countenance or ascendency to any one sect over another.[84]

The tentative proposal for a professor of divinity had been dropped only because such a provision would have necessarily been sectarian, and unless all the denominations were to have equal faculties of their own within the university theology department, a partial provision would be offensive to the state constitutional guarantee of equality of religious freedom and exercise which, for Jefferson, extends into education itself. At that time ("at this point") the commissioners were satisfied that those religious truths which were an essential ingredient of the Jeffersonian concept of education could be taught by the professor of ethics on the universal basis of rational persuasion as distinct from the dogmas peculiar to various creeds. In the earlier report of 1818, Jefferson saw the dangers of preferment in one or some sectarian teaching by state law. In 1822 Jefferson goes further: "The want of instruction in the various creeds of religious faith . . . presents therefore, a *chasm* in a general institution of the useful sciences."[85] The significance of this very serious judgment on instruction in the various creeds is sharpened by the sentiments which Jefferson at that time was expressing in private correspondence. Scarcely four months earlier he had written to Dr. Benjamin Waterhouse, venting his spleen against "impious dogmatists" and "false shepherds" who had adulterated the genuine doctrine of Jesus with "the *deliria* of crazy imaginations," and he "trusts that there is not a young man now living in the United States who will not die an Unitarian."[86]

The dogmatically intolerant Jefferson could insist in the full stature of a great statesman on the equal right of all the faiths before the law and, as an educator, appreciate the beneficient effects of bringing the various faiths together on a university level. In 1818 his solution to the knotty problem was to be content with religious study and investigation by the ethics professor and leave it to each sect to provide further instruction in its own peculiar tenets. In 1822 Jefferson studiously formulates a remedy that is as positive in its provisions in favor of religious studies as it is in guarding against a favoritism that encroaches upon anyone's religious conscience. The detailed suggestions are: that the various denominations "establish their religious schools on the confines of the University,"[87]—in 1818 they had been asked to attend to their own peculiar instructions without the present specific invitation that they do so on state university property; that their students have "ready and convenient access and attendance on the scientific lectures of the university; that students of the university may have reciprocally equal access to the "religious exercises with the professor of their particular sect, either in the building still to be erected . . . or in the lecturing room of such professor." The visitors of the university "would think it their duty to give every encouragement, by assuring to those who might choose such a location for their schools, that the regulations of the University should be so modified and accommodated as to give every facility of access and attendance to their students, with such regulated use also as may be permitted to the other students, of the library, which may hereafter be acquired, either by public or private munificence."[88] Jefferson then concludes with the inviolable principles and premises within which all such dispositions must take place: "But always understanding that these schools shall be independent of the University and of each other."[89] He is satisfied that "such an arrangement would complete the circle of the useful sciences embraced by this institution, and fill the chasm now existing, on principles which would leave inviolate the constitutional freedom of religion."[90] Let us bear in mind that Jefferson is writing not only for himself but also for the commissioners (of whom ex-President Madison was one) and the visitors of the university. A more compact epitome of the intricate and necessarily involved

80

relations between religious beliefs and state schools, one expressed with a more precise constitutional guarantee of the equality of religious freedom and its exercise in education, can scarcely be imagined. The 1822 report is the most telling commentary by Jefferson on his metaphor of the "wall of separation of church and state." The problem of religious freedom and public education engaged Jefferson's mind tenaciously, and with the patience of a great statesman he resolved it without seeking refuge in educational neutralism which, let it be noted, is far from neutral and decidedly offensive to the religious conscience.

Jefferson can barely contain his resentment and anger at the misconstruction placed on his educational provisions despite the meticulous care with which he explains his reason.[91] Three weeks later, on Nov. 2, he wrote to Thomas Cooper:

In our university you know, there is no Professor of Divinity. A handle has been made of this, to disseminate an idea that this is an institution, not merely of no religion, but against all religion. (He then lists the recommendations of Oct. 7, perhaps asking his friend how could he possibly be misunderstood.) In our annual report to the legislature . . . we suggest the expediency of encouraging the different . . . sects to establish, each for itself, a professorship of their own tenets, on the confines of the university, so near as that their students may attend the lectures there, and have the free use of our library, and every other accommodation we can give them; preserving, however, their independence of us and of each other. This fills the chasm objected to (in) ours, as a defect in an institution professing to give instruction in all useful sciences.[92]

And what is equally puzzling is that a century later Jefferson's clear record should have been construed contrary to his explicit meaning by members of the highest tribunal in the American judiciary. The wry irony is that Jefferson's appointment of Cooper, a scientist, to the university faculty was to be blocked by the hue and cry raised by the Virginia Presbyterians for *his* religious views.

In 1824 Jefferson, now rector of the State University of Virginia, draws up the regulations[93] for the university which was scheduled to open within a year. It had taken six years to build and it would not actually open its doors until March of 1825 after a postponement of its original date, Feb. 1, because faculty members from across the ocean had not yet arrived. One would think that he had amply disposed of the university cooperation with religious education in his 1822 report, but he recurs to it again with stronger stipulations. In the 1818 plan the proper solution was "to leave every sect to provide . . . further instruction in their own peculiar tenets."[94] In 1822 the "(v)isitors (of the University) . . . think it their duty to give every encouragement, by assuring those who might choose such a location for their schools, that the regulations of the University should be so modified and accommodated as to give every facility, etc."[95]

In 1824 the opportunity offered the religious sects to build on the university grounds is referred to as "according to the invitation held out to them."[96] In 1822 the arrangements and accommodations are to be such as to provide "greater advantage of enabling the students of the University to attend religious exercises."[97] In 1824 "the students of the University will be free, and expected to attend religious worship at the establishment of their respective sects, in the morning, and in time to meet their school in the University at its stated hour."[98] This statement is surely a very pointed commentary on those persons who today objected to released-time programs on or away from public school property and in the same breath quote Jefferson's "wall of separation!" In 1822 the religious schools may build "on the confines of the University."[99] In 1824 they

82

are invited to build "within or adjacent to the precincts of the University, schools for instruction in the religion of their sect."[100] And as if to erase every doubt as to the status of the students of divinity who also attend any school of the University, they "shall be considered as students of the University, subject to the same regulations, and entitled to the same rights and privileges."[101] A conscientious reading of the various educational plans of Jefferson should leave no room for the misconstruction with which Jefferson has been visited in our times. And if the students of religion should be in want of a room for religious worship as well as for lectures and examinations, the 1824 regulations provide that "one of its (university's) larger elliptical rooms" may be used for such purposes.[102] A year after its opening, on the Fourth of July, 1826, fifty years after he had penned the theological premises justifying the American Declaration of Independence, forty years after discriminatory preferments of the church establishment in Virginia were annulled, Jefferson was to breathe his last. In 1822 and 1824 he had worked toward a positive construction of a formula and its special detailed concrete implementation for the free exercise of religion in education, just as assiduously as he had labored for the removal of the impediments for the equality of religious freedom for all creeds.

THE MODERN PROBLEM

Two considerations remain for our final reflections. Any reference to Jefferson's position on the relations of religious rights and state supported education must be historically correct. It was a problem to which he gave repeated attention and he was not content to avoid the difficulties of

83

formulating a solution by withdrawing into a specious neutrality. As an individual, he was as firmly convinced of his own religious correctness as he was certain that the "various creeds," "sects" and "denominations" were in their expressions of supernaturalism decidedly wrong and a falsification of the "genuine teachings of Jesus." He was, in a word, personally and dogmatically intolerant. He was opposed to error in any form. He was neither a skeptic nor indifferent in religious matters. On the contrary, he held firmly to the ability of reason to attain to religious truths. He saw, however, no contradiction in his mind that public law provisions should guarantee equality of religious freedom for all these creeds, however obnoxious they were to him. That Jefferson was misunderstood in his own time, as he complains in his letter to Cooper, can be explained in part by the limitations of publication in his day. There is no such excuse for scholars today—or for jurists on and off the bench—who engage in quoting Jefferson.

The second consideration is to decide what Jefferson would hold today. He would definitely not compromise the two principles he held inviolable—the equality of religious freedom for all believers and the rights of religious conscience and its free exercise, guaranteed by law, in education. Would he hold today for the same concrete implementations he specified in his own times for the public schools of Virgina? The answer may vary from the affirmative to that of a doubt, a doubt that would extend to almost all of his thoughts, namely, as to whether Jefferson would be so "Jeffersonian" today, a century-and-a-half after his own historic times. This is a question which we think no one can settle convincingly about any historical personage. But there are certain lessons which we can learn from the Jefferson of a century-and-a-half ago which we think are abiding and

84

permanent characteristics of the American formula of church-state relations.

The "wall" that keeps governmental powers from preferential treatment of a religion must be impregnably high. The "wall" that protects the free exercise of religion must be just as high and impregnable. The provisions of public law must be uniformly nondiscriminatory, universally applicable and impartially favorable. Neutrality is not impartiality[103] and that ghostly evasive reference should be confined to limbo once and for all. Nor should the baffling difficulties of implementing the two inviolable principles afford any rational excuse for retreating into that neutrality which is the benign disguise for wholly secular education. Such education, besides being defective, as Jefferson held, cannot but be a contrary influence upon the necessary religious involvements of various disciplines, viz., literature, history, philosophy, value judgments, political science.

Legally the problem today is how to adjust legislative and judicial action to the resolution of the thorny problem of satisfying the legal requirements of the American type of separation of church and state in a manner in accord with the social and religious demands of American history. The problem is complicated not only by the difference in federal and state histories on church-state relations but also by the operation of the religious clauses of the First Amendment through the Fourteenth upon states who disagree among themselves on the constructive interpretation of financial aids.[104]

The First Amendment couples an express declaration of no delegation of power whatsoever to Congress to pass laws respecting religion with just as strong an affirmation of religious freedom—no preference and no interference. The amendment prohibits not only establishment but also any other encroachment upon religious liberties. It is the broad federal meaning of religious liberty which is transferable through the Fourteenth Amendment, not the meaning of any particular state law of any time in our national history. Historically part of the explanation of the bizarre pattern of discriminatory and nondiscriminatory practices in the states and, comparatively, among the states, derives from the fact that the states, unlike the federal government, began with establishments and disestablishments and the transition has been to a religious liberty scarcely discernible from tolerance. Further, the states have maintained through the decades, until recent times, religious tests and qualifications for state public office. The federal government, on the other hand, began with a clear and clean slate of no establishment, no restriction on religious freedom and no religious test for federal office. Consequently, it was able to adopt more easily from the beginning a policy of nondiscriminatory financial assistance to religion, religious activity and religious institutions. The federal government was therefore able to escape the consequences of the tensions of a pluralistic religious society which came to the fore whenever a church or a religion enjoyed a preferred status in law and the other churches and religious societies strove to obtain (with an increase in numbers) an equality before the law. Federal incompetence and impotence to prefer a religion or church and to interfere with the free exercise of religious conscience has never meant, in law and in fact, federal neutrality toward religious life.

We must be confident as Jefferson was in working out an implementation that satisfies all requirements of principle and law. And above all the suspicion that the dogmatically intolerant, the nonbeliever as well as the believer, cannot be politically tolerant, through the provision of public law,

86

should be dispelled by the example of Jefferson who formulated detailed accommodations of state university facilities for the benefit of the various religious denominations whose supernaturalism he disparaged so relentlessly in private correspondence. Jefferson's stature as a statesman concerning the function and scope of public law touching on religious life is more than matched by the grandeur and nobility of his character.

87

3

Religion in Public Education

THE PROBLEM

"Congress shall make no law respecting an establishment of religion, or prohibiting the free exercise thereof." This part of the First Amendment explicitly affirms what Hamilton, Madison and Jefferson held to be implicit in the Constitution, namely, that Congress was not delegated the power to make laws respecting the establishment of religion or the prohibition of its free exercise.

Relevant to this part of the First Amendment are a number of controversies though the years on the legitimacy of the use of public funds for religious purposes; and on the legitimacy, propriety and desirability of religion in publicly supported schools. In accordance with the expressed meaning and significance of the First Amendment, there is unanimity among all Americans against national establishment of religion and against interference with the free exercise of religious beliefs, save for those restraints which the just exigencies of social order require.

Of these two controversial aspects that are discussed with alleged reference to the no establishment clause, this study is concerned primarily with the latter, since this problem will aways continue to persist. It cannot be set aside as readily as proscribed by court rulings on formal religious exercise and instruction.

Recent events have focused a most vexing problem that bristles with many issues, and its complexities present a challenging and almost discouraging affront to an equitable solution. It is imperative that we first take cognizance of the educational, religious, sociological and constitutional issues and their mutual involvement. After that we will suggest a tentative approach toward a solution that will both satisfy our rights and our consciences, and be in accord with our laws. The problem is unavoidable, and to dismiss it is in effect to decide in favor of one contention against another. Perhaps there is not even *a* Catholic solution to the concrete situation, much less *the* Catholic solution except on the level of principle.

EVENTS FOCUS A PROBLEM

On Nov. 30, 1951, the New York Board of Regents issued its *Statement on Moral and Spiritual Training in the Schools,* which opened: "Belief in and dependence upon Almighty God was the very cornerstone upon which our Founding Fathers builded." The Regents maintained that such fundamental belief and dependence are the best securities against the dangers of these difficult days and the adoption of their recommendations the best way of insuring that this government and our way of life shall not perish from the earth. The Regents recommended that in every public school in the state the day begin with a brief prayer as part of a program stressing the moral and spiritual heritage of our country. Of the nine hundred school boards in the state, scarcely one hundred and fifty adopted this pro-

89

posal, according to a report of the State Department of Education.[105] The Regents' Statement contemplated the issuance of a Supplemental Statement setting forth recommendations for programs in the schools emphasizing America's moral and spiritual heritage.

On March 6, 1952, the New York City Board held an open hearing on the Regents' statement and directed that the fourth stanza of "America" be sung daily in connection with the salute to the flag.

The following Jan. 15, the Board of Education passed a resolution requesting the Superintendent of Schools to review the curriculum with a view toward insuring inclusion of appropriate programs of instruction emphasizing the spiritual interest and patriotic motivations of our pioneering ancestors; and the devotion and self-sacrifice of the Founding Fathers and their abiding belief in the principles of democracy.

Supplementary to its Statement of Nov. 30, 1951, the Board of Regents on March 28, 1955, made public its recommendations for school programs on America's moral and spiritual heritage. It prefaced its 1955 Statement with the caution:

In putting such recommendations into effect teachers will be mindful always of the fundamental American doctrine of the separation of church and state, and careful at all times to avoid any and all sectarianism or religious instruction which advocates, teaches or prefers any religious creed. Formal religion is not to be injected into the public school. It is a matter for the church and the home, for the religious leaders and the parents of the child.

Under the synoptic title, "Fundamental Beliefs, Liberty Under God, Respect for the Dignity and Rights of Each Individual, Devotion to Freedom, the Brotherhood of Man under the Fatherhood of God," the Regents gave select citations concerning relevance of religion to our Republic from the Declaration of Independence; from Presidents Washington, Lincoln, Wilson and Eisenhower; from the Supreme Court's ruling in the Zorach Case; from the religious inscription on American money; and from the Constitution of the State of New York. The Regents made two recommendations:

First: That periods be set aside at frequent intervals during the school year which will be devoted to the intensive study of the foregoing and great American documents and pronouncements. The same will give to the student an understanding and appreciation of his role as an individual endowed by his Creator with inalienable rights and as a member of a group similarly endowed; of respect for others, particularly parents and teachers; of devotion to freedom and reverence for Almighty God. Thus, as we heretofore stated, "the school will fulfill its high function of supplementing the training of the home, ever intensifying in the child that love for God, parents and for home which is the mark of true character training and the sure guarantee of a country's welfare."

Second: The development of moral and spiritual values through all the activities and lessons of the school day and particularly by the good example of the school staff . . . Thus our children, inspired by the example of their ancestors, guided by the faith and love of their parents and encouraged by their spiritually sensitive teachers, will renew in their daily lives America's Moral and Spiritual Heritage: Liberty under God, Respect for the Dignity and Rights of Each Individual, Devotion to Freedom.

Here, clearly and unequivocally expressed, is the position that the dependence of our country's welfare upon character training based upon the religious nature of man, as repeatedly professed in American documents, should be taught in public schools in fulfillment of their high function of supplementing the training given by family and church. The Statement rejects the futility and pretensions of laic morality.

91

The Board of Superintendents unanimously approved these recommendations on June 14, 1955, and released for publication in November its "Guiding Statement for Supervisors and Teachers" on "Moral and Spiritual Values and the Schools." This Statement begins with a summary review of the abundantly rich historical evidence that the "American people are, characteristically, a religious people, who derive their accepted moral and spiritual values from religion." The Statement then proceeds to examine the nature of these religious values and to reaffirm their relevance to the preservation and survival of our democracy. It also sets forth the responsibility of publicly supported schools in the transmission and cultivation of these values:

To the public school, as to the home and the church, the full life is, in the final analysis, the objective of all education for all children. This implies that the public school must use every means properly at its disposal to develop in its pupils the cultivation of those values accepted by American society for its welfare and for the good of the individual. These are the moral and spiritual values. It implies, further, that the program of the public schools must reinforce the program of the home and church in strengthening belief in God. At the same time, the schools must also cultivate a respect for adherents of different religions and belief.

After outlining the means and resources in public school curriculum and activities for the inculcation of moral values rooted in religion, the Statement concludes:

At appropriate levels and in appropriate contexts, the public schools teach the role of religion and encourage factual study about religion, but they do not undertake religious instruction. They teach the moral code and identify God as the ultimate source of natural and moral law. They encourage children to discover and develop their relationship to God, referring them also to their families, churches or synagogues. In their programs of moral and

92

spiritual education the public schools maintain a climate favorable to religion without making value judgments about any particualr religions. Thus, the public schools devote their primary efforts to the development of the values and objectives of our American democracy, recognizing their spiritual and religious motivations.

This Statement of the Board of Superintendents of the Public Schools of the City of New York provoked various reactions.[106] Obviously it was not countenanced by secularists and educational neutralists. But most significant was the varied reaction among religious believers. Msgr. John J. Voight, secretary of education of the archdiocese of New York, praised and endorsed the Statement. The Brooklyn Catholic Teachers Association supported it enthusiastically. The Protestant Council of the City of New York gave it tentative approval with the proviso that a revised version consider those who "take a nontheistic attitude" regarding moral and spiritual values. The Board of Rabbis of New York expressed vigorous opposition, and on Dec. 3, five hundred orthodox, conservative and reform rabbis in the New York metropolitan area devoted their Sabbath sermons in support of their opposition. They contended that to bring religious values into teaching would violate the doctrine of separation of church and state, would be a divisive factor among students, and would import a vague theism offensive to all believers. Because of the vigorous opposition it stirred,[107] the report was put to further study by the Committee of Instructional Affairs of the Board of Education, which was expected to return it to the Board of Superintendents for possible modification.[108]

A new controversy[109] developed in the last week of December, 1955, with the distribution of a 158-page publication, an official Board of Education bulletin, entitled,

93

"Curriculum Development in the Elementary Schools." The new dispute centered around an introductory sentence: "Belief in God and the place of religion in the life of the child are essential factors underlying the public school program." The Board of Superintendents' report had been sharply criticized by various Jewish groups, the New York Civil Liberties Union, the Teachers Guild of the AFL-CIO, the United Parents Association, and the Public Education Association. Protesting the new curriculum guide were the New York Board of Rabbis, the New York Regional Chapter of the Anti-Defamation League of B'nai B'rith, and the New York Council of the American Jewish Congress. School Superintendent Jansen had noted, however, that the curriculum guide was in no way related to the superintendents' report.

THE INEVITABILITY OF THE PROBLEM

Apart from the question of the desirability and propriety of religious influence in education according to one's educational philosophy, what renders the problem inevitable is the actual involvement of religion in education—a fact which some Protestants have since come to recognize upon Nicholas Murray Butler's[110] delineation of the problem some years ago, and which has been acknowledged in our day with equal force and persuasion by Dr. Nathan Pusey of Harvard. This blunt fact of the involvement of religion in education is independent of the position generally taken by the Board of Rabbis as to the adequacy, competency and exclusive prerogative of home and church or synagogue regarding religious training.

The involvement of religion in education arises from

94

the nature and content of the subjects taught; from the role of the teacher as educator; from the moral and formative objectives of teaching as well as learning; from the impossibility of departmentalizing the spiritual life of the student as citizen and believer; and from the very theological quality of secularism itself and of educational neutralism. And, as though the problem is not thorny enough, there are also the rights of parents and children who are believers, and the rights of parents and children who are not believers, concerning the quality of public school education which both support by taxes. There are, moreover, the rights of public authority in deciding what kind of education will be given its future citizens in accordance with state and national, official and authoritative professions regarding the basic relevance of religious belief to the founding and continued well being of the Republic.

On Oct. 4, 1956, the New York Board of Education adopted a revised and diluted version of the Statement on Moral and Spiritual Training in Schools. In order to mollify critics the revised New York statement eliminated from the original such passages as "The public schools encourage belief in God," or "The public schools reinforce the program of the home and church in strengthening belief in God." The most radical changes were made in the summaries of the two versions. Even so, there were still objections to such passages as "the concept of infinity cannot do other than lead to humbleness before God's handiwork" and that pupils should be "deeply conscious of the religious underpinning of our moral and spiritual ideas, our western culture and our American democracy."

A disturbing undercurrent is the unpleasant contention that religious influence, if sufficiently definite, would be divisive, and if indefinite and vague, would be meaningless

95

and useless. In addition there are the difficulties which may befall the teacher,[111] rarely a nonbeliever, and his function in the pro-religious orientation in public schooling. Even beyond such expedients as dismissed-time and released-time religious arrangements, the involvement of religion in education, private or public, remains a stubborn and basic fact.

THE SUBJECTS TAUGHT

In the teaching of American history, neither student nor teacher can avoid the many references to the religious and spiritual foundations of our nation, as contained, for instance, in the Mayflower Pact or the Gettysburg Address. Can these facts of American life be excised from the public school textbooks? Is there not a duty of the public schools to transmit the American heritage, with its deep wellsprings of religious and spiritual life, to the young citizenry? What of the questions that inevitably arise in the study of our national history as to the meaning and significance of the doctrine that men are equal because they have been endowed by their Creator with inalienable rights? These are strictly theological terms and religious judgments. And in teaching European history is not the teacher cast in the very delicate role of discussing Christendom, the Age of the Reformation, the rise of totalitarian governments? Determinative norms of judgment will be used in the condemnation of certain absolutist polities. Are not value judgments of right and wrong, good and bad, truth and falsehood inextricably bound up with the study of literature and with the appraisal of human activities and conduct? And does not the disciplinarian function of the public

96

school presuppose in the development of character and integrity a right norm with a moral compulsion in conscience because it comes from something higher than man? Will ideals sustained without religious motivation be strong enough to give direction to a recalcitrant and mobile free will? Will the validity of norms of right and wrong, true and false, rest on conventional mores which vary in time and place, or on state laws which may be changed by majority determination; rather than on "self-evident" religious truths, eternal and unchanging, which compel in conscience because of their divine origin? Evident today in certain sections of our country is the shameful ugliness which our communal consensuses, mores and laws have brought about in racial relations. As we sow we shall reap. Apparently home and church have not sufficed for the rectitude of conscience.

THE PROBLEM IS UNAVOIDABLE

Some educators would meet the problem by seemingly avoiding and ignoring it as nonrelevant and dispensable. Such a position is validated in terms of the prepossessions of a philosophy of life or of a school of pedagogy popular among secular humanists and educational neutralists. But when their position is submitted to rational analysis their argument appears illusory and self-deceptive, though with a spurious facility for deceiving others. In the first place they raise illegitimate issues to which, in addition, they not infrequently give invalid answers. There can be no neutrality because neutrality is impossible. Secular humanism is not religion as the word deserves to be understood; it is neither a substitute for religion nor its equivalent. Both

97

secularists and educational neutralists would inculcate humanitarianism without the divine image; charitable benefactions without the divine commandment; fraternity without the Fatherhood of God; equality before the law without the equality which was before the law.

To escape the relativism and dire consequences of temporal mores and community ethics, secularists are driven to an absolute and this they seek to achieve, evidently without any embarrassment, by investing politics with theological virtues and by constructing a democratic faith and a democratic ethics.

Secular humanism is atheistic humanism—that is to say, it transfers to men the divine prerogatives concerning the ways of men. Faith, hope and charity no longer reach outside and above men for the "substance of things unseen," for "the vision of things to come." The energizing force and motivation of the social order must come wholly and exclusively from the vast potentialities of man as they are increasingly revealed by the exciting adventures of the natural and empirical sciences. One would think that history had recorded sufficiently convincing and tragic lessons from purely human creative politics. A strictly secular education belongs in a strictly secular state where it is necessary and apt for its existence and survival. The American Republic is not a strictly secular state. Adolf Hitler reared his secular state upon a secular education and out of divided souls evoked a blind obedience in fealty to a national faith. There is no room for a purely secular education in our democracy for the secularists are unable to transmit to public school children the religious and spiritual heritage of the American people and the role religious truths have played in our national history. One of America's leading

98

authorities on constitutional law, Dr. Corwin, has said:

> Primarily democracy is a system of ethical values, and that this system of value so far as the American people are concerned is grounded in religion will not be denied by anybody who knows the historical record. And that agencies by which this system of values has been transmitted in the past from generation to generation, the family, the neighborhood, the Church, have today become much impaired, will not be seriously questioned by anybody who knows anything about contemporary conditions. But what this all adds up to is that the work of transmission has been put more and more upon the shoulders of the public schools. Can they then do the job without the assistance of religious instruction? At least, there seems to be a widely held opinion to the contrary.[112]

The denial of human rights, natural and civil; the affirmation of race supremacy; discrimination and the restriction and elimination of "undesirable" minorities have come from purely secular polities and from believers whose consciences have not been in accord with their presumably religious convictions. In terms of constitutional law the secularists commit themselves to absurdities. If American democracy alone was the religion, faith and ethics of the public schools, the First Amendment would then read to mean: "Congress shall make no laws respecting the establishment of democracy nor prohibit the free exercise thereof."

An even more deceptive distortion of American law occurs when secularists would have the no establishment clause of the First Amendment mean, not what it meant to the drafters and ratifiers of the Amendment and continued to mean for one hundred and sixty years thereafter— freedom of religion for religion—but, exclusively, freedom from religion.[113] Invoking Jefferson's metaphor of the "wall of separation" (and blandly ignoring Jefferson's statement

99

regarding facilities in the matter of religious instruction for the publicly supported University of Virgina), they construct a wall of complete separation, impregnably high. But their separatism does not prevent them from having a legal passkey of their own. They read into the no establishment clause their own exception, the establishment of secularism—an unmistakably theological position. Again, their misinterpretation of the no establishment clause leads them to do violence to the free exercise of religion assured to believers by constitutional law, especially its affirmation of the natural law right of parents to direct the education of their children. This inviolable parental tutelage has been upheld by our supreme judicature. Secularism, even as sectarianism, is incompatible with the First Amendment. When the Constitution acknowledges the incompetency of political power in spiritual matters, it is not tolerating but upholding religious liberty.

The educational neutralists, like the secularists, are involved in similar inconsistencies and contradictions. Whereas the secularists would read a theological position of atheism into a denial of the delegation by the people of political empowerment to the national Congress, the educational neutralists would read an educational theory into the First Amendment. But the blunt truth of the matter, of course, is that educational neutralists are, like the secularists, decidedly not neutral; they are positively partial and partisan. It is pretentious to maintain that not to teach a subject is to be noncommittal about it; to omit subject matter is a silent form of teaching which surreptitiously establishes its insignificance and irrelevance. Like social discrimination, doctrinal discrimination avoids and so affirms loudly by its silence an inequality and an intolerance. Educational segregation of subject matter is a positive

100

position. Educational neutralism like secularism is an assault upon the paramount American principle of religious freedom designed to ensure religious belief and practices, and the no establishment clause is a political policy instrumental to that supreme purpose.[114]. The First Amendment was not intended to be, nor has it been for over a century and a half of American life, destructive or hostile to the practice of religion. Secularists and educational neutralists by their silence would excise American history of the countless professions of the nexus between religious and civil liberties asserted by all American presidents and many responsible national leaders. A neutral education is as impossible as the professed neutrality of a nation whose borders are contiguous to nations at war and with whom she carries on commerce and continues relations as usual.

A STUDY OF THE ISSUES

Admitting, therefore, the inevitability of the involvement of religion in public education and rejecting the pretensions of the self-sufficient secularist and the prejudicial neutrality of some educators, the problem then is to give direction to this unavoidable problem in a matter which will respect the rights of conscience and accord with the laws of the American nation.

THE LAW

Sectarian or denominational teaching in public schools was specifically prohibited by most states even before the McCollum decision. Therefore, the teaching of distinctly Catholic, Protestant or Jewish religious tenets in public schools would

101

be in contravention of the religious freedom guaranteed by the First Amendment and made applicable to the states by the Fourteenth Amendment and state constitutions. This prohibition would also interdict the formal teaching of agnostic, skeptical or atheistic tenets in public schooling for acceptance by the students.

The prudence as well as the justice of the law is obvious to anyone who respects the sincerity of the religious beliefs of others. Legally, there is no specific prohibition that the public schools may not teach the meaning of religious terms that appear in basic national documents, nor can there be.

A separate question is the pedagogic and legal propriety of teaching those common fundamentals of religious belief which prevail in the American community. This was the position of Horace Mann,[116] foremost promoter of the public school system. Mann vigorously protested the purely secular form of education, as well as sectarian doctrinal instruction in the public schools. On one occasion he even said that he was in favor of religious instruction "to the extremest verge to which it can be carried without invading those rights of conscience which are established by the laws of God, and guaranteed to us by the Constitution of the State." Mann regarded hostility to religion in the schools as the greatest crime he could commit.

But this question is scarcely distinguishable in the concrete from the teaching of the theological references in our historic documents which give expression to the broad religious consensus of the nation. The problem may prove to be too elusive even for the Supreme Court and its distinction between explanation and doctrine-inculcation. When are informations and explanations, essential and primary functions of teaching, wholly separable from the

102

consequences of some indoctrination? The dilemma will never leave us, nor will we ever be fully secure against the hazards of either choice—to teach or not to teach the religious heritage of our country.

Sectarian teaching of religion in public schools is, of course, sociologically and theologically offensive. The reality of religious pluralism and the respect due to the sincerity of believers as to the truth of their faith militate against sectarian indoctrination. Doubly offensive and inexcusable would be the instilling of agnostic and atheistic suspicions and doubts in the minds of the students.

NEITHER VAGUE NOR DIVISIVE

Two questions arise: what constitutes nonsectarian religious fundamentals? Would their teaching be divisive? If religious fundamentals are understood as the least common denominator, the risk is taken of watering down certain substantial characteristics of different faiths so as to be offensive to their adherents. If by fundamentals is meant those religious truths which are intelligible to the vast majority of Americans and whose acceptance is discernible by their reactions to the religious protestations of our public officials or to occasional religious celebrations and commemorations, then surely there is nationwide concordance in the existence of God; in the equality and inviolability of men who are created and divinely endowed with inalienable rights; and in an ultimate rendering according to God's universal law of justice and charity.

A recent criticism of the "Guiding Statement" of the Board of Superintendents charged that it "substitutes for the belief in God a vague theism, to which, it implies, we

103

all subscribe."[117] This criticism falls wide of the mark. The religious truths in question are far from vague in the minds of the Jewish, Protestant and Catholic believers attending public schools when they hear and read of them as they inevitably must in the study of American history. What is more to the point is that these religious truths, fundamental because they are formally part of the Jewish, Protestant and Catholic faiths, far from dividing have drawn our students together in silent prayer in public school exercises and in the salute of allegiance "under God" to the flag.

Oddly enough and contrary to their protestations, it is the separatists, neutralists and secularists who are truly divisive for they have raised issues that in the past have not troubled the students of public schools; and they have pointed loudly to the differences between the various faiths which students in their generosity keep to themselves. It is their bond which is vague and threateningly dangerous monism, a mechanical unitarism in a spiritual and intellectual vacuum.

As for the role of the teacher, whatever his personal faith he is bound to teach correctly the religious propositions repeatedly affirmed by our government. There is nothing divisive in the idea of brotherhood of men by divine creation, of fraternity by divine commandment of charity and justice binding in conscience. Far from being vague, these are definite religious truths which have bound our nation in peace and in war and have aroused our consciences against injustices in our midst as well as in other countries. A purely secular education is false to the nature of man and to God; false to American history; false to that philosophy of life and education[118] which refuses to departmentalize what is inseparably one—the continuity of the spiritual life and moral development of the whole person, whether at home, at church or synagogue, or at school.

RIGHTS OF CONSCIENCE

One of the most sensitive of considerations of the problem, one that causes immediate reactions of caution, questioning, doubt and warning, is the rights of conscience of believers and unbelievers, of teachers and students. Unfortunately, this problem is usually formulated in an emotional and prejudicial manner as the "rights of the majority v. the rights of the minority." These are fighting words. Democracy has been defined as the rule of the majority in defense of the rights of the minority. The defense of the rights of the minority is the universally accepted test of impartial justice familiarly expressed as equal protection before the law.

Sociological studies show that the vast majority of Americans[119] have been believers. American state and federal courts have repeatedly acknowledged that this fact affects our laws and institutions. As the Court said in the Zorach case: "We are a religious people whose institutions presuppose a Supreme Being . . . We cannot read into the Bill of Rights (such) a philosophy of hostility to religion." Another very significant fact is that in this same case the nation's highest court maintained that state cooperation in the adjustment of school schedules to accommodate sectarian religious needs away from public property "follows the best of our traditions . . . For it then respects the religious nature of our people and accommodates the public service to their spiritual needs."

The force of the argument is not lost or diminished when state cooperation in accommodating sectarian religious needs outside state property is made applicable to nonsectarian religious needs on state property. For the involvement of religion in public education and the equally

105

important fact that American institutions presuppose a Supreme Being must be positively considered in the pedagogy of public schools for the transmission of our religious heritage as a major factor in the formation and growth of the Republic. Pedagogically speaking, there is no special difficulty preventing a teacher, regardless of his faith or lack of it, from teaching correctly to students, regardless of their faith or lack of it, the meaning of words and expression, of facts and factors of American national history which are theological and traditional. This does not mean that teachers are asked to teach sectarian religion, or even teach "about religion," but only that they simply explain what needs to be explained doctrinally in the course of teaching secular subjects. To argue from the legal position of "no state religion" to "no religion at all in public schooling" is not only absurd but also opposed to American legal and national history, and in direct contradiction of the history of education in American schools, public as well as private.[120]

The artificial formulation of the problem can be examined in terms of a vexing and antagonizing antithesis: majority rights v. minority rights. Rights of conscience are those prerogatives of individual consciences which are acknowledged to be inviolable, and are secured and guaranteed—not granted—by law. The history of religious persecution could have been spared many of its wasteful tragedies had it been borne in mind that, theologically speaking, an act of faith is invalid unless free; that according to sound moral philosophy the individual conscience, firmly convinced of the righteousness of its own persuasion, is bound by the dictates of that conscience; and that, expressed sociologically, political allegiance is not contingent upon religious conformity. If the rights of the minority of the nontheistic conscience are subjectively inviolable, so too are the rights of the religious conscience of the majority. Does justice forbid the violation of the nontheistic conscience of the minority but for its sake require, at its request, the submerging of the rights of the religious conscience of the majority? Because of one boy's alleged social embarrassment, the rights of eight hundred and fifty children —eight hundred Protestant, about twenty Catholic and thirty Jewish—as well as the five-year-old arrangement by the Champaign Council of Religious Education (a voluntary association of Jewish, Catholic and Protestant faiths permitted by the School Board of Champaign, Ill., acting under the authority given them by the laws of Illinois, and upheld by the Illinois courts), were effectively challenged before the Supreme Court for their use of public school facilities for their lawful religious instruction. Bearing in mind the case of the Jehovah Witnesses, whose conscientious protest again the salute to the flag was upheld by the Supreme Court, is it not conceivable that one atheist boy might be able to eliminate from all public schools with more reason than the Jehovah Witnesses the pledge of allegiance to the flag, which by Congressional enactment includes the formula "under God?" Why would insistence by the minority on having its way be any less arbitrary than having the "preferred" right of the believing majority equally respected?

The position of the Board of Rabbis is equally incongruous concerning its denial of the inevitability of the involvement of religion in public schooling, to say nothing of its defective concept of philosophy of education and of character formation. The outcry of the nontheist is grossly unfair for it seeks to prevail at any cost, and with complete disregard for the rights of others.

107

Is the religious freedom of the believer who wishes to be educated in the religious heritage of his country less a preferred right than the preferred right of the educational neutralist? In the Zorach case the Supreme Court upheld released time, an arrangement of cooperation between public schools and religious sects for religious instruction away from school premises, and asserted that to deny this adjustment of school programs once a week would be reading into the Constitution a preference for "those who believe in no religion over those who do believe." With what grosser inequity would preference be given to nonbelievers over believers than by denying public schools the right to teach not sectarian religion, or even "about religion," but the very religious deposit of our national history!

Moreover, who is actually going against the grain: the majority of believers who wish to be educated in our national tradition, or those who want to excise God from the texture of our national history? Surely the majority should not prevail in violation of the inalienable rights of the minority, but neither does the converse strike the chord of justice. How then shall this artificial formulation of an antagonizing antithesis be resolved?

First of all, it is misleading to contrast majority rights and minority rights. Rights are harmoniously coherent and if they are otherwise, either the law is defective or the alleged claim is discordantly spurious. The anti-thesis belongs in an entirely different context, "majority rule v. minority rights," a meaning which is irrelevant to the present issue. Equal protection of laws must surely apply to the "majority" as well as to the "minority."

The plain fact is that *there is no violation of the nontheistic conscience*. It is simply being taught the truth about the influence of religious life upon American social and political institutions. Nontheistic students should be taught the American heritage and this task is one of the responsibilities of public schools. Would secularism or educational neutralism do away with the chapels built with government funds or government property at our military, naval and merchant marine academies?

The Supreme Court frequently applies the clear-and-present-danger test to determine whether an individual's religious freedom—one of the preferred rights—has been justifiably restricted. In so doing the Court has maintained that religious freedom may be constrained only if its exercise creates a clear and present danger of an evil that public authority has a right to suppress. The question arises: what substantial harm to the righteous demands of social order, the suppression of which would justify the curtailment of religious freedom, can possibly ensue from the teaching and explanation of America's religious heritage? On the contrary, does not the teaching of America's religious heritage provide the occasion for mutual respect for the sincerity of one another's religious conscience? The point is that students are confronted with the fact of religious pluralism every day and will continue to be for the rest of their lives. Should not the schools assist in the development of a genuine reverence for one another's religious conscience?

PARENTAL DUTIES AND RIGHTS

There is the further question of the rights of parents, to whom the laws of God have entrusted the guidance and education of their offspring. The courts have affirmed this prerogative to be inviolable and primary. Must parents then be obligated not only to support by taxes a secularized

109

public school system but also, in obedience to state compulsory educational laws, to send their children—when they cannot afford to do otherwise—to schools which offer a radically defective education, and which violate their religious beliefs by fostering a statism called democratic faith?[121] Parents, church and state share in the obligation to educate, and parental rights are paramount where the young are concerned. May not religious parents who hold for a religious moral education assert their rights as taxpayers as to the schooling their children should have? Parents may delegate their right to teach but they may never shirk the responsibility of demanding an account from those to whom they have delegated this right. Ultimately, it is a question of a philosophy of education or, more comprehensively, a philosophy of life. Either one does or does not believe that every moment of man's life is religious, that there is no human endeavor which may insulate itself against the all-pervading dominion of God. To educate is to develop an individual as he is meant to be by God. Religious training at home and in church and synagogue, and a purely secular education in godless moral and spiritual values are simply not complementary.

A SOUND FUNCTION OF LAW

A paramount function of sound law is to recognize the sociological panorama of the religious life of the American people and its involvement in the social and political context of the American way of life. The courts have acknowledged this fact in the past and in the Zorach case. The Supreme Court disallowed that the no establishment clause meant neutrality between believers and nonbelievers to the disadvantage of religious believers. The Court held that not to respect the religious nature of the American people and not to accommodate public service to their spiritual needs would constitute a callous indifference on the part of public authority to religious groups. "That would be preferring those who believe in no religion over those who believe." If, as the Court said, the state follows the best of traditions when it encourages religious instruction or cooperates with religious authorities by adjusting the schedule of public events to sectarian needs (away from public property), how much more faithful to American tradition is the state when it requires that its own schools teach America's heritage to its young citizens and future guardians of the Republic? If the vast majority of believers supported the pro-religious orientation outlined in the recommendations of the Board of Regents of the State of New York and of the Board of Superintendents of the City of New York, they too would be acting in accordance with our national tradition.

A novel interpretation of freedom of religion is freedom from religion, and the attempt is sometimes made to give this interpretation precedence over the idea of freedom for religion. Secularism and educational neutralism are not neutralist, much less separatist. The exclusion of religious influence from public schools is an influence against religion.[122] Pro-religious orientation in public schooling is a matter of public concern, for public education is for the public common good as well as for the private good of the individual. Only a loyalty to this "nation under God" can convey the spiritual malice of treason. Only a religious ethics can convey the immorality and the illegality of crime, and make the religiously binding obligations of charity and justice compelling in conscience. Which is more likely to resist "brainwashing," a religious or a godless education in American patriotism?

111

Even before the outbreak of the Korean hostilities on June 25, 1950, the United States Army realized the importance of stressing the religious foundations of moral training. On Jan. 20 of that year the Army had issued its Character Guidance Program for all Army trainees in accordance with Army Regulation 15–120. The preface of the text (Army Pamphlet 16–8) reads in part " . . . the character-development programs stress . . . the moral principles that sustain the philosophy of American freedom, particularly as it is set forth in the opening paragraph of the Declaration of Independence. That philosophy regards man as a creature of God." Possibly in reaction to the appalling spiritual deficiencies of many American soldiers, the U.S. Air Force issued its own statement on the religious presuppositions of the loyal soldier in its new 1955 training manual, *Living for Leadership:*

There is an objective truth which we can discover with our own intellects concerning the nature of man, and of society, and of the purpose of life. There is a natural law and order . . . There is a God who has created man with rights and duties and a purpose in life.

Will the proponents of absolute separation of church and state call into question before our judiciary the constitutionality of teaching these religious truths to soldiers by the tax-supported military forces? (Cf. also the new *Code of Conduct for Prisoners of War* issued in 1955 by a commission appointed by President Eisenhower.)

FIRST AMENDMENT

The constitutional separation of church and state is uncompromisingly precise regarding laws "respecting an establishment of religion or prohibiting the free exercise thereof."

112

Concerning these two intrusions upon religious freedom let the Jeffersonian wall be high and impregnable. But between these two walls there has been from the earliest days of our national history a spacious corridor of cordial concourse, a mutually friendly cooperation manifest in countless ways between government and religion that was born of the conviction that this nation was conceived under God and for its survival and the preservation of its liberties must endure under God. According to the Court in the Zorach case:

> The First Amendment, however, does not say that in every and all respects there shall be a separation of Church and State. Rather, it studiously defines the manner, the specific ways, in which there shall be no concert or union or dependency one on the other. That is the common sense of the matter.

By what right, therefore, shall education in publicly supported schools be exorcised, as from an evil influence, from the allegedly divisive and vague religious protestations of American presidents in order to keep the students in the dark about the spiritual heritage which underlies our democracy? The interrelation between religion, education and government has been repeatedly affirmed ever since the Northwest Ordinance of 1787: "Religion, morality, and knowledge, being necessary to good government and the happiness of mankind, schools and the means of education shall forever be encouraged."[123] Historically and politically, religious and civil liberties have been interdependent. Where freedom for religion and pro-religious orientation have been gradually narrowed, neutralized and insulated, so too have civil liberties been correspondingly undermined. This is a fact which no schooling, least of all publicly supported education, may ignore.

113

CONCLUSION

"Freedom is not free." For the preservation of American religious and civil liberties and for the survival of majority "preferred rights" the public schools, together with home discipline and sectarian religious instruction, must educate the future guardians of our Republic in the truth that the political freedom of men issues from their freedom as children of God. It is the godless state which in our times has lowered the Iron Curtain between free and captive peoples and which advocates without reservation its mission to bring all the nations of this earth to its secular and materialistic way of life. Its schooling is geared to this universal mission by a purely secular education which banishes God from its books, its lessons and its instruction. Our public schools have the responsibility of strengthening the American way of life against this threat whose major barrier is at this time the very same American way of life. Those believers who are critical of and who oppose the original recommendations of the Board of Regents, and who maintain that only moral and spiritual values without reference to their theological presuppositions should be taught in public schooling would do well to recall the words of Washington:

Of all the dispositions and habits which lead to political prosperity, religion and morality are indispensable supports . . . reason and experience both forbid us to expect that national morality can prevail in exclusion of religious principle.

On Nov. 23, 1952, the Rt. Rev. Horace W. B. Donegan,[124] Bishop of the Protestant Episcopal Diocese of New York, charged in a sermon that public education "has come, by and large, to be dominated by an educational philosophy grounded in naturalism . . . The Roman Catholic hierarchy

114

has brought to the fore an issue that all American citizens and especially those of religious convictions, can no longer ignore." Asserting that an education which excludes the religious understanding of man's nature and destiny "does in fact shape the child's mind and spirit in a secularist mold," Bishop Donegan added:

The Roman Catholic Bishops[125] are right in their recognition that this is not healthy for the nation and for the maintenance of a free democratic society. We should encourage efforts to provide more adequate hearings for the Judeo-Christian heritage in public education and also encourage our church schools in their efforts to provide education which is explicitly Christian in its orientation to acknowledge [sic].

In November, 1955, the National Conference on Religion and Public Education convened in St. Louis to discuss this very problem. Four major Protestant groups participated. It maintained:

Since religious truth is a part of our heritage of truth, it should be included in the child's education wherever relevant to the subject matter of public education.[126]

This Protestant conference made no exception, as did the Protestant Council of the City of New York, for "the nontheistic attitude" toward moral and spiritual values. "The public school must recognize," it said, "that most American people believe in the existence of God, and it must treat the influence of this belief, in history and in contemporary society."

Deeply religious believers who are committed to the proposition that education should be directed to the whole of life, civic and religious, would do well to support official recommendations that assist the continuity of spiritual development at school, home and church. Otherwise they may

115

find themselves unhappily allied[127] with secularists and educational neutralists in the promotion of a godless education; in the transmission of a maimed American heritage; and in the communication of knowledge not rooted in religious wisdom.

Public school education is the universal concern of all faiths, Catholic, Protestant, Jewish.

In 1802 Thomas Jefferson wrote of the "wall of separation" in a private letter to the Baptists of Danbury, Conn. But Jefferson also said that "religion is the Alpha and Omega of the moral law."[128] And Jefferson touched upon the question of our own day when, in 1822, he discussed the teaching of religion at the University of Virginia, a publicly supported institution:

It was not, however, to be understood that instruction in religious opinion and duties was meant to be precluded by the public authorities, as indifferent to the interests of society. On the contrary, the relations which exist between Man and his Maker, and the duties resulting from those relations, are the most interesting and important to every human being, and the most incumbent one is study and investigation.[129]

Jefferson also wrote:

Can the liberties of a nation be thought secure, when we have removed their only firm basis, a conviction in the minds of the people that these liberties are the gifts of God?[130]

Surely public schooling must share the responsibility of conveying this conviction to the rising generation of Americans especially since its immediate task—not that of home or church—is to teach[131] the historical origins of our civil liberties and the religious motivations requisite for their continued preservation.

116

4

PRAYER IN PUBLIC SCHOOLS

It is important at the outset of this discussion to define the constitutional issue involved in *Engel v. Vitale*.[132] The issue was not simply prayer in public schools. No legal power can prevent a student from reciting privately his prayers while sitting in the school library or while standing in the schoolyard—provided he does not interfere with any academic assignments or with prescribed recreational employments. All prayer is personal; it is a religious exercise, wheresoever it is said, in private or public institutions, and on any occasion. No description of prayer as ceremonial deprives it of its religious nature and meaning. Only the internal disposition or outward demeanor of a private individual or of a public official indicate whether he is truly praying or not. Prayer is always and on every occasion a religious exercise or it is not prayer at all. A ceremonial prayer which is not a religious act is a contradiction in terms.

Prayer is individual when a person prays by himself or in the midst of others for his own intentions. And prayer is corporate when several persons pray together in unison for one another, or for a common purpose. Corporate prayer may be at home, as when a family prays together, or in a house of worship, as when a congregation professing the

117

same creed takes part in a common liturgy. Corporate prayer may also be civic, as when fellow citizens voluntarily unite to pray to God for divine blessings upon their country. From the earliest days of our history, it has been a time-honored and cherished tradition of the American people to respond in prayer at the official request of government authorities on solemn public occasions, in time of impending peril, during war and peace. Men, women and children of different religious confessions and church affiliations, united by the common bond of belief in God, have joined their hearts and minds in a corporate act of prayer for the preservation, survival and prosperity of America. Civic corporate prayer has been one of the most effective unifying spiritual bonds in our national history. In the Engel case, no one disputed that prayer was a religious act. The Court admitted the absence of regulatory compulsion and punitive coercion.

Justice Douglas made these detailed admissions in his concurring opinion:

> First a word as to what this case does not involve. Plainly, our Bill of Rights would not permit a State or the Federal Government to adopt an official prayer and penalize anyone who would not utter it. This, however, is not that case, for there is no element of compulsion or coercion in New York's regulation requiring that public schools be opened each day with the . . . prayer. . . . The prayer is said upon the commencement of the school day, immediately following the Pledge of Allegiance to the flag. The prayer is said aloud in the presence of a teacher, who either leads the recitation or selects a student to do so. No student, however, is compelled to take part. The respondents have adopted a regulation which provides that "neither teachers nor any school authority shall comment on participation or non-participation . . . nor suggest or request that any posture or language be used or dress be worn or be not used or not worn." Provision is also made for excusing children, upon written request of a parent or guardian, from the

saying of the prayer or from the room in which the prayer is said. A letter implementing and explaining this regulation has been sent to each taxpayer and parent in the school district. As I read this regulation, a child is free to stand or not stand, to recite or not to recite, without fear of reprisal or even comment by the teacher or any other school official. In short, the only one who need utter the prayer is the teacher; and no teacher is complaining of it. Students can stand mute or even leave the classroom if they desire.

The prayer in its simple wording was a solemn declaration of belief in the existence of Almighty God and a public acknowledgment of our dependence upon God as a nation and as individuals. There was no intent or effect of "teaching" a new belief in God.[133] The prayer was an open affirmation of a faith already possessed by every participant. The approval of the parents incontestably upholds this fact. The prohibition against any comments on the prayer was to ensure this fact. Voluntary participation and liberty of exemption gave the widest possible scope to personal response of conscience.

AN ESTABLISHMENT OF RELIGION

The Supreme Court ruled that because the prayer had been composed by a governmental agency it fell under the ban of the no establishment clause. However, this cardinal argument of the Court on governmental composition may not be as telling as it seems. If by composition it is understood that the prayer originated in wording and meaning wholly with the New York Board of Regents and entirely on their own initiative, then the argument is without foundation. The New York educational authorities were motivated in part by the broad public consensus authentically embodied in American national documents on the religious

119

foundations of the Republic and, in part, by the rights and anxieties of religious-minded parents of students in the public schools. The Regents were guided in the writing of the prayer in context and in words by state constitutions, by congressional resolutions and laws, by presidential acts, and by practices in the judiciary. Fifty state constitutions, in one way or another, acknowledge their dependence upon Divine Providence, express their gratitude to God as the Author of American civil and religious liberties, and pray for His continuing guidance and counsel in their governmental deliberations.

In addition to legislative and military chapels and chaplaincies, acts of the national Congress and other deliberative assemblies have called for days of prayer through executive proclamations. The day after the national Congress passed the proposal which became the First Amendment, it passed a resolution calling for the designation of "a day of public thanksgiving and prayer." This tradition of civic corporate prayer at the invitation of government officials has been, with but two exceptions, unbroken from the days of George Washington to the present administration. More pertinent to the issue at hand, Congress has officially prescribed and adopted the divine invocation on American coinage and currency, in the national anthem and motto, and in the Pledge of Allegiance to the flag. What the New York Board of Regents did was neither novel nor original. Only in a minimal sense—almost in the capacity of an amanuensis—may the prayer be called the Regents' composition. They simply gave expression to what the American people and their duly elected representatives have ratified and adopted in every decade of our national history.

While the majority opinion written by Justice Black

120

pivots the decision technically on governmental composition of the prayer, construed as one of the exercises of a proscribed state-established church under the ban of the First Amendment, Justice Douglas, on the other hand, settles upon governmental financing of religious exercises. Both the majority and concurring opinions isolate elements of state-church establishment, elements which by themselves are not necessarily derivative of or conducive to state-church establishment. Indeed, governmental composition of a prayer—though not any prayer—and certain governmental financing of religious exercises may be justifiably sustained by the religious liberty clause. (In this instance, there was greater use of what was already financed: the schools. An additional specific expenditure of public funds was not entailed by the optional recitation of the New York prayer.) In severing these elements from one another, the way is paved for absolutizing an isolated element into a constitutional barrier, whether or not anyone suffers an infringement of religious liberty and without regard for the equal protection the law extends to all, believer and nonbeliever, consentient and dissident. Such an absolutizing process gradually expands from a narrow legalism to a broad premise of proscription. For example, the New York Commissioner of Education has ruled that a part of "The Star-Spangled Banner" may not be used as a school prayer.

The radical source of the antinomies which have been inserted by court interpretation into the religious clauses of the First Amendment is the as yet unsettled legal question (historically, there appears to be less doubt about it) of whether the two clauses dealing with no establishment and free exercise so correspond to one another that an adjudication under one clause may not be at the expense

121

of the legal guarantees of the other; or whether the two clauses may be interpreted in exclusive isolation to one another. Until and unless this question of the interrelationship of the two clauses is resolved, the absolutist construction of the no establishment clause which Justice Wiley Rutledge put forth in his dissenting opinion in Everson and which the Court adopted in McCollum is likely to prevail over the original authentic meaning of no establishment as explained by Madison in his rejoinders to questions put to him in the debates of Congress. The danger involved in the absolutist interpretation is that the judiciary may over-reach itself by pre-empting the democratic political process and embodying on its own initiative public policy into constitutional law. In Zorach, the possibilities of harmoniously relating the two religious clauses to one another in specific programs of mutual accommodation appeared to be an implementation of Justice Black's assertion in Everson about "the interrelationship of these complementary clauses" and his warning against interjecting a religious discriminatory norm into the First Amendment.

Another source of ambiguity is the extent to which governmental aid to religion may be given. Thus far the Court has not formulated practical norms beyond which the political process may not extend. The wide variety of legislative precedents, from the beginning of the Republic to this day, of governmental financing of religious life directly, indirectly or incidently offers the greatest obstacles to the judicial construction of such norms. Perhaps as a last resort, public opinion may provide the practical wisdom to which intercredal dialogues hope to make sensible contributions. Some constitutional lawyers have formulated a "neutral principle" as opposed to the principle of neutrality in the area of federal aid to education. This neutral principle

122

looks to the standard of public function and does not allow religion to be the cause for action or inaction, since the religious clauses of the First Amendment prohibit classification that would entail conferment of a benefit or the imposition of a burden. Under this neutral principle, the prayer case might have considered the question of whether civic corporate prayer was a constitutionally justifiable exercise for the promotion of an educational program to foster in school children moral and spiritual values which have been traditionally part of our national heritage. The determination of this issue would in turn rest on the ulterior question of whether it is part of the public function of tax-supported schools to transmit the spiritual heritage of the nation as it is authentically embodied in the official acts and the authoritative documents of American history.

One optimistic argument is that the Court decision might not proscribe the optional recitation of a prayer composed by non-officials. But the fact and the law are that whatever takes place permissively in a state school under official supervision or conduct necessarily involves governmental responsibility to some degree. It is quite possible that the high tribunal overexaggerated the significance of the role of the New York Board of Regents in the construction of the prayer and foresaw potential dangers to church and state wholly out of proportion to its real intent. Not every and any government involvement in a religious act is *eo ipso* suspect and tainted with unconstitutionality. One must look to the context, purpose and concrete circumstances of the religious act to ascertain its constitutional propriety. It would seem that an officially prepared civic corporate prayer, publicly known, approved and consented to in advance, might have been favorably viewed as a calculated precaution to ensure the necessary constitutional safeguards

123

against any surprise encroachments upon a sectarian conscience by the impromptu prayer of a well meaning student or teacher. Of the two likely opposing interpretations, the Court chose the negative one. The pivotal question may well have turned on the rights of religious-minded parents and school children to choose freely to participate in an official prayer modeled on the country's national documents.

ANCIENT HISTORY AND MODERN LAW

As though to substantiate its fears about an official prayer, the Court reached back to sixteenth century England and the *Common Prayer Book* which an established church imposed upon a nation. The employment of history in the determination of cases should be subject to more rigorous canons of constitutional relevance than was exercised in the ruling on prayer. The *Common Prayer Book* and its succeeding amended versions were composed by the Established Church of England with the deliberate intent of effectuating revolutionary doctrinal changes—at first upon those unsuspecting faithful who still clung to articles of faith according to papal teaching after the breach with Rome, and in the following century upon alert and vigorously resisting Puritans. It was deliberately designed not only to change ancient ceremonial administration of the sacraments, but its wording was calculated to instill in the people the new theological doctrines of the Episcopal Church that touched upon the meaning, substance and validity of the sacramental rites. The *Common Prayer Book* was an instrument of radical credal changes prescribed for the willing and the unknowing, and the English government was a party to this.[134]

124

The New York prayer, however, was not a surprise en-croachment upon sectarian confessions. It conformed with beliefs already held; it was imposed on no one; it was recommended to all; it was freely adopted by the local school board; and in the case in point, it was voluntarily participated in by all school children with the approval of their parents, with but one exemption—the highest degree of near unanimity possible.

The constitutional relevance of sixteenth and seventeenth century English history was without any substantive anal-ogy to the New York case. The resort to the historical past does not enlighten if it serves to evoke ancient fears and premonitions out of tune with the times and popular sensi-bilities. Americans have a right to fashion their own con-stitutional history in church-state relations without being burdened by the memories of religious wars and animosities of their distant forebears.

Perhaps in an effort to bolster the weakness of the his-torical analogy, the Court sought to bridge the span of centuries and the disparity of national experiences by the use of a "bad tendency" rule together with an agreement based on indirect coercive pressure. The majority opinion said that "a union of government and religion tends to destroy government and to degrade religion." But when government encourages religious life as part of its spiritual heritage, it strengthens itself and enhances religious liberty. And both the dark and bright lessons of history will illus-trate that the governments which show impartial accommo-dations for the free exercise of religious liberty are the wonder of mankind and the hope of all churches. As for the indirect coercive pressure, it is no more—and perhaps even less—than what might be inferred from a voluntary salute to the flag with or without the divine reference, or in

125

the singing of the national anthem and in the program of released time for religious instruction.

It is no small cause for wonder then that in all of the First Amendment cases touching upon education and religion, only once does the Court, in resorting to Jefferson, consider his plans for lower and higher education which he drew up for his own state of Virginia upon his retirement from the presidency. His educational plans of 1814,[135] 1817,[136] 1818,[137] 1822[138] and 1824[139] disclose three principles to be permanent in Jefferson's mind. First, that a totally non-religious education is defective. Secondly, government is to offer impartial encouragement and, if need be, accommodations for the expression of religious life in state schools. Thirdly, in the manner of mutual accommodation and cooperative relationship, neither government nor religion is to lose any measure of its proper competence and independent jurisdiction.

Jefferson never construed such cordial arrangements and mutual adjustments as tantamount to a union of church and state which would tend to destroy the one and degrade the other. If the high tribunal was in search of Jefferson's mind on a practice that bore some substantial constitutional analogy to the New York prayer case it might have examined his draft for the establishment of state elementary schools which the Virginia Assembly enacted into law in 1817. Part of the eleventh provision of the act reads:

> The said teachers shall, in all things relating to education and government of their pupils, be under the direction and control of the visitors; but no religious reading, instruction or exercise shall be prescribed or practiced inconsistent with the tenets of any religious sect or denomination.

For Jefferson there was only one absolute and all-controlling restriction on any religious exercise or instruction in the elementary grades: that it be not inconsistent with the confessional tenets of the school children. He was most anxious to guard the religious conscience of all minors against the more learned persuasion of adult instructors. All of his educational plans insist upon a positive doctrine of impartial and mutually beneficient accommodation between the religious conscience and the state schools. The New York prayer gave offense to no denominational confession. On the contrary, it was willingly recited precisely because it was in full accord with professed beliefs. This does not mean that Thomas Jefferson should be considered the constitutional oracle of governmental relations with religion in education. But if the Supreme Court chooses to quote him, it ought to have recourse to the very documents that give his own explicit, direct and pertinent testimony. Whether the Court might then still wish to follow him remains an open question.

One of the most engaging enterprises of the high tribunal is the frequency with which it employs James Madison's justly famed *Memorial and Remonstrance Against Religious Assessments* of 1785 and the ease with which its meaning is bent beyond its authentic purpose. In 1784 Patrick Henry had proposed to the Virginia Assembly a "Bill Establishing a Provision for Teachers of the Christian Religion" with the expectation that such a comprehensive tax support would find acceptance with all Christians, for it would take the place of the abrogated provision for the support of Anglican ministers only. It was against this preference through tax support of a religion, a broadly defined Christianity under the benign mantle of the Anglican Establishment, that Madison directed his famed *Memorial:*

127

Who does not see that the same authority which can establish Christianity, in exclusion of all other Religions, may establish with the same ease any particular sect of Christians, in exclusion of all other Sects? That the same authority which can force a citizen to contribute three pence only of his property for the support of any one establishment, may force him to conform to any other establishment in all cases whatsoever.[140]

The New York prayer was singularly free of any of these Madisonian premonitions. It allowed Christians of every denomination and non-Christians of any confession to join in a unifying corporate prayer wholly of their own choice and in accord with their own religious conscience. Fifty signers of the Declaration of Independence—thirty-four Episcopalians, thirteen Congregationalists, six Presbyterians, one Baptist, one Quaker and one Catholic—confessed publicly to self-evident truths in the common patrimony of human nature which the Creator had endowed with certain inalienable rights. And Paul of Tarsus, Jewish Apostle of Christianity among the Gentiles, taught that knowledge of God is open to human reason apart from the teachings of divine revelation.

As for the Court's reference to James Madison, apart from its misleading use of his *Memorial,* it scarcely takes any cognizance of Madison's own unequivocal explanation of the scope and meaning of the no establishment clause recorded in the congressional debates.[141] And further, it takes no note of the significant fact that ex-President Madison was one of the commissioners of the University of Virginia for whom Jefferson drafted the educational plan of 1818 for submission to the legislature of the state. The plan declares that:

(T)he proofs of . . . God, the creator, preserver and supreme ruler of the universe, the author of all the relations of morality, and

128

of the laws and obligations these infer, will be within the province
of the professor of ethics; to which adding the developments of
these moral obligations, of those in which all sects agree, with a
knowledge of the languages, Hebrew, Greek, and Latin, a basis will
be formed common to all sects.

PSYCHOLOGY AND LAW

The establishment clause, the Supreme Court said, does
"not depend upon any showing of direct governmental
compulsion and is violated by the enactment of laws which
establish an official religion whether the laws operate directly to coerce the non-observing or not." Perhaps the
Court was simply saying that, as in England today, direct
governmental compulsion need not be a necessary incidence
of proscribed establishment even though it almost always
entails at least indirect coercive pressure. In a word, the
Court ruled the element of compulsion to be constitutionally non-relevant and not as controlling as it had opined in
the McCollum and Zorach cases.

Indirect coercive pressure upon the religious noncon-
formist is everywhere, apart from those circumstances
where there is governmental provision for religious expression in public institutions. It takes its strongest emotional
experience in a constraining feeling of embarrassment. This
is generally the concomitant of most acts of dissent and
nonconformity. Public law is committed to the defense of
individual rights, to the remedy and redress of hurt rights,
not to hurt feelings unless the hurt is such that it effectively
impedes the free exercise of personal choice. Public law is
not required to convert the psychology of dissent into a
constitutional principle. It is not the function of law to
remove the situations wherein contrary choices may en-

129

gender contrary feelings. The dissenter must be the first to acknowledge that the condition for his own dissent is to live and let live. Good will in a community rests in great measure on people leaving others to their own choices. No man is an island to himself in society. Robinson Crusoe was seemingly free from any social inhibitions until one day he noticed the footprints of another person and from that moment on the law of mutual adjustment and tolerance set in. The right of the conscientious objector is to shield his own conscience, not to strike down the religious rights of his neighbors. Everyone is a conscientious objector and no one should enjoy an exclusive privilege to the prejudice of others.

Jewish Orthodox want an exception for their ritual slaughter of animals in humane slaughter laws. Jehovah Witnesses are exempt from the salute to the flag. Pacifists object to combatant and noncombatant military service. Christian Scientists are excused from hygiene courses. One atheist child wiped out a voluntary cooperative arrangement of five years standing for religious instruction in public schools. Sabbatarians oppose Sunday Laws. Catholics oppose the use of public funds for the promotion of birth control instructions at home and in any foreign aid program. The Amish raise religious objections to the Social Security tax. These are but a handful of the instances of legally and politically effective protests. Is there any room for conscientious protest against godless education in public schools? Would Thomas Jefferson's protest be heeded today?

If words have substantive meaning, a captive audience is an audience whose involuntary presence is forcibly detained or whose involuntary participation is compelled. To have denied the school children the choice of joining in the

130

recitation of the prayer was to have denied them the opportunity of sharing in the spiritual heritage of the nation. The governmental denial of freedom of choice is as much coercion as the imposing of an action. The argument that public law is required to uphold the conscientious dissenter who is impervious to indirect coercive pressure, divisiveness, and the likelihood of social stigma and isolation that may possibly follow upon a governmental program of religious accommodation, bears within itself a premise of assault upon the salute to the flag in the public schools to which the Jehovah Witnesses oppose their religious conscience.

There has been a full and truly vicious circle, from religious persecution, intolerance and church establishment to benign tolerance; to disestablishment; to equality of all faiths before the law; to equality of belief and nonbelief before the law; and now to the secularists' and the religious dissenters' intolerance of religious belief in public law. The wry irony is that this is being done in the name of and for the sake of religious liberty.

American believers are losing by default. They have taken their spiritual heritage for granted. They have allowed a creeping gradualism of secularism, under one specious pretext or another, to take over their public schools. A vociferous and highly organized pressure group is exerting its own form of indirect coercive pressure upon the American community. Determined to deflect American national traditions and heritage from their authentic historic course, this group is cutting a devisive swath across the nation, advertising for clients to challenge in court what is obnoxious to them. Whoever works for the destruction of the positive doctrine of accommodation and mutual adjustment must shoulder the blame for uprooting the bonds of concord and friendship and for forcibly injecting bitter antagonisms into the

131

nation's pluralistic society. Political and legal action alone cannot create the moral and social impulses which are the conditions of harmony in a community. With full regard for the radical and primary rights of all parents to guide the education of their children in public or in private schools, members of a local community can strive, with persevering good will, to find a reasonable accommodation and mutual adjustment of one another's choices. In this way law becomes—as it ought—the formal expression of the practical wisdom of a self-regulating community. Dissidents and consentients should be motivated to the exercise of cultivated rights of men living in fellowship, not as strangers in a contest of absolute and conflicting claims.

The more the context of the New York prayer and the circumstances attending its optional recitation are examined, the more can be discerned the vast possibilities it offered for the increase of friendly community life.

First, the children and their approving parents of different faiths and church affiliations came together in a prayer based on the common bonds of their religious beliefs. Their religious sectarianism was in no way experienced as a barrier to the brotherhood of all men under the Fatherhood of God. One would suppose, with all the adult incantations about the intercredal relations and the counsels—on all sides—of charity and good will against divisiveness, that here was a truly unitive bond of intercredal relations in the most sensitive time of the school children's formative years.

Secondly, it provided an opportune and excellent educational training and habituation to the exercise of individual choice in the midst of others according to the vaunted American boast of individualism and free self-expression. Religious differences are a very broad fact even for the most enlightened adults, and social adjustment in this matter is essential to good community relations. Should not the

132

youngsters mature gradually in this delicate experience with civility toward one another without resentment and without inhibition? The circumstances for the corporate prayer provided an early schooling both for the dissidents and for the consentients to advance in mutual reverence for one another's religious choices.

Thirdly, the dissenter and the minority must surely be shielded from majoritarian imposition. So too must the majority be protected from the unilateral dictation of the absolute dissenter. It is a strange pathology that when people in increasing numbers freely choose to act agreeably in unison there is less cause for public gratification than in the uncompromising protestations of the dissenter. The numerical superiority of a consensual agreement should not be constitutionally suspect, and if conformity is the flower of human freedom, the wider the area of religious consensus among the variety of religious confessions, the greater will be the harmony among men of good will. Only when the dissenter treasures the liberties of others as his own and insists on equal freedom and the same legal immunity for opposing choices that he demands for himself, will he act in the name of law and justice.

No one can deny that public law is burdened with an almost insurmountable task when it is confronted with the problems of religious pluralism. The voluntary nondenominational prayer was possibly one of the best and, at that, a minimal resolution of this thorny moral-legal problem.

SEPARATION AND RELATION

Separation of church and state in American law is uniquely an American experience. Its meaning derives from the constitutional history of the days of the Northwest Ordinance to the construction of the interfaith chapel at the

Air Force Academy in Colorado. Separation of church and state is a positive affirmation, not a negative protestation. Its paramount purpose is to preserve unimpaired and inviolable the freedom and independence of both church and state. It is but the counterpart of an orderly and harmonious relationship of friendly powers, a relationship of cordial cooperation and of benevolent accommodation, not a relationship of mutually exclusive isolation. In Everson the Court held for equal benevolent impartiality to believers and unbelievers alike. In Zorach a positive doctrine of accommodation was opposed to a neutrality of total abstention, of indifference, of suspicion and hostility.

We are a religious people whose institutions presuppose a Supreme Being. We guarantee the freedom to worship as one chooses. We make room for as wide a variety of beliefs and creeds as the spiritual needs of man deem necessary. We sponsor an attitude on the part of the government that shows no partiality to any one group and that lets each flourish according to the zeal of its adherents and the appeal of its dogma. When the state encourages religious instruction or cooperates with religious authorities by adjusting the schedule of public events to sectarian needs, it follows the best of our traditions. For it then respects the religious nature of our people and accommodates the public service to their spiritual needs. To hold that it may not would be to find in the Constitution a requirement that the government show a callous indifference to religious groups. That would be preferring those who believe in no religion over those who do believe (*Zorach v. Clauson*, 343 U.S. 306, 312, 1952).

In the Zorach opinion which Justice Douglas wrote, he listed, with apparent approval and as though giving substance to his argument, several tax-supported religious exercises by public officials and in public institutions:

Prayers in our legislative halls; the appeals to the Almighty in the messages of the Chief Executive; the proclamations making

134

Thanksgiving Day a holiday; "so help me God" in our courtroom oaths—these and other references to the Almighty that run through our laws, our public rituals, our ceremonies, would be flouting the First Amendment. A fastidious atheist or agnostic could even object to the supplication with which the Court opens each session: "God save the United States and this Honorable Court."

In *Engel v. Vitale,* Justice Douglas forgot the fastidious objector and attached himself to an absolutizing principle of governmental financing of religious activity (and every governmental action is tax-supported) that would abrogate the multitude of governmental involvements in those religious exercises he had cited with approval in Zorach. Now, apparently, a taxpayer may have a stronger case before Justice Douglas as a fastidious financier than as a fastidious conscientious objector.

The New York prayer was a reasonable and proper accommodation to the spiritual needs of the American people in accordance with the spiritual heritage of the country. What absolute right does a dissenter have to protest against such an orderly harmony when the government acts to foster the relevance of religion to our national existence? To what purpose then may a court reason, "If this is allowed to take place, dire consequences will therefore inevitably follow." Politics, social relations and public law cannot be regulated solely by narrow legal ergotisms. Each human experience is invested with sensibilities of its own times and the present may presage a future wholly alien to the heavy hand of the past. The law of progress is as applicable to public law as to other human enterprises. Far from being a dark beginning, a first experiment on national liberties, a portent of dangers to come, the New York prayer was, on the contrary, a refined product of American constitutional history on church-state relations. It was also sensi-

135

tive to the rights of conscience of all—of parents and their children; of participants and nonparticipants; of equal neutrality between believer and nonbeliever; of impartiality among all the religious confessions, with due regard to the government's role to foster in public schools the relevance of belief in God to our national existence—and it gave immunity for personal choice.

Every generation of Americans has admitted to the role of the government in attesting to the religious foundations of the Republic. Occasionally, though, one hears and reads of statements that religious inscriptions on coins and currency are a profane use of divine invocations. Of course, no one can argue conclusively that there must be religious inscriptions on coinage. But given the fact by congressional enactment, one may question the charge of the impropriety of employing divine references on currency. Radically speaking, it is really a question of asceticism. Optimistic asceticism affirms that the original goodness of divine creation forever retains the image of godliness against any evil-doing. All things remain sacred and for this reason St. Paul wrote that all creation calls out "Abba Pater," and our Divine Lord said that the stones would cry out in His praise if the jubilant shouts of the children had been stifled. Through the centuries men have quarried stones and marble to raise magnificent houses of worship. Most of the tangible articles used in divine services are of gold, silver and the finest raiment. There is also a somber asceticism once prevalent among the English and American Puritans which saw in these instrumentalities the danger of distraction or interference with direct communication with God. This view, however, is not relevant to the issue.

The charge of profane use rests logically upon a presupposition of Manichaeism which considers corporeal and material things as somehow vitiated, tainted and imbued with a radical principle for evil in eternal contest with the spiritual principle of Goodness for the allegiance of men. In this view, material things in no way can give glory to God. Optimistic asceticism affirms, on the contrary, that the source of evil does not spring from things—*falsitas non ex rebus sed ex peccatis* (St. Augustine) but from a love that is not God-centered—*nonfaciunt bonos vel malos mores nisi boni vel mali amores* (St. Augustine). Optimistic asceticism does not demand or require that there be divine invocation on currencies. But it does deny that such inscriptions on coinage are a profane use. They are in accord with the dominical prayer for daily bread and may serve as a telling reminder that commercial instruments of exchange are not to be debauched by dishonest trafficking. Also, religious-minded citizens may wish divine blessing and providence for the national economy.

If federal and state governmental officials and public institutions engage in religious activity, why should the First Amendment operate to greater duress upon a local school board and the school children who wish to say a prayer together? The New York prayer was no more a violation of the no establishment clause in public school activities than optional participation in the singing of the national anthem, the Pledge of Allegiance, the released time religious instruction program, and the statutory alternate of testifying under oath or by affirmation in court proceedings. In Zorach we were told that the "problem, like many problems on constitutional law, is one of degree." But in the prayer case, the Court perceived an absolutizing principle which posed a threat to government and religion.

137

ONE NATION UNDER GOD

It is not in any way intimated that a civic corporate prayer so much in evidence in public institutions and in national documents would, if excluded from public schools, bear within itself a "bad tendency" rule that might inexorably work to the development of a godless state in America. But in our times we have seen a highly civilized society whose government gradually restricted in its civil institutions the official profession of belief and dependence upon God and has handed over religious exercises exclusively to churches and homes. But when the tragic hour of conflicting allegiances bore upon its citizens, they obeyed, with passioned submission and gratified acquiescence, a supreme and absolute statal authority to the complete destruction of the state and to the enduring shame of their religious confessions.

Perhaps the United States Supreme Court might have allowed a "good tendency" rule to be imminent in the civic corporate prayer to impress on all alike—on participants and nonparticipants—that there is a higher allegiance to God under which men must rule; that no patriotism may obey against the moral law; that personal immunity against arbitrary power is a divine mandate. It is not without profound symbolism that public authority should be a party to an acknowledgment of dependence upon God.

138

Footnotes to Part One

[1] *Cambridge Medieval History,* xx 529: "The effects of the Church upon the Empire may be summed up in one word, 'freedom.' In a word, authority was seen to be a form of service according to God's will and such service was freedom. It was, however, not from Seneca but from Christ and St. Paul that the Fathers took their constant theme of the essential equality of men before which slavery could not stand. . . . Not only did the Fathers establish the primitive unity and dignity of man, but seeing slavery as the result of the Fall, they found in the sacrifice of Christ a road to freedom that was closed to Stoicism."

[2] Otto von Gierke, *Political Theories of the Middle Ages,* (Maitland's translation, 1927), 81–2: "In this Medieval Doctrine was already filled with the thought of the inborn and indestructible rights of the individual. The formulation and classification of such rights belonged to a later stage in the growth of the theory of the Natural Law. Still, as a matter of principle, a recognition of their existence may be found already in the medieval Philosophy of Right when it attributes an absolute and objective validity to the highest maxims of Natural and Divine Law. Moreover, a fugitive glance at Medieval Doctrine suffices to perceive how throughout it all, in sharp contrast to the theories of Antiquity, runs the thought of the absolute and imperishable value of the Individual; a thought revealed by Christianity. . . . That every individual by virtue of his eternal destiny is at the core somewhat holy and indestructible even in relation to the Highest Power; that the smallest part had a value of its own, and not merely because it is a part of a whole; that every man is to be regarded by the Community, never as a mere instrument, but also as an end; all this is not merely suggested, but is more or less clearly expressed."

139

[3] The earliest expressions of secularism in America are to be found in the writings of Tom Paine, John Taylor and Benjamin Rush. The current widened with the victory of Jeffersonian Democracy in 1800. All sorts of philosophical isms have dominated most of our higher institutions of learning and have seriously threatened to secularize our national culture. Prevailing today in many of our colleges and universities, though not without challenge in some quarters, is power politics in international relations, pragmatic functionalism in educational studies, skepticism in philosophy, agnosticism in religion, behavorism in the social sciences, hedonism in literature. Despite the increasing efforts to interrelate the various branches of the social sciences and of the natural sciences, there is scarcely an equal concern to relate these in turn to philosophy and theology. In general, there is widespread among intellectuals an aversion for dogma in religion, philosophy and the sciences. Secular humanism is offering the strongest challenge to the American religious heritage which in the past has provided a general consensus for that public morality which our law must embody as the moral foundations of the American Republic.

[4] Clinton Rossiter, *Seedtime of the Republic* (New York: 1953), 352.

[5] *Works,* Congress edition, I, 250, 251.

[6] *Writings of Thomas Jefferson* (Ford edition) (New York: 1899) X, 343.

[7] *The Works of Burke* (Oxford), II, 185.

[8] Anson Phelps Stokes, *Church and State in the United States* (New York: 1950), 3 vols., I, 451.

[9] *Messages and Papers of the Presidents,* compiled and edited by James D. Richardson (1897), I, 212.

[10] *Ibid.,* 221.

[11] *Ibid.,* 258.

[12] *Ibid.,* 275.

[13] *The Public Papers and Addresses of Franklin Delano Roosevelt,* compiled and collated by Samuel Rosenman, 1939 volume (1941), 1–2.

[14] Chief Justice Kent in *People v. Ruggles,* 1811, 8 Johns., 290. Also 296, that the Constitution "never meant to withdraw religion in general, and with it the best sanctions of moral and social obligation, from all consideration and notice of the law."

[15] Justice Brewer in *Church of the Holy Trinity v. United States,* 143 U.S. 457 (1892).

[16] Joseph Storey, *Commentaries on the Constitution,* no. 1874 (1833): "Probably at the adoption of the Constitution, and of the amendment to it, now under consideration, the general, if not the universal sentiment in America was, that christianity ought to receive encouragement from the state, so far as was not incompatible with the private rights of conscience, and the freedom of religious worship. An attempt to level all religions, and to make it a matter of state policy to hold in utter indifference, would have created universal disapprobation if not universal indignation."

[17] "The Supreme Court as National School Board" in *14 Law and Contemporary Problems,* 21 (1949).

[18] Zorach et al v. Clauson et al., Court of Appeals of New York, 1951, 100 N.E. 2d 463. Cf. Judge Desmond's concurring opinion.

[19] 343 U.S. 306 1952.

[20] See, for example, J. Roland Pennock, "Reason, Value, and the Theory of Democracy" in *American Political Science Review,* October, 1944, 855–875; Willmore Kendall, "Prolegomena to Any Future Work on Majority Rule" in Journal of Politics, XII, November, 1950, 694–713; J. Austin Ranney, "Toward a More Responsible Two-Party System: A Commentary" in *American Political Science Review,* XLV, June, 1951, 488–99; J. Austin Ranney and Willmore Kendall, "Democracy: Confusion and Agreement" in *Western Political Quarterly,* IV, September, 1951, 430–39; Sidney Hook, *Heresy, Yes—Conspiracy, No* (New York: 1953).

[21] For example, Justice Cardozo in *Palko v. Connecticut* spoke of "immunities implied in the concept of ordered liberty" and lists the four freedoms. 302 U.S. 319, 324–5.

[22] *New York Times,* March 29, 1955.

[23] *Zorach v. Clauson* 343 U.S. 306 (1952).

[24] *Everson v. Board of Education,* 330 U.S. 1 (1947).

[25] *McCollum v. Board of Education,* 333 U.S. 203 (1948).

[26] Costanzo, "Federal Aid to Education and Religious Liberty" in 36, *University of Detroit Law School Journal* (1958).

[27] Padover, *The Complete Jefferson,* 955 (1943). She was the wife of the newspaper publisher whom Jefferson induced to transplant his printing establishment from Philadelphia to Washington. Rumor had divulged the contents of Jefferson's letter to Thomson

earlier that same year that he had compiled a scrapbook of the teachings of Christ and speculations stirred that Jefferson had "changed" to Christianity.

[28] *Ibid.*, 414. Consult too his letter to David Barrow on May 1, 1815: "We are not in a world ungoverned by the laws and the power of a superior agent. Our efforts are in his hand, and directed by it; and he will give them their effect in his own time." 9, *The Writings of Thomas Jefferson*, 516 (Ford edition, 1892–1898).

[29] Padover, *The Complete Jefferson*, 1104 (1943).

[30] Padover, *Democracy by Thomas Jefferson*, 178 (1939), in a letter to J. Fishback written in 1809.

[31] "Reason and free inquiry are the only effectual agents against error. Give a loose to them, they will support the true religion, by bringing every false one to their tribunal, to the test of their investigation." Jefferson, *Notes on the State of Virginia*, c. 17 (Stockdale edition, 1787). These notes had their origin in the fall of 1780, when Jefferson, as governor of Virginia, undertook to reply to a questionnaire addressed to the several American states by Francois Marbois of the French legation in Philadelphia. Jefferson's replies to Marbois' twenty-two inquiries are a valuable sourcebook on eighteenth-century Virginia. In three pages Jefferson states his argument for freedom of religion based upon natural rights, the fallibility of governments in religious matters, the futility of control and suppression, the inevitability of truth and the competence of reason if left free of hindrance, of compulsion and of coercion. These notes were first published privately in Paris in 1785 and later edited and published at Jefferson's request by John Stockdale of London in 1787. For a rather recent American edition based on Stockdale, see Jefferson, *Notes on the State of Virginia* (Peden edition, 1955).

"Your own reason is the only oracle given you by heaven, and you are answerable not (only) for the rightness but the uprightness of the decision." So Jefferson counseled his own nephew in searching for religious truths. 4, *The Writings of Thomas Jefferson*, 432 (Ford edition, 1892–1899); consult, too, Padover, *The Complete Jefferson*, 1104 (1943), about the "proofs of the being of a God, creator, etc." to be "within the province of the professor of ethics."

[32] Padover, *The Complete Jefferson*, 946 (1943).

[33] Padover, *Democracy by Thomas Jefferson*, 184 (1939), in a letter to Adams written in 1823.

[34] 15, *The Writings of Thomas Jefferson*, 274–275 (Bergh and Lipscomb edition, 1904).

[35] Padover, *Democracy by Thomas Jefferson*, 184 (1939). A year earlier, he had written to Short that he was an Epicurean in philosophy, adding that he meant Epicurean in the genuine and original sense. 15, *The Writings of Thomas Jefferson*, 219 (Bergh and Lipscomb edition, 1903–1905). The next month he repeated the same to John Adams. Padover, *The Complete Jefferson*, 1036 (1943), in a letter dated Nov. 7, 1819.

[36] For a contrary appraisal consult Koch, *The Philosophy of Thomas Jefferson*, 34 (1943), where Jefferson is set down as a "conservative materialist"—an odd conjunction of political and philosophical terminology.

[37] Padover, *Democracy by Thomas Jefferson*, 187 (1939), in a letter to Hopkinson written in 1789. Also consult a letter to E. Styles written in 1819: "I am of a sect by myself as far as I know." *Ibid.*, 188.

[38] *Bowers, Jefferson and Hamilton*, 103 (1930): "He planned at least one church and contributed to the erection of others, gave freely to Bible Societies, and liberally to the support of the clergy. He attended church with normal regularity, taking his prayer book to the services and joining in the responses and prayers of the congregation." Consult also Smith, *The First Forty Years of Washington Society*, 13 (1906). During the winter of 1800, before the regular Sunday services were established in the capitol, Jefferson was a frequent attendant of the small Episcopal church in Washington.

[39] Padover, *The Complete Jefferson*, 1032–1034 (1943), in a letter to Thomas Law dated June 13, 1814.

[40] Padover, *The Complete Jefferson*, 1057–1058 (1943), in a letter to Peter Carr dated Aug. 10, 1787. Scarcely adequate cognizance has been taken of the influence of the Scottish school upon Jefferson especially in his earlier years. In his memoirs, Jefferson speaks of his early education at William and Mary College under Dr. William Small of Scotland who gave him his "first views of the expansion of science, and of the system of things in which we are placed." 2, *Memoir, Correspondence, & Miscellanies*, from the papers of Thomas Jefferson, 2 (second Randolph edition, 1830). The philosophy of common sense which was worked up in Scotland

by Reid and Beattie in opposition to Hume and Berkeley held that there are certain first principles or dictates of common sense which are either simple perceptions or seen with intuitive evidence. This Scottish school had its stalwart advocate in colonial times in the person of John Witherspoon who had come over from Scotland and become president of Princeton. Jefferson's preference was obviously not for the Scottish thinkers of the antisceptical and non-sentimental type but for the moral sense of Shaftesbury, Hutcheson and Hume, which was but a modification of the same, minus all assumptions of the supernatural (the Reformer's "personal inspiration") and with the additional identification of moral sentiment with utility.

[41] Padover, *Democracy by Thomas Jefferson*, 177–178 (1939), in a letter to Fishback written in 1809. "Reading, reflection and time have convinced me that the interests of society require the observation of those moral precepts only in which all religions agree (for all forbid us to murder, steal, plunder, or bear false witness) and that we should not intermeddle with the particular dogmas in which all religions differ, and which are totally unconnected with morality. . . . The varieties in structure and action of the human mind as in those of the body, are the work of our Creator, against which it cannot be a religious duty to erect the standard of uniformity. The practice of morality being necessary for the well-being society, he has taken care to impress its precepts so indelibly on our hearts that they shall not be effaced by the subtleties of our brain. We all agree in the obligation of the moral precepts of Jesus."

[42] Padover, *Democracy by Thomas Jefferson*, 187 (1939).

[43] Padover, *The Complete Jefferson*, 955 (1943), in a letter to Dr. Benjamin Rush dated April 21, 1803; also Padover, *Democracy by Thomas Jefferson*, 186 (1939), in a letter to W. Short written in 1820.

[44] Padover, *Democracy by Thomas Jefferson*, 181 (1939).

[45] *Ibid.*, 185: "It is the innocence of his character, the purity and sublimity of his moral precepts, the eloquences of his inculcations, the beauty of the apologues in which he conveys them, that I so much admire." Consult also Padover, *The Complete Jefferson*, 949 (1943): "His parentage was obscure; his condition poor; his education null; his natural endowments great; his life correct and inno-

cent; he was meek, benevolent, patient, firm, disinterested, and of the sublimest eloquence."

46 Padover, *Democracy by Thomas Jefferson*, 186 (1939).

47 *Ibid.*, 185–186.

48 *Ibid.*, 184–185.

49 Padover, *The Complete Jefferson*, 948: "Their ethics were not only imperfect, but often irreconciliable (sic) with the sound dictates of reason and morality, as they respect intercourse with those around us; and repulsive and anti-social, as respecting other nations. They needed reformation, therefore, in an eminent degree."

50 Padover, *The Complete Jefferson*, 951 (1943), in a letter to John Adams dated Oct. 13, 1813; 10, *The Writings of Thomas Jefferson*, 294 (Ford edition, 1892–1899); Padover, *A Jefferson Profile*, 251 (1956), in a letter to Charles Thomson dated Jan. 9, 1816; as late as 1820, he is still calling for this work of restoration. Padover, *Democracy by Thomas Jefferson*, 181 (1939), in a letter to Van der Kemp written in 1820.

51 Padover, *The Complete Jefferson*, 951 (1943).

52 His final achievement is "an octavo of forty-six pages, of pure and unsophisticated doctrines" which are easily distinguished as "diamonds in a dunghill" from what he called "the deliria of crazy imaginations," referring to St. Athanasius, no less. Padover, *The Complete Jefferson*, 951, 956 (1943).

53 Padover, *Democracy by Thomas Jefferson*, 185 (1939), in a letter to W. Short written in 1820.

54 Padover, *The Complete Jefferson*, 956 (1943) in a letter to Dr. Benjamin Waterhouse written in 1822.

55 His untiring complaint was that the "simple religion of Jesus" was disfigured beyond recognition by Christ himself by the "jargon of Plato, of Aristotle, and other mystics." Padover, *Democracy by Thomas Jefferson*, 180 (1939).

56 Consult Padover, *The Complete Jefferson*, 948–950 (1943) (Syllabus of an Estimate of the merit of the Doctrines of Jesus Compared with those of others), written in April, 1803; *ibid.*, at 950–951, in a letter to John Adams dated Oct. 13, 1813; Padover, *Democracy by Thomas Jefferson*, 187 (1939), in a letter to C. Thomason written in 1816; *ibid.*, 188, in a letter to E. Styles written in 1819; *ibid.*, 185, in a letter to Short written in 1820.

57 Padover, *Democracy by Thomas Jefferson*, 179 (1939), in a

letter to De la Motte written in 1820: "(I am) happy, in the restoration, of the Jews particularly, to their social rights, and hope they will be seen taking their seats on the benches of science, as preparatory to their doing the same at the board of government."

[58] *Ibid.*, 179, in a letter to Joseph Marx.

[59] *Ibid.*, 184, in a letter to John Adams written in 1823.

[60] *Ibid.*, 183, in a letter to Short written in 1820: "The Presbyterian clergy are the loudest; the most intolerant of all sects, the most tyrannical and ambitious; ready at the word of the lawgiver, if such a word could be now obtained, to put the torch to the pile, and to rekindle in the virgin hemisphere, the flames in which their oracle Calvin consumed the poor Servetus, because he could not find in his Euclid the proposition which has demonstrated that three are one and the one is three, nor subscribe to that of Calvin, that magistrates have a right to exterminate all heretics to Calvinistic Creed."

[61] Jefferson, *Notes on the State of Virginia*, c. 17 (Stockdale edition, 1787).

[62] Padover, *The Complete Jefferson*, 947 (1943).

[63] *Ibid.*, 397–946. The date is not certain. Jefferson dated the manuscript "scraps" early in the revolution.

[64] *Ibid.*, 942.

[65] *Ibid.*

[66] *Ibid.*

[67] *Ibid.*, 943.

[68] *Ibid.*, 944.

[69] *Ibid.*, 946.

[70] *Ibid.*, 946–947.

[71] "Can the liberties of a nation be thought secure, when we have removed their only firm basis, a conviction in the minds of the people that these liberties are the gifts of God?" Morris, *Christian Life and Character of the Civil Institutions of the United States Developed in the Official and Historical Annals of the United States*, 35 (1864). *Notes on Virginia*, Query XVIII.

[72] Padover, *The Complete Jefferson*, 518–529 (1913).

[73] Padover, *Democracy by Thomas Jefferson*, 177 (1939); consult too his letter to Elbridge Gerry written 1799: "I am for freedom of religion, and against all maneuvers to bring about a legal ascendancy of one sect over another." 10, *The Writings of Thomas*

146

Jefferson, 78 (Lipscomb edition, 1904); and in the following year 1800, he listed among his services to his country, "I proposed the demolition of the church establishment, and the freedom of religion." Padover, *The Complete Jefferson,* 1288 (1943).

In the same letter to Levi Lincoln referred to above, Jefferson says that he had hoped to explain in the same letter to the Danbury Baptists why he had not continued the practice of his presidential predecessors of proclaiming days of fasting and thanksgiving. Padover, *Democracy by Thomas Jefferson,* 177 (1939). (The occasion was not opportune.)

He repeats his stand again during his second inaugural address of March 4, 1805; but it is not until Jan. 23, 1808, that he explains in a letter to Reverend Samuel Miller that he considers such an act on his part as "intermeddling with religious institutions, their doctrines, discipline (and) exercises," and let us note, while he allows such practice to be within the proper jurisdiction of state governments, he, as President of the United States, has "no authority to direct the religious exercises of his constituents." *Ibid.*

Whatever may be the merits of Jefferson's rationale on a practice which, with the added exception of Jackson, has continued uninterrupted into the proclamations of days of prayer and thanksgiving by all subsequent presidents, we must not lose sight of Jefferson's sensitive concern against interference with anyone's religious conscience. We might reflect that Jefferson's eudaemonism hardly inclined him to penitential practices. *Ibid.,* 184–86, in a letter to Short dated 1820.

Jefferson's contemporaries did not share his construction of the powers of the presidential office. The day—Sept. 24, 1789—that both Houses adopted a resolution to recommend the new amendments to the states, a resolution was adopted that a joint committee of both Houses request the President to proclaim a day of thanksgiving and prayer.

74 Padover, *The Complete Jefferson,* 544 (1943).

75 I *American State Papers,* 687 (1803).

76 4 *American State Papers,* 687 (1803). In 1789 the first Congress appropriated funds for the support of Christian missionaries among the Indians in implementation of a recommendation made by General Knox, the Secretary of War, and approved by President Washington: "The object of this establishment would be the happiness of Indians, teaching them the great duties of religion and

morality, and to inculcate a friendship and an attachment to the United States."

[77] Padover, *The Complete Jefferson*, 1064–1069 (1943).

[78] *Ibid.*, 1072–1076.

[79] *Ibid.*, 1076.

[80] *Ibid.*, 1097–1105.

[81] *Ibid.*, 1104.

[82] *Ibid.*, 957.

[83] *Ibid.*

[84] *Ibid.*

[85] *Ibid.*, 957–958.

[86] *Ibid.*, 956.

[87] *Ibid.*, 958.

[88] *Ibid.*

[89] *Ibid.*

[90] *Ibid.*

[91] *Ibid.*, 956–957, in a letter to Dr. Benjamin Waterhouse dated June 26, 1822.

[92] 10, *The Writings of Thomas Jefferson*, 243 (Ford edition, 1892–1899), in a letter to Thomas Cooper dated Nov. 2, 1822.

[93] Padover, *The Complete Jefferson*, 1106–1112 (1943).

[94] *Ibid.*, 1104.

[95] *Ibid.*, 958.

[96] *Ibid.*, 1110.

[97] *Ibid.*, 958.

[98] *Ibid.*, 1110.

[99] *Ibid.*, 958.

[100] *Ibid.*, 1110.

[101] *Ibid.*

[102] *Ibid.*, 1111.

[103] cf. Chapter 3, below.

[104] cf. Part II, Chapter 1, below.

[105] *New York Times*, March 29, 1955, "Teaching Is Urged On Moral Values."

[106] *New York Times*, Nov. 25, 1955, "School Spiritual Guide Approved by 2 Faiths, Opposed by Rabbis."

[107] Perhaps no more discordant reflection was expressed than the one by Professor Blau of Columbia University which appeared in the *Columbia Spectator*, Dec. 14, 1955. In an address to the Students

for Democratic Action he saw cause to attack "creeping clericalism." He said that "if schools take over the role of Church and parents there will be no non-believers in a generation." "We are convinced that if we can get a test case on the 'under God' (Pledge of Allegiance) we can get it declared unconstitutional." " 'Creeping clericalism' would lead, as I see it, to an America about the year 2000 with an established Roman Catholic Church with possibly the Papacy in America and the absolute suppression of all religious opposition."

[108] *New York Times,* Dec. 16, 1955, "3 Religious to Aid in School Report."

[109] *New York Times,* Dec. 22, 1955, "Schools' Bulletin Stirs New Dispute."

[110] Nicholas Murray Butler in his Report of President of Columbia University (1934), 21–22: "The school child . . . is entitled to receive . . . that particular form of religious instruction and training which his parents and natural guardians hold dear. This cannot be done if the program of the tax-supported schools is arranged on the theory that religion is to be excluded from the educational process or treated merely incidentally as an element in home life." Also in "The Place of Religion in American Education" in *Modern Churchman,* June, 1941, 116–118: "In this day and generation we are beginning to forget the place which religious instruction must occupy in education if that education is to be truly sound and liberal. We seem to forget that until some two hundred years ago religious instruction everywhere dominated education; religion guided education, shaped education and selected the material for education in every part of the world—in the Orient, in Europe and in the Americas. Then began, as a result of the rise of Protestantism and the spread of democracy, those sharp differences of religious opinion and of religious worship which unfortunately exhibited themselves in highly controversial form. One consequence was to lead men to turn aside from religious study and religious teaching in the attempt to avoid those unfortunate contentious differences which had become so common. Then, particularly in this democracy of ours, a curious tendency grew up to exclude religious teaching altogether from education on the ground that such teaching was in conflict with our fundamental doctrine as to the separation of Church and State. In other words, religious teaching was narrowed down to something which might be called denominationalism, and therefore because of

differences of faith and practice it must be excluded from education. The result was to give paganism new importance and new influence . . ." Dr. Butler then proceeds to endorse heartily the released-time statute then passed by the legislature of the state of New York in 1940.

[111] *New York Times,* Nov. 27, 1955, "School Religion Draws Criticism," an address by Philip Jacobson of the American Jewish Committee to a meeting of the National Council for Social Studies, a department of the National Educational Association.

[112] "The Supreme Court as National School Board" *14 Law and Contemporary Problems,* 21 (1949).

[113] Luther A. Weigle, formerly dean of Yale Divinity School, in an address delivered at the 1940 Annual Meeting of the International Council of Religious Education, said: "The principle of religious freedom is designed to protect religious belief, not to hinder or destroy it. It is meant to insure the free exercise of religion according to the dictates of conscience, not to limit that exercise by forcing secularism upon American citizens. For the state even tacitly to deny religion in its schools would be to impair the religious liberty of that vast majority of American citizens who believe in God and desire that the education of their children give proper place to religious belief."—Public Education and Religion (pamphlet) quoted by Leo Pfeffer, *Church, State, and Freedom* (Boston: 1953), 292. Professor Wilbur G. Katz, of the University of Chicago Law School: "One must expect that where strict separation is incompatible with the free exercise of religion, individuals deeply concerned for the protection of civil liberties would prefer protection of religious freedom to the maintenance of strict separation. This is not always the case, however, as witness Justice Rutledge's opinion in the bus fare case, and the position of the American Civil Liberties Union in all of the recent cases. Speculation is invited as to why absolute separation is supported in quarters such as these, apparently regardless of the resulting restraint of religious liberty."—"Religion and State Neutrality," 20, *U. of Chicago Law Review,* 426 (1953). And we recall Storey's *Commentaries on the Constitution,* 1874 (1833): "Probably at the time of the adoption of the Constitution, and of the amendment to it, now under consideration, the general, if not the universal sentiment in America was, that Christianity ought to receive encouragement from the state, so far as was not incompatible

with the private rights of conscience, and the freedom of religious worship. An attempt to level all religions, and to make it a matter of state policy to hold all in utter indifference, would have created universal disapprobation if not universal indignation."

[114] Ernest Johnson, "Some Crucial Contemporary Issues" in *Social Action* (Nov. 15, 1947), 14: "One of the expressions most frequently heard in current religious discussions is the 'separation of church and state.' Those words are commonly taken as defining a principle that is at once basic in the federal Constitution and central in Protestant doctrine. It should be clear that a phrase which is taken to define both a secular political principle and a religious principle is less than truly definitive. I suggest that the basic principle is freedom, and that the separation of Church and state is a political policy designed to effectuate religious freedom on the one hand and political freedom on the other. As a policy it grows out of practical necessity due to the fact that our population is religiously heterogeneous. If we were all of one faith the distinction between church and state would be only a functional one: 'separation,' in its present context, would be unknown. Thus, espousal of the separation of church and state by a religious group is not the affirmation of a religious principle, but is rather acceptance of a public policy designed to protect religious freedom and to prevent the domination of the state, at any level, by any one church or combination of churches."

[115] *The Public Papers and Addresses of Franklin Delano Roosevelt,* compiled and collated by Samuel Rosenman, 1939 volume (1941), 1–2.

[116] Raymond B. Culver, *Horace Mann and Religion in the Massachusetts Public Schools* (New Haven: 1929), 235.

[117] See the Letter to the *New York Times* dated Dec. 7, 1955, and appearing Dec. 12, 1955, by Charles A. Siepmann, chairman, Board of Directors, New York Civil Liberties Union.

[118] Dr. D. Campbell Wyckoff, chairman of the Department of Religious Education of New York University addressing the twenty-seventh annual luncheon of the Protestant Teachers Association, Nov. 15, 1952, declared that the country's schools, with few exceptions throughout the years, had recognized that sectarian neutrality must not mean hostility to religion or to the churches. "The purposes of American education are rooted in the religious faith of the Jewish-

151

Christian tradition underlying our whole culture. Behind the need for maintaining sectarian impartiality is a positive need to maintain the moral and religious truth upon which our national life has been built. Especially in critical times like ours, the character of the future citizen depends on friendly mutual understanding even among institutions that must forever remain separate. The aim of education is not to produce children and youth who are merely informed and skilled but without moral and religious commitments. The aim of education is rather to produce the citizen of deep and intelligent convictions. This is the heart of the public schools' task, and without question it involves implications that are moral and religious in nature."—*New York Times,* Nov. 16, 1952.

[119] Will Herberg, *Protestant-Catholic-Jew* (New York: 1955), 85: "What do Americans believe? Most emphatically, they 'believe in God;' 97 per cent according to one survey, 96 per cent according to another, 95 per cent according to a third." Cf. also 59, 62.

[120] Howard K. Beale, *A History of Freedom of Teaching in American Schools* (New York: 1941).

[121] For example: *American Education and Religion: The Problem of Religion in the Schools,* F. Ernest Johnson (ed.), (New York: 1952). Vivian Thayer, 30: Secularism is "a faith that conflicts with the tenets of traditional religion . . . we should recognize it for what it is: an affirmation of faith, a religion, if you will, which entitles it to the right of competition in the marketplace, with all the privileges and limitations that apply to the propagation of other religions." Also cf. Conrad Moehlman, *School and Church: The American Way* (New York: 1944).

[122] For a defense of wholly secular education in American public schools see Leo Pfeffer, *Church, State and Freedom,* 288: "The American public school is a secular school . . . The Catholic Church, and probably most of the Protestant Churches, as well, undoubtedly do not approve of its secularity. Yet secular it is, in curriculum, method and spirit." Pfeffer's own prepossessions lead him to absolutize about a factual situation which is still under study and a matter of concern to all, as well as to dispense rather cavalierly with the wishes of the vast majority of Americans whose philosophy of education is fundamentally religious, not of course to refer to the tradition of American education since the days of the Northwest Ordinance.

152

123 The Ordinance of 1787 for the government of the Northwest Territory continued in effect by act of Congress Aug. 7, 1789, after the adoption of the Federal Constitution and formed the basis of government provided by Congress for all the territories of the United States. The Southwest government provided by Congress for all the territories of the United States. The Southwest Ordinance of 1790, setting up "The Territory of the United States, south of the River Ohio" contained the same guarantees as the Ordinance of 1787, and applied to Tennessee and, later, to the Mississippi Territory prior to their becoming states. Article III of the Northwest Ordinance has been retained in the constitutions of Michigan, Mississippi and Ohio.

124 See *New York Times,* Nov. 24, 1952, column headlined "Catholics' Stand On Schools Backed" and subtitled, "Bishop Donegan also deplores 'Shift' from Religion but Fears 'Entering Wedge'."

125 For the test of the Statement by Catholic Bishops on Secularism and Schools see *New York Times,* Nov. 16, 1952.

126 *International Journal of Religious Education,* March, 1956, 24.

127 An American sociologist has suggested an explanation for the defensive attitude of the minority-consciousness of the American Jewish community which may explain at least in part the general alarm of some Jews, believers and nonbelievers, toward the recommendations of the Board of Superintendents of the City of New York. Cf. Will Herberg, *Protestant-Catholic-Jew,* 254–55.

128 *The Writings of Thomas Jefferson,* edited by H. A. Washington (New York: 1857), I, 545: VII, 339.

129 *The Complete Jefferson,* edited by Saul K. Padover (New York: 1943), 957.

130 Quoted by B. F. Morris, *Christian Life and Character,* 35.

131 The recorded reflections of Orestes Brownson, one-time secularist and later a convert to the Catholic faith, are not without significant bearing upon the educational promotions of modern day secularists: "It is far easier to educate for evil than for good, for children since the fall take to evil as ducks take to water. The enemies of religion and society understand this perfectly well, and hence whenever in their power they seize upon the schools, and seek to control the education of the young. To accomplish their purposes, they have only to exclude religion from the schools, under the plea of excluding sectarianism, and instead of teaching religion, teach as Frances Wright was accustomed to say, know–*ledge,* and

they may soon have a community whose thoughts and affections will be exclusively of the *earth earthy*. It is not without design that I have mentioned the name of Frances Wright, the favorite pupil of Jeremy Bentham . . . I knew this remarkable woman well, and it was my shame to share, for a time, many of her views, for which I ask pardon of God and of my countrymen. I was for a brief time in her confidence, and one of those selected to carry into execution her plans. The great object was to get rid of Christianity, and to convert our churches into halls of science. The plan was . . . to establish a system of state—we said national—schools, from which all religion was to be excluded, in which nothing was to be taught but such knowledge as is verifiable by the senses, and to which all parents were to be compelled by law to send their children. Our complete plan was to take the children from their parents at the age of twelve or eighteen months, and to have them nursed, fed, clothed, and trained in these schools at the public expense; but at any rate, we were to have godless schools, for all the children of the country, to which the parents would be compelled by law to send them . . . For this purpose, a secret society was formed, and the whole country was to be organized somewhat on the plan of the carbonari of Italy, or as were the revolutionists throughout Europe by Bazard preparatory to the revolution of 1820 and 1830. This organization was commenced in 1829 in the city of New York, and to my own knowledge was effected throughout a considerable part of New York State. How far it was extended in other states, or whether it is still kept up I know not, for I abandoned it in the latter part of the year 1830, and have since had no confidential relations with any engaged in it; but this much I can say, the plan has been successfully pursued, the views we put forth have gained great popularity, and the whole action of the country on the subject has taken the direction we sought to give it . . ." "Liberal Studies" in *The Works of Orestes A. Brownson* (Detroit: 1904), XIX, 441f.

[132] 370 U.S. 421 (1962).

[133] Justice Douglas, in his concurring opinion, stated: "In the present case, school facilities are used to say the prayer and the teaching staff is employed to lead the pupils in it. There is, however, no effort at indoctrination and no attempt at exposition. Prayers of course may be so long and of such a character as to amount to an

attempt at the religious instruction that was denied by the McCollum case. But New York's prayer is of a character that does not involve any element of proselytizing as in the McCollum case."

[134] Hughes, *The Reformation in England,* 111–13, 121–26 (1954).

[135] Jefferson, "Plan for an Educational System" in *The Complete Jefferson,* 1064–69 (Padover edition, 1943).

[136] Jefferson, "An Act for Establishing Elementary Schools" in Padover, 1072, 1076.

[137] Jefferson, "The University of Virginia, Aim and Curriculum" in Padover, 1097, 1104.

[138] Jefferson, "Freedom of Religion at the University of Virginia" in Padover, 957–58.

[139] Jefferson, "Regulations for the University" in Padover, 1106–11.

[140] 2, *The Writings of James Madison,* 184–88.

[141] 1, *Annals of Congress,* 727, (1789).

PART TWO

FEDERAL AID TO EDUCATION

5

FEDERAL AID TO EDUCATION AND RELIGIOUS LIBERTY

In the context of governmental aid to church-related schools, the word "school" is here meant to comprise the several component factors that constitute it: the state which has an interest in the education a school provides and a supervisory role over it; the parents who are legally held responsible for the attendance of their children at a publicly accredited school; the school buildings; the instructional facilities, the faculty, the officially prescribed curriculum; and, of course, the school children, for whose benefit the school is conducted.

The present nationwide controversy concerning such aid cannot be totally disengaged from its historical legacy. Both the opponents and advocates of aid to church-related schools have forged stubborn arguments from history and, unfortunately, have thereby given rise to the sympathies and resentments which this sort of disagreement inevitably engenders.

The arguments of the opponents are both old and new. For a complete understanding of them, they must be projected against the repeated failures of the Blair educational bills of the 1880s; the unsuccessful Blaine amendments to the federal constitution, whereby any tax support for sectarian purposes would have been forbidden; similar adoptions to state constitutions; and the failure of Congressman Bryson's bill of 1947 to reintroduce substantially the same proposal as Blaine's for federal adoption. The old argument at least acknowledged, however, that the Constitution as it stood did not proscribe what they thought it ought to forbid. The new approach is to affirm, and with a very great assist from Justice Rutledge, that this proscription has all along been immanent in the First Amendment—even though it may have escaped the critical eye of American jurists for more than a century and a half.

The advocates of aid to parochial schools also have old and new arguments. They have always insisted that these schools are truly part of national education; that they serve the public purpose no less effectively than the state schools in preparing the students for the public life of citizenship; that their educational process fulfills the requirements set down by state educational authorities in the very environment of a general and particular religious orientation; and that they thereby enjoy an advantage of enormous significance by the exercise of religious liberty in education. This right is severely restrained and subject to many compromises and restrictions in governmental schools, not because the ideal of public education requires restraint but because of the very real difficulties created by the plurality of diverse claims of conscience which prevails therein. In a word, the advocates want the implications of the juridical status of the nonprofit school with religious affiliation fully brought out and acknowledged. The new argument is that a federal program of aid to general education as presently contemplated would threaten the existence of church-related schools, would be divisive of that unity of ultimate common goal to which our dual system of national education should be ordained, and would be disruptive of the American community by weighting one type of schooling with the prestige, power, influence and enormous financial resources of the federal government. This consideration is more real than apparent since the majority of parochial schools are Catholic and therefore the constitutional argument is for the most part identified in the popular mind as a Catholic protest. Many other arguments of reasonable persuasion can be marshaled for both sides and with an earnestness to match.

Apropos to the controversy, then, is a survey of the complex and intricate question of federal aid to education broadly considered—direct, indirect, auxiliary—and an outline of the distinctly different issues and the premises from which each issue legitimately depends and validly may derive its force of rational persuasion. From such an analytical-critical examination the conclusion will emerge that whatever may be the political determination of our national congress on federal aid to education in no wise should its legislative policy portend an interpretation of the religious clause of the First Amendment contrary to its authentic meaning. Part of the responsibility for conjoining these two questions rests with the Supreme Court which in the Everson[1] and McCollum[2] decisions stirred up blinding confusion about what kind of "aid to religion" the First Amendment allowed. The Court upheld in 1947 the constitutionality of a New Jersey statute which provided at public expense bus transportation to all school children whether they attended governmental or nongovernmental schools, as a legitimate exercise of state police power. Benefits of public welfare legislation were extended "to all its citizens without regard to their religious belief." Not content with satisfying the requirements of law, the Court, in acknowledgment of the appellant's contention, also considered whether public aid to religion was constructively a violation of the First Amendment:

160

The establishment of religion clause of the First Amendment means at least this: Neither a state nor the Federal Government can set up a church. Neither can pass laws which aid one religion, aid all religions, or prefer one religion over another. Neither can force nor influence a person to go or to remain away from church against his will or force him to profess a belief or disbelief in any religion. No person can be punished for entertaining or professing religious beliefs or disbeliefs, for church attendance or non-attendance. No tax in any amount, large or small, can be levied to support any religious activities or institutions, whatever they may be called, or whatever form they may adopt to teach or practice religion.[3]

Even at first reading a glaring incongruity confronts the reasonable mind. Government establishment of religion, which the Court correctly identifies with the legal preferential status of one state established church or religion and its concomitant incidents of coercion and civil incapacitations for nonconformists, is simultaneously equated in the same breath with impartial governmental aid of all religions. On the basis of such reasoning, the Court should have consistently voided the New Jersey statute. The following year in *McCollum v. Board of Education*[4] the high tribunal adopted Justice Rutledge's construction of absolute separation as enunciated in his dissent in the Everson[5] case with full logical consistency by declaring unconstitutional a released-time religious program on public school property.

Notwithstanding the Court's improvised proscription of "any" aid "large or small" to "all religions" and "any religious activities" in "whatever form," state and federal authorities are confronted with a vast panorama of governmental aid, "large and small," to "all religions" and "religious activities"—especially in our national history—in varied forms, financial and non-financial, direct and indirect. Nonetheless, the Court's pronouncement of no governmental aid at all to any religion has caused confusion in the minds of Congressmen and state officials.

161

Among the states, where all with but one exception, the state of Vermont,[6] rule out indirect as well as direct aid to sectarian schools and denominational institutions—some provide or allow auxiliary services and others do not—and even where permitted, a bizarre and inconsistent pattern prevails. Surely, auxiliary services may very properly be distinguished from indirect aids inasmuch as they are intended to relieve the nonreligious needs of school children. But in the place of clearly established and reasonably well founded definitions of law, supreme, uniform and universal, there is instead the exercise of discretionary judgments of state attorney generals or of local school boards.

In 1952, in *Zorach v. Clauson*[7], the Court retreated somewhat from Rutledge's revolutionary doctrine on church and state to explain the specific type of separation implied in the First Amendment:

The First Amendment within the scope of its coverage permits no exception; the prohibition is absolute. The First Amendment, however, does not say that in every and all respects there shall be a separation of Church and State. Rather, it studiously defines the manner, the specific ways, in which there shall be no concert or union or dependency one on the other. . . .

We are a religious people whose institutions presuppose a Supreme Being. We guarantee the freedom to worship as one chooses. We make room for as wide a variety of beliefs and creeds as the spiritual needs of man deem necessary. We sponsor an attitude on the part of government that shows no partiality to any one group and that lets each flourish according to the zeal of its adherents and the appeal of its dogma. When the state encourages religious instruction or cooperates with religious authorities by adjusting the schedule of public events to sectarian needs, it follows the best of our traditions. For it then respects the religious nature of our people and accommodates the public service to their spiritual needs. To hold that it may not would be to find in the Constitution a requirement that the government show a callous indifference to religious groups. That would be preferring those who believe in no religion over those who do believe. Government may not finance religious groups nor undertake religious instruction nor blend secular and sectarian education nor use secular institutions to force one or some religion on any person. But we find no constitutional requirement which makes it necessary for government to be hostile to religion and throw its weight against efforts to widen the effective scope of religious influence. The government must be neutral when it comes to competition between sects. It may not thrust any sect on any person. It may not make a religious observance compulsory. It may not coerce anyone to attend church. . . .[8]

The Zorach decision marks a retreat from the reasonings of the Everson and McCollum cases. The Court upheld governmental "encouragement" and "accommodation" with religious life because our "institutions presuppose a Supreme Being." While rejecting unequivocally "partiality," "compulsion," "coercion" or "force" in favor of one religion, it disowns governmental neutrality between believer and unbeliever as the equivalent of preferential treatment for nonbelievers. Further, the Court finds no constitutional requirement that conduces the government to throw "its weight against efforts to widen the effective scope of religious influence."

Admitting therefore that religious education is an effort (perhaps one of its strongest) to widen the effective scope of religious influence, does governmental "encouragement" and "accommodation" allow the inclusion of federal financial aid to it? And if so, what sort? What would or would not be lawfully permissible? Surely, religious education is one of the "forms" of religious exercise and the First Amendment guarantees "the free exercise thereof" of which one vindication is the constitutionality of church-affiliated schools upheld in *Pierce v. Society of Sisters.*[9] Yet the Court said in Everson:

163

No tax in any amount . . . can be levied to support any religious activities, whatever they may be called, or whatever form they may adopt to teach or practice religion.[9a]

It seems to us that the question of religious education is involved in the "free exercise thereof" clause of the First Amendment. Whether or not the exclusion of religious education from a federal aid bill—and what separate answers may be given to the different sorts of aid—is a reduction of that freedom constitutionally guaranteed, and constitutes a preferential status for secularized education, and a discrimination against publicly accredited education precisely because it is religious as well as secular, or church-affiliated—cannot conclusively be resolved from the Everson-McCollum-Zorach reasonings. We must turn to American constitutional history to ascertain what have been the governmental relations to religious exercise and in this studious endeavor subject the rulings of the present Court to a critical appraisal. From the high tribunal have come words of encouragement. Justice Frankfurter in his dissent in *Bridges v. California* said:

. . . (J)udges must be kept mindful of their limitations and of their ultimate public responsibility by a vigorous stream of criticism expressed with candor however blunt.[10]

CONSTITUTIONAL CONSENSUS

A. Legislative History — Textual Evidence and Intentions

A careful scrutiny of the various drafts of the religious amendment submitted to either or both Houses of Congress discloses the meaning which the framers strove to fix into

164

legal language. Such a responsible task against a vivid background of state establishments and disestablishments and the use of concepts and words clearly intelligible to their contemporaries, to the framers and to the adopters of the First Amendment, would reveal through the various successive versions proposed prima facie and inferentially the original and authentic meaning of the First Amendment.[11]

Since in our times an alleged principle of absolute separation of church and state is facilely invoked without surcease, it is remarkable that neither "separation" nor "church" nor "state" (in the generic meaning) occurred at all to the men who strove with great care to express their meaning with literal accuracy. A reflective rereading of the various versions discloses these constants: the Congress of the federal government is declared impotent to legislate into existence a "national religion," that is to say, "articles of faith or a mode of worship," "One Religious sect or Society in preference to others," "particular denomination in preference to another"—or simply, a preferential status by law to one religion or church to the disadvantage of all the others. The uniform intention underlying all the various versions of "no establishment" is to guarantee the equality of all religions and churches in two complementary ways—one indirectly, by rendering the national government impotent to bring about an inequality of religions before the law by political "establishment;" and secondly, the over-all preoccupation of the First Congress to guarantee inviolable the "free exercise thereof," under federal jurisdiction—that is to say, not only freedom of belief is secured against national conformism of religious profession, but also religious worship and activities, the outward exercise of religious belief, is guaranteed freedom of public expression. In view of the reference made today in discussions of federal aid to education, of religious education to the First Amendment, let us observe a matter of fact and a question of interpretation. The fact is there was absolutely no mention at all made in any way of education, religious or non-religious, nor aid for it, in the entire deliberations of the Congress on the First Amendment.

Now we must consider the question of interpretation. Educational neutralists and secularists are wont to read, on their own, federal aid to religious education into the prohibition of the no establishment clause. An interpretative construction which would refer the question of federal aid to non-governmental schools of religious affiliation to the First Amendment can reasonably do so only by including it with in the "free exercise thereof" clause. Religious education is in response to the dictates of religious conscience and it is undoubtedly an exercise of religious liberty which the law better preserves by removing the possibility of establishment and its inhibiting incidence. The paramount principle of the First Amendment was a federal guarantee of religious liberty and the no establishment clause was a political decision of a public policy instrumental for the insurance of the religious liberty on the federal level.

B. *Madisonian Federalism and Religious Liberty*

There is much discussion in the federal aid question about James Madison's mind on church-state relations and much more controversy about what is relevant and non-relevant from his lifetime testimony and actions. However, no one may reasonably question the telling evidence of the

166

Annals of the First Congress which has preserved for us Madison's mind on the religious amendment. It is to his lasting credit that despite his personal doubts on the constitutional necessity for such an amendment, he championed its passage. Madison initiated the congressional proceedings of the subject with his own formula:

> The civil rights of none shall be abridged . . . , nor shall any national religion be established, nor shall the full and equal rights of conscience be in any manner, or on any pretext, infringed.[12]

When the House debated an altered version of Madison's which omitted his adjectival "national," questions arose which seem to have justified Madison's original inclusion of the term. Mr. Sylvester of New York feared the amendment " . . . might be thought to have a tendency to abolish religion altogether."[13]

> Mr. Madison said, he apprehended the meaning of the words to be, that Congress should not establish a religion, and enforce the legal observation of it by law, nor compel men to worship God in any manner contrary to their conscience. Whether the words are necessary or not, he did not mean to say, but they had been required by some of the State Conventions, who seemed to entertain an opinion that . . . the clause of the Constitution, which gave power to Congress to make all laws necessary and proper to carry into execution the Constitution, and the laws made under it, enabled them to make laws of such a nature as might infringe the rights of conscience, and establish a national religion; to prevent these effects he presumed the amendment was intended, and he thought it as well expressed as the nature of the language would admit.[14]

In his response, Madison discloses what is paramount in his mind, namely, the constitutional guarantee of religious liberty affirming explicitly what the original organic act achieved by its omission, the legislative impotence of the federal government to confer a preferential status on one

167

religion together with the accompanying restraints of religious and civil liberties for nonconformers. He stresses the federalist character of the proposed amendment to assure those who feared it might operate to intrude into each state's own settlements on religion.[15]

That same day, Aug. 15, 1789, Representative Huntington of Connecticut averred that he personally understood Madison's meaning clearly but he feared " . . . that the words might be taken in such latitude as to be extremely hurtful to the cause of religion . . . " by others who " . . . might find it convenient to put another construction upon it."[16] Mr. Huntington voiced the fear that a federal court might not uphold local by-laws which authorized the financial support of "ministers" and the "building of places of worship" by their congregation.

> He hoped, therefore, the amendment would be made in such a way as to secure the rights of conscience, and a free exercise of the rights of religion, but not to patronize those who preferred no religion at all.[17]

Madison's rejoinder reiterates the federalist character of the law, the technical meaning of establishment, and the over-all purpose of securing religious liberty against governmental religious dictation.

> Mr. Madison thought, if the word "national" was inserted before religion, it would satisfy the minds of the honorable gentlemen. He believed that the people feared one sect might obtain a pre-eminence, or two combine together, and establish a religion to which they would compel others to conform. He thought if the word "national" was introduced, it would point the amendment directly to the object it was intended to prevent.[18]

Madison's insistence on the federalist character of the amendment and the inviolability of the sovereignty of the states should foreclose any endeavor to read the dispositions of one state on church-state relations (settled upon

168

three years before the ratification of the Constitution) into the federal organic act. The blunt historical fact is that the Virginian legislature found the amendment "totally inadequate, and betrays an unreasonable, unjustifiable, but a studied departure from the amendment proposed by Virginia. . . ."[19] The supposition of continuity between Madison's conception of church-state relations in his own state of Virgina brought about three years before the ratification of the Constitution, and Madison's meaning of the First Amendment is only possible by a process of thinking unrelated to reality.

In colonial times, the Anglican Church was the established church in Virgina with the attendant incidents of the legal preferential status, civil privileges, tax support, and for the dissenters, compulsory religious attendance, occasional penalties and civil disabilities. Even toleration, at first an unavoidable concession to a growing society of religious pluralism, and the beneficent consequence to the common cause against England, still retained many of the disabilities of the existing establishment. But, when the increasing number of dissenters reduced the Anglicans to a minority, Patrick Henry in 1784 proposed to the Virginia Assembly, a Bill Establishing a Provision for Teachers of the Christian Religion with the expectation that such a comprehensive tax support would find favor with all Christians whether of the establishment or not to take place of the abrogated provision for the support of the Anglican ministers alone. It was against this preference through tax support of *a* religion, the Christian one, under the benign mantle of the Anglican establishment that Madison directed his famed *Memorial and Remonstrance Against Religious Assessments* of 1785. The reading of the text[20] makes evident that Madison's primary concern is religious liberty for all through equality for all beliefs before the law and he

169

considers tax support of one religion (latitudinarian) Christianity, in itself or (incongruously) as part of the Anglican establishment then still existing in Virgina, as a violation of that equality before the law which he considered a precondition of religious liberty. Madison's success in defeating the religious assessment bill encouraged him to reintroduce Jefferson's Bill for Religious Freedom of 1779, and its passage on Jan. 16, 1786, brought to an end the establishment in Virginia.

Justice Rutledge's enterprising manipulation of Madison's *Memorial and Remonstrance* to mean no governmental aid at all to religion as such and to infuse this meaning into the federal First Amendment of four years later drew Dr. Corwin to comment:

All in all, it is fairly evident that Justice Rutledge sold his brethren a bill of goods when he persuaded them that the "establishment of religion" clause of the First Amendment was intended to rule out all governmental "aid to all religion."[21]

C. The Jeffersonian "Handle"

On June 13, 1779 Jefferson introduced a Bill for Establishing Religious Freedom into the Virginia Assembly[22] and because of the opposition it aroused, its passage was delayed until Madison reintroduced it successfully in 1786. Since in the previous year Madison's *Memorial and Remonstrance* had prevailed against state favoritism of one religion, latitudinarian Christianity, in his home state, the persuasion of logic, from the greater to the less, brought about the end of the establishment of the Anglican church in Virginia. For Jefferson as for Madison, church establishment epitomized the compulsions, coercions and disabilities whereby religious liberty might be discouraged, diminished, or even destroyed. Disestablishment for both was instru-

170

mental and subservient to the paramount right of religious liberty.

Today we are confronted with an unusually remarkable fact. Educational neutralists and secularists who quote Jefferson's "wall of separation" (a very admirable metaphor), ignore Jefferson's expressly defined mind on state relations with religious education the very precise issue before us. Not once but several times and hammering upon the same issue, Jefferson has not only stated his position with argumentative reasoning but pointedly warned his contemporaries against the very misrepresentation that he is being subjected to by the educational neutralists and secularists of our times.

1. PLAN FOR AN EDUCATIONAL SYSTEM, A LETTER TO PETER CARR, SEPTEMBER 7, 1814[23]

In this letter, Jefferson fulfills a promise made to the "trustees" for a plan of education for "our native State" to be supported by state public funds for three specified types of schools, the elementary, general and professional. Among the several provisions for the latter, he stipulates a department for "Theology and Ecclesiastical History" to which "the ecclesiastic" will repair as the "lawyer," "physician," the "military man," the "agricultor," etc., to his own appropriate studies.

2. AN ACT FOR ESTABLISHING ELEMENTARY SCHOOLS, SEPTEMBER 9, 1817

Jefferson's draft for the establishment of state-supported elementary schools passed the Virginia Assembly three years later. The eleventh provision of the Act registered a change in the original plan of 1814:

171

The said teachers shall, in all things relating to education and government of their pupils, be under the direction and control of the visitors; but no religious reading, instruction or exercise, shall be prescribed or practiced inconsistent with the tenets of any religious sect or denomination.[24]

Clearly Jefferson is careful to preserve inviolable the rights of religious science against sectarian teaching in a state-supported school that would be offensive to pupils of other faiths.

3. THE UNIVERSITY OF VIRGINIA, AIM AND CURRICULUM, AUGUST 10, 1818

The following year, Jefferson drew up a plan for the University of Virginia in which he makes a notable change from the tentative proposals of 1814. Then he had provided for a department of theology and ecclesiastical history to which the ecclesiastic could repair as the lawyer, physican, etc., would to his own studies. Now he argues against state provision of sectarian teaching:

In conformity with the principles of our Constitution, which places all sects of religion on an equal footing, with the jealousies of the different sects in guarding that equality from encroachment and surprise and with the sentiments of the Legislature in favor of freedom of religion, manifested on former occasions, we have proposed no professor of divinity; rather, as the proofs of the being of God, the creator, preserver, and supreme ruler of the universe, the author of all the relations of morality, and of the laws and obligations these infer, will be within the province of the professor of ethics; to which adding the developments of these moral obligations, of those in which all sects agree, with a knowledge of the languages, Hebrew, Greek, and Latin, a basis will be formed common to all sects. Proceeding thus far without offense to the Constitution, we have thought it proper at this point to leave every sect to provide, as they think fittest, the means of further instruction in their own peculiar tenets.[25]

172

The change from the 1814 plan is most reasonably explained with due regard for the equal rights of an inviolable religious conscience and for the laws that guard "that equality from encroachment." There is no change in principle but only in prudential choice to guard against the "surprise" that may compromise religious liberty. Further, Jefferson makes it clear that the fundamental truths, theological and moral, philosophically knowable, will be taught by the professor of ethics, who, as a professor of a branch of philosophy, is bound to follow the light of reason in his expositions as distinguished from the evidences of supernatural revelation, the proper province of a professor of divinity.

4. THE FREEDOM OF RELIGION AT THE UNIVERSITY OF VIRGINIA, OCTOBER 7, 1822[26]

In 1814 Jefferson included a department of theology and ecclesiastical history within his state-supported educational system for the training of clergymen. In 1817 Jefferson advised against such religious instruction for elementary schools as would be violative of the rights of religious conscience of any sect or denomination. In 1818, moved above all by the supreme concern for religious liberty for every sect, Jefferson withdrew his original proposal for a school of divinity in the 1814 plan while he retained the study of the ontological and moral relations of man to God as within the proper domain of philosophy wherein human reason can ascertain those truths which are cognizable by the intelligence of any believer. Because his change of plan was being misunderstood despite his clear and painstaking explanation on the basis of principle, Jefferson four years later in his Report to the Legislature defined his position in words and content which no educational neutralist and secularist could receive with satisfaction. No one should infer from his change of plan that public authorities are unconcerned about the relevance to society of man's relations to God. A totally nonreligious education is a defective one. If the dangers imminent in the public provision of religious instructions ("ascendancy of any sect over another") are to be removed on the one hand, on the other a remedy is proposed for this total abstention (which he describes as "evils of less danger") by a cooperative relationship between religious life and studies and the state, a type of cooperation that is equivalent to the "full benefit the public provisions made for the instruction in the other branches of science." This cooperation is filled out in detail within the two broad premises that public authority acknowledges the place of religious life in society, and that religious studies are necessary to an integral concept of education. The details suggested are: that believers establish their religious schools "on the confines of the university" so that students attending these religious schools may have "convenient access" to other University lectures; that other University students may "attend religious exercises with the professor of their particular sect, either in the rooms of the building still to be erected . . . or in the lecturing room of such professor;" those "who might choose such a location for their schools (sectarian schools of divinity on the confines of the University) are to be assured that the University regulations will be modified in order to accommodate those divinity students with the same facilities as the other University students," such as, access to and use of the University library. And then the

174

telling line: "But always understanding that these schools shall be independent of the University and of each other." The facilities on state property which the State University offers the sectarian schools of divinity established on the confines of the University are to entail no compromise of their independence. As he began his explanation so he ends:

Such an arrangement would complete the circle of the useful sciences embraced by this institution, and would fill the chasm now existing, on principles which would leave inviolate the constitutional freedom of religion, the most inalienable and sacred of all human rights, over which the people and authorities of this state, individually and publicly, have ever manifested the most watchful jealousy. . . .[27]

5. LETTER TO THOMAS COOPER, NOVEMBER 2, 1822[28]

That same year Jefferson felt compelled in private correspondence to express his resentment against the misconstruction which was being placed upon his change of plans for the University of Virginia. "In our university you know there is no Professorship of Divinity. A handle has been made of this, to disseminate an idea that this is an institution, not merely of no religion, but against all religion."[29]

Here Jefferson singles out his opponents, educational neutralists ("not merely of no religion") and secularists ("but against all religion") as the ones who are seizing upon a part of his proposal as a "handle" to misconstrue his purpose and to confound the people. In his letter to Thomas Cooper, Jefferson repeats almost verbatim the provisions of the new plan to remedy the "chasm" which the withdrawal of the professorship of divinity might bring about.[30]

175

6. REGULATIONS FOR THE UNIVERSITY, OCTOBER 4, 1824[31]

Two years later, Jefferson, as rector of the State University of Virginia, again sets down the cordial and cooperative relations between the sectarian schools of divinity established "within, or adjacent to, the precincts of the University." He is not content to say only that the University students are "free to attend religious worship at the establishment of their respective sects" but they are "expected" to do so. Students of the religious schools are to be "considered as students of the University, subject to the same regulations, and entitled to the same rights and privileges."[32] University classrooms are made available for theology lectures and religious worship when the facilities of the divinity schools do not suffice.

7. LETTER TO THE DANBURY BAPTISTS, JANUARY 1, 1802[33]

In the second year of his presidential office, Jefferson received an address of congratulations and good wishes from a committee of the Danbury Baptist Association of the State of Connecticut. If we bear in mind that Connecticut did not disestablish its Congregational church until 1818, sixteen years later, that Jefferson was the original author of the proposal for the disestablishment of the church in Virginia, that he was the constant foe of the privileged status of a religion or church in law, that he repeatedly championed equality of religion before the law (and especially so in education), the patent meaning of Jefferson's use of the metaphor of the "wall of separation between church and state" was to express his disapproval

176

of the disadvantageous status of the Baptists within the terms of the Congregationalist establishment in Connecticut. He objected, in a word, to state support, not indeed of religion (for which his educational plans provided) but to a discriminatory favoritism of one religion with rights and privileges denied to nonconformists and dissenters. He therefore studies "with sincere satisfaction the progress of those sentiments which tend to restore to man all his natural rights (the right of conscience) convinced that man has no natural right in opposition to his social duties." If the educational neutralists and secularists whom Jefferson resentfully marked as his interpolators could seize upon a "handle" in Jefferson's own lifetime, it is not surprising that their modern heirs do so with more boldness many decades after his demise with a metaphor taken out of context.

FEDERAL AID TO RELIGION

Across the panorama of American history hangs a brilliant rainbow of religious dedication illuminated by frequent professions, lay and official, individual and corporate, of dependence upon and gratitude to Divine Providence. In response to the religious life of our nation, and in the continuous acknowledgement of individual, social and political dependence upon the providence of God, federal and state governments in numerous and different ways have financially supported and encouraged religious activities.

The federal tradition has its authentic beginnings in the Continental Congress' Ordinance for the Government of the Northwest Territory. The statesmen of the time give expression to the prevailing religious convictions of their day in Article III of the Ordinance of 1787:

177

Religion, morality and knowledge, being necessary to good government and the happiness of mankind, schools and the means of education shall forever be encouraged. . . .[34]

Lot Number 16 of every township, including six hundred forty acres, was set aside for the support of the schools (at that time characteristically religious and for that reason supported), Lot Number 29 for the support of religion, and two townships for the benefit of a university. The provisions of the Northwest and the later Southwest Ordinances are highly meaningful because they were incorporated into the constitutions of the several states which arose from these territories. For example, the Ohio Constitution of 1802, twelve years after the adoption of the First Amendment, provided in Section 26:

The laws shall be passed by the legislature which shall secure to each and every denomination of religious societies in each surveyed township which now is or may hereafter be formed in the State, an equal participation, according to their number of adherents, of the profits arising from the land granted by Congress for the support of religion, agreeably to the ordinance or act of Congress making the appropriation.[35]

It was not until 1860 that the land grants for higher education were restricted to the "State University" and the grant for schools only to "common schools" which though officially undenominational were under the direction, control and publicly avowed influence of Protestant Christianity. In 1789 the First Congress appropriated funds for the support of Christian missionaries among the Indians in implementation of a recommendation made by General Henry Knox, the Secretary of War, and approved by President Washington. "The object of this establishment would be the happiness of Indians, teaching them the great duties

178

of religion and morality, and to inculcate a friendship and attachment to the United States."[36]

President Jefferson continued this governmental policy of supporting, with public funds, religion, religious education and religious worship when in 1803 he asked the Senate to ratify the treaty with the Kaskasia Indians which included the following passage:

And whereas the greater part of said tribe have been baptized and received into the Catholic Church, to which they are much attached, the United States will give annually, for seven years, one hundred dollars toward the support of a priest of that religion, who will engage to perform for said tribe the duties of his office, and also to instruct as many of their children as possible, in the rudiments of literature, and the United States will further give the sum of three hundred dollars, to assist the said tribe in the erection of a church.[37]

In this historic instance the President and Congress supported the subvention of one religion and one church without any intent or effect of conferring upon it a preferential status in law or discriminating advantages by benefit of law. In 1897 Congress abandoned this century-old policy of subsidizing Christian missions among the Indians and by the Act of June 7[38] decided no longer to make appropriations for sectarian education, with a proviso, however, that such financial assistance continue in diminishing sums until 1900. There was no question raised about the constitutionality of the century-old practice and the change was one of policy unless someone would rather infer that the National Congress legislated a three-year moratorium on constitutionality. It is easier to point to federal support of a congressional chaplain, of the support of chaplains in the armed services, on land and sea, in peace and in war, and the construction at federal cost of chapels on government property. Religious publications enjoy mail-

179

ing privileges. Federal and state pentitentiaries provide facilities for preserving uncompromised the constitutional guarantee of religious liberty in circumstances where the exercise of other civil rights is gravely curtailed. A number of Congressional financing programs have been directed to remedying a need defined and acknowledged whatever its religious or proprietary affiliation. The National Youth Administration program of 1935,[39] the Reserve Officers Training Corps program,[40] the federal school-lunch program,[41] the G.I. Bill of Rights[42] (which included education for the ministry and rabbinate), the Legislative Reorganization Act of 1946[43]—all provided out of federal funds financial assistance, military opportunities, food and education, with due respect for the personal choice made in accordance with individual conscience. Federal projects of research are assigned to institutions of higher learning with or without any avowed religious affiliation. The Hill-Burton Act[44] makes federal funds available to any hospital on the basis of predefined need and demonstrated fiscal ability. The seemingly endless enumeration of specific illustrations of programs of federal aid which consistently has maintained throughout our national history the traditional policy of absolute equity in sensitive deference to rights of conscience is an exceptionally agreeable instance of etceteration. The policy is not only authoritative (the effect of national legislation), it is also authentic, the representatives of the nation acting in response to the national religious mind. The strength and vigor of this federal policy prevailed in the 1870's over the challenges of President Grant and Congressman James Blaine and again against the proposal of Congressman Bryson[45] in 1947. Amendments to the Constitution have been proposed to prohibit the extension of federal aid to religious institutions and in

180

every instance the Congress refused. Opponents of federal aid to religious schools, having failed for almost a century to change the Constitution to achieve their objective, now pin their hopes on a realignment of nine justices of the Supreme Court to interpret the First Amendment contrary to its authentic meaning. Their hopes rested with the potentialities of the reasoning in the Everson case in 1947 and soared with the triumph of the Rutledge doctrine in the McCollum case the following year. But the American constitutional consensus reasserted itself when a year after the McCollum decision President Truman signed a Congressional bill which appropriated $500,000 for the construction of a chapel at the Merchant Marine Academy, Kings Point, New York.[46]

CATEGORIES OF AID

Government financial support of religion is ordained directly for religious life as such, that is to say, no one church or religion is singled out exclusively for preferential treatment to the disadvantage of the others. In acknowledgment of the religious foundations of our country and in recognition, public and official, of the need for divine guidance for the just government, prosperity and preservation of our Republic, federal funds provide for chaplains and chapels for Congress and the military, and make available facilities for religious exercise and worship in penal institutions. Public funds pay for the printing of the annual presidential Thanksgiving proclamations and, in recent years, for the Army Character Guidance Program and the United States Air Force training manual which state without hesitation the religious presuppositions of the American way of life.[47] Technically and in the strict mean-

181

ing of words tax-exemption and tax-deductible benefits are not considered direct positive aids in law. Only the appropriation and subtraction from public revenue and its conveyance to an institution fulfills the meaning of financial support by law. These exceptional benefits befall churches and synagogues, schools of divinity, universities, hospitals, orphanages, etc., inasmuch as they are included within those benevolent, nonprofit institutions and associations, educational,[48] cultural, charitable, scientific, literary, which the law sets apart.

Governmental financial aid is said to be indirect when the disbursements of an authorized appropriation of public funds are directly ordained for the remedy, alleviation, amelioration, of a predefined good by whomsoever it is achieved, whether the agency and its affiliation be religious (of any denomination) or nonreligious.[49] Indirect aids are said to be incidental to express the indirection by which the institutional agency may benefit as a consequence of the aid directly given to a defined objective. The G.I. Bill of Rights, the N.Y.A., R.O.T.C., Hill-Burton Act, government research projects, etc., while ordained for the good of individuals regardless of their faith or lack of it, may result in some advantages to the institutional agency. Indirect aids at times are described as accidental aids to emphasize that it is by chance, it is not part of the legislative intention, that a particular denomination of the institutional agency is indirectly benefited. The indirect assistance chances to be the operations of an unavoidable double effect.

"Auxiliary aids" "help out" financially all needy school children with governmental provision of free bus transportation, lunches, health and welfare services, nonsectarian textbooks for the purpose of equalizing educational opportunities in a democratic society and with due reverence for the rights of conscience in education. The Supreme Court has refused to consider "auxiliary aids" within the category of "indirect aids" which almost all state constitutions proscribe, and the states through their courts and attorney generals are fairly evenly divided on this point and not always consistently within each state. At present the federal government provides free lunches to needy school children either with state cooperation or through a federal administrator. State governments either provide some, or all, or none of the auxiliary aids. The Supreme Court has upheld the constitutionality of state supplied nonsectarian textbooks to all school children in *Cochran v. Board of Education*[50] as a legitimate exercise of state police power for public welfare. In the Cochran case, the Court denied the contention of the appellants that inclusion of school children attending privately owned schools constituted the taking of public property for a private purpose in violation of the due process of the Fourteenth Amendment. In the Everson case, the Court rejected the contention that provision at public cost of bus service to children attending religious schools was constructive of establishment within the meaning of the First Amendment. In this case, too, the Court for the first time in its entire history raised the nonrelevant position (since it upheld the bus service as a legitimate exercise of police power for public welfare) in recognition of the appellant's contention, whether any tax support of all religion was constructive of establishment and in the face of past and present history, held that it did. On the identical ground of police power for public purpose, the health and welfare services provided by some states would, if ever contested before the court, be equally upheld. Opponents of federal provision of aux-

183

iliary services for children attending church-affiliated schools object to federal provision of other auxiliary services besides school lunches on the ground that it would be violative of the First Amendment when as a matter of fact the Supreme Court has already upheld their constitutionality.

SECULARIZATION OF STATE SCHOOLS

Today all states, with the possible exception of Vermont, prescribe, one way or another in constitutional or statutory law, that no direct or indirect state financial aid may go to a sectarian school or denominational institution. Despite this express prohibition, many states grant or permit one or more of the auxiliary aids and these practices have been upheld by state courts and attorney generals and further confirmed by the Supreme Court of the United States. These states do not agree with others states that auxiliary aids are to be counted among the proscribed indirect aids and rightly so since auxiliary aids provide nourishment, safety, medical care and textbooks for the benefit of the child in alleviation of a predefined need wheresoever it is found without prejudice to creed.

What has been the story of public support of religious education in the states?

In the history of public support of education, federal and state policies have been neither identical nor consistently parallel to one another. The traditional federal policy has been uniformly and universally nondiscriminatory. State policies, on the other hand, whether in law or practice, have been discriminatory. The earliest American schools were church schools. With disestablishment, the intermingling of religiously pluralist population, and the

184

growing need for making education more available, the financial limitations of the church groups could no longer support the educational burdens adequately, nor could various religious groups agree on the religious influence that was to dominate. In 1818 Connecticut first introduced the public or common school which is not by proprietary title under church control. From 1820 to 1870 the states assumed more and more the responsibilities of education by supporting from public funds their own public schools and other non-church schools sponsored by school societies. All these schools were, in the original American tradition of education, religiously orientated and where one denomination predominated, its sectarian beliefs were taught. But where the frictions of religious pluralism would not countenance such a partisan dictation, a compromise among the Protestants settled upon the teaching of fundamentalist doctrines of Protestant Christianity. Horace Mann is looked upon as the champion of nonsectarian religious public schools and his plan for Massachusetts which precluded public funds from nonpublic schools was widely adopted by other states. But what of the Catholics? The teaching of nonsectarian Protestant Christianity in state-supported schools was a matter of public policy and approved in some instances expressly by law and at times upheld in some places by the local courts, even in the absence of positive law. With the influx of the Catholic immigrants, Catholics voiced publicly a rightful protest against the imposition of fundamentalist Protestantism upon their children attending state schools. Since they were being asked to support a public school system which Protestantism—if not officially prescribed at least authoritatively permitted or even approved[51]—controlled and influenced, it is not surprising that members of the Catholic hierachy

185

would request to participate equitably in the disbursement of state funds earmarked for compulsory education. While Protestants and Catholics agreed that education is religious, Protestants would not allow the application of state funds except for the support of public education that was under the influence of Protestant Christianity. The episcopal requests in the cities of New York and Philadelphia aroused the rage of the nativists of the 1840s and again in the 1850s of the Know-Nothings, and in Philadelphia and Boston, Catholics were assaulted and killed and church properties destroyed.[52] The ugliness of the Know-Nothings' animus moved President Lincoln to write to Joshua Speed, under date of Aug. 24, 1855:

I am not a Know-Nothing, that is certain. How could I be? How can any man who abhors oppression of negroes be in favour of degrading classes of white people? Our progress in degeneracy appears to me pretty rapid. As a nation we began by declaring that "All men are created equal." We now practically read it "All men are created equal, except negroes." When the Know-Nothings get control, it will read "All men are created equal except negroes and foreigners and Catholics." When it comes to this, I shall prefer emigrating to some country where they make no pretense of loving liberty.[53]

In *A History of Freedom of Teaching in American Schools*, Howard K. Beale has given us a trenchant account of the religious educational tensions in the mid-nineteenth century:

While sectarianism was increasingly discouraged, practically all schools still included religion in their curricula. School opened with prayer. The Bible was read and portions of it memorized. Hymns were sung. The principles of Protestant Christianity, so far as they were accepted by all Trinitarian sects, were instilled into children. . . .[54] These religious requirements of schools decidedly affected teachers. In religious schools where children were now allowed to attend the worship of their parents' choosing, teachers were still

186

expected, on the contrary, to adhere to the denomination that controlled the school. In many communities local public opinion, even in the face of a state prohibition of sectarianism for the pupils, still required public school teachers to be orthodox according to the local conception of orthodoxy. In places where the sects were mixed, sectarian restrictions disappeared, but a teacher still had to be a fundamentalist Protestant Christian without Unitarian taint. Most states had constitutional provisions guaranteeing religious liberty. But this had not yet come to mean religious equality. If it had really been interpreted to mean what it said, most early state constitution makers would have opposed as destructive of the integrity of the state that provision of the Wisconsin Constitution of 1848 that declared that "no religious test shall ever be required as a qualification for any office of public trust under the State." But "religious tests" usually meant only sectarian tests among Protestant Christians. Most original constitutions included restrictions that violated this principle in regard to important state functionaries. It is doubtful whether local public opinion permitted its fulfillment in regard to teachers even in Wisconsin in 1848. In any case, the public school requirements concerning religious instruction, Bible reading, and prayers would have made it impossible for the teachers to accept, and unwise for the school to offer, a position to any but orthodox Protestant Christians. . . .[55]

All would have been well, however, in the best of Protestant school worlds, had not this period brought a great influx of Roman Catholic immigrants who objected to Protestant schools and who had the power in some cases to make men heed their objections. There had always been a few Catholics, a few Jews, a few deists, and many who were indifferent to religion. But the indifferent had not objected to a system that excluded them from teaching and taught their children Protestant Christianity. The indifferent had merely accepted the situation, because, after all, religion did no harm. The Jews, Catholics, and deists had accepted the situation because they did not have the power to alter it. The Protestant sects, therefore, had been able to meet the religious problem by agreeing to teach in the schools not the sectarian dogmas on which they disagreed but the Protestant Christian principles upon which they could unite. . . . The Catholics had always had a few schools of their own. As democratic influence increased their desire for education, they built more. When thousands of new Catholics arrived from Europe, they built still more. In days when all education was in private hands, this arrangement had been satisfactory. Their teachers and their children had been on equal terms with Protestants. Under a system of public education, however, they contributed in taxes to the support of schools in which their teachers were not allowed to teach and could not have taught the required subjects anyway without violating their own consciences. Furthermore, the Catholics were not satisfied to have religion excluded from the schools. Like the Protestants, they wanted to teach religion to children, but, again like the Protestants, they wanted to teach their own religion. Since in America Catholic control of the public schools seemed impossible, they preferred a parochial school system in which each denomination trained its own children and supplied its own teachers. If, however, they were to be taxed for the support of the public schools, then, since schools that taught Protestant religion could not satisfy them, they demanded a share of the school fund to pay their own teachers to teach their own children in schools that taught Catholic doctrine. There were American precedents for state aid to religious schools. But Protestants objected to having public tax money used to spread "dangerous" Papist power, and nationalist democracy objected to contributing to schools that were controlled neither by the local community nor by the nation but by a "foreign sovereign."[56] . . . The net result of all this agitation was that the status of the teacher remained about what it had been. A Catholic teacher was still barred from the public schools, as was a Jew, and in many places a deist or a Unitarian. Trinitarian Protestant Christians, however, retained the liberty to teach the Bible and the general principles of Protestant Christianity in the schools with no further restraint upon them than the prohibitions against sectarianism. Here was freedom for a particular group—freedom that in many places is denied today, but freedom exercised at the expense of other groups. In this controversy, the first blows were struck in a struggle that was to bring sufficient secularization of the school curriculum so that some day men could be qualified to teach in public schools whatever their religious views might be.[57]

Where the multiplicity of sects made the dominance of public schooling by one sect difficult to assert itself, the contrivance was attempted to funnel the disbursement of

188

tax funds through a Public School Society. But since this organization was under Protestant domination and indeed chartered to forward fundamentalist Protestant tenets, not only were church-affiliated "religious" schools thereby excluded from participation in public funds allotted to education, but the public schools were avowedly stamped with the religious character of nonsectarian Protestant Christianity.

The abandonment of state support for religious education in public schools was historically not motivated by any "principle" of "separation of church and state" or the "wall of separation" or the fear of the camel's nose, but the phantasmagoria of papist, popish plots that danced in revelry in the minds of nativists and Know-Nothings and their progeny in succeeding decades. Expediency dictated a forced compromise. True, prior to the adoption of the Fourteenth Amendment in 1868, there was no limitation in the Constitution upon the powers of the states on the subject of religion. After its adoption, even then, it was not until 1940 that the Supreme Court in *Cantwell v. Connecticut*[58] handed down the first decision categorically holding that the religious freedom embraced in the First Amendment was applicable to the states. It was in 1947 that the Supreme Court for the first time in its entire history considered any governmental aid to religion constructive of establishment within the prohibited meaning of the First Amendment.

FEDERAL AID TO EDUCATION

There is no mention of education in the Constitution and despite some earnest talk of a national university in the Convention of 1787 and for some years thereafter in and out of Congress, nothing came of it. The original governmental policy dating from the Northwest and South-west Ordinances, and continuing to the middle of the nineteenth century, was financial support in the form of land grants and the income deriving therefrom for general education. In the earlier years the general education was neither general in curriculum nor generally available. Theological and moral studies predominated. In the 1860's, a new governmental policy was initiated which has continued to our times. The Morrill Act of 1862[59] set the first precedent of land-grant colleges and universities for the benefit of agricultural and mechanical arts. Since that time the federal government has established state agricultural and mechanical arts colleges, experiment stations, vocational promotions, extension services, and has financed a variety of specialized training programs and numerous research projects both in private and government owned schools of higher learning. The aftermath of the Civil War and the two World Wars awakened the national conscience to the promotion of a federal program of aid for general education. American citizens who never had the equivalent of even an elementary education, the newly enfranchised Negro population, and the successive waves of immigration to our country posed a grave problem of educating citizens to their responsibilities of achieving a decent minimum of literacy, and of satisfying a legitimate demand for a process of Americanization among diverse ethnic groups of varied national origins.

In the 1880s Senator Blair successfully championed several federal aid programs for general education in the Senate but none of his bills ever reached the House. After the First World War, and more insistently since the Second World War, scores of bills were introduced in both Houses, which generally have expired from constant revisions in response to criticisms, or failed to win the vote in either

190

or both Houses of Congress. Summarily and cumulatively the objections which have frustrated the passage of a federal aid bill for general education are as follows: the express or effective exclusion of religious schools from the benefits of federal general aid programs or the exclusion of even auxiliary aids for parochial school children: fear of federal control of education incident to or, if provided against by the terms of the legislation, inherently potential in the power of the purse which court interpretation might uphold as legitimate jurisdictional supervision and direction; opposition to "creeping socialism" in government; suspicion of federal encroachments in a domain traditionally entrusted to local communities and states; the dread of increased taxation; and, most recently, the stipulation that federal funds be available only to such states as manifest concrete evidence of a gradual and effective cooperation with the desegregation decision. Our study concentrates only on an examination of the constitutional question which turns upon the inclusion or exclusion of parochial school children as beneficiaries of "auxiliary services" provided by a federal general aid bill and secondarily, the broader, all-comprehensive, underlying fundamental question of constitutionality of governmental support for education whatever its proprietary or religious affiliation.

A. Divisions and Distinctions

Specific federal aid to education may be for a specialized type of education and since the 1860's the federal government has to this day established a large variety of such programs. Specific aid may also be earmarked for an auxiliary aid and as such it is not an aid to education but a general welfare benefit for the remedy of a need and also one type of equalization of educational opportunities.

General federal aid to education was the original tradition which gradually diminished toward the middle of the nineteenth century as local communities assumed the responsibility for providing public school education and after the 1870s institutions of higher learning were increasingly founded by individual philanthropists and by the states. "General aid" is a comprehensive term which may reach out to any expenditure-building construction, provision, extension and improvement of facilities, scholastic and athletic, libraries, laboratories, and the supplementation of teachers' salaries. General aid may be restricted to current expenditures which may or may not include auxiliary aids and if provided, may or may not extend to children attending nongovernmental schools. Federal grants in aid to the states and government territories for educational purposes have been established in principle. The policy, however, of fixing upon the revenue resources, the methods of allocation, and the procedures and distribution formulae varied in the different legislations and proposals in response to a variety of circumstances. Suffice for our study to designate the general usages and preferred kinds. Prior to the middle of the nineteenth century federal support of education was in the form of land grants and the revenue deriving therefrom allocated to the states on the basis of uniform amounts to defined geographical units. This was the original pattern of financing education which began with the Northwest and Southwest Ordinances and which continued in practice as the Western territories were incorporated as states in the Union. Approximately three-fourths of the states were beneficiaries under the federal land grant plans. In the 1880s the federal government followed a new policy of money grants which were distributed in proportion to population figures, and this type of grant and method of allocation has been the general practice for subsidization of the

192

various specialized educational programs as well as for the school lunch program. These money grants may be outright, flat grants or, as in recent years, may follow an equalization formula. In order to relieve the poorer states the grants are made on a per capita basis but inversely in proportion to financial ability. The Hill-Burton Act[60] by which the federal government aids all hospitals whatever their affiliation on the basis of defined and demonstrated needs and supplementary to local fiscal capacity is an exemplary illustration of this inverse relationship. Most of the federal aid to education bills which have been proposed unsuccessfully for the past twenty years have followed the equalization formula.

B. The Problems Presented

The fact is that the federal government in a long line of valid acts has supported directly and indirectly religion, religious activity and church-affiliated institutions of a great variety. On the other hand, almost all the states have laws, constitutional or statutory, which expressly forbid in one way or another, direct and indirect aid from state revenue to sectarian schools and denominational institutions. Many of the states do not consider auxiliary aids (we concur in this interpretation), one or the other or all of them, within that prohibition. Other states do. Since the contemplated bills for general aid to education require that federal funds be made available to the states provided that the states match such funds from their own fiscal resources, the problem arises how to resolve the conflict between the federal laws which constitutionally allow extension of these benefits to children attending church-affiliated schools and those state laws which expressly or interpretatively forbid such an application. In cooperatively financed programs the problem is real and inevitable and a just solution must

193

respect the supremacy of laws and legitimate jurisdictions within the proper domain of federal and state governments. Neither one nor the other should be compromised.

The complexity of the problem and the facility with which different issues deriving their legitimacy from disparate sources are unwittingly confounded establishes the necessity for raising questions in order to ascertain the nature and significance of the many issues of the problem. Is there a grave need for financial assistance for education from sources beyond the local communities and state supplementary to their own provisions?[61] Should there be federal subsidization for education? That is a matter of political decision. No one questions that the legislation providing appropriation for education is one for the national Congress to decide upon by the political process of majority decision. Must these aids—and of what sort—extend to church-affiliated schools? Should auxiliary needs, which are not properly educational aids nor for that matter even indirect aids for sectarian schools but, as the Supreme Court has upheld, constitutionally valid child welfare programs—should these auxiliary aids be extended to children attending church-affiliated schools by the federal government in an interlocking federal-state educational program? In a conflict of laws which may arise in a federal-state cooperatively financed program, equity and distributive justice would so dictate. There is no legal compulsion to include nor legal requirement to exclude. Here again, it is one of political decision embodying a policy which binds in legal justice because of the general will of a democratic society to abide by majority decisions. An equitable solution should satisfy the jurisdictional rights and responsibilities of state and federal governments.

Many factors besides legality enter into the promotion

194

of legislation. Is the contemplated measure desirable, expedient, wise, feasible? These are strongly felt considerations and any combination of them can effectively block the passage of the proposal. Should we allow the federal government to enter into a domain traditionally a concern of the local communities and states? Will not federal subventions entail supervision and direction that potentially and gradually may assume the proportions of control or dominance of education? Will not the American taxpayer be overburdened directly by an increase in income and realty taxes, or indirectly by taxes attached to commodities and luxuries? Should the disbursement of federal funds be contingent upon state cooperation with the desegregation decision? What of the animus surely of some secularists and educational neutralists toward any federal beneficence however related to church-affiliated schools? What of the fears of a "creeping socialism?" Whatever may be the degree of reasonableness of each of these considerations and the substance of reality behind them they can block a measure because of the emotional climate they engender and the strength of will to choose as one pleases. However, we are concerned in this study solely with the question of constitutional law.

THE CONSTITUTIONAL QUESTION

A. The Basis of Opposition

The constitutional issues raised by the controversialists on federal aid to education touch upon several provisions and amendments to the United States Constitution. These are:

195

Article I. Section 8. The Congress shall have power to lay and collect taxes, duties, imposts, and excises, to pay the debts and provide for the common defense and general welfare of the United States.

Article VI. This Constitution, and the laws of the United States which shall be made in pursuance thereof . . . shall be the supreme law of the land.

Amendment I. Congress shall make no law respecting an establishment of religion, or prohibiting the free exercise thereof.

Amendment V. No person shall . . . be deprived of life, liberty, or property, without due process of law.

Amendment X. The powers not delegated to the United States by the Constitution, nor prohibited by it to the States are reserved to the States respectively, or to the people.

Amendment XIV. Section 1. All persons born or naturalized in the United States, and subject to the jurisdiction thereof, are citizens of the United States and of the State wherein they reside.

No State shall make or enforce any law which shall abridge the privileges or immunities of citizens of the United States; nor shall any State deprive any person of life, liberty, or property, without due process of law; nor deny to any person within its jurisdiction the equal protection of the laws.

B. The Key to the Solution

The key to the solution is to be found in the constitutional prescriptions of American federalist government and dual citizenship. A conflict, therefore, between what the federal laws allow and what state laws prohibit is not only legally possible, but also, strange as it may seem, legally compatible. Two sovereignties converge upon one and the same individual. Both are invested with their own proper plenary powers—the federal government with its delegated and enumerated powers, expressed and implied, and the states retaining what was never delegated. The American citizen owes obedience to the laws of both governments which the

196

general will of their respective constituents brought to pass through their duly elected representatives. Each individual citizen enjoys privileges and immunities corresponding to his dual citizenship and not infrequently there is also a concurrence.

Within these constitutional premises, federal aid to religious education—interlocked with state finance—is not only feasible but also legally possible. The National School Lunch Act aids all children who attend publicly accredited nonprofit schools whatever their proprietary and religious affiliation. The federal government offers to the states funds in proportion to the population of all school children which the states must match dollar for dollar from their own resources for the provision of free lunches. In twenty-eight states where state laws prohibiting direct and indirect aid to sectarian education are interpreted by their own courts and attorney generals to preclude such a matching arrangement, the National School Lunch Act stipulates that a federal administrator withhold the amount proportional to the number of school children in church-affiliated and private schools and then disburse the amount withheld directly to the parochial and private schools, who then in turn supplement the federal contribution for the expenses incurred *in toto* in serving lunches to their school children. This withholding proviso preserves intact the traditional federal policy of nondiscriminatory benefactions while at the same time it does not interfere with contrary state practices. Another model statute which embodies this same nondiscriminatory policy of the federal government is the Hill-Burton Survey and Construction Act of 1946. Congress provides an annual appropriation for the construction and expansion of facilities and equipment of nonprofit hospitals whatever their proprietary or religious affiliation on the basis of defined minimum standards and demonstrated needs relative to the community and in inverse proportion to the respondents' fiscal ability. Both these legislative enactments of 1946 have been highly successful in their objective, and are exemplary embodiments of the traditional federal policy of nondiscriminatory action, and on that basis, of the governmental acknowledgement of the right to participate equitably in the disbursement of federal funds, of the governmental definition of a good whatever the affiliation of the agency, and of the equality before the law of the institutions serving such a good.

C. States' Rights

Almost all of the numerous proposals concerning federal aid fall into one of three categories on the point here under study. The Taft-Thomas bills[62] provided a federal offer of funds to the states to be matched by them on an equalization basis so that the poorer states receive a greater proportion of funds per capita than the richer states. They embodied no withholding of funds but rather left it to the states to decide whether any part of the federal funds received by them would reach church-affiliated schools for the provision of auxiliary services. A second and meager class of proposals, the Aiken-Mead proposal of 1945,[63] the first of its kind, extended to all children attending state and private schools the auxiliary services which were specifically included in the appropriation for current expenditures. Where the interpretation of state laws would not allow this disbursement because of the federal-state cooperatively financed benefit, the federal government empowered a National Board of Apportionment to make the allotment of funds directly to the nongovernmental schools. This bill, too, followed the equalization formula. Foremost among the opponents of the Aiken-Mead Bill was the National Education Association. In general, the third category includes the pre-Taft proposals and the Barden bill.[64] Whereas the Taft-Thomas type left it to the states to decide whether any share of the federal allotments should reach the children of nongovernmental schools, the pre-Taft proposals generally excluded the nongovernmental school from any sort of benefit from the public funds, auxiliary or otherwise. The Barden Bill has the singular and unenviable distinction of frank discriminatory definition. It was a general aid bill limited to "current expenditures," a term which as customarily used has included auxiliary services. The Barden Bill explicitly incorporated a restriction of its own, with obvious intention, that "current expenditures" does not include in the definition given the auxiliary services. In two other ways the bill excluded children of nongovernmental schools from the federal benefits that would otherwise have accrued to them in the absence of the inserted restriction. In the apportionment of funds the total school children population from five to seventeen years of age, in each state, attending parochial schools as well as state schools was counted in, but in the disbursement of funds the children of the church-affiliated schools were counted out. To make certain a third time the exclusion of children attending parochial schools, a judicial review section empowers a taxpayer to proceed to a federal court on one count: when in his judgment any of the money appropriated is being applied to nongovernmental school children. The Barden Bill foreclosed entirely not only what the nondiscriminatory School Health-Services Bill[65] (introduced by Senator Thomas as subsidiary to the Thomas General Aid bill and approved by the Senate) provided universally to

199

all school children—it incorporated the "withholding proviso" of the School Lunch Act of 1946—but it also would
not allow what the Taft-Thomas proposals would leave to
the states to decide for themselves. The Representative from
North Carolina did not trust even the alleged states' rights
argument! This proposal deservedly never left the full House
Committee on Labor and Education. It was repeatedly
affirmed that the underlying principles of the Taft-Thomas
general aid bills were in accord with states' rights. Leaving
it to the states to decide whether any of the federal funds
should be allocated for the children attending nongovernmental schools was a respectful regard of the sovereign
jurisdiction of each state and of its laws. To incorporate a
withholding proviso such as the School Lunch Act of 1946
had embodied, and to disburse funds directly to the institutional agency on an equalization formula such as both the
School Lunch Act and the Hill-Burton Act of 1946 provided
was denounced as "by-passing" the states, "sidestepping"
the states, "diverting" public funds. Besides, such a pattern
of federal allocation of its own funds was a violation of the
"principle" of noninterference with the educational systems
of the states! We must bear in mind that in the controversies
of the 1940s the benefactions in question were auxiliary
services such as bus transportation, nonreligious textbooks,
medical services and school lunches, which the Supreme
Court had repeatedly upheld as legitimate expressions of
the police power of the state for the nondiscriminatory
provision of public welfare benefits. All of these services,
with the exception of the textbooks, are noneducational in
purpose. They are welfare and safety measures. There is no
whisper at all here of direct or indirect aids to religious institutions in a federal-state interlocking financing program,

200

aids which the federal government by itself has and does provide in a variety and number of ways.

D. *Federal Rights*

The antinomy of federal v. states' rights is unnecessary and artificial. We should all be advocates of states' rights but we should all be equally advocates of federal rights. Within the context of American federalism there is no irreconcilable conflict between the two. National citizenship is primary and paramount over state citizenship, and the Constitution and the laws of the United States made in pursuance thereto are the supreme law of the land. Where an apparent conflict emerges it is for the courts to ascertain whether the federal government is usurping powers reserved to the states or whether the states are encroaching upon the powers delegated to the federal government. And where both sovereign powers legislate for the same individual in a field of action which the law has not pre-empted exclusively to one jurisdiction or the other, the concurrence of responsibilities and rights must be mutually preserved intact through the function of the judiciary. Both governments for obvious reasons have a serious interest in and corresponding grave duties for the education of an intelligent and responsible citizenry; and the federal government can help to equalize the educational opportunities among the poorer and wealthier states. Traditionally it is left to the states and their local communities to determine their own educational systems. There is no discernible conflict between state educational systems and federal nondiscriminatory legislative policy of financial aid for education as such. In an interlocking federal-state financial program for education, the federal government may not require that states match the federal offer of funds in disregard of state laws and policies. But neither should the laws and policies of any state interfere with the laws and policies of a higher sovereignty of the federal government. The "withholding proviso," far from "bypassing" and "side-stepping" the states, assiduously respects the laws and policies of each state while at the same time it preserves undamaged with equal reverence the laws and legislative policies of a higher jurisdiction and of a superior law operating for the benefit of a higher citizenship. "Leaving it to the states" is in fact a surrender of federal responsibilities and subordination by default to the unilateral dictation of state laws and policies. The real difference is between federal nondiscriminatory legislative policy in the disbursement of federal benefits for education—as witness the G.I. Bill of Rights, R.O.T.C., N.Y.A., National Reorganization Legislative Act, federal research programs, the School Lunch Act, etc.—and state policy which discriminates between state and nongovernmental schools as the beneficiaries of state direct and indirect aid in education. But this real difference is not a conflicting one since the federal government can pursue its own policy and at the same time leave untouched the state laws and policies by means of a "withholding proviso" in any federal-state fund matching subsidization of educational needs.

E. Rights of Citizens

As the middle term of all exercise of authority and operation of laws and policies stands the American citizen endowed with federal and state rights. Invested with citizenship, he is entitled to the rights and the benefits of both governments as he is without arbitrary exception to obey the laws, pay the taxes, be subject to military duty, and fulfill all the obligations which each government may rightly demand of him. The most prized of the constitutional rights is the "exercise of religious freedom."[66] In American law, religious liberty means the right to believe and the right not to believe. The wording of "exercise" of religious freedom was sedulously chosen by the drafters of the amendment to embrace not only articles of faith which may be contained within one's conscience and mind, and modes of worship which as external manifestations are locally expressed in houses of prayer and worship, but also all such human conduct and activity which the religious conscience may dictate in conformity with the dogmas of its faith with due regard for the legitimate demands of social order and peace. The Supreme Court has upheld the constitutionality of religious schools which comply with state requirements to satisfy the state compulsory school attendance laws.[67] While it did not expressly rest its ruling on the free exercise clause (and it did not do so until 1940),[68] the Court declared inviolable "the liberty of parents and guardians to direct the upbringing and education of children under their control." No one can seriously contest that the motive of parents for sending their children to parochial school is religious, since in fact the parents' compliance with state compulsory attendance laws by sending their charges to public schools would be at no financial burden to themselves. The significance of the Court's striking down state education compulsory laws seems to be completely lost on those who recognize only state education as the truly American type of education.[69] Equally lost on public school advocates is the implication which the Court drew from any pattern of state monopoly of education: "The child is not the mere creature of the State; those who nurture him and direct his destiny have the right, coupled with the high duty, to recog-

203

nize and prepare him for additional obligations."[70] Since 1940, when *Cantwell v. Connecticut* categorically included for the first time the "free exercise" clause of the First Amendment in the content of the "liberty" of the Fourteenth Amendment, the Court has jealously guarded religious "exercise" even to uphold in *West Virginia Board of Education v. Barnette*, as an expression of that free exercise, an objectively wrong conscience on the significance of flag-saluting provided in the given instance there is no danger to public order. While scarcely anyone would openly contest the rights of parents to send their children to a parochial school in response to the dictates of religious conscience, in the matter of federal aid even when restricted to auxiliary aids, there are many who would place a disabling price upon such religious liberty. Attendance at church-affiliated schools becomes *eo ipso* for these opponents a liability before the law. Contrary to the intentions of the framers of the First Amendment and its subsequent history, they would insert an antinomy into the "preferred" right of religious liberty. What the no establishment clause intended to do—to remove any actual or potential impediments to religious liberty and to the equality before the law of all believers—these opponents would annul by converting the right of free exercise of religion in education into a religious test of exclusion from the disbursement of federal aids. National and state governments are enjoined by the Fifth and Fourteenth Amendments from depriving a person of life, liberty or property without due process of law. Not only is religious liberty in education contracted by the proponents of exclusion without any culpability before the law, but the right to property is conditioned in the disbursement of federal funds on a discriminatory basis of religious affiliation. In the words of Cardinal Francis Spellman, this is

204

equivalent to "taxation without participation." Let us bear clearly in mind we are still restricting our discussion to auxiliary aids which are vital services—health, welfare, and safety—for the child, not for the church-affiliated school, for the alleviation of needs, not for the support of a creed. To say that government responsibilities to children cease when in compliance with their religious conscience they attend parochial schools is to pervert our national law and the underlying moral principles which have inspired the federal nondiscriminatory policies traditional in our history. Furthermore, the "leave-it-to-the-states" argument seriously jeopardizes impartiality in federal government. Since there is no consistent and uniform pattern among the states, and even within each state, on auxiliary services, the federal government in a federal-state financing program would become accessory to their bizarre variations. If the federal government permitted its own share of funds to be disbursed in accordance with the contradictory policies that exist among the states, it would be partner to the unequal treatment of its own federal citizens.

F. American Constitutional Consensus

A general and summary view of the American constitutional consensus of the national government's relation to religion and religious institutions readily brings to mind the more obviously known facts:

1. DIRECT FINANCIAL SUPPORT

In the Ordinances for the Northwest and Southwest territories in the period immediately prior to and continuing after adoption of the Constitution, land grants were set aside for the support of religious education. From the presidencies of Washington and Jefferson until 1900 Congress supported with tax funds religious education by Christian missionaries among the Indians. Throughout our national history, chapels and chaplains for Congress (a system which Madison helped establish) and for the armed services on land and sea in war and peace have been traditional. One month after the McCollum decision, Congress passed and President Harry S. Truman signed a bill which appropriated public funds for the construction of a chapel at the Merchant Marine Academy at King's Point, New York. In circumstances where the exercise of civil rights are justly restrained by due process of law, provisions for religious exercise in penal institutions are conscientiously made for the privileged right of religious liberty.

2. INDIRECT FINANCIAL SUPPORT

The National Youth Administration Act of 1935 extended public fund benefits to all high school and college students whatever the school of their choice. The Reserve Officers Training Corps program conducted by the military may be incorporated into the curriculum of any college. The Legislative Reorganization Act of 1946 provided at federal cost for the choice of religious education of congressional pages in the District of Columbia.[71] War surplus at nominal prices was available to religious institutions as well as to other defined nonprofit organizations. And above all, the G.I. Bill of Rights provided at federal cost for the higher education of veterans at any educational institution of their choice not excluding preparation for the ministry and rabbinate. The federal government supports numerous research projects at institutions of higher learning whatever their

206

proprietary and religious affiliation. The Hill-Burton Act extends federal funds to all nonprofit hospitals for the expansion and improvement of their facilities regardless of their proprietary and religious affiliation.

Not the least significant admission of the constitutionality of federal aid to religion and its free exercise is the unsuccessful and repeated action of those who would alter the Constitution by amendment in order to reverse the government's traditional policy of nondiscriminatory disbursements.

3. AUXILIARY SERVICES

The Supreme Court has upheld the constitutionality of auxiliary aids by the states as a legitimate exercise of police power for the nondiscriminatory provision of public welfare benefits. The Court upheld the state statutes as neither violative of state law, prohibiting direct and indirect aid to sectarian schools and denominational institutions, nor of the First and Fourteenth Amendments of the Constitution. At present nonreligious textbooks are provided free by the states to all school children in Louisiana, Mississippi, New Mexico, Rhode Island, and in West Virginia only to indigent parochial school children. Free transportation is provided by nineteen states: California, Connecticut, Illinois, Indiana, Kansas, Kentucky, Louisiana, Maine, Maryland, Massachusetts, Michigan, New Hampshire, New Jersey, New Mexico, New York, Oregon, Rhode Island, West Virginia and Wyoming. The exemplary Federal School Lunch Act provides free lunches to children whatever the school of their choice either directly through a federal administrator in twenty-eight states, or in cooperation with the other twenty-two states and the four jurisdictions under

U.S. control—the District of Columbia, Puerto Rico, the Virgin Islands and American Samoa—whose policy of disbursement concurs in this instance with the federal government's. The Supreme Court has upheld the free textbooks and bus transportation. The Federal School Lunch Act has so far not been contested and it is to date the only federal auxiliary provision. In the 1940s many insisted that health and welfare benefits, bus transportation and free nonreligious textbooks be included among the federal provision of auxiliary services and extended to all children without discrimination.

Such has been the magnificent panorama of the federal government's support of religion—not to mention the countless evidences of the authoritative and official professions of our country's dependence on divine providence for its foundation, survival and prosperity. Scarcely the masonry of a wall of absolute separation (which Jefferson disowned as a misleading "handle" for the understanding of his thought on the subject), it is more like the corridor constituted by two walls, political government and religion, each a distinct jurisdiction and proper competency, mutually respectful and cooperative for the benefit of one and the same individual citizen and believer.

G. What Is Education?

One of the many slogans which is repeated in the public debates on federal aid is the constant reference to the "American type" of education, as if parochial schools were not quite as much American as the state schools. As a matter of fact, the parochial schools are a more indigenous development in America than in any other part of the religious world, and a pro-religious oriented education was the original prevailing American conception of education which has suffered by default in the state schools because of unresolved religious tension. We may properly speak of the American type of education in the same sense that we speak of the English school system, the German *gymnasium* and the French *lyceum*, namely, a distinctive pattern of intellectual disciplines directed to an academic achievement. Broadly speaking, there is only one American system of education in the sense that all publicly accredited schools, state and privately owned, must comply with the required standards of teaching, of curriculum and of school facilities, and generally, pass the final examinations provided by the state educational authorities. For this reason the student of any publicly accredited school is given recognition in a transfer to another school before or after graduation. The differences that exist between state schools and church-affiliated schools do not affect these common standards and requirements. Both schools are obviously under the greater supervision incident to proprietary and religious affiliation. The slogan, "American type of education," is supposedly bolstered by invoking in the same voice the "American principle of separation of church and state." There is an American type of separation which precludes presumptuous interference beyond the competence of one jurisdiction upon the other, which differentiates it from say, the French absolute separation of the laic state and, within the context, a subordinate church. But the conjunction of these two slogans makes a seriously misleading assumption that the relation of government to church is the same as the relation of government to education.

In the American type of separation, two separate jurisdictions are recognized by law, each supreme in its own domain, and between the two a traditional policy of co-

209

operation and mutual assistance, moral and fiscal, has been a standing testimonial that the two separate jurisdictions must operate in harmony for the integral good of citizen and believer. On the other hand, the government has real jurisdiction, although not an exclusive one, as well as an interest in education so much a constituent part of general welfare. The conjunction of these slogans has logically led to the insertion of a religious test in the definition of education, of educational needs, and of the common good to which education contributes. Does education become less educational and less American because it also provides religious instruction? Do educational needs cease to be needs and lose their significance because of the religious affiliation of the school? Do schools lose their efficacy to contribute to the common good because their students are taught the love and fear of God? And if an appeal be made to Americanism, well then, which of the schools, the secularized state schools or the religious schools, are in accord with the religious heritage of America and with the religious nature of our people, whose institutions, as the Court said in the Zorach case, presuppose a Supreme Being? Which of the two educational arrangements, religious or secularized education, "completes the circle of the useful sciences . . . and fills the chasm" which Jefferson decried in a school which did not provide for religious instruction and facilities, let us note, for religious exercise and worship on state property? Jefferson held that the students of religious education on or near the confines of the state university should be "entitled to the same rights and privileges!" Yet a new brand of Americanism ignores Jefferson on governmental aid to religious education, rejects the nondiscriminatory policy traditional in the federal government, and is remarkably divisive by inserting a religious test in a general federal aid bill.

H. Federal Aid to Education and Religious Liberty

One consideration emerges as paramount with increasing clarity from this study: one cannot totally separate the problem of federal aid to education from religious liberty. If the objective is to assist education, remedy educational needs, and equalize the educational opportunities among the poorer and richer states, for the good of the American nation, then it is extremely difficult and potentially dangerous to settle upon a norm of participation, of inclusion and exclusion, by reason of religious affiliation. The exercise of religious liberty must not become a liability before the law in the disbursement of the benefits of law.[72] To allow this is to incur through the exercise of religious liberties one of the "civil incapacitations" of which Jefferson spoke as the incidents of a state established church. In a reverse spin, the First Amendment, originally intended to deny the national legislature any power to grant a preferential status in law for a church or a religion, comes now to mean that Congress shall have the power to pass laws that may operate to the disadvantage of the exercise of religious liberty. *The controlling provision of the constitutional organic act for federal aid to education is the general welfare clause of Article I, § 8.* The First Amendment is a guarantee that the exercise of federal power for general welfare should not abridge the free exercise of religion. The Court in the controversial Everson reasoning felt the artificial tensions which it had created for itself when it incorporated in its reasoning the novel Rutledge doctrine of absolute separa-

211

tion. It would not allow that a religious test be controlling in the exercise of a general welfare provision:

New Jersey cannot consistently with the "establishment of religion" clause of the First Amendment contribute tax-raised funds to the support of an institution which teaches the tenets and faith of any church. On the other hand, other language of the amendment commands that New Jersey cannot hamper its citizens in the free exercise of their own religion. Consequently, it cannot exclude individual Catholics, Lutherans, Mohammedans, Baptists, Jews, Methodists, Non-believers, Presbyterians, or the members of any other faith, *because of their faith, or lack of it,* from receiving the benefits of public welfare legislation. While we do not mean to intimate that a state could not provide transportation only to children attending public schools, we must be careful, in protecting the citizens of New Jersey against state-established churches, to be sure that we do not inadvertently prohibit New Jersey from extending its general state benefits to all its citizens without regard to their religious beliefs.

The Court therefore does not deny that a state may adopt a restricted policy in the disbursement of public welfare benefactions, but it refuses to allow that the motive for such a restriction be a religious test. In the Zorach case, the Court tries earnestly to extricate itself from the unreality of the Rutledge absolute doctrine and to reaffirm in broad sweep the American constitutional consensus on the relation of government to religion. It rejects the conception of absolute separation as one which would connote preference for those "who believe in no religion over those who do believe."

I. Law and Policy

Constitutionally there is no real problem at all for the federal provision of auxiliary services to all school children. Constitutionally, there has not been any real problem on

212

federal indirect aid to religious educational institutions. In fact, the practices of the national government are lavishly uniform and universal. What of direct federal aid to religious educational institutions? One would think that no legal objection would be raised for doing the less when in fact the federal government has from the inception of the Republic done the greater, the provisions of chapels and chaplaincies which are a direct financial support of religion.

During the war the federal government constructed "temporary" buildings on the campus of private educational institutions whatever their religious or proprietary affiliation. Yet there may be reasons of great weight why there should not be a policy of direct federal aid to religious schools; certainly not a policy of equal aid to all schools. Ecclesiastical authorities have made advance disclaimers of participation in any federal bill of direct support, such as capital outlays for construction, payment of teachers' salaries, etc. But such disclaimers may be for prudential reasons, for reasons other than constitutional. It is here precisely where the unsuccessful Kelley Bill[74] for "construction," and other similar proposals failed to meet the constitutional issue. They think to evade this issue; actually they submerge it. May educational institutions of religious affiliation be included constitutionally? We submit that they may. Must they be so included? There is no legal compulsion to do so, but likewise there is no legal barrier against such an inclusion. *The reason and motive for noninclusion must never be the fact of religious affiliation.* Concretely, there might never be a bill proposed or promoted by anyone for direct financial aid to religious educational institutions. But the answer must be unequivocally given even if it never descends from the speculative to the order of actual events for the supreme purpose of keeping the authentic meaning

213

of the First Amendment inviolate from misconstruction. The choice by the democratic political process of majority decision of one policy in preference to others must always be within the comprehension of the law. The choice of a specific policy or the change of a prevailing policy is usually motivated by a combination of conditioning factors, expediency, wisdom, desirability, feasibility, fiscal and social, etc. But if ever the choice of restricted policy of disbursement of general welfare benefactions to education, direct, indirect or auxiliary, should operate in the concrete to interfere with religious liberty, conduce to inequalities before the law, as to constitute a discriminatory preferential status against believers, then we hold it to be the solemn duty of the courts to affirm the primacy of religious liberty before the law. The courts have yet to decide whether restricted general welfare policies can in certain circumstances be constructive of the violation of the free exercise thereof clause.

J. An Argument of Law

One of the causes contributing to the confusion in many minds on the problems of federal aid to education is the unjustifiable reference to a so-called Catholic position. A careful survey of expressions by Catholics on the rights to participate in federal aid will disclose no unanimity on the extent of federal aid to parochial schools. There are Catholics who would rather rely completely on the resources and generosity of the parish for all the school needs, including the auxiliary services. In rejecting any sort of public aid they are not questioning its constitutionality. Many Catholics and non-Catholics insist upon the legality and provision of auxiliary aids for all school children but either will not

214

allow or do not want any direct public support for the school itself which is church-affiliated. There are Catholics who share with many non-Catholics the conviction that governmental intrusion into the educational field should be restricted only to necessary aid for the needy areas in the economically poorer states. Here, there is a difference of opinion whether such necessary aid should be applicable to all publicly accredited schools or not. This author's position is: the controlling constitutional provision for federal aid to schools is the general welfare clause of the organic act. The determination of the provision and extent of federal aid to schools is a matter of policy which is fixed upon by the democratic process of majority decision. The Supreme Court has sustained the contitutionality of state provision of auxiliary services in the Louisiana textbook case and the Everson bus fare case. On the same grounds it would uphold, if challenged, the federal provision of free school lunches both directly to the children through a federal administrator and, where interpretation of state laws allows, through state cooperative finance and distribution. There is no question about the constitutional consensus of the federal direct support of religion in Congress and in the armed services. The problem centers on support of religious schools. There is no question on federal indirect aid to religious schools. The federal policy of nondiscriminatory indirect aid to religious institutions of learning is an established policy and thriving in our times. What of federal support of religious institutions? In the noneducational area, the Hill-Burton Act provides federal supplementary aid for the construction, extension and maintenance of hospital facilities on a nondiscriminatory basis. The pointed question: what of direct federal aid to religious educational institutions? This author's position, unequivocally stated, is that the noninclusion of religious educational institutions may not be motivated by an objection to their religious profession and affiliation. This would be a violation of the religious liberty guarantee of the First Amendment, and if the appeal be to the First Amendment, it constitutes a misconstruction of the authentic meaning of the entire amendment. This author personally prefers that religious educational institutions draw their vigor from the free financial support of the faithful. Where avoidable, it would be wiser not to have governmental support because of the governmental control it may entail and for other reasons mentioned elsewhere. But we must insist that this additional question be asked and duly considered: whether, in any given concrete circumstance, the exclusion of a religious school from public funds does or does not operate as a restriction of the exercise of religious liberty in education. The courts have not to date faced this issue. But it has not gone wholly without notice among jurists. Professor Wilber G. Katz has reflected:

No case in the Supreme Court has directly involved the question of the validity, under the First Amendment, of tax support for parochial schools. In the New Jersey bus fare case, however, both the majority and the minority clearly assumed that such support is unconstitutional. Until recently, it seemed to me that this assumption was a sound application of the "no aid" rule. It seemed to me that direct payment for educational costs was something more than action to avoid discrimination against religion. Two years ago, I suggested that to protect the freedom of parents in their choice of schools, a tax deduction of some kind for tuition paid to such schools would be permissible. It seemed to me, however, that affirmative aid to religion would be avoided only if religious schools were limited to the support of individuals paying tuition and voluntary contributions.

This position no longer appears to me to be tenable. The "no aid to religion" rule is a rule prescribing neutrality, forbidding action which aids those who profess religion as compared with those who do not. If one assumes that the religious schools meet the state's standards for education in secular subjects, it is not aid to religion to apply tax funds toward the cost of such education in public and private schools without discrimination. Like the dissenters in the bus fare case, I am not now able to distinguish between the minor payments there involved and payments for educational costs. I believe, therefore, that none of such nondiscriminatory uses of tax funds are forbidden by the First Amendment.[75]

If the Supreme Court may consider, as it needlessly did in the Everson case, whether any public support of religion may be construed a violation of the no establishment clause —and it did so in the face of American constitutional consensus to the contrary—then it may with greater relevance ask itself whether the exclusion of a religious school in a federal policy of aid to schools does or does not operate to a real governmental restriction and intervention of the free exercise thereof clause. But neither natural nor legal justice requires equal aid, uniform and in the same amount to all schools in a nondiscriminatory policy of aid to schools. But distributive justice does require that there be equal right to proportionate aid the computation of which rests on a number of confluent factors. The Hill-Burton Act is an exemplary illustration of one such sort of computation for all hospitals whatever their proprietary or religious affiliation.

Federal aid to education which excludes religious schools from its beneficiaries precisely because of their religious profession and affiliation may place Congress in the incongruous role of promulgating a law prejudicial to the free exercise thereof clause; of establishing a preferential status for a secularized education as more worthy of its benefits than religious education, and find itself in the unenviable position of constructively setting a religious test

217

as a norm for inclusion among the beneficiaries in the exercise of its general welfare powers; and, lastly, allow, if not actually intend, that exercise of religious liberty in education become a liability before the law in the disbursement of the benefits of the law. This would convert the no establishment clause into an affirmative official action in favor of nonreligious education.[76]

K. *The Residual and Delegated Rights to Educate*

The right of parents to educate their children is primary, personal and inalienable. The high tribunal has acknowledged this connatural investiture of parents, and in 1944 the court noted: "It is cardinal with us that the custody, care and nurture of the child reside first in the parents, whose primary function and freedom include preparation for obligations the state can neither supply nor hinder."[77] When, therefore, parents cannot provide a private education, they delegate some of their responsibilities to the government, whose right to exist derives in great measure from the purpose of civil society to implement the inadequacy of means and the incompetence of parents to fulfill their parental obligations. Besides, the state has its own stake in education. The common good is the realization of a good society and this moral excellence derives from the moral development of its citizens. When the government aids education which also provides religious instruction it is assisting itself. For the government would otherwise have to provide at public cost the classrooms which religious communities are providing at their own expense. If, as all agree, it is an expression of social justice when the government provides the total cost of public school education, why should the lesser provision of partial support

218

of nonprofit private schools be offensive to anyone? The Canadian, Dutch and English educational systems make these provisions to the consternation of no one in countries predominantly Protestant. We maintain that the controlling constitutional premise for federal aid to education is the general welfare clause of the organic act. The First Amendment is secondary and qualifying. The motive for the noninclusion of church-affiliated schools in a governmental policy of aid to education may not be the religious profession and affiliation.

All must jealously regard the "wall of separation" for the sake of religious freedom. Civil and religious jurisdictions must be kept distinct and separate. Neither the political nor the ecclesiastical authorities should be allowed to encroach upon the legitimate and proper jurisdiction of the other. Neither one should hinder the operations of the other. This is a two-faced coin. All, too, should in their vigilance be just as jealously sensitive against any sort of educational establishment which would be prejudicial to and diminish the exercise of religious liberty that the no establishment clause was intended to secure. Even those who for many good reasons of policy—and they number among the different faiths—are opposed to federal direct aid to religious education should be just as responsive to the effects of such a policy. Any evidence—not abstract or hypothetical, but real and substantive—which shows that the exercise of religious liberty in education becomes a liability before the law and operates as a sort of religious test, results in an inequality before the law, for the benefits of law should arouse the anxieties of all of both sides of the debate. The civil rights of believers should not be abridged because the first civil right is exercised. Federal educational favoritism of an educational policy cannot be justified in reason or law to the disadvantage of religious liberty in education. To date, the courts have yet to weigh this consideration.

The distinctive meaning of the First Amendment, which Madison helped define and explain, is that the federal Congress is declared impotent to legislate on establishment which may be such as to infringe upon the religious liberty (as state constitutions allowed for many years) and to ensure against a restricted liberty, the free exercise thereof clause was inserted. When the First Amendment is taken, as it should be, together with the "no religious" test of the organic act, its meaning has a sharper precision than the religious liberty guaranteed by the state constitutions which in its earliest history was scarcely distinguishable from tolerance and which for decades prescribed in some form or another a religious profession for public office. The incorporation therefore of the freedom of religious exercises of the First Amendment into the liberty of the Fourteenth if it is to convey the original and authentic meaning of the First should be equally prohibitive of any state action in the field of education no less than in any other human activity that would constructively operate as a religious test as a liability before the law for the benefits of the law. In the absence of such a conformity will be found the radical reason for the disparity between the traditionally uniform federal policy of nondiscriminatory beneficence, and the bizarre patterns of partly discriminatory and partly nondiscriminatory policies and laws of the states. It is precisely at this juncture that the unsuccessful Kelley Bill and others like it to be proposed fail to conform with the authentic purpose of the First Amendment. A bill which for very good and valid reasons does not include religious schools within its capital outlays should make acknowledgement of their contribution to American education and in this way or another officially disown that the reason for their noninclusion is not their religious affiliation.

State and federal courts have at various times upheld in the interest of religious freedom governmental administration or provision of funds in such circumstances which favored religious education. In *Quick Bear v. Leupp*,[78] the Supreme Court sustained the authorization of the Commissioner of Indian Affairs to pay from treaty funds for the education provided by the Bureau of Catholic Indian Missions lest the free exercise of religion be otherwise constrained among the Indians. On this same constitutional principle courts have upheld state statutes which committed delinquent, neglected or dependent minors to institutions under the auspices of the same religious profession as the child and to which the state paid from public funds for their care. The courts have struck at the restriction of religious liberty even when freedom of movement is controlled by government authority; it has not spelled out entirely how far government may favor religion positively. The high tribunal has upheld auxiliary services; the federal government provides many indirect aids to religious education; the federal government gives direct financial support to religion in Congress and in the armed forces. How far may it go in direct subsidy of religious education, if at all? No one really knows the answer.

L. How Far?

The affirmation of a constitutional right is not disowned because of the advance disclaimers to benefit by that right. Nor does the validity of a constitutional right lose meaning because the question how far it extends has not yet been answered. Within the broad comprehensive scope of the general welfare clause of the constitutional organic act, the federal government may choose for valid reasons of expediency, feasibility, wisdom, social considerations, economy, underlying religious tensions—not to extend direct and to church-affiliated schools in a general federal aid program for education. But we emphasize that this restriction may not derive from the First Amendment. Such an appeal would be a serious distortion of the original and authentic meaning of the amendment. Secondly, since the *Cantwell v. Connecticut* ruling of 1940, the religious liberty guarantee of the First Amendment was categorically made operative through the Fourteenth Amendment upon the states. May not the broader meaning of the federal free exercise of religion at least suggest that it serve as a normative correction of the state laws and correspondingly, their policies, on governmental relations with religious activities not excepting religious education? May not the traditional federal policy of nondiscriminatory benefits through the efficacy of the operation of the First Amendment upon the states achieve a corresponding nondiscriminatory state practice, at least as far as auxiliary services are concerned, services which the high tribunal has already upheld as in no way offensive to federal and state laws? Finally, the Supreme Court has yet to consider whether a federal aid program limited exclusively to government schools (and, let us grant, for valid reasons) may not operate in a particular concrete circumstance to an "unreasonable interference" with religious liberty exercised in education. This last consideration should engage the serious reflections of jurists and nonjurists for the preservation of the original and authentic meaning of the First Amendment and its relevance as a qualifier upon the exercise of the general welfare clause of the Federal Constitution for aid to education.

6

The Administration's Memorandum on Aid to Education

On Feb. 20, 1961, the late and beloved President of the United States sent to Congress his Special Message on a federal program of aid to education. Taking a realistic and total view of our national needs and potentials, President Kennedy said:

> Our progress as a nation . . . will require the maximum development of every young American's capacity. The human mind is our fundamental resource. A balanced federal program . . . must include equally determined measure to invest in human beings.

He detailed specifically the needs of children and youths, classroom shortages, underpaid teachers, the inadequate financial resources of institutions of learning, unequal and inferior educational facilities; lastly and above all he insisted on freedom of individual choice:

> Our twin goals must be: a new standard of excellence in education—and the availability of such excellence to all who are willing and able to pursue it.

It was regrettable to many loyal Americans that such universal affirmations of educational needs in the case of students, teachers and facilities, all unequivocally related to our nation's progress, should have been so quickly contradicted by the President himself in outlining discriminatory norms for the disbursement of federal funds.

President Kennedy proposed that colleges and universities be benefited by the expansion of an existing program of loans for the construction of faculty and student residences and the establishment of a new long-term, low-interest loan program for the construction of academic facilities, such as classrooms, laboratories, libraries and related structures. He also recommended a new federal program of state-administered scholarships for talented and needy young people accompanied by additional allowances to the college or university of their own choice. All these financial aids, federal construction loans and scholarship grants would be made available under his program without prejudice to institutions of higher learning under religious auspices whether they benefited thereby or not.

For the lower levels of education, the elementary and secondary schools, the President recommended to the Congress a three-year program of general federal grants for classroom construction and teachers' salaries. Parochial schools were explicitly excluded from these subventions.

In accordance with the clear prohibition of the Constitution, no elementary or secondary school funds are allocated for constructing church schools or paying church school teachers' salaries.

With this, the President erected a wall of absolute separation between schools in what was otherwise a cohesive comprehension of American education, its national needs and objectives. An exclusionary rule was founded on religious affiliation.

On March 28, 1961, Abraham Ribicoff, then Secretary of Health, Education, and Welfare, in response to a request made by Senator Wayne Morse, chairman of the Senate Subcommittee on Education, sent the latter a memorandum discussing the constitutionality of loans to private schools including sectarian institutions and a summary of existing federal legislation which benefits sectarian institutions. Because the memorandum is, in its own way, an official document of opinion, it could be easily misconstrued as an authoritative interpretation of the historical practices of governmental aid to education. Actually it is no more than a cabinet officer's report committed *a priori* and *ex officio* to the support of his chief executive. To acknowledge frankly the restricted purpose and loyal service of the memorandum is not to deride it. There is much to admire in this earnest effort of a staff of counselors to assume the burden of piecing together into a seemingly coherent presentation the undeniable antinomies which have risen throughout our national history between some Supreme Court rulings and dicta and the wide variety of governmental aid to religion and to activities and institutions under religious auspices. At no time, however, do they proffer even a mild criticism of any Court opinion. Neither do they suggest, however respectfully, the slightest doubt about the President's position. And this, be it noted, in an area of constitutional controversy which has divided many of the country's most eminent jurists into opposing camps. But the memorandum is distinguished for the singleness of its purpose—to sustain the presidential position.

Whether or not precollegiate education under religious auspices will be included in federal general aid legislation covering religiously professed institutions of higher learning, or will be separately subsumed in a revised and extended version of Title III of the National Defense Education Act, the constitutional debate will be far from settled. For this reason, the memorandum is deserving of critical study. Cogently and with legal *expertise* it has hardened a position that is not likely to dispel disquietude about governmental aid to church-related educational institutions.

THE CONSTITUTIONAL PRINCIPLES

In a preface to a discussion of the judicial precedents[79], the memorandum calls attention to the three constitutional limitations relevant to the problem before us. They are: first, the legislative incompetence of the national Congress and of the states to pass any law respecting an establishment of religion; second, the constitutional denial of any power to pass a law infringing upon the free exercise thereof; and third, the due process clause of the Fifth Amendment and the due process and equal protection clauses of the Fourteenth Amendment which operate as restrictions upon the laws that the federal and state governments may pass and accordingly forbid an unreasonable discrimination in governmental programs. These three limitations are so closely associated as to make it extremely unlikely that a governmental action would be sustained which did not satisfy all of them.

Within the freedom constitutionally guaranteed by these three restrictions upon governmental action, the American system of dual education is securely situated. Education may not be exclusively reserved to state schools nor may government schools provide instruction in any specific religion contrary to the religious conscience of the students. In its genuinely earnest effort to explain government neutrality and impartiality in matters of religion in education, the memorandum gives expression to an ambiguity that suggests more than may have been intended. It says in part, ". . . there seems little doubt that Government may not use

226

its authority in the field of education in order to instruct children in religion generally." It is still far from a settled question whether moral values necessary for civic peace and order should be taught without theological reference, or whether relative, conventional mores will suffice; nor does it yet seem practically possible to disengage certain subject matters from their religious factors, history, for example, in any public school curriculum. One might observe also that certain American educators hold that behind the need for maintaining sectarian impartiality is the further positive one to maintain the moral and religious truths upon which our national life has been built. Either we hold that state schools are and should be wholly non-religious, in which case we stir up a hornets' nest of constitutional problems touching upon parental rights and upon the religious conscience of the students; or we decide that the religious heritage in American national history should be taught and thus lay to rest for ever all pretense to a wholly secular education; or we insist on a wholly secular education even at the cost of mutilating the substantive content of a subject matter; or we frankly admit that tax-supported education is not and cannot be neutral and impartial but only and decidedly anti-religious. Each of these considerations gives its own distinctive direction to constitutional reasoning on religion in schools. The memorandum provides no inkling as to which of these alternatives it chooses to hold. Not until we have fixed upon a clear and definite meaning of the relation of religious historical factors and religious moral values to the public school curriculum can we arrive at a precise appreciation of the implications of governmental neutrality and impartiality. The memorandum does not attempt to establish whether there is in fact, or can possibly be, a truly neutral

227

ground equally impartial to the religious and nonreligious student in a state school curriculum and in any program of character development. The memorandum admits to the religious orientation of American national life and is acutely sensitive to the need of drawing a line between what is permitted and what is constitutionally prohibited to a "society in which aspects of religion are inextricably entwined with knowledge and culture." However, in focusing the problem immediately on the precise issue at hand—governmental relations with schools under religious auspices—it does so with an omission that lends emphasis to the statement:

The difficult problem is posed by the dual constitutional mandate: that the state must recognize these schools (parochial) as part of its educational system for purposes of compulsory attendance laws, but it cannot support them in ways that would constitute an "establishment of religion"—

To which should be added for full constitutional perspective: "and without converting the exercise of religious liberty in education into a liability before the law in the disbursement of government benefits." Throughout the memorandum the major emphasis is repeatedly on the no establishment clause. The free exercise is apparently of little interest, and scarcely any consideration is given to the instrumentality of the former for the latter.

THE JUDICIAL PRECEDENTS

The memorandum notes that the rulings in both the Pierce and Cochran cases occurred before it had been decided that the establishment of religion clause of the First Amendment operated upon the states by virtue of the due process

228

clause of the Fourteenth Amendment, and proceeds to argue that:

> For this reason the Cochran case is dubious authority for the proposition that textbooks may be provided by a state to parochial school students. The crucial question of whether the establishment clause of the first amendment prohibits the expenditure of public funds for textbooks to be used by church school pupils was not presented to the Court in this case, and the Court therefore had no occasion to rule upon the question (9, n. 4).

This manner of reasoning seems to minimize the constitutional precedent of Cochran as a legitimate point of departure of the constitutionality of other forms of aid to all school children. But the cursory reference to Pierce and Cochran does less than justice to the full significance of the reasonings of the Court.

In 1925 the Supreme Court ruled upon two companion cases, *Pierce v. Society of Sisters* and *Pierce v. Hill Military Academy*. The Society of Sisters, a Catholic congregation, empowered under Oregon law to conduct schools and orphanages, along with the Hill Military Academy, a private organization operating under state law an elementary, college preparatory and military training school, had successfully prayed the District Court of the United States for Oregon to enjoin the enforcement of an Oregon statute, effective Sept. 1, 1926, whose manifest purpose was to compel general attendance at public schools by normal children between eight and sixteen, who had completed the eighth grade. The Supreme Court unanimously sustained the action of the District Court and agreed with its ruling.[80] Though the case is justly celebrated for the pronouncements of the Court on the paramountcy of the rights of parents to direct the education of their children,[81] only corporations and no parents were party litigants. The

Court, in fact, disposed the case on the ground that the private corporations were being deprived of their property without due process of law.

There are two observations customarily made suggesting that less reliance should be place upon the Pierce ruling in the present discussion of aid to all schools. It is said that the statement on parental rights in education was no more than a dictum and that the First Amendment was never argued or even mentioned. But the point is that the non-religious character of the Pierce ruling is precisely what constitutes the importance of the case. In ruling upon both cases together, the Court in effect denied that the religious affiliation of the parochial school distinguishes it from the private school as an educational institution capable of fulfilling a public purpose as prescribed by state educational laws. Both are subsumed as private corporations with equally inviolable property rights not merely in education but in public education. Private proprietary title and church affiliation do not derogate from or diminish the ability to fulfill public law requirements of school curriculum, standards of teaching, and other education facilities, or render the educational process less competent, less truly public in purpose and achievement. By denying to the state a monopolizing role in education, it implicitly affirms that parents, church and the state are all contributors to public education. While the First Amendment was not mentioned in the Court's opinion, the Court did overrule the underlying objection that the parochial school could not be public education because a religious and therefore necessarily private organization benefited thereby. The Court took cognizance that the schools of the sisters were remunerative and that the Hill Military Academy was conducted for profit.

230

The Court's affirmation of the primacy of parental rights is more than a dictum. In upholding private corporation property rights to engage in public education the Court considered these rights dependent upon patronage, "the free choice of patrons, present and prospective." One cannot sustain the opportunity to exercise one right without holding inviolable the other corresponding right. The Court, in a word, was protecting real, not abstract, doctrinaire rights.

Two years earlier[82] the Court had sustained in similar terms the necessary correspondence of the right to teach as a remunerative occupation and the right of parents to engage teachers.[82] While the subsequent absorption of the religious clauses of the First Amendment into the Fourteenth seems to make the case relevant to the question of their proper interpretation, the original nonreligious character of the Court's ruling in Pierce may suggest a serious consideration concerning the practical impact of a vast comprehensive scheme of federal assistance at all levels of education that would place at enormous economic disadvantage a significant part of American public education. No one could contend that a governmental program of financial subvention may never under any circumstances risk consequential disadvantages to private interests. But when government defines national educational needs, relates them to the achievement of a national purpose and then proceeds to exclude as beneficiaries of government assistance elementary and secondary schools (not the colleges and the universities) conducted under religious auspices, then their property rights in these concrete circumstances in conjunction with the free exercise of religious liberty in education take on a larger dimension. To risk property rights because of religious affiliation as a result

231

of the impact of the immense financial resources of the government may well argue to a "hostile state action," by which government would be forsaking its avowed role of neutrality and impartiality to believers and nonbelievers alike. The constitutional import of a massive federal aid program to education which would seriously imperil the property rights of church-affiliated schools has not been to date fully weighed. This author has never been entirely sympathetic to Chief Justice Marshall's remark, "The power to tax is the power to destroy," because he has constantly viewed the power to tax purposive to the common good, the general welfare of the nation. But where this purpose is defeated through an exclusionary rule based on religious profession, the power to tax may indeed operate as a destructive force.

The nonreligious character of the Pierce case, far from weakening its constitutional usefulness in the present national debate on federal aid, clearly strengthens it. The right to send children to parochial schools rather than to public schools is based by the Court on the right of parents to guide the education of their children, a right protected by the presence of the word "liberty" in the Fourteenth Amendment. Briefly, it is not the religious or nonreligious conscience that is made to prevail but it is the parental right, whether exercised out of religious motivation or not, that limits the state to a partnership, and denies it an exclusive role in public education. The Pierce case may properly suggest that the present program of federal aid should in the method and reach of its disbursement have equitable regard for all taxpayers in the parental exercise of directing their children's education. And if the religious issue is to be raised at all, it may surely not be used as the basis of an exclusionary rule. Instead, the parental right must be considered as an element inherent in "the free exercise" of their religion which the First Amendment guarantees to all, believers and nonbelievers alike. The Pierce case upholds logically the coherence of real rights.

A Total View of Public Education

Whereas in the Pierce ruling the principal stress was upon the correlation of real rights, in the Cochran case the Court emphasized a total view of public education as the legitimate objective of a general welfare benefaction. The appellants had brought suit to restrain the Louisiana state officials from expending any part of the severance tax fund in purchasing textbooks and in supplying them free of cost to parochial school children of the state, contending that taxation for the purchase of school books constituted a taking of private property for a private purpose. The Supreme Court took cognizance of the nondiscriminatory language of the state statute which authorized without religious qualification "supplying school books to the school children of the state" and the directive to the Board of Education to provide "school books for school children free of cost to such children." "The purpose is said to be to aid prviate, religious, sectarian, and other schools *not embraced* in the public educational system of the state by furnishing text-books free to the children attending such private schools."

The Court rejected this contention:

Viewing the statute as having the effect thus attributed to it, we cannot doubt that the taxing power of the State is exerted for a public purpose. The legislation does not segregate private schools, or their pupils, as its beneficiaries or attempt to interfere with any matters of exclusively private concern. Its interest is education,

233

broadly; its method, comprehensive. Individual interests are aided only as the common interest is safeguarded.

Referring to this case in *Carmichael v. Southern Coal Company,* the Supreme Court observed:

The end being legitimate, the means is for the legislature to choose. When public evils ensue from individual misfortune or needs, the legislature may strike at the evil at its source. If the purpose is legitimate because public, it will not be defeated because the execution of it involves payments to individuals. Individual interests are aided only as the common interest is safeguarded.

Denominational and nonsectarian, private and governmental schools are all embraced in the conception of public education and the differential of religious affiliation or profession does not detract from the common purpose, the public service.

No Religious Exclusionary Rule

In *Everson v. Board of Education,* 1947, the Court upheld the constitutionality of a New Jersey statute which authorized that parents be reimbursed from public funds for their children's bus transportation to schools, public and parochial. Everson sustained use to tax funds to provide transportation to church schools as a legitimate exercise of state police power for general welfare. Not content with satisfying the requirements of the law, the Court, in acknowledgment of the appellant's contention, also considered whether public financial aid to religion was constructively a violation of the First Amendment. In complete disregard of the historical record of American legal practice since the founding of the Republic, the Court subscribed to Justice Rutledge's absolute separation of church

234

and state but stopped short of applying this novel pronouncement to the issue before the Court. Needless to say the result is a precarious balance of tensions between seemingly disjointed factors—liberty and no establishment clauses. The inherent harmony of the First Amendment religious clauses which rested on the paramountcy of religious liberty and the instrumentality of no church establishment to securing this liberty was disturbed. Fortunately the traditional judicial sensitivity against religious discrimination proved superior to the logical consequences of a doctrinaire construction of no establishment.

New Jersey cannot consistently with the "establishment of religion" clause of the First Amendment contribute tax-raised funds to the support of an institution which teaches the tenets and faith of any church. On the other hand, other language of the amendment commands that New Jersey cannot hamper its citizens in the free exercise of their religion. Consequently it cannot exclude individual Catholics, Lutherans, Mohammedans, Baptists, Jews, Methodists, Non-believers, Presbyterians, or the members of any other faith, *because of their faith, or lack of it,* from receiving the benefits of public welfare legislation. While we do not mean to intimate that a state could not provide transportation only to children attending public schools, we must be careful, in protecting the citizens of New Jersey against state-established churches, to be sure that we do not inadvertently prohibit New Jersey from extending its general state benefits to all its citizens without regard to their religious beliefs.

Of course cutting off church schools from these services, so separate and so indisputably marked off from the religious function, would make it far more difficult for the schools to operate. But such is obviously not the purpose of the First Amendment. That Amendment requires the state to be neutral in its relations with groups of religious believers and non-believers. It does not require the state to be their adversary. State power is no more to be used so as to handicap religions than it is to favor them.

Here the Court disallows that the motive for the inclusion or exclusion of a class of citizens from a government benefit is to be a religious test. Impartiality forbids such an exclusionary rule.

Cochran-Everson

Be it noted that in both Cochran and Everson provision is made at public cost for educational facilities. While no one can entertain any doubt about the educational character of textbooks, the reimbursement of parents for their children's transportation to schools is no less directed to an educational purpose.

Children like all others are under the general mantle of municipal police and safety protection, wheresoever they choose to wander or travel. The further provision, however, under state law for the reimbursement to parents of expenditures for transportation of their children to public and Catholic schools on regular buses operated by the public transportation system, while a safety measure in kind, is more than that—it is specifically directed to fulfilling an educational service. This added safety measure while not educational in itself is intended as an aid to education. The plaintiff taxpayer took full cognizance of this and directed his constitutional objection to the church affiliation of the parochial schools. The Court disallowed that this affiliation disparaged the status of parochial schools as accredited schools together with other nonprivate schools, and ruled, on the contrary, against an exclusionary religious test in the disbursement of public welfare legislation, under which education and safety among others are to be subsumed.

236

Constitutional History Remade

Let it be noted at the outset that whenever the memorandum cites opinions of the United States Supreme Court Justices these are always cited *as given;* it then proceeds to argue therefrom apparently with complete agreement. While the interpretations of law, its enlargements, its contraction and reversals are within the competence and jurisdiction of the high tribunal, the remaking of history is not. It would seem, therefore, to exceed the proper bounds of due deference to the high tribunal to cite without critical comment the Court's reading of history, thus leading the reader to assume its historical accuracy. For example, under the heading, "Judicial Precedents," the memorandum refers to Justice Rutledge's dissenting opinion in Everson as follows:

On the basis of his evaluation of the historical material and his view of the objectives of Madison and Jefferson, leading proponents of the Amendment, he stated that—

"The Amendment's purpose was not to strike merely at the official establishment of a single sect, creed or religion, outlawing only a formal relation such as had prevailed in England and some of the colonies. Necessarily it was to uproot all such relationships. But the object was broader than separating church and state in this narrow sense. It was to create a complete and permanent separation of the spheres of religious activity and civil authority by comprehensively forbidding every form of public aid or support for religion. In proof the Amendment's wording and history unite with this Court's consistent utterances whenever attention has been fixed directly upon the question.

Since the memorandum cites Justice Rutledge without critical comment or appraisal of his reading of American history it in effect uses his manner of reasoning to adopt the position that the First Amendment was intended to go far

237

beyond interdicting a preferential status in public law for a church or a religion with disabilities or civil incapacitation for nonconformists and dissenters.

Scholars ever since Everson have disclosed the historical inaccuracies and fallacies of Justice Rutledge's understanding of Madison and Jefferson. All this is or should be by now old cloth. Since the First Annals of Congress the intent and scope of the religious clauses of the First Amendment as understood by James Madison emerge clearly from his reassuring rejoinders to allay the anxieties of Peter Sylvester of New York,[84] Mr. Huntington of Connecticut,[85] and Mr. Tucker of South Carolina.[86] The proposed amendment, his fourth, against an establishment of religion was directed solely against the national government, and was not intended in any way to interfere with state financial assistance to religion nor to conflict with state-church establishments. Madison's scope and meaning of the federal religious guarantees are further clarified by his original fifth amendment which guaranteed religious freedom against encroachment by the states without at the same time requiring state disestablishment.[87] Despite Madison's repeated reassurances that the federal amendment left untouched state dispositions of religious life, Justice Rutledge attributed the converse to him, reading his mind as to the disposition of religious matters in his own state of Virginia, expressed in his *Memorial and Remonstrance* of 1785, six years before the final ratification of the ten amendments, as interpretative of the intent of the federal First Amendment.

As for Jefferson, his plans for education in the state of Virginia, drawn with meticulous care years after the First Amendment had been ratified and years after his two terms as chief executive, disclose a persevering and uncompromising endeavor to protect the rights of religious conscience in tax-supported education. His plans of 1814, 1817, 1818, 1822 and 1824 are classic apologias for state financial assistance and state administrative accommodations of the most intimate and involved sort concerning religious instructions and religious practices in the state University of Virginia. If the President's legal counselors felt constrained *ex officio* to follow the Court's assertions of what the law is henceforth to be, there is no rational, justifying explanation for following the Court in a remaking of American history. This is to harden and to perpetuate the initial errors.

Justice Black in the opinion of the Court compounds the error by intermingling Justice Rutledge's pronouncements with an assortment of his own, rejecting governmental favoritism to a church together with impartial and equal treatment, and any aid in any amount to support religious activities or institutions.[88]

From the time of the administrations of Washington[89] and Jefferson and continuing for over a century, the federal government supported the propagation of Christianity among the Indians in a nondiscriminatory program of annual congressional appropriations made available to Christian missionaries and organizations of various denominations for the civil, moral and religious instruction of the Indians.

As for the prohibition of the establishment of religion by Congress, certain eminent constitutional authorities still maintain that it is not convertible into a similar prohibition on the states under the authorization of the Fourteenth Amendment unless the term be given an application which carries with it an invasion of someone's freedom of religion, that is, interference with religious liberty.

239

It is easier to recall to mind the traditional and still vigorously extant government financial support of congressional chaplains, of chaplains in the armed forces, on land and sea, in peace and war, and the construction of chapels on government property with funds appropriated from the public treasury. Many religious and ecclesiastical items and equipment, stationary and portable, necessary to the religious services of the major faiths in the armed forces are made available through an across-the-board appropriation of public funds. Some of these are furniture, altars, chalices, altar linens, crucifixes, sacramental wine, grape juice, wafers, candles, rosaries, cruciform medals, charcoal and incense, and such publications as testaments, missals, church folders, character education literature.

It is a facile but scarcely knowledgeable retort to say that these governmental provisions are intended as compensatory measures for the enforced restricted movement of servicemen. For the greater part of the history of military chaplaincy there has never been a sufficiency of chaplains for all faiths or, for that matter, for any faith, and even up to the Civil War congressional law did not allow for every faith. The first Roman Catholic priest for Army services was appointed in 1846 by President James Polk during the Mexican War and only three had been named by 1856. Jewish chaplains were first authorized during the Civil War when Congress at the recommendation of President Lincoln removed the restrictive requirement that chaplains be Christians. The idea of military chaplaincy merely as a governmental compensatory measure for the restrictions placed by military command on freedom of movement and therefore on freedom to exercise one's own religious faith is also contradicted by the original and still prevailing tradition of the volunteer recruit as compared with the conscripted serviceman. With the exception of Massachusetts and Virginia, which resorted to conscription, the American Revolutionary War was fought and won by volunteer recruits. It was not until April, 1862, that the Southern Confederacy initiated conscription, the Union doing so on March 3, 1863, with the congressional enactment of the Enrollment Bill. In addition to the nearly three million who were inducted through the Selective Service Act of May 18, 1918, the first national wartime conscription in American history, approximately one million enlisted voluntarily in the Army, while almost the entire Navy and Marine Corps were made up of volunteers. Volunteer recruiting has always been and still remains the primary source and the core of military manpower; conscription is designed to supplement it.

The unvarnished fact is that military chaplaincies have primarily a symbolic meaning in addition to other motives for their existence, namely, an official acknowledgment that a patriotic duty to risk life and limb, if necessary, for one's country far transcends mere human command. Attendance at church services is compulsory at both the military and naval academies. Chaplains of the United States Senate and House of Representatives are chosen by these bodies and receive annual stipends. There is obviously no suspicion here of any compensation for the restriction of movement of our Congressmen in the exercise of their religious liberty. Legislative chaplaincies, state as well as federal, of which the memorandum seems scarcely aware, are an official affirmation that our governments seek and depend upon Divine Providence in their deliberations and decisions.

In addition to the direct governmental support of religion in general and in particular because of its salutary in-

241

fluence upon a variety of national interests, religious institutions are encouraged by tax preferment benefits, tax exemptions and tax deductible gifts—thereby relieving them of the statutory burdens which other income and property groups in the country ordinarily bear. It is true that in the federal tax system religious institutions are exempt together with other institutions that operate exclusively for charitable, scientific, literary or educational purposes. But the inclusion in a class group does not render the intent less definite or specific. The contrary is the case. This is borne out by the many state statutes which extend exemption only to such property of religious institutions as is used for religious purposes, or to such property as is exclusively used for religious purposes. It is also true that the inclusion of religious institutions among the tax-exempt beneficiaries is often justified because some of their activities frequently perform services identical with those of charitable and educational institutions. Thus church-sponsored relief and charities, old people's homes, orphanages, hospitals and schools relieve the state of many of its own obligations in these activities. But this only means that religious organizations, with their undoubted religious influence and environment, perform public services, as do nonprofit organizations, and may share equally in tax preferment benefits without prejudice to their religious apostolate. An impressive number of state court decisions have upheld tax exemption encouragement to religion as such apart from its social welfare activities. State court decisions upholding tax preferment benefits for denominational schools of divinity, sectarian colleges, churches and religious printing businesses apparently do not consider them divisive forces of society. Can this lesson be lost upon those in the federal government who have a myopic fear of establishment? In a remarkable and significantly elevated point of view state courts have seen all churches and their religious schools as contributing to the common public benefit in the very exercise of their distinctive religious influences. Scarcely a monetary benefit but far more significant of the federal government's favor to religion is the exemption from military service of the nonordained students of divinity as well as ordained clergymen in peace and war.

In the field of education, every conceivable sort of financial assistance has been given by state and federal governments to educational facilities that are church-supported. To the students of lower grades, nonreligious textbooks, school lunches, health and welfare services, and bus transportation have been provided. Federal tuition grants have been allotted for congressional pages. On the collegiate level there have been state scholarships, federal fellowships, research grants and if necessary G.I. tuition grants. Parents have been reimbursed for the expense of bus transportation of their children to parochial schools, and tax deductible benefits have been allowed for contributions to church-school building funds. Schools have received construction loans for college dormitories, faculty residences and campus centers—all revenue earning—in the care of institutions of higher learning. Contract and research grants have been made. Private elementary and secondary schools have received loans for the acquisition of laboratory and other special equipment for science, mathematics, or modern foreign language teaching, and for minor remodeling of laboratory or other space to be used for such equipment. Tax exemption and tax deductible benefits have been granted to all private nonprofit institutions of learning.

243

To all of these must be added those aids which in their flow of multiple effects bring incidental benefits to religious institutions.[90]

In the noneducational field, the amount of financial assistance from the federal government through the terms of the Hill-Burton Survey and Construction Act for the construction and expansion of facilities and equipment of nonprofit hospitals under religious auspices is beyond calculation. The vast program of state assistance to all social welfare agencies which care for the sick, the blind, the indigent, the aged, orphans, delinquents, minors and so on, and which are conducted by religious organizations, is hardly calculable. Without state assistance on a per capita basis religious institutions could not possibly cope with the financial burden of caring for the same number of dependents. The fact that these agencies are performing services for society, which the state itself would otherwise have to bear directly, cannot conceal the evident fact that the state is also subsidizing indirectly religious institutions which engage in these services out of a religious motive, in a religious environment and under religious jurisdiction, and which gather membership to their organization by the appeal of these very charitable works. To appraise rightly the indirect aid given to religious institutions by past and existing programs of government assistance, one need only conjecture how long these religious agencies could continue to conduct these activities, educational and noneducational, to the same extent as they now do if they were to be deprived of these governmental benefactions. Direct, indirect or incidental, such benefits constitute undeniably substantial assistance to religious institutions and their influence.

244

McCollum, the Fiction of Coercion

The Everson ruling could have contented itself, in complete constitutional propriety, with the general welfare motivation for public provision of transportation to all school children without any religious exclusionary test defining the recipients of this public benefaction. Not content with satisfying the requirements of law, the Court, in acknowledgment of the appellant's contention, also considered whether any public aid to religion in any of its activities was constructively a violation of the no establishment clause. The Court decided that a single passage bore the tantalizing consequences of the McCollum case. Here the Court held that use of tax-supported property for a voluntary cooperative plan of religious instruction through the state's compulsory education machinery fell under the ban of the First Amendment as it had been interpreted in Everson. One would have supposed that the constitutionality of the Champaign released-time plan would have been subsumed as a minor under the unanimous Pierce ruling. It seems that the right of parents to direct the education of their children in response to the dictates of their religious conscience is not as inviolable for those who are economically constrained to send them to government schools as it is for those who send them to schools that are church-sponsored.[91] Logically McCollum is incompatible with Pierce. The children who were attending religious instructions were doing so at the written request of their parents whose consent must, by law, be imputed to the child. No one's religious liberty was being curtailed, nor for that matter any other personal liberty. There was no legal compulsion to attend nor any threatened or imposed penalties. Terry McCollum, whose parents and counselors protested that he was being singularly embarrassed, was free to immunize his nonreligious identity among other students whose parents had not requested religious instruction for their children. Yet a lone atheistic conscientious objector was allowed to prevail over eight hundred and fifty Protestant, Catholic and Jewish religious conscientious objectors in a voluntary cooperative plan between tax-paying parents and tax-supported schools. McCollum notwithstanding, the parental right which Pierce upheld when conjoined, as it ought to be, with the constitutionally guaranteed right of the free exercise of the parents' religion still awaits a judicial resolution of government neutrality in education that is truly impartial to religious and nonreligious alike.[92]

Zorach—Toward Impartiality

In the reasoning of the Court's opinion and of the dissenting justices in Zorach in 1952, it becomes clear that Justice Black's conjunction of the use of tax-supported property for religious instruction with the operation of the state's compulsory education machinery was not to be considered a disparate element in the McCollum case. Justice Douglas, speaking for the majority, insisted, "We follow the McCollum case." Justice Black, dissenting, wrote sharply, "I see no significant difference between the invalid Illinois system and that of New York here sustained. . . . As we attempted to make categorically clear, the McCollum decision would have been the same if the religious classes had not been held in the school buildings." Justice Jackson dissented: "This released time program is founded upon a use of the State's power of coercion, which, for me, determines its unconstitutionality. . . . The distinction attempted between that case (McCollum) and this (Zorach) is trivial,

246

almost to the point of cynicism, magnifying its non-essential details and disparaging compulsion which was the underlying reason for invalidity." Justice Frankfurter, too, in his dissent made the finding of the presence or absence of coercion controlling. Perhaps the justices of the Court were unduly captivated by the constructive inference of "coercion," "compulsion," "restraint" both in McCollum and Zorach in the employment of the state's compulsory public school machinery. The fact is that truant officers check equally on absentees from state and private schools. And as far as the children's own wish is concerned, most of them, if they had their way, would consider themselves as much "captive" for being compelled to attend public school by the state law and by their parents as to attend religious instruction, if not more so.

The Court divided on the existence or absence of coercion in the operation of the state school machinery in releasing school children during one school hour a week for religious instruction off school premises upon the written request of the parents. Reports of the children's presence at religious instruction classes were made to the school authorities in order to see that the excuses were not taken advantage of and the school deceived. Apparently all the members of the Court agreed implicitly that use of tax-supported property by itself was not a controlling factor constitutionally. No less could be expected from a Court habituated to sustaining use of public parks and street corners for sectarian religious proselytizing, even if the restraining arm of the police force was visibly within reach to guarantee order. In some instances the right to propagate a sectarian religion was scarcely distinguishable from provocative, offensive attacks upon the faiths of others. Consequently, it seems rather dubious for the mem-

247

orandum to ignore the taint of coercion with which allegedly the use of tax-supported classrooms through the operation of the state's compulsory school machinery was legally infected and proceed to make the taxpayers' use of public school classrooms for religious instruction the premise for denying the legality of federal provision of property value in the form of loans to church-affiliated schools. No element of coercion can possibly be discerned in such use of government property. It might have been noted, on the other hand, that the impartiality of the Everson ruling which refused to allow religious affiliation to be made the basis of an exclusionary rule and which was reduced to a questionable neutrality in McCollum, was restored to that stance which looks with equal favor upon all.

Circular Arguments

The memorandum notes that two state court cases which have been decided since Everson have interpreted that case together with McCollum and Zorach as forbidding use of public funds to pay tuition at sectarian schools. *Almond v. Day* maintained that state payments to sectarian elementary and secondary schools for the education of war orphans violated the First Amendment because such payments were opposed to the principles laid down in Everson.[93] But this only illustrates the legal antinomies let loose by the absolute separatist dicta of Everson. A federal program of War Orphans Educational Assistance does provide educational opportunities for children of wartime veterans who died from a service-incurred disease or injury.[94] The student must be pursuing an approved program of education in an institution of higher education or in a vocational school below the college level. Payments are made directly

248

to the student to meet in part the expense of his tuition and subsistence. Also, under Section 243(a) of the Legislative Reorganization Act of 1946 the secretary of the Senate and the clerk of the House were authorized to arrange with the Board of Education of the District of Columbia for the education of the congressional pages. The District was to be reimbursed for any additional expenses:

(c) Notwithstanding the provisions of subsections (a) and (b) of this section, said page or pages may elect to attend a private or parochial school of their own choice: provided, however, that such private or parochial school shall be reimbursed by the Senate and House of Representatives only in the same amount as would be paid if the page or pages were attending a public school under the provisions of paragraphs (a) and (b) of this section.

In *Swart v. South Burlington Town School District,* the constitutionality of a state statute was challenged which required town districts to maintain a high school or furnish secondary instruction at schools selected by the parents.[95] Under another section of this law, South Burlington was authorized to pay the tuition of Catholic and non-Catholic students attending two Catholic high schools. The Vermont Supreme Court took cognizance of the fact that the district did not maintain a public school and that non-Catholic students were not required to attend religious instruction classes. In a paraphrase of a dictum from Zorach the Court raised in the form of a question what the original dictum asserted positively:[96] "Does the payment of tuition to a religious denominational school by a public entity finance religious instruction, to work a fusion of secular and sectarian education?"[97] Acknowledging that the parent-right and tuition-payment plan was within the "literal provisions of the (state) statute" it concluded

249

nonetheless that it "exceeded the limits of the United States Constitution."

Tax support, which historically was one of the incidents of state-church establishments, is repeated here in the wake of Everson to be constructive of church establishment forbidden by the First Amendment. We have seen the variety of ways in which federal and state governments subsidize religious life. Whereas in McCollum and Zorach tax support was interdicted in circumstances in which the element of coercion allegedly ensued, in Swart tax support is proscribed where it operates to a fusion of secular and sectarian education. Separation of church and state is construed to require separation of education and religion, an impossibility which many educators and the late Justice Jackson have insisted upon. The no-blending doctrine is vulnerable on many accounts, theoretical and practical. Physics, chemistry and mathematics are probably the only sciences that are wholly nonreligious in content, but literature, the esthetic arts and, above all, history are necessarily involved with religious factors, values and events. On another count, where supposedly separation of church and state is understood as jurisdictional, it is also not wholly complete and absolute. The state does set at times certain values and interests of its own as superior to a church dogma or claim of religious conscience. American law forbids polygamy, may compel vaccination upon conscientious objectors, and may force objecting parents to permit blood transfusions for their children. Religious services which require the handling of snakes may be proscribed. Absolute separation, then, seems to be a myth on several accounts—in matters of governmental financial assistance, of the religious involvements in education, and in some exceptional instances of competing interests on questions of competent jurisdiction.

But the central and controlling issue in Swart is submerged almost beyond notice in the questionable consideration of aid in the form of tuition payment operating to a fusion of secular and sectarian education. According to the Vermont law of 1915, the state assumed the duty to provide secondary education and in addition allowed the parents a choice of schools. *De facto* there was no public high school in South Burlington.[98] Although it is fair to surmise that Catholic parents welcomed the opportunity of sending their children to Catholic high schools, the fact is that in the absence of a public high school Catholics and non-Catholics alike were in effect compelled to attend the only school available in South Burlington, the religious school. This was a return in full circle to McCollum, coercion in reverse. Further, doubly to compound legal and economic duress, it would seem that the Court might uphold tuition payments to private nondenominational schools. What has happened to the primary, preferred right of parents and children to the free exercise of religion in education? Although the tuition payments were directly paid to the private religious schools, the state was actually paying for the children's education *in loco parentis*. These were really payments for services rendered, services which were required and approved by public authorities. But the right to impose a compulsory school attendance law and the duty to provide the educational facilities from its own public funds are legitimate exercises of state general welfare powers. No more nor less was undertaken and achieved by Vermont state law. Beneficiaries of the state tuition payment plan were the students and the benefit bestowed by the state was a public welfare benefit. If an incidental benefit may be shown to accrue to the private school that is church-affiliated—a rather dubious task since the payment in this instance covered only part of the cost of educating the pupils—Pierce, Cochran and Everson would allow that consequence as an inevitable and unavoidable incidence of any public welfare benefit. The Vermont Supreme Court might have asked whether tuition payment was one such benefit and whether in the light of Everson it might be denied precisely because of faith or the lack of faith.[99]

Concerning the contending considerations of public welfare benefactions and religious confession a Mississippi court had held:

> The state is under duty to ignore the child's creed but not its need. It cannot control what one child may think, but it can and must do all it can to teach the child how to think. The state which allows the pupil to subscribe to any religious creed should not, because of his exercise of this right, proscribe him from benefits common to all.[100]

If the legal antinomies let loose by some of the Supreme Court's dicta have inserted a specious conflict between the Court's reading of "separation of church and state" and the free exercise of religion, the resolution of the issue should not be to duress in the exercise of that liberty, much less to allow, as in the Swart decision, financial advantage to non-denominational private schools over private religious schools.

Oddly, the conjunction of education and religion seems to stir legal aversions not to be found in the conjunction of religion and public health. In 1955 the highest court of New Hampshire upheld the constitutionality of a statute giving state aid to denominational hospitals for the education of nurses:

> The purpose of the grant . . . is neither to aid any particular sect or denomination nor all denominations, but to further the teaching of the science of nursing . . . The aid is available to all hospitals

252

offering training in nursing without regard to the auspices under which they are conducted or to the religious beliefs of their managements, so long as the aid is used for nurses' training "and for no other instruction or purpose." . . . If some denomination incidentally derives a benefit through the release of other funds for other uses, this result is immaterial. . . . A hospital operated under the auspices of a religious denomination which receives funds under the provisions of this bill acts merely as a conduit for the expenditure of public funds for training which serves exclusively the public purpose of public health and is completely devoid of sectarian doctrine and purposes.

The fundamental position that public moneys shall be used for a public purpose has not prevented the use of private institutions as a conduit to accomplish the public objectives.[100]

In Kentucky the Court of Appeals upheld the federal statute against the contention that the federal-state grant to church-affiliated hospitals violated both federal and state constitutions.

. . . (4) private agency may be utilized as the pipe-line through which a public expenditure is made, the test being not who receives the money but the character of the use for which it is expended. . . . The fact that members of the governing board of these hospitals, which perform a recognized public service to all people regardless of faith or creed, are all of one religious faith does not signify that the money allotted the hospitals is to aid their particular denominations. . . . Courts will look to the use to which these funds are put rather than the conduits through which they run. If that use is a public one . . . it will not be held in contravention of sec. 5 merely because the hospitals carry the name or are governed by the members of a particular faith.[101]

The difference between religion and public health and religion and education is not so broad as to warrant, despite certain obvious dissimilarities, a contrary attitude toward those who approve of government aid to church-affiliated schools.[102] The fact is that Catholic ethics is taught in

253

nursing schools under Catholic auspices, Catholic moral theology is all-controlling in permissible operations in Catholic hospitals, and religious garbs and symbols are everywhere in evidence. What the state court rulings of New Hampshire, Kentucky, Mississippi and others have stressed is that a public purpose can still be served through a private agency despite or together with its patent religious profession and environment and even allowing for incidental benefits to the religious institution itself. It is not without significance that in *Craig v. Mercy Hospital* the Supreme Court of Mississippi in upholding federal-state appropriations for Catholic hospitals reached back twenty years to reaffirm its ruling which approved public provision of free nonreligious textbooks to all school children inclusive of those attending parochial schools.[103]

In its summary discussion of the Swart case, the memorandum might have adverted to the dilemma in which parents of the children who attend the only high school in South Burlington find themselves—a dilemma not unlike the one which the late Justice Jackson scored in delivering the opinion of the Court in *West Virginia Board of Education v. Barnette.*[104] "The State asserts power to condition access to public education on making a prescribed sign and profession and at the same time to coerce attendance by punishing both parents and child." The Vermont Court recognized that a substantial number of the district school children attend the church-sponsored high school. Should some parents be unable to support the education of their children without state aid and their children be unable to attend the secondary school, in the absence of any other public or private accommodations would these parents be subject to the punitive consequences of failing to comply with the state compulsory attendance laws?

254

CRITERIA

The largest sector of the memorandum is a discussion of criteria for evaluating the constitutionality of government aid to education which entail some benefits to religion. The criteria are:

1) How closely is the benefit related to the religious aspects of the institution aided?
2) Of what economic significance is the benefit?
3) To what extent is the selection of the institutions receiving benefits determined by Government?
4) What alternative means are available to accomplish the legislative objective without resulting in the religious benefits ordinarily proscribed? Could these benefits be avoided or minimized without defeating the legislative purpose or without running afoul of other constitutional objections?

Whatever the source of these criteria, they are not likely to be found in the Supreme Court decisions on which the memorandum rests its defense of the President's discriminatory program and are far less likely to find support in past and existing legislative programs. The criteria, however, do reveal an embarrassing task for the government lawyers. They must try, *ex officio,* to reconcile the wide variety of governmental aid to religion and to activities sponsored by religious institutions with the generalizations of Everson and the President's federal aid program, which includes religious colleges and universities but excludes religious parochial schools. The legal counselors half succeed as they strive to escape the legal incongruities and antinomies with which they must contend but fail to set up legal safeguards for government impartiality toward religion. The overruling preoccupation is with the establishment clause as constructively interpreted with an acknowledgment of

255

scarcely equal, if not superior, regard for the free exercise of religion clause.

Throughout the criteria an extreme anxiety dominates a discussion of means for the realization of a government-defined objective in such a way as would minimize or make remote or even remove the possibility of any benefit accruing to the religious institution through whose agency the governmental purpose is fulfilled. The sort of means adopted is entirely a political and discretionary choice of the national Congress. The constitutional test is whether the objective defined by Congress is within or among its constitutional empowerment, neither more nor less. Every sort of aid in one form or another has existed in government practice. Tax preferment benefits, grants and loans to religion in general, to religious sectarianism, to general welfare activities, educational and noneducational, sponsored by churches and religious groups exist under state and federal laws. And benefits accrue intentionally or unavoidably to religious life in general and to particular religious institutions, either directly, indirectly or incidentally. The recipients intended by law have been religion, schools, parents and students. To turn the test of constitutionality on the sort of means adopted or upon the degree of immediacy, mediacy or remoteness with which government benefits reach the religious institution borders on legal casuistry. The distinctions are rationally valid but they do not constitute barriers of legality. Law cannot control the overflow of benefits beyond its declared intention and there is no need for any legal or intellectual embarrassment in admitting this. It would be a very narrow philosophical and legal mind indeed that would stop the flow of benefits to religious life. One would suppose that multiple good effects would be a welcome regard for any human enterprise, govern-

256

mental or private, and if they fall upon religious life, so much the better in a country whose national documents and government officials give frequent testimonies to its religious foundations. In no other public discussion do we hear any reasonable objection to multiple good effects. If a public national purpose can be realized through the offices of religious agencies, then so much the better for the spiritual life of the nation. And if the public service is fulfilled by a religious institution to the satisfaction of public authority should there reasonably be any repugnance to a benefit that reaches it by forseeable chance or even intent?

The memorandum notes approvingly that Everson upheld as permissible the incidental advantage which public provision of transportation for parochial school children afforded the church school. But is incidental aid constitutionally permissible because it is a remote consequence, insignificant in amount, "indisputably marked off from the religious function?"

These criteria of what is permissible can be applied to a cooperative arrangement between the city and state of New York with Yeshiva University.[105] In 1950, Yeshiva University, a group of secular and religious schools, secondary, undergraduate, graduate and professional, affiliates of the parent school, the orthodox rabbinical seminary, was granted a state charter authorizing the opening of medical and dentistry schools. In 1953, when Yeshiva had not yet built its medical school, the city of New York contracted to affiliate with the University the Bronx Municipal Hospital Center[106] which it was constructing at the cost of $45,000,000. According to the terms of the agreement:

(the city) offered to affiliate the said Hospital Center with the University whereby the professional care of the patients will be under the jurisdiction and the responsibility of the Faculty of Medi-

257

cine of the University, which said offer by the City has been accepted by the University.

(Whereas) The Faculty of Medicine of the University will have the exclusive responsibility of nominating the members of the clinical and other professional staff of the Hospital Center.[107]

The University agreed to furnish complete services (item 1) and in turn the city agreed that it will physically equip and maintain entirely the laboratories and furnish all supplies necessary (item 5). In addition (item 6):

... the University may receive and accept grants, gifts, bequests, devises and contributions from any source in support of the professional services and scientific activities to be carried on in the Hospital Center which the University may conduct in conjunction with similar work conducted elsewhere in the Medical School, other divisions of the University or other institutions.

The City agrees that during the next ten years it will pay to the University for services to be performed hereunder the sum of $531,000 for the period commencing July 1, 1954 and ending June 30, 1955 and the sum of $750,000 per annum thereafter during each of the remaining nine years. . . .

Late in the summer of 1955 the first approved applicants to the Albert Einstein School of Medicine registered to begin classes in September. In 1957, when the medical school was in its second year of operation, the state of New York began construction of a state mental hospital adjacent to the medical school at a cost of $70,000,000, consisting of six buildings and a dozen auxiliary structures, inclusive of a school of nursing. According to cooperative arrangements similar to the ones between the Bronx Hospital Center and the medical school, research and training programs of the psychiatric center were entrusted to the Albert Einstein College of Medicine. In 1959 the medical school had its first graduates.

These agreements entrust staffing, medical services,

laboratory experiments, analysis, operations, research projects to the exclusive jurisdiction and supervision of the medical school of Yeshiva University. All provisions of equipment, services and maintenance are furnished by the city and state. Such an arrangement is both desirable and proper. A less generous arrangement might make efficient and expert service for the sick and afflicted less than likely. It might also deprive the hospitals of all the possible and full advantages of advanced research. Still, when is such comprehensive arrangement not an indirect aid to the medical school of a university under religious auspicies?[108] Who can deny that enormous and incalculable benefits accrue to the University thereby? The use of a hospital is an indispensable condition for a medical school in the training of its students. A hospital center completely under the school's jurisdiction and supervision and furnished entirely by public funds is a benefit that cannot be measured. The great variety of excellent and most modern facilities, vast opportunities for research grants, the promise of attracting thereby eminent men of science to a new and untried school of medicine, even the initial staggering costs of constructing and operating a new school of medicine and the hospitals it would need in order to function, an annual stipend of three-quarter million dollars—are these incidental aids, remote, insignificant, wholly unintended, bearing no substantial fortunes to the academic status of the Jewish Orthodox Seminary, the parent school of Yeshiva University? Can the forest be ignored like a tree?

Nor will it do to argue that only a relatively small number of Orthodox students attend the Einstein School as compared with the nonobservant and the non-Jewish students, or even to point to the religious indifference of some members of the medical faculty. Whether or not a school is church-affiliated or under religious auspices is not to be determined by the counting of the faithful, but by the officially professed religious commitments of the corporation to which the charter of the university has been granted by the state.[109]

A more comprehensive perspective of federal aid to education might have also suggested these criteria—especially in the light of the national welfare objectives outlined by the President:

1) Are private elementary and secondary schools under religious auspices educational facilities? If not, why are they approved and so accredited?
2) Have they and do they still contribute to national education?
3) Are they capable of contributing to the educational objectives which the President set forth in his Message to Congress?
4) Can an exclusionary rule based on religious affiliation be constitutionally upheld in the light of the First, Fifth, and Fourteenth Amendments? Specifically, may such an exclusionary rule reach out to the child, the parents, to the school itself—separately or cojointly considered?

The real issue at bottom is not governmental aid to private schools but the acknowledgment on the part of the government of their role in American education, and the further admission that their religious functions contribute to the spiritual life of the nation. The Constitution forbids a state religion. There is nothing in it that forbids a religious state. Such a perspective might provide the basis for considering the propriety of one general, all-inclusive aid program which did not differentiate between schools. Whatever might be obtained by an extension of Title III of the National Defense Education Act could just as well be stipulated in an omnibus bill under differentiating terms and specifying conditions. What is demanded is not an identity of provisions but a parity of equivalence. Free education

260

heavily weighted by the enormous resources of the national treasury can destroy freedom of education. It is pretentious talk to uphold legally freedom for religious education and then to turn that choice into a liability before the law in the disbursement of the benefactions of the law. The constitutional right of the free exercise of religion in education is designed to protect religious belief, not to hinder or destroy it by conferring a preferential status upon supposedly secular public schools. The argument is not for parochial school children but for all school children.

The constitutional issue does not depend on a specific form of aid—tax deductions, nonreligious supplies and services, tuition, construction loans, grants, teachers' salaries; nor upon the recipient—the child, the parent, the school. These are the various means of concretely implementing a national welfare program in aid of educational needs. Almost all of these instances already exist. But there is no basis in law to differentiate either as to means or as to recipients between colleges and universities that are church-sponsored and the lower levels of education. If governmental loans for college dormitories, campus centers, faculty residences—all revenue-earning and all undeniably releasing substantial private funds for other purposes—can be sustained, then construction loans for elementary and secondary school classrooms may be equally upheld; more so, in fact, since these classrooms are more truly educational facilities than are dormitories.

LEGISLATIVE PROGRAMS AND PROPOSALS

In none of the wide variety of existing legislative subsidies for education is there any across-the-board grant or loan nor, as far as we can determine, has an ecclesiastical authority or lay advocate of federal aid suggested that there be federal grants or loans to an educational institution to be spent as it judges for itself without obtaining in advance government approval for the use of public funds. Secondly, the implementation of educational needs as detailed by the President of the United States is sufficiently specific and only within these explicit terms is a claim being made for the inclusion of parochial schools, the school children and their parents. Thirdly, in the existing congressional provisions of funds available also to religious educational institutions, such as construction loans, there is an undoubted releasing of private funds which the religious institution is free to use as it sees fit even for religious purposes. Despite the memorandum's effort to discount this, it is obvious that a several million dollar construction loan does make increasingly possible the application of limited private funds to purposes which could not otherwise be afforded. The prospect of this sort of substantial indirect aid to religious institutions, clearly forseeable, has not in the past deterred Congress from including them in a nondiscriminatory disbursement of public funds. Fourthly, whether Congress exerts its tax-spending power for national defense or general welfare, the religious clauses of the First Amendment are equally operative upon all its legislation. If, as government officials allow, federal loans to precollegiate private schools under religious auspices for scientific equipment and facilities as made available under Title III of the National Defense Education Act are constitutional without offense to the religious clauses of the First Amendment, then similar construction loans for nonreligious educational facilities other than the scientific subjects are just as specific in purpose. Science subjects do not pre-empt or exhaust the educational process for the objective which the President set in his educational aid program, namely, "the maximum development of every young American's capacity." No discussion about a particular form of aid or manner of conveyance should therefore distract from the central issue, the direct and principal beneficiary of a government-sponsored educational aid program howsoever devised or formulated, namely, the intellectual and spiritual benefits of the child or adult student upon whose realization the progress of the nation depends.

The labored reasoning of the memorandum on the unconstitutionality of across-the-board grants and loans is not only wholly irrelevant to the discussion but may suggest, unfortunately, a calculated misdirection of argument. The prospect of an overflow of benefit to religious educational institutions *qua* religious, which may serve efficiently as a conduit of a public purpose defined by the national legislature, has not in the past led Congress to exclude them, nor has any of the congressional acts been construed by the Supreme Court as violative of the no establishment clause of the First Amendment.

HIGHER EDUCATION

This section of the memorandum is intended to show that the constitutional principles are identical for elementary and secondary school education and for higher education but that factual circumstances surrounding the application of the principles lead to radically diverse consequences. It looks to the history of education to justify the administration's discriminatory constitutional position for supporting higher levels of education under religious auspices and for refusing it to the lower levels. But the argument is heavy-footed and awkward.

To begin with, the policy of state support of elementary

263

and secondary public schools was never intended to supplant but to supplement the private religious schools which were the original traditional schools in our country. The necessity for public support of these schools was largely due to the lack of private resources to cope with the educational needs of the nation enlarged by the successive wave of immigration and by the newly enfranchised Negro, as well as by the conflicting claims of religious conscience which religious pluralism posed. Even state-supported schools were for many decades religiously oriented and some still are to this day. Historically, tax support of private denominational schools antedated this practice, as witnessed by the provisions of the Northwest and Southwest Ordinances and by the first constitutions of some of the states that emerged from these territories. Private institutions of higher learning, most of them religiously affiliated, were, on the other hand, fortunate beneficiaries of the generosity of private philanthropies. Statistically, there is a wide distribution today of private, state and church-affiliated colleges and universities with a large variety of faiths represented. The fact that in grammar and secondary education Catholic parochial schools far outnumber all other religious schools combined and that Catholic school children will be the chief beneficiaries in an all-inclusive federal aid program may be the real force of the opposition and not any constitutional qualm. The parents of these children constitute a proportionately larger group of taxpayers who, in addition to supporting the public schools and the parochial schools, would be required by law to contribute a third time to the increased government expenditures. In no other program of governmental benefactions are recipients referred to according to ethnic origins or credal profession. If Catholic parochial schools constitute the vast majority of religious schools

264

it simply means that they have made a substantial contribution to the educational needs of the nation. To them as to Jefferson, a nonreligious education is not only defective but bears within itself a secularizing process of the meaning of human existence harmful to the individual and to society. Legally, the parental right which Pierce upheld must be reckoned to be an element of the right which the Constitution guarantees to all to the "free exercise" of their religion. This right in fact should obtain even in public schools. There is nothing in the Constitution which says that tax-supported education must be nonreligious. The difficulty of relating these rights in circumstances where religious pluralism may set up conflicting claims of conscience accounts historically for the rise and growth of private religious schools. These schools do not exist as a concession or compromise or by tolerance of public law. They fulfill the law on every count of parental right, of religious conscience, of compulsory school attendance, of private corporation right to engage in publicly approved and accredited education. It is rather the public school which is a comparative compromise and a necessary one. Both schools are integral parts of what is basically a dual system, serving the same public interest. There is nothing in the divergent histories of higher and lower education that warrants the establishment in public law of an exclusionary religious test for any school in the disbursement of government funds. Governmental subsidies of public schools to the exclusion of parochial schools is a direct threat to their survival. This should be a matter of utmost concern to the nation and to the government, not merely to Catholic ecclesiastical authorities. It is precisely at this point that the memorandum fails seriously to focus upon the central role of church-affiliated schools as one of the principal instruments serving national educational needs.

265

Without the graduates of these schools, which supply the majority of students for Catholic colleges and universities, these institutions of higher learning would not long survive. Of the paramount necessity to preserve private higher education under religious auspices the memorandum entertains no doubt. Why does it not express equal concern for the parochial schools, which supply a large part of the student body for church colleges?

Next, we are treated to a deft but curious exercise in dialectical reasoning whereby we are led to suppose that the right of parents to guide the education of their children, operating as it does in compliance with compulsory attendance laws for minors, is to be viewed in a less favorable light when compared with the wholly voluntary choice of the college student. This is almost too ludicrous to be considered seriously. In the first place, one would reasonably expect that, where a constitutionally guaranteed parental right when conjoined with a "preferred" freedom of religious exercise is made to operate under a legal constraint, public law would offer compensatory remedies protective of these rights rather than subject them to additional liabilities. Parents may be forced by economic factors to send their children to public schools against the dictates of their religious conscience. Parents who send them to church schools must pay taxes to support the education of other children in public schools and must bear the additional burden of paying the educational expenses of their own children in the religious schools. A federal program that excludes these taxpayers and their children (after counting them in) may subject them to a third tax burden to defray the increased government expenditures. Secondly, the parental choice is by law imputed to minors. Fortunately, to date, the Courts have not yet emancipated children from parental authority and responsibility. As for the wholly voluntary choice of the college student one may question it in the numerous instances where parents pay fully the tuition fees. The memorandum's interpolation of the constitutional import of the exercise of parental rights under compulsory laws is meaningless in the context of federal aid. Evidently, for the administration's legal staff, the effect of legal compulsion under which students attend public schools with or without real freedom of choice for the parents does not bear with equal logic on their exclusion from federal aid. Underneath the pretense lies the real and poorly concealed objection that the choice has been directed to a religious education.

Here and elsewhere, the religious involvement in the institutions of higher learning is considered not so pervasive as on the lower levels. But this is not a correct appraisal. In Catholic colleges and universities not only theological courses but also philosophical courses ancillary to religious belief are mandatory for Catholic students. These studies are intellectually more exacting and more intensive than the religious indoctrination of the lower levels. Furthermore, the religious facilities and devotions in evidence on the religious college campus are the same as those that are to be found in parochial schools. If the existence of institutions of higher learning with religious professions is essential to the national interest, as the memorandum strongly contends, so too are the church grammar and secondary schools which supply the great majority of graduates without whom these institutions would not long survive.

To set national goals of education in broad terms; to refer to the maximum development of every student and to his free choice; to relate these educational objectives to our national progress; to extend federal aid to all private

267

and religious colleges and universities, and to all elementary and secondary schools but to deny any sort of aid whatsoever to parochial schools because of religious affiliation (after counting in their students); and, finally, to require by law that all taxpayers support this national program, is neither just law, good reason, nor sound policy but deep-rooted bias and discrimination. It is high time that the astigmatic vision of the advocates of secular education be readjusted to normal and balanced sight, if need be, by congressional law. There is nothing in the history of higher and lower education to warrant a constitutional basis for an exclusionary religious rule in the disbursement of government subsidies. On the contrary, there is an abundance of practices and precedents within which acceptable forms of aid can be devised for all school children. Whatever the specific form of aid—tuition grants, construction loans, tax credits, government provision of nonreligious facilities, and so on—the direct and primary intention and objective remain always the educational needs of the student in terms of whom all educational goals are defined, whether the aid goes directly to the parent or child or to the school for the benefit of the parent and child.

JUDICIAL REVIEW

In general, with the one notable exception of federal grants and loans to hospitals, federal subsidies which entail some benefit to religious institutions have not been subject to judicial review by the Supreme Court of the United States. And so it might be suggested that we should refrain strictly from referring to them as constitutional while admitting their legality. However, such a reservation of judgment is not as telling as it may seem at first sight. True, the

Supreme Court is the ultimate arbiter of constitutional interpretation; it is equally true that the Supreme Court has frequently reversed itself. Consequently, the appeal to the high tribunal is itself subject to a similar reservation of judgment, a reservation which is further deepened by the fact that much of the present confusion must be traced to recent Court reasoning in Everson, McCollum, Zorach. There is, too, a considerable area of government political activity that is beyond the reach of judicial review.[110] Exemption from court adjudication does not necessarily render the action in question constitutionally suspect. Separation of powers grants to each branch of government some areas of supreme and ultimate authority.

Congressional laws are invested with the presumption of constitutionality. Should an eventual test before the Supreme Court strike down the enabling act as unconstitutional, this would not destroy the validity of the presumption. The presumption of constitutionality does not derive from the absence or silence of judicial notice and review but from the authoritative sovereign source of governmental action. It is therefore not ambivalent, which would suppose that the judiciary is the only sovereign branch of government, and only the Supreme Court of the United States at that. Indeed, the courts themselves approach the constitutional test of a congressional or state legislative enactment with this favorable presumption of constitutionality and justify judicial interference with legislative action only on clear and demonstrated usurpation of power. This judicial self-restraint is not a discretionary self-imposed limitation on the part of the Court but a corollary of the constitutional separation of sovereign powers.

For a justiciable action the Court has set down three certain requirements. First, there must be a case or controversy.

269

Judicial power is capable of acting only when the subject is submitted in a case, and a case arises only when a party asserts his right in a form prescribed by law. Controversies may be distinguished from cases to the extent that they include only suits of a civil nature.

By cases and controversies are intended the claims of litigants brought before the courts for determination by such regular proceedings as are established by law or custom for the protection or enforcement of rights, or the prevention, redress, or punishment of wrongs. Whenever the claim of a party under the Constitution, laws or treaties of the United States takes such a form that the judicial power is capable of acting upon it, then it has become a case. The term implies the existence of present or possible adverse parties whose contentions are submitted to the Court for adjudication.

These definitions were quoted with approval in *Muskrat v. United States*[111] where the Court held that the exercise of judicial power is limited to cases and controversies and emphasized "adverse litigants," "adverse interests" and "actual controversy," and conclusiveness or finality of judgment as essential elements of a case. In Muskrat the Court ruled that Congress cannot through legislation create a case or controversy merely by stating an issue and by designating parties to present each side.

In the present nationwide controversy as to the constitutionality of federal aid to parochial schools under a general federal aid program, suggestions have been made by both sides that a statutory requirement be built into a federal aid law that would bring about a court test of the constitutional question. Such an insertion would be not only ill-advised but useless as well.

Moreover, such a statutory requirement would have no mandatory force whatsoever. Admittedly there would be adverse parties, an actual, real, genuine controversy, an

270

antagonistic assertion of rights, presented in a form prescribed by law. But there would be wanting the third requisite: substantial interest. The Court has ruled that a resident taxpayer may bring suit against a municipality because of his direct and immediate interest in the application of its public funds. It has also maintained that the right to challenge the constitutionality of an appropriation by a state legislature or an expenditure by a state officer depends upon whether or not state law permits such suits. In the same celebrated case, the Court, however, denied the standing to sue a taxpayer who challenged the constitutionality of a federal statute authorizing expenditures from the national treasury, stating that:

> ... the relation of a taxpayer of the United States to the Federal Government is very different. His interests in the moneys of the Treasury—partly realized from taxation and partly from other sources—is shared with millions of others; is comparatively minute and indeterminable; and the effect upon future taxation, of any payment out of the funds, so remote, fluctuating and uncertain, that no basis is afforded for an appeal to the preventive powers of a court of equity.[112]

Further, the Court denied to a state the requisite standing to sue by assuming the role of corporation representative of all its resident taxpayers and thereby cumulatively enlarging the impact of federal expenditures upon the generality of its residents—the taxpayers. The hurt interest must be personal, and the effect upon an individual federal taxpayer would not amount to a substantial interest. *De minimis non curat lex.* A built-in statutory requirement for a Court test of constitutionality is ineffective for it can have no mandatory effect in the light of the Muskrat and Mellon rulings. It is, besides, ill-advised. By its very presence it prejudices the proposed congressional legislation in the popular mind by robbing it of that presumption of constitutionality with which every congressional enactment is invested and which the courts themselves have repeatedly acknowledged save in the patent showing of usurpation of power by the legislature. Further, it places the law in double jeopardy by suggesting that Congress itself has doubts about it. Nor could such a determination of constitutionality obtain by the proceedings of a declaratory judgment since the question of substantial interest would still be controlling a taxpayer's standing to sue. The degree of controversy necessary to establish a case for purposes of jurisdiction remains always within the discretionary powers of the court to determine and in every instance the Court is under no compulsion to exercise its jurisdiction. The request for a built-in statutory requirement for a court test of constitutionality is a political pressure upon the judiciary to perform a duty which is within the proper competence and constitutional empowerment of Congress itself to exercise. The case of *Swart v. South Burlington Town School District* bore constitutional issues strikingly similar to the ones involved in the present federal aid controversy, and offered opportune occasion for review by the United States Supreme Court. The high tribunal denied review without comment.

Advocates of federal aid in some form or another to children who attend parochial schools are just as sensitive about allegiance to the Constitution as are those who oppose such aid. They feel convinced that Congress can devise ways and means according to established practices and precedents that would uphold immune from legal liability the parental right to guide the education of their children and ensure the inviolability of the free exercise of religion in education within the context of a national program of improving and promoting education for the sake

272

of the national interest. And, on the other hand, they are as sincerely desirous of preserving beyond jeopardy the future of public elementary and secondary schools as they are of the survival of the corresponding church schools which could not possibly cope with the enormous economic resources of the national government weighted against them.

The latter-day willingness of administration spokesmen that aid to public schools be considered first by Congress and that then aid to private and parochial schools be taken up separately, while placing one bill presumably above constitutional reproach, officially weakens the other with constitutional qualms. In an educational aid program that reaches out to all the educational needs related to national defense and welfare, in a cohesive view that embraces all students, all taxpayers and all educational facilities and is carried out by the powers of Congress defined by a national purpose to be supported by national taxation, the test of constitutionality falls equally upon all recipients and beneficiaries with prejudice to none. If private and parochial schools may be included in an amended form and extension of the National Defense Education Act, as many are ready to allow, it may with equal legal propriety be included in the same general federal aid bill. To insist on a separate bill for private and parochial schools—if at all—is undoubtedly an act of disparagement of the legal status of these schools as beneficiaries of government subsidies, and of the equality of all students in a national program directed to the "maximum development of every young American's capacity." Have the parochial school children, America's future citizens, no role to play in the general welfare of their country? Will the demands of the country upon them in peace and war be less because of their religious training? Have the religious schools no contribution to make to the progress of the nation for national defense and general welfare? What distinguishes parochial schools from public elementary and secondary schools except that in addition to state educational requirements of curriculum and standards of teaching they also instill in students religious belief in God, and spiritual values and moral obligations? Can that be the source of unconstitutionality?

CONCLUSION

There is no basis in constitutional law, in the history of higher and lower education, or in sound reason to warrant the distinction whereby the federal government may favor with financial assistance in any form church-related colleges and universities and on the other hand be required to deny it in all forms to their subsidiaries in the precollegiate grades. The constitutional principle on which federal subsidies to the church colleges and universities are based also justify the extension of governmental assistance to their grammar and secondary schools. A constitutional principle which defends support of sectarian schools on the one level and denies it on another level—both of which in the minds of the churchmen themselves cohere as a continuous educational process—cannot be established validly. And if the unabashed objection is to religious teaching and practices on the lower level but not on the higher, will the dispensers of the administration program first eliminate every religious practice and observance now prevailing in a variety of ways in public schools across the country? What then happens to the parental rights of children attending public schools? Would not the process not only of secularizing the public school but also of constitutionalizing irreligion be inevitably

274

begun? What of private schools which are not church-owned—are they to be denied governmental aid, if in need of it, because the corporation or board of trustees determines that belief in God, obedience to His divine commandments, and imitation and practice of the Christian counsels be encouraged in the students without sectarian indoctrination? And what of private schools which teach sectarian dogmas without proprietary ownership by a church or ecclesiastical authority? The Kennedy administration built for itself a veritable hornet's nest of constitutional entanglements. The unalterable experience of American education is that governmental aid to church schools and religious education has a more ancient and enduring history than many may care to acknowledge.

No one has asked nor does anyone expect across-the-board grants and loans from the government, that is, for subsidies unconditioned by a prior governmental approval of a specified purpose whose use would be wholly left to the discretionary choice of the beneficiary institution. This was an unreal issue conjured up by Mr. Ribicoff's legal staff to serve as a premise of an evolving sorites whose apparent intent and effect was to cast doubt upon the legality of other forms of aid by the process of dubious equations and equivocal analogies. No aid is being sought which is not based on existing practices and long-standing precedents. Equating governmental loans to the use of public classrooms which McCollum denied for sectarian religious instructions seems to ignore the full significance of the presence or absence of the element of coercion supposedly implied in a voluntary cooperative use by taxpayers of the state's compulsory school machinery which the majority and dissenting justices insisted was controlling in both the McCollum and Zorach cases.

275

We see no distinction of constitutionality between the validity of federal grants and loans to church-affiliated institutions of learning, nor has the abundant record of congressional enactments disclosed such a difference. For that matter, the late President of the United States himself did not do so when he proposed construction loans for higher education and in addition grants supplementary to scholarship awards to be made directly to the institution to help meet full educational costs. The test of constitutionality of a general welfare program is not determined by a religious test; or by a specific type of aid—every variety suggested is already in existence; or by the manner of conveyance—whether the aid be given directly to the student, or in the case of minors to the parent, or directly to the school for the benefit of the student. Educational goals are defined in terms of the needs of the student. Any federal aid that is not directed to the achievement of these goals is not an aid for education. Both the type of aid and the manner of conveyance are entirely decisions of policy and rest wholly within congressional competence and discretion. The sole controlling constitutional test is whether the Congress is exerting its taxing and spending powers to serve the national interest within the terms of its general welfare powers. When, then, the federal government proposes to promote education by its economic resources as a means of furthering national defense and the common welfare there is no constitutional dictate that impels it to identify national educational needs in the lower grades with public schools alone. Unless and until the government is ready to demonstrate that church-related grammar and secondary schools, unlike their counterparts in higher education, do not make a contribution to the intellectual and, let it be said, the spiritual progress of the country, do not actually render real

276

public service, it may not presume to identify education with the public schools alone nor restrict the meaning of educational needs to their students only. That these church grade schools perform a public service is already a legally recognized fact in every state of the Union, as witnessed by their accrediting agencies and by the tax-preferment benefits which they enjoy precisely because of that public service. The federal government need only act in accordance with this broad legal fact. Parents who contribute to church school building funds are granted tax deductible allowances. The wry irony is that there is inherent in the current educational aid program a very serious threat to the separation of church and state on which supposedly the administration professes to base its rules of inclusion and exclusion. Government is certainly not neutral when it taxes all to aid some and excludes others by a religious test; it is surely interfering with the free exercise of religion in education when it denies parents a share in governmental subsidies unless they send their children to a school not of their choosing nor in accordance with the dictates of their religious conscience. The federal government is scarcely impartial toward believers and nonbelievers when it converts in effect the exercise of religious liberty into a liability before the law in the disbursement of governmental general welfare benefits. Worse still, the government plan poses a serious and grave threat to the survival of parochial schools themselves. Unless there be separation of church and state with benevolent impartiality toward all equally subsumed under a broadly defined educational aid program, governmental action may be directly responsible for destroying the coherence of constitutionally guaranteed rights. The exercise of one right ought not to nullify or harass the exercise of another simply because of governmental action.

Freedom to attend parochial schools is a choice equally between alternatives. It is more than the freedom to attend or not attend. Rather it is a choice under law to attend any of the publicly accredited schools—church, state, and private. And the parental choice which by law is imputed to the minor is no less a legally protected free choice than the choice of the college student to whom the memorandum seems to ascribe a higher degree of independence and volition. The comparison should be between the parental choice and the choice of the college student, not between the minor and the adult student. Further, parental choice for minors operating under a compulsory school attendance law should be redressed with compensatory provisions, not rendered more onerous by governmental action. American citizens have come to realize that a merely formal guarantee of the political right to vote is not sufficient unless there is correspondingly effective legal protection against arbitrary interference with the exercise of that right. No freedom is self-sustaining. To survive and prosper it must be legally immune from liability and allowed to thrive in the equality of treatment, opportunity and protection.

It is of concrete, real, operative rights we speak, not of abstract religious liberty. We cannot legally prejudice one right without disparaging another. Parental choice, religious liberty in education, corporate property rights of religious education—all these cohere with an inner associated bond and strength.

If the federal government were to throw the enormous weight of its economic resources on the side of the public elementary and secondary schools to the exclusion of the religious schools it would bring about a substantial disparity between one segment of American education and another; it would be directly responsible for favoring by law certain schools and disfavoring others, for patronizing one sort of parental choice and prejudicing another. In no government-citizen relationship of rights and duties—for instance, those of taxation, voting, eligibility to public office, military service, administration of justice in the courts, public law and order—does there exist a religious exclusionary rule to divide one beneficiary of governmental aid from another. This is clearly indefensible in terms of constitutional law, and certainly not made defensible through a pretentious reference to the religious clause of the First Amendment.

In the case of both higher and lower education the federal government has already provided financial aid without regard to creed. It sedulously avoided such an injustice in the G.I. Bill for veterans' educational benefits and in the law governing the cost of education of page boys serving in the Houses of Congress. For the pages who choose to attend a parochial school, the U.S. Code provides that tuition payments shall be made from federal funds to the school chosen. In neither provision was there any suspicion of an establishment of religion; on the contrary, there was sensitive regard for religious liberty. Governmental loans for the construction of college dormitories, campus student centers and faculty residences are available to all private institutions of higher learning. Construction loans for parochial school classrooms where secular subjects would be taught would be far more educational in service. It is not beyond the ingenuity and competence of Congress to devise aids to parochial schools within the terms of already existing practices and precedents. The constitutionally guaranteed religious liberty must be equally guaranteed to all, equally protected for all. Its very exercise should not constitute an incapacitation for governmental benefits. Concretely this means that the formal guarantee of a right must be implemented to secure immunity from interference or liabilities in the exercise of that right. A massive educational aid program that excludes parochial school children because of a religious test not only offends that right but declares it to be an inferior, not a preferred primary right, as the United States Supreme Court has held.

Governmental aid to church-related schools is not in itself an aid to the church nor does the overflow of benefits to the educational religious establishment constitute an establishment of religion. Far from interfering with the religious liberty of anyone it ensures it for everyone. The time has come when all Americans must rethink the relations between freedom of religion and freedom of education and in the process shed the hidden, obdurate bias against church schools. Perhaps more and more Americans will come to admit to the necessity of religious education for the spiritual life of the nation. It is a strange pathological condition of our times that in a country whose national history is abundant with official and authoritative protestations of the religious foundations of our institutions, our civil liberties, and democratic way of life, an administration should not want to include in an educational aid program the very wellsprings of the country's spiritual life. The blunt fact is that it is in the national interest to support that education which sustains religious life. Church schools are not a compromise or concession which the state tolerates. They exist by right and not by privilege. Parenthetically, one might venture to say that the public school is the compromise which has not yet been satisfactorily adjusted as far as the religious problematic is concerned. In terms of number of students, educational facilities, teaching staffs, financial cost of construction and maintenance, number of graduates for higher education, professional schools and governmental

280

service, church-sponsored schools constitute a monumental contribution to national education and one of the most glorious achievements of private enterprise, as well as an enormous saving to taxpayers and public treasuries. It is on these lower grade schools that the church colleges and universities depend in large part for their student body. They make possible that higher education under religious auspices about which the memorandum speaks when it refers to the "disastrous national consequences in terms of improving national educational standards which could result from exclusion of, or discrimination against, certain private institutions on grounds of religious connection."[113] In the minds of the Catholic hierarchy there is no doubt of the continuity of the educational process between the lower and higher levels of these institutions of learning. Should not the government, too, have the good judgment and sound reasoning to consider the students of parochial schools as potentially apt candidates for the higher education under church sponsorship which it holds essential for the national interest?

Neither natural nor legal justice requires equal aid, one that would be uniform and in the same amount to all schools in a nondiscriminatory policy of aid to education. But distributive justice does require that there be equal right to proportionate aid, the computation of which rests on a number of confluent factors. Construction aid to schools may be modeled after the formula of the Hill-Burton Survey and Construction Act program. Tuition aid to students might imitate the provisions of the G.I. Bill of Rights and the tuition grants for congressional pages. There are extant federal and state legislative practices for the provision of nonreligious textbooks, building of science facilities, reimbursement for bus transportation. Where state court rulings and state attorney generals do not allow state-federal matching funds programs, federal statutes have the School Lunch Act as a worthy precedent to follow. Tax preferment benefits and exemption credit on deductions are some of the ways of aiding parents. There is no theoretic need nor is there any legal requirement for the national Congress to go beyond its own existing precedents and practices in order to devise legally correct means of financially assisting school children attending the lower grades of church schools either directly or indirectly through their parents or the schools. It hardly becomes the *parens patriae* to be itself a divisive force by means of a religious test of students, schools and taxpayers as beneficiaries of the public treasury. For these reasons one federal aid omnibus bill is the best solution. This would be just law, sound reason and good morality. It would symbolically affirm that we are what in war and peace we profess to be, one nation under God. There is no legal necessity for separate bills. Different stipulations for private and state schools can be written and have been written into one and the same bill. In this way, the government would officially disown and disassociate itself from the divisive forces which would accentuate and set in opposition to one another those equally important segments of American education, the state, church and private schools, and thereby acknowledge the necessity and contribution of each to the national interest. Construction loans for nonreligious specialized educational facilities and for the provision of identical general welfare services is one excellent example, for it is difficult to conceive of a more important government investment with full return of capital outlay and interest to cover all government cost.

Unfortunately, the discussion has been partly obfuscated in the popular mind by uncritical and specious associations.

A religious establishment is not an establishment of religion. The Constitution forbids a state religion; it does not proscribe a religious state. There is nothing in the Constitution that requires tax-supported education to be wholly secular and divorced from religious influence and orientation nor any requirement that public education and general welfare be identified with state schools exclusively. Separation of church and state is not and cannot ever be separation of religion and education. Church schools are not religious schools as are seminaries, ministerial and rabbinical schools. They are truly educational facilities that comply with state educational standards and requirements of teaching and curriculum—even when considered within their own religious orientation, environment and influence. Religious instruction in accredited private schools needs no apologia within the context of America's religious heritage. The national interest depends as much upon their vigorous survival as it does upon state schools.

A religious and moral imperative is at the heart of American culture. Successive generations of Americans have prided themselves on the spiritual and religious wellsprings of their democratic way of life. It is not without profound significance that the most revered and time-honored document in our national history is the Declaration of Independence, which protests to the whole world the birth of a new nation in terms of self-evident religious truths. In the international struggle to contain Communist totalitarianism and dehumanization Americans look to religion as a principal ally and major defense for the preservation of the free way of life. At home there is a general consensus among the people and government officials that the nation's democracy rests more firmly upon religious foundations and that its civil liberties are ultimately justified by the spiritual concept of the dignity of man, the validity of which is beyond any social mores to arrest or majoritarian determination to defeat. The unique American experience has been to hold fast to these religious presuppositions of our institutions, on the one hand by exercising no legal constraint over the consciences of its citizens and on the other by providing equal protection of laws and legal immunity for the free exercise of religious liberty. It is in the national interest for all schools to retain this relevance of religious life and the spiritual values implied in our democratic institutions. No legal prejudice or disability should be visited upon those who do.

The constitutional question is not whether the church has any claim to educational aid from the federal government but whether some elementary and secondary schools must be denied a share of governmental subsidies in a congressional program for the betterment of national education solely because they teach religious beliefs and morality in addition to all the legally prescribed studies. No official vision of constitutional prohibitions should be blind to the clear and definite interdiction which the First Amendment places upon Congress against interfering with the exercise of religious liberty.

284

7

Religious Schools and Secular Subjects

Prior to the National Defense Education Act of 1958, the only federal assistance to reach elementary and secondary schools were noneducational child welfare benefits. Under the terms of the National School Lunch Act and the Special Milk Program of the Agricultural Act, the federal funds were appropriated for the provision of midday meals and milk to students attending schools of high school grade and under. Both these programs were administered with or without the concurrence of state agencies and were available without distinction to both state and church-related schools. Where new or increased federal activities resulted in substantial increases in school membership, Congress provided funds for the construction and operation of school facilities in these federally affected areas. Apart from these exceptional circumstances, in which the enlarged educational needs of a locality had been brought about directly by activities of the national government, it was not until 1958 that any federal financial assistance was extended for educational purposes in the lower grade schools. Under the terms of Title III of the N.D.E.A. the federal government made available grants to state educational agencies and loans to nonprofit private schools so that they could acquire laboratory and other special equipment, suitable for use in providing education in science, mathematics or modern foreign languages, and for minor remodeling of the laboratory or other space used for such materials or equipment. Whether or not church-related schools have availed themselves of these loans to any great extent, their inclusion in the N.D.E.A. symbolized for them a gratifying acknowledgment by the federal government that they were a part of national education and that they too should contribute to the objectives of the national defense through educational programs.

The presidential Special Message to Congress on Feb. 20, 1961, on a general federal aid program to education reopened wide the national controversy on the constitutionality of including children of parochial schools in such a program. Among the legislative precedents cited in favor of parochial schools were the provisions of Title III, Section 305, of the N.D.E.A. The argument ran that similar provisions for the secular studies in church-related schools would not run counter to the constitutional rquirements of the First Amendment.

In the spring of 1962, the first press notice appeared of a forthcoming publication of a study[113a] which purported to demonstrate that the supposition on which the constitutionality of loans to parochial schools rested—the promotion of secular studies—was empirically false. An analysis of the textbooks used would disclose many evidences of religious permeation. If the advocates of a nondiscriminatory federal aid program to education had ever intended to develop an argument of prolongation which, proceeding from the alleged constitutionality of federal loans for science and language equipment, extended to the advocacy of governmental loans for the construction of classrooms set aside for the study of these secular subjects designated in Section 305 of Title III,[114] the study had within the convolutions of

286

its own argumentation a similar argument of extension, but in reverse. If it could be shown by empirical evidence that the rationale of the purely secular subject premise on which the constitutionality of the N.D.E.A. loans allegedly rested, then *a fortiori* federal loans for the construction of classrooms for parochial schools and, analogously, other educational aids, would wither on the constitutional vine. By being struck at its roots the tender plant would never grow strong with an accumulation of substantive precedents. Either way the efficacy of the argument would be far-reaching and telling in its application. The main difficulty with the study may prove to be that it was not radical enough. It certainly did not enter into the nature and quality of the roots as thoroughly as it ought and the detachment professed by the empirical analysis was in fact a profound commitment to a philosophy of education of enormous magnitude.

While the purely secular subject concept is apparently accepted by George LaNoue, the author of the study, as his own personal conviction—he never raises critically the question of its validity, neither for himself nor for others—the occasion for its legal supposition is supplied handily by two governmental sources. The first is a passage from the Memorandum on the Impact of the First Amendment to the Constitution upon Federal Aid to Education which was prepared by the legal staff of the Department of Health, Education and Welfare in cooperation with the attorney general in response to a request by Senator Morse in the aftermath of the President's Special Message to Congress. The passage reads:

To what extent a special purpose provides constitutional legitimacy to assistance to elementary or secondary schools depends on the extent to which the specific objectives being advanced are unrelated

287

to the religious aspects of sectarian education. The problem is complicated because assistance for one purpose may free funds which would otherwise be devoted to it for use to support the religious functions and thus, in effect, indirectly yet substantially support religion in violation of the establishment clause. At the present time, the National Defense Education Act permits the U.S. Commissioner of Education to make loans to private schools to acquire science, mathematics, or foreign language equipment. We believe such loans are constitutional because the connection between loans for such purposes and the religious functions of a sectarian school seems to be nonexistent or minimal.

Whether or not on this passage may be said to rest the constitutionality for Title III, Section 305 loans under N.D.E.A. a purely secular subject concept is an inference that is far from conclusive and beyond question. It states that the "constitutional legitimacy" of such assistance "depends on the extent to which the specific objectives being advanced are unrelated to the religious aspects of sectarian education." Does this mean that what matters is whether the specific objective is attained despite or together with or only in complete insulation from any religious reference? Does the phrase, "unrelated to the religious aspects of sectarian education," mean "unrelated to the religious aspects of the general curriculum of education in a parochial school?" Hardly, for how could that be possible? "Unrelated to the religious aspects of formal sectarian religious instruction" would be a clumsy tautology. Should the objectives be unrelated, that is to say impervious, to any moral-religious import of the secular subjects designated in Title III? By no conscientious analysis of the passage may such a rationale be ascribed categorically to the authors of the memorandum. Admittedly, on the other hand, the passage, thanks to its ambiguities, does not preclude the possibility of such an interpretation.

The second governmental source, however, does provide

LaNoue with an unequivocal statement of the purely secular subject concept. Roman Pucinski, Congressman from Illinois, in his interrogations of two witnesses appearing before the House Joint Subcommittee on Education and in his own testimony as a witness before the House General Subcommittee on Education and Labor, allows no suspicion of a doubt in his personal commitment to the purely secular subject supposition on which he categorically rests the constitutionality of the loan provisions of the N.D.E.A. to parochial schools.

MR. PUCINSKI: Mr. Witness, do you have any reason to believe, or do you have any evidence that would indicate, that these 162 loans that were approved by your Department, totaling more than $2 million for the special purpose of science, language, or mathematics, that any of this equipment was used for courses and purposes other than purely secular instruction?

MR. LUDINGTON: We have no such evidence at this time.

MR. PUCINSKI: Have you made any effort to ascertain that?

MR. LUDINGTON: The loan application which is submitted by the interested school states that this equipment will be used for instruction in mathematics, science, or modern foreign languages.

MR. PUCINSKI: Therefore, you have no reason to believe that it is used for any other purpose except that the law provided.

MR. LUDINGTON: Due to the types of equipment, I would find it difficult to find ways of using it in other types of courses.

MR. PUCINSKI: So, based on your experience with the act so far, you have no reason to believe that the lending of this money to private schools, although they may be church related, has in any way interfered with the separation doctrine?

MR. LUDINGTON: I go by the applications and the kinds of equipment that they have listed on these applications, and it is our belief that these are held to math, science, and foreign languages.[115]

As is apparent, Ludington's testimony assumes that the equipment requested was of such sort that it could only be used for the specific purpose prescribed by Title III.

Other witnesses, however, raised the question of the general permeation of religious influence in a church-school and the pervasion of a particular religion in all of the subjects that are taught. To this pressing objection Pucinski insisted on knowing how religious doctrine could be brought into an algebraic formula.[116]

The Congressman from Illinois, appearing as a witness before the House General Subcommittee on Education, expressed his own convictions in a forthright statement:

These loans should be made available for the specific purpose of developing science, math, and language facilities. And I certainly think that it would be in order to suggest that they include also loans for construction of facilities and physical fitness and perhaps cafeterias.

We heard testimony yesterday from Coach Wilkinson, who stressed the great importance of physical fitness in this country. And yet these are things that are completely divorced from any sectarian teaching. These are subjects that, as I have said many, many times, it would be extremely difficult to try to impugn, or to associate with these secular subjects any religious dogma.

As a matter of fact, so far as I know, the textbooks which are used for the teaching of these subjects in the private schools, even though they may be church related, are the same textbooks that are being used by the secular, by the public schools. So there is no conflict there.[117]

Despite some questionable underlying assumptions of this statement, Pucinski's subsequent comments offer fruitful opportunity for second thoughts on what had just been stated:

I believe it is certainly fair to point out that we know from the youngsters going on to higher education that those youngsters who get their education in private schools, in these particular fields, are just as qualified to carry on their higher education in the scientific fields in colleges as youngsters who get their education in public schools.

Certainly, then, if anyone was to presume that the training that

290

these youngsters get in these particular subjects is in some way deficient, or is in some way different, or is in some way altered by religious dogma in the course of the educational process, this would very quickly be reflected when these youngsters go on to higher education. And yet we can show records and we can show proof and we can show evidence, and I am sure we can bring in thousands of cases of youngsters who have gotten their basic training in private schools, church-related if they be so, and went on to college, and took courses over there, and graduated, and reached great positions of prominence in their scientific field.[118]

These statements might have suggested to both Pucinski and LaNoue (who omits quoting these two paragraphs) some profitable second thoughts on the preceding statements, namely, that the controlling question should be whether the end result of the science courses in parochial schools adequately prepares the student to meet the requirements set for these sciences in higher grades in schools which are not church-related. This in turn may have suggested the consideration of the indefectibility of the subject matter of a science course in an educational process whose ultimate values are theistic and Christian. Pucinski's own illustration of athletic exercises as "completely divorced from any sectarian teaching" should easily have brought to mind parochial school children wearing religious medals and blessing themselves before plunging into the pool.

Apparently, LaNoue adopts the purely secular subject concept since he at no time examines the question of its validity either for himself or for others. And since the possibility of the neutrality of science courses must underlie any insistence, arguing from the Constitution, on a neutral presentation, the possibility will have to be examined in all of its ramifications. Prior to that, however, some preliminary observations can be made.

First, the loan provisions of Title III are for equipment,

291

not textbooks, although the illation from equipment to text-books is provided by Pucinski. LaNoue dispenses with this difference in a footnote:

> Any claim that equipment as opposed to the other essentials of teaching is necessarily nonreligious is a meaningless distinction from a church-state point of view. It would be the same as claiming that the state could contribute bricks for a church building and wood for the pews because these two elements were in themselves not religious. The essential criterion is the purpose for which the elements are used, be it church equipment or school equipment. To know that, one must examine the actual content of the subject matter. For an example of a court making this kind of analysis, see *Dickmen v. School District*, Oregon City, 366 P2d 553 (1961)[119]

The broad fact is that federal funds are expended for the construction of chapels on government property and for the provision of many of the instrumentalities of worship of the various faiths. There seems to be at present no real threat to this traditional congressional practice. The constitutional sensitivity on the part of opponents of federal aid to parochial schools seems to be for the most part restricted to the educational area and even then largely to the infra-collegiate level. The religious purpose and sectarian uses to which brick, mortar and wood are put in the construction of chapels at governmental expense are beyond all question. It seems doubtful in arguing by analogy from the extensive aptitude of a subject matter for religious orientation that one can conclude to similar utilization of school equipment material. Such an illation, from equipment to textbooks, as noted above, was provided by Pucinski.

Furthermore, the federal government as the original and sole donor of outright grants for science equipment to public schools would have the right to stipulate for a reasonable time the exclusive purpose and use of the science equipment in the public schools. Nonprofit schools, on the other hand, in obtaining these science facilities through a governmental loan, to be repaid in full with interest, are from the very beginning co-owners and should not be denied all say in the use of these equipments.

Secondly, a word might be said about the testimonies before the House hearings. LaNoue makes no mention of those witnesses who did not, of their own accord, raise any objections to the continued inclusion of parochial schools in the N.D.E.A. program. It is safe to suppose, therefore, that the religious orientation of the curriculum of church-related schools was too broad a fact for them to be ignorant of. Among those witnesses were eminent educators and jurists. And while outside the time-limit of Mr. LaNoue's survey-study, notice should nonetheless be given to such educational savants as Walter Lippman and Robert Hutchins and in some instances reversal of positions since the publication and wide publicity given to his survey study. Apparently his permeation argument has not weakened the conviction of many persons that the secular aspects and secular functions of science subjects remain inviolably intact for public purpose even though invested with religious values and judgments. For many observers the pedagogic distinction between theological instructions in a religion course and religious moral values in nontheological studies is too formidable to be obliterated by a nonblending formula.

Thirdly, an impartial study would have inquired into the value permeations in public school textbooks and in the light of the Supreme Court ruling in *Torcaso v. Watkins,* which raised the inevitable question of the role of public law in relation to the spiritual content of the educational process.

Fourthly, at no time does Mr. LaNoue ask whether the science subjects are taught and learned proficiently in parochial schools according to existing empirical tests or by any standard of measurement that he could suggest, so as to satisfy the objective and national interest for which the N.D.E.A. was passed by Congress.

THE MYTH OF NEUTRALITY
IN EDUCATION

Since the time of Socrates pedagogues through the centuries have conceived of the educational process as a spiritual experience of eminent significance for the person and his community. Educators have differed on the ultimate premises and the substantive content of the moral ideals to which all learning is ordained. Political authorities no less than ecclesiastical officials have insisted on their interest in the education of their subjects. The stake of democratic societies in education is such that their survival is publicly professed to be dependent largely upon the loyalties engendered in school children for their free institutions. Totalitarian governments with logical consistency dictate not only the subject matters taught but define the ideals that are to be inculcated in the young. Any education worthy of its high purpose is above all else humanist and, therefore, presupposes ultimates about human existence and destiny. Even the serious-minded and well-intentioned construction in recent times of "neutral principles of adjudication" to help resolve the national controversy over the constitutional propriety of extending federal aid to church-related schools has not gone unchallenged. Even nonbelievers have had to admit this raw and unfair fact.

294

Professor Joseph Tussman of Syracuse University has observed:

> The charge that public education in its secular form is irreligious may have some substance. As a nonbeliever I may find this convenient. But I am not sure that it is altogether fair or that it justifies, in the name of "neutrality," the rejection of the claims of our religious citizens to public support for their efforts at providing education that is religious in spirit. The neutrality of the public school should not, I suggest, be considered beyond challenge.[120]

And from a critic who holds fast to absolute separation of church and state we hear a complaint about the uneven struggle for the spiritual control of public education:

> If teacher-education colleges in the past generation in this country had attended more to the religious enlightenment of their students and had restricted themselves less exclusively to the thought and language patterns of a non-theistic scientific naturalism, it is altogether possible that the churches would not have been driven to the only recourse that lay within their grasp. Their demand for sectarian religious education in the schools, and when possible, in teacher education, is a reasonable and democratic demand for just as long as the secularists insist on dominating the educational system and excluding, neglecting or depreciating the religious dimension in American culture.[121]

The best-intentioned but nonetheless misguided efforts of those persons who seek a solution for public schooling in a purely secular education call to mind the militant secularism that has fought to prevail in our public schools from Francis Wright to Vivian Thayer.[10] There is no inclination on the part of secular humanists and ethical culturists to disown the spiritual content of their nontheistic beliefs. It is precisely here that LaNoue's study falters badly. He does not give even a passing nod to the problem of value permeability in public schooling or raise the constitutional

295

question of governmental aid in support of these "religious" orientations.

THE MYTH OF THE PURELY SECULAR SUBJECT CONCEPT

A broad fact that most educators acknowledge—that the educational process as an integral whole is at its core pre-eminently spiritual and a commitment to value-judgments of one sort or another—does not, of course, settle *a priori* the distinct question of whether every subject matter for study is permeated with moral ultimates. Nor does Pucinski's and LaNoue's assumption of the validity of the purely secular subject concept of specified branches of learning make the concept valid. It is, therefore, imperative that the meaning and content of secular studies in general and of secular subjects in particular be examined to ascertain whether they are to be distinguished from religious studies and, if so differentiated, whether they bear within themselves any grounds for relations with sacral studies.

A subject of study is defined by its formal object which, in turn, prescribes the appropriate methods of teaching which are conducive to efficient learning. For example, spelling is the correct lettering of words. The methods employed are oral or written exercises naming each letter component of the word. It is easily distinguishable as a natural science, *de naturalibus;* that is, it is not *de divinis,* not about the existence, nature and attributes of a transcendental being. It reaches out to all words, inclusive of words that designate sacral subjects, such as God, the angels, the sacraments, items of worship and liturgy, and so on. The spelling of sacral terms does not convert spelling from a natural into a sacral study. The number of sacral terms

296

required for spelling exercises in a church-related school would probably be more extensive than what is required in a public school, however. Nonetheless, provided the list of words designating secular objects is not less than what is required by a state educational curriculum or what is necessary for daily concourse with people and for the needs of advancing in other subjects of study, the greater inclusion of sacral terms is understandable and might be considered as an enlarged vocabulary. (Conversely, it would be equally understandable that less sacral terms would be included in a public school spelling list although, by the same token, less sacral terms are being learned.) Spelling does not become a religious subject because parochial school children are called upon to spell such words as "Trinity," "Sacrament," "tabernacle," "host," "chalice," "extreme unction," "rosary."

The formal object of the study of arithmetic is to add, subtract, divide and multiply numerals. Numerals may be employed as substantives or adjectivals. Whether the things computed are potatoes or marbles or rosary beads the effective teaching and efficient learning of multiplication, division, subtraction and addition remains unimpaired by the use of sacral illustrations. Arithmetic is not thereby transformed from a natural science to a theological science nor does it, as a natural science, require the exclusion of sacral illustrations. While spelling reaches out to all words, sacral and secular terms, the range of employment of sacral illustrations in arithmetic poses at most a question of intellectual temperance, restraint, balance and common sense.

There are, however, natural sciences where referrals to religious dogmas and morals, whether of reason or of revelational theology, may not be entirely excluded because they are patently relevant questions that will unavoidably arise in class with direct reference to the subject matter. For example, in biology, the natural science of organic life, vegetable, animal and human, the question of the ultimate origin of life may properly arise. Biology teachers in public schools as well as in church-related schools are faced with a choice: either rule out the question or give the theistic or nontheistic version of the origin of life. The fact that some textbooks do not touch upon the question does not preclude it from the minds of the interrogating students. Whether or not the answer given in a public school classroom is an affront to the religious conscience of some of the students is a problem that does not obtain in church-related schools.[122]

Biology textbooks used in public schools make the dutiful distinction between voluntary and involuntary muscles. There is, however, generally no mention of free will and moral responsibility despite some discussion of the manner whereby a "bad habit" is replaced by a "good habit." The text simply notes that one habituation is reversible by the opposite habituation. There is an obvious restraint from mentioning freedom of choice and personal moral responsibility and hardly any explanation of the difference between a "bad" habit and a "good" habit. Whether intentional or not a subtle form of naturalistic behaviorism pervades public school textbooks. In church-related schools there is a frontal approach to these questions and the provided answers constitute no concealed threat to the religious conscience of the students. A textbook on a natural science like arithmetic could be entirely devoid of sacral illustrations without the subject matter or the student being the worse for it. But biology teaching and textbooks cannot block out completely from the minds of students in public and church-related schools all questions of religion and morality which are properly stirred by some aspects of the

298

subject matter. In biology there are a number of points of study where the secular and religious aspects of a natural science are intertwined. There is some persistent talk among enlightened educators of the need for sensible sex instruction. In many schools students are warned of the dangers of self-restraint on the nervous system and health of the body. At least the instructions given in church-related schools on the morality of the use of sex faculties are in accordance with the religious conscience of the students and their parents.

There are subjects of study in the curriculum of public schools and church-related schools where the degree of religious permeability is such that it could not be disengaged without mutilating the subject matter itself. So many of the classic masterpieces and lesser works in sculpture, painting, architecture and music give expression to a religious theme. If with Plato and other eminent educators we insist that schooling should include esthetics, then should Handel's "Messiah;" illustrations of world-renowned cathedrals and basilicas, Gothic, Baroque, Byzantine, with their crucifixes and statuaries; and the prints of Michelangelo, Raphael and many others be banned from schooling in order to be constitutionally eligible for federal assistance? One could correctly reply that these are objects of study, but let us also note that with every gratifying appreciation of a religious work of art of undeniable beauty some attraction is experienced. That these questions are not raised to embarrass unduly a common sense approach to the arts can be illustrated by the protests of the plaintiff in the Maryland Bible case, which included among its complaints an illustration of the head of Christ by Velasquez in a public school textbook.

The secular subjects in which religious factors are so

299

much in evidence and so intimately intertwined with the subject matter as to constitute an integral part of it are literature and history. Many of the literary classics, poetry, drama, epics, essays and novels, have a religious story or are expressive of religious and moral values. Would the reading of selected excerpts from these classic compositions entail a legal disability? History, above all, a uniquely secular study, is most permeated with religious facts and influences whose presentation cannot but entail religious interpretations, prepossessions and loyalties. Surely history must be numbered among the necessary studies and of all the subjects history is least capable of being expurgated of religious life without serious mutilations of the subject matter. Western history can scarcely avoid the advent of Christianity, the Crusades, the Inquisition, the Reformation, the religious wars. In American history many of our basic national and organic documents are solemnly vibrant with religious professions and dedications.

Justice Jackson in his concurring opinion in McCollum warned at some length those who might be encouraged by the Court's ruling to hope with the plaintiff for the insulation of every secular study from every religious connotation:

> While we may and should end such formal and explicit instruction as the Champaign plan and at all times prohibit the teaching of creed and catechism and ceremonial and can forbid forthright prose-lytizing in the schools, I think it remains to be demonstrated whether it is possible, even if desirable, to comply with such demands as plaintiff's completely to isolate and cast out of secular education all that some people may reasonably regard as religious instruction. Perhaps subjects such as mathematics, physics or chemistry are, or can be, completely secularized. But it would not seem practical to teach either practice or appreciation of the arts if we are to forbid exposure of youth to any religious influences. Music without sacred music, architecture minus the cathedral, or painting without the

300

scriptural themes would be eccentric and incomplete, even from a secular point of view. Yet the inspirational appeal of religion in these guises is often stronger than in a forthright sermon. Even such a "science" as biology raises the issue between evolution and creation as an explanation of our presence on this planet. Certainly a course in English literature that omitted the Bible and other powerful uses of our mother tongue for religious ends would be pretty barren. And I should suppose it is a proper, if not an indispensable, part of preparation for a wordly life to know the roles that religion and religions have played in the tragic story of mankind. The fact is that, for good or ill, nearly everything in our culture worth transmitting, everything which gives meaning to life, is saturated with religious influences, derived from paganism, Judaism, Christianity— both Catholic and Protestant—and other faiths accepted by a large part of the world's peoples. One can hardly respect a system of education that would leave the student wholly ignorant of the currents of religious thought that move the world society for a part in which he is being prepared.

But how can one teach, with satisfaction or even with justice to all faiths, such subjects as the story of the Reformation, the Inquisition, or even the New England effort to found "a Church without a Bishop and a State without a King," is more than I know. It is too much to expect that mortals will teach subjects about their contemporaries with the detachment they may summon to teaching about remote subjects such as Confucius or Mohammed. When instruction turns to proselytizing and imparting knowledge becomes evangelism is, except in the crudest cases, a subtle inquiry.

The task of separating the secular from the religious in education is one of magnitude, intricacy and delicacy. To lay down sweeping constitutional doctrine as demanded by complainant and apparently approved by the Court, applicable alike to all school boards of the nation, "to immediately adopt and enforce rules and regulations prohibiting all instruction in and teaching of religious education in all public schools," is to decree a uniform, rigid and, if we are consistent, an unchanging standard for countless school boards representing and serving highly localized groups which not only differ from each other but which themselves from time to time change attitudes. It seems to me that to do so is to allow zeal for our own ideas of what is good in public instruction to induce us to accept

301

the role of a super board of education for every school district in the nation . . ."[123]

It is well to note that Justice Jackson is discussing the unavoidable religious implications of secular studies in the elementary and secondary public schools of the state. The problem arises from the moral implications of the secular studies themselves in varying degrees of involvement, from the tangential to the necessary and the unavoidable. Public schools are confronted with the almost insuperable task of not offending the rights of conscience of all their students and of their parents. Because of the religious identity of creed of the children attending church-related schools, these schools at least have the merit of offending no religious conscience. It is, therefore, puzzling when their pedagogy thereby raises constitutional questions.

Lastly, however neutral some natural sciences may be in themselves, such as physics and chemistry, once the products of these natural sciences are put to human use, they immediately become invested with a moral and spiritual import. One need only note in the various communications media the debates current on the national and international level on the moral aspects of the use of nuclear weapons, contraceptives, abortion of defective foetuses, birth control program information, etc. The likelihoood that such moral-science questions would arise in infra-collegiate studies should be gauged by the all-pervasive impact of the communications media—newspapers, magazines, cinema and radio and television programs which almost compel youngsters to take notice of these serious adult controversies.

For better or for worse neutrality in the educational process is a myth. The conversion of this myth into a constitutional principle would seem to be an unwarranted distortion of the function of public law. The assumptions

302

of the purely secular subject concept on which some testimonies before the House hearings apparently based the validity of the loan provision of Title III are intrinsically false. The data of the study simply discloses what may have been reasonably expected: that the spiritual orientation in religious schools would be in conformity with credal confessions while the moral context of public school education would have to contend with the authentic challenges of religious pluralism.

Before proceeding to a review of LaNoue's construction of the religious permeation in parochial school studies, let us first observe parenthetically that direct financial aid to formal religious activity seems to afford no serious constitutional challenge outside of the area of education. Tax support of chaplains in the armed forces and in state and national legislative houses continues with the approval of the legislative and executive branches of the American government, and some justices of the United States Supreme Court have given reassuring explanations that these practices were not threatened by the Court ruling in recent decisions on prayer and Bible reading. If it is technically correct to hold that tax exemption for religious institutions and their nonprofit religious, social and educational enterprises are not a direct formal participation in governmental funds, it most assuredly constitutes an enormous governmental encouragement for religious activities in a manner no less concrete for the vitality and expansion of the religious apostolate. There is an undoubted religious preferment in the tax exemption laws which is clearly distinguishable from the social welfare functions and services of the churches which nonreligious agencies also perform. Even in the educational area, opposition for the most part is directed to the lower levels. The higher institutions of learning with religious profession and affiliation—colleges, professional schools, universities—receive governmental subsidies in a wide variety of ways whether they reach the institution directly by construction loans or indirectly through the student and research projects on the broad basis of a public purpose or utility. We have not yet brought completely to the surface, however, all the nonrational forces beneath that formally rationalized opposition which denies to the parochial schools the same legal distinctions of direct, indirect, incidental, consequential benefits, secular aspects and functions which they do not begrudge the higher institutions of learning, despite the interdependence of these church-related schools for their student enrollment.

AN ANALYSIS OF LaNOUE'S STUDY

LaNoue observes at the start that there was remarkable silence on the part of some witnesses who testified before the House hearings in behalf of parochial schools about the religious permeation of the school curriculum in general and in the science subjects covered by Section 305. This silence, he notes, is in marked contrast to the forthright statements of Leo XIII and Pius XI on education for Catholics. One should seriously pause before suggesting that silence about an obvious broad fact, known and easily understood by anyone, was a calculated omission. Parochial schools are open for inspection by the state educational authorities and at set intervals are visited by the appropriate officials. The textbooks used in parochial schools are not a guarded secret. The presence of religious garb, religious symbols and, of course, a uniformity of religious confession are religious factors which do not

304

evanesce as students go from one subject matter to another. It is simply that Catholics hold to the indefectability of secular aspects and functions of science studies in an integrated educational process which culminates for them in the primacy of religious ultimates. This philosophy of education has an ancient tradition reaching back even to pre-Christian Plato and is still advocated in many reputable institutions of learning outside the Catholic Church. To talk of the religious pervasiveness of studies in parochial schools is a pointless belaboring of the obvious.

LaNoue observes that the term "sciences" is nowhere precisely defined in the N.D.E.A. He assumes that more likely than not it refers to the natural sciences rather than to the social sciences. He notes, too, that there are borderline studies such as geography, physiology and experimental psychology which would defy exclusive classification. Whether this is true or not, LaNoue intends to show that "even into subjects which are undeniably scientific, parochial schools inject a considerable amount of religious interpretation and even some sectarian doctrine."[124] By an editorial use of the verb "inject" he seems to suggest a forcible intrusion of religious considerations as wholly alien to a science study. He finds that at the elementary school level most of the religion in textbooks is generally a simple theism, expressed in a variety of ways: use of religious symbols, scriptural quotations and repeated references to God as creator. The theistic theme is specifically Christian in its view of the ultimate ends of man. Children are reminded in the textbooks that they are accountable to their Creator for the use they make of their bodies and souls. Children are given an integrated perspective of the harmonious relationship of religion and science, of the interdependence of creatures, of the orders of nature and

305

grace, and of the personal responsibility they have as stewards of God's creatures. In a word, they are taught the holiness of everything and a veneration and grateful use of the things of this earth.[125]

One need not apologize for teaching elementary school children a reverential regard for everything about them, by stressing the "importance of everything God made," "even the tiniest creatures," much less admit to a legal disability for inculcating a motive of conscience for that responsibility and disciplined conduct that are so necessary for the proper behavior of energetic youngsters in a community. It is the task of all schooling, state and independent, to do this. To provide additional religious reasons for that correct conduct on which the good order of the local community must rely would seem to foster with greater moral strength the inculcation of civic virtues than to do so in complete disregard of them. There is evidence to suppose that the Founding Fathers of our Republic welcomed religious motivation as an ally of public welfare. As for purely theistic references distinct from Christian theism, many of our national basic and organic documents are permeated with belief in and dependence upon Almighty God for the well being of the nation. LaNoue may correctly respond that these documents are not scientific treatises, but what is more to the legal point, they are or may be subject matter of study at tax-supported public schools.

In Catholic parochial schools, a Christian motivation, that is, a compelling motive of conscience, is provided for social conduct.

In the pursuit of Catholic Action the spiritual and corporal works of mercy are the guide; in the pursuit of conservation the proper use of soil, water, minerals, forests, and wildlife is the guide.[126]

Such teaching may prove to be more effective guidance than, say, the posters in conveyances which depict Papa Bear begging us not to set the woodlands on fire while picnicking. Christianity is not behaviorism. Sluggish human nature needs to be prodded as much from within by conscience as from without by law. Whichever of the motivations, religious or nonreligious, may prove to be the controlling factor in every instance of the actions of youngsters is a matter of speculation. The law does expect that some motivation be inculcated in our school children for proper civic conduct. But there is no reason to suppose that in view of the good effect intended the law thereby chooses between the religious and the nonreligious. No value deleterious to society is being taught, no harm to one's neighbors urged, or any waste of natural resources encouraged by relating good conduct to a theistic creed. Intellectual temperance should counsel against unnecessary frequency or forced insertions. But surely there is nothing in the passages quoted which relates human use of natural resources to a religious responsibility, which is against the national interest, which is bad pedagogy, which opposes the general and specific purposes of a publicly accredited education. To base civic conduct, warranted by the communal good, on a religious motivation might, on the contrary, be reasonably construed as a public service of religion rather than as a sectarian private interest liable to legal disabilities.

The immense moral significance and imperative need in our times to call upon the spiritual resources of the nation to eradicate the deep-rooted racial antipathies now disturbing the very foundations of American society cannot be stressed enough.

What is not clear, however, is whether LaNoue objects

to the Catholic answer or to any answer to the problems facing the nation, or whether he would insist, rather, that both kinds of answers be given the youngsters in the elementary and secondary grades. But what he unfortunately takes no cognizance of in pointing to sectarian interests is that these teachings are ordained to foster the common good. LaNoue has not understood that the public welfare has many diverse spiritual tributaries. And his concept of sectarianism as private religious interests is radically false. The presence of a private desire and interest is not *eo ipso* to be opposed to a public need. Values to be gained by religious teachings are not merely private, and reasonable men and men of law can judge whether a faith has social significance. We would suppose that Christianity had long ago been acknowledged as the foundation of western civilization, even taking into account the religious animosities of misguided Christians at variance with one another.

There have not been wanting eminent educators and jurists in America who have stressed the need for public schools to teach the religious foundations of our democracy. No less a constitutional authority than Dr. Corwin has written:

> Primarily democracy is a system of ethical values, and that this system of values so far as the American people are concerned is grounded in religion will not be denied by anybody who knows the historical record. And that agencies by which this system of values has been transmitted in the past from generation to generation, the family, the neighborhood, the Church, have today become much impaired, will not be seriously questioned by anybody who knows anything about contemporary conditions. But what this all adds up to is that the work of transmission has been put more and more upon the shoulders of the public schools. Can they then do the job without the assistance of religious instruction? At least, there seems to be a widely held opinion to the contrary.[127]

308

Those persons who insist on a released-time program for sectarian religious instruction during a school hour and away from public school properly—a position sustained by the Court in Zorach—do so in order to stress the nexus of religious instruction, albeit sectarian, to a public school education. When parochial schools include formal sectarian religious instruction in their general curriculum they are thereby fulfilling one of the avowed educational purposes of sectarian instruction in a released program during a school hour, and fulfilling their religious apostolate as well. Further, there is an area of concordance between the religious heritage of America and what is taught in parochial schools. In addition, specifically Catholic dogma gives no evidence whatever of being adverse to the national interest, and there is much in it that fosters an ardent patriotism that has characterized parochial schools.

Christianity is not behaviorism. The charity that should distinguish the Christian will not ensue without deliberate personal effort and repeated spiritual exercise. To call forth this effort against the instincts of selfishness may require a strong doctrinal information of the young conscience. Failure to live up to the ideals of the Christian faith for the benefit of society can be better remedied by an environment and schooling which integrate the educational process and infuse it with the high vocation of Christian dedication. A nontheistic humanitarian, wonderfully generous in his daily living, may be edified but not awed by our Savior's warning, "Whatever you do to the least of mine, you do unto me." And if Catholics are to check their prejudices and biases they shall need more than their own instincts of generosity to help them overcome deep-rooted social and moral infirmities. Whatever nonbelievers and non-Christians may consider to be "the way, the truth, and the life," Catholics are convinced that they can better serve their country as practicing Catholics. The religious orientation of parochial schools is intended for the benefit of society as well as for personal sanctification. "By their fruits shall you know them." This evangelical counsel might be profitably applied even by law to the beneficent consequences of religious pluralism in America. This pluralism is not, to be sure, an equality of religious doctrine or an unconcern with dogmatic differences. But with the passage of time, Americans have become the wiser and have succeeded in eliminating gradually the intercredal frictions and intolerances to a remarkable degree. More than that, they have come to acknowledge that each faith, firm in its own creed, can contribute to the well being of our country. LaNoue has entirely missed the full merits of religious schooling in harmony with American public law and order. He has construed sectarianism too narrowly as a private interest completely separated from the public interest which depends upon it. He has not seen the forest for the trees.

If the constitutionally-eligible-for-federal-aid-pedagogy was stripped of all theistic reference and motivation the resultant educational process would be not only a moral and legal affront to the religious conscience of the students but also a subtle assault upon the spiritual foundations of our nation. By subtraction, if not by openly formal instruction, a consequent behaviorist psychology would by calculated omission instill in youths an apathetic amoralism at a period of life when instincts and passions are strongest. It is high time that the moral role of religion in schooling is recognized in the public interest. The religious neutrality of public schools is not a good incident to their educational process but rather a constraint which religious pluralism forces upon them.

At the high school level, religious doctrine is most prom-

310

inent in the science textbooks when creation and evolution are discussed. But LaNoue contends that the compatibility between religion and science can only be that between the Catholic creed and Catholic-taught science. He does not question the propriety of discussing creation and evolutionary theory in science courses. The origin of life would be an obvious albeit profound question in biology. LaNoue sees a different basis for constitutional issue:

Certain interpretations given to the student are held uniquely by Catholics, or, at least, by Christians; and the context of the material is all Catholic . . . Subjects like birth control, sterilization and euthanasia are usually mentioned only in terms of the Church's judgments.[128]

Left unexplained is what precisely generates the constitutional issue: whether the subjects ought not to arise, whether they should be blacked out or completely ignored, whether only the Catholic answer is given, or whether, as is more likely, all the answers are not given. But if this last criticism is the case, then it ought to be directed at every public school textbook as well. And even the most earnest of pedagogues would be taxed in giving a comprehensive, impartial and acceptable presentation of each of the numerous answers. Moreover, certain questions arise not only from the very nature of the subject matter, but also from wide publicity given by the communciations media to such issues as thalidomide babies, abortion and sterilization laws, or the use of contraceptives. Such publicity can scarcely escape the attention of school-age youngsters. At least the answers given in parochial schools have the merit of being in conformity with the religious confession. No one can vouch with equal assurance that the answers given in public schools, however euphemistically expressed— mercy killing, euthanasia, birth control—are not a subtle attack upon the religious conscience of the students. Surely if Darwin's evolution can have its day in class and in court, then too may creationist evolution fare with equal favor.

LaNoue also points to the cultural concentration in some elementary geography textbooks on the Catholic contributions to western civilization and culture[129]—for example, the popes as patrons of science, the Catholic faith of some scientists, Catholic activities in various countries with no mention about the contributions of other faiths and churches. Here it is hoped that LaNoue was making a good case for counseling intellectual temperance and for attaining a comprehensive perspective, rather than raising more evidence for the apparent unconstitutionality of federal loans for science teaching.

The question rightly framed, however, is one of pedagogy, not of law. Though difficult, the task of a balanced presentation which takes appreciative cognizance of all agencies for good living among men should be the overriding concern of all textbook writers. However, one can sympathize with the Catholic cultural stance. In less enlightened circles and even in public school textbooks as recently as the first World War, the Church was directly or indirectly pictured as an obscurantist, parochial society. Public school textbooks were wont to begin American history with the landing of the Pilgrims, and with little proportionate cognizance of the Italian, Spanish and French Catholic discoverers, explorers and missionaries who surely were among the first and principal settlers. On matters of religious intolerance and persecution in European and American history the weight was decidedly cast against the Church of Rome despite the highly creditable record of Catholics derived from the Toleration Act of Lord Baltimore and consistent professions of church-state separation

312

by the Catholic hierarchy. In any public discussion of the two traditions of church-state relations, the major tradition which grants a preferred status in law to "true" religion, and the minor one which confers equality before the law, the preferred status position is more often than not identified with the Catholics, despite the consistent disavowals of the Catholic hierarchy since the days of John Carroll. Yet both traditions have been part of the other major faiths: Protestant (in Sweden today and in American history almost down to the Civil War) and the Jewish Orthodox (State of Israel).

It is true that one imbalance does not redress another, but it does bring about a change of sentiment. When a people has all along been on the receiving end of a calculated campaign of professionally organized nativism; portrayed as un-American or as suspect; its churches, convents and schools burned; its loyalty questioned despite a very proud boast of American citizenship, enormous sacrifices in war, and a wide participation in public service and community life, then partisan enthusiasm is easily understandable. LaNoue might have been reminded that even on the higher levels of learning in the early part of this century, scholars and historians were still referred to as Protestant or Catholic in order to designate the direction of their favorable prejudices and their adverse biases. Learning and scholarship was, openly or not, committed to an apologetic purpose. Persevering endeavors at intercredal dialogue have lessened much of this partisan championship of historic causes and have brought about the brightest prospects of cooperative intellectual enterprises.

There will always be room for a balanced writing of elementary and secondary high school textbooks for private and public schools. Today voices are being raised for a fair and proportionate accounting of the contributions to the American community by ethnic and racial minorities who have thus far been completely neglected. LaNoue's study on cultural and religious emphases should stir serious thoughts in the direction of a truly catholic presentation. What is needed is not the obnoxious weighting of interest but a balanced perspective correspondent to the broad sweep of history. LaNoue has posed an authentic problem which may prove highly troubling and overwhelming in resolution. But it is essentially and entirely a pedagogic problem better left to educators and scholars. Constitutional law and the judiciary have neither the jurisdiction nor the competence to serve as the national board of education.

MATHEMATICS AND INTELLECTUAL TEMPERANCE

Perhaps subjects such as mathematics, physics or chemistry are, or can be, completely secularized.[130] But religious facts, factors and influences are so much a part of history that they could not possibly be exorcised without maiming the subject matter. They are so prominent in esthetics that to concentrate on secular works of art is to study esthetics inadequately. And religious-moral value judgments and spiritual conflict cannot be completely banned from literature without deforming human experience. And as noted above, the science of biology, whenever it touches upon human action however physical, cannot disengage itself from the spiritual dimension. Apart then from the products of mathematics, physics, chemistry and engineering, which raise at time inescapable moral questions when their results are put to human use or destruction, these natural sciences do not immediately and certainly on elementary and sec-

314

ondary levels of education do not warrant any religious reference. The use of sacral illustrations in adding, subtracting or multiplying may be in bad taste but it certainly is not required by any degree of relevance to the subject matter itself.

At best LaNoue has raised a question of intellectual temperance, and more likely than not the use of sacral illustrations in mathematics will instill an aversion for religious references in the minds of the youngsters rather than foster religion itself. But the point remains that the use of sacral illustrations does not raise a constitutional issue of eligibility for federal assistance in the study of these subjects. Only one question is all-controlling: does the use of sacral illustrations in mathematics obstruct proficiency in the teaching and learning of the subject? If mathematics is learned whether the illustrations are religious or nonreligious, the purpose set down by Congress in Section 305 of Title III of the N.D.E.A. is truly and fully achieved. The insertion of law to determine constitutionally permissible illustrations in mathematics would be a grotesque and foolish function of law. Sacral illustrations do not convert mathematics into a sacral subject matter or transform its purpose into a religious one. LaNoue's criticism deserves to be heeded and it is not improbable that it may have already suggested corrections.

MODERN LANGUAGES

The teaching of modern languages entails the teaching of grammar rules, spelling and sentence structure.[131] Here too the efficiency with which these exercises are taught and mastered by the students remains unaffected by the cultural and religious emphases that may be found in some textbooks. Whether one learns to translate into French the phrase, "the cow jumps over the moon," or "St. Francis of Assisi spoke to the birds and the fishes," all these words are part of a language, and we have no reason to suppose in the absence of attested evidence that modern languages in parochial schools are being taught in such a way as not to prepare the students for the reading of literature without or with any cultural emphasis or religious theme.

ENGLISH LANGUAGE AND LITERATURE

In the expectation that "English is almost a certainty to be the first extension if the National Defense Education Act is expanded," LaNoue discusses the integration of religion in the study of the English language and literature in some parochial school textbooks.[132] But LaNoue is belaboring the obvious. Language study whether foreign or domestic has among its classic works religious themes. Here too intellectual temperance and pedagogic prudence would counsel proportionate measure of literary exercise in religious and nonreligious themes. But it is difficult to see how the study of excerpts from Chesterton and Belloc or Dante's *Divine Comedy* can be in less legal favor for federal loan assistance than the study of Longfellow's "Evangeline" or selections from Charles Lamb. What should be considered is not whether there is evidence of sacral themes studied in literature, but whether there is such an excessive emphasis as to deprive students of acquaintance with other literary studies that are expected of a well informed and properly educated elementary or secondary student. It is not so much the presence of the religious literary studies as the absence of nonreligious literature in a well balanced curriculum that should stir constructive criticisms. At no

316

time does LaNoue suggest that students in parochial schools are being kept in the dark about such literary studies as a well rounded curriculum would require. On such a score a legal argument against aid to a schooling which state educational authorities found defective would hardly be contested.

One cannot argue for academic freedom and at the same time require the exclusion of religious themes in English and modern language studies in order to qualify for federal educational aid.

THE NON-CATHOLIC SCHOOLS

LaNoue tells us[133] that his study has concentrated on the integration of religion in Catholic science, mathematics and language textbooks because the Catholic parochial schools constitute by far the larger part of church-related schools and, secondly, because the church-related schools of Protestant and Jewish faiths are opposed to "accepting public money for their schools on constitutional and policy grounds." This admission seems to avoid the question of law. Law does not require anyone to apply for governmental assistance. The question is whether the secular aspects and secular functions of formally nonreligious studies of the sciences and modern languages which congressional legislation offers to assist can be realized in a Christian integration of learning. Further, one must consider whether Catholic parochial schools—which enroll 91 per cent of all nonpublic school students and one sixth of the nation's school children—are not such a significant part of national education that an exclusion of them from governmental assistance works to cross purposes with the congressional intent of promoting the knowledge of sci-

317

ences and languages among the students of America. Whether or not many Protestant and some Jewish organizations choose to receive governmental assistance may be likened to some extent to the action of Baptists who will apply "on principle" for loans and not grants under the Hill-Burton Act for their church-affiliated hospitals.

Integration of religion in the science subjects of Protestant church-related schools is openly professed by their textbooks. For example:

> A Lutheran elementary school teacher will insist that all areas of the curriculum reflect an adequate philosophy of Christian education. Thus he will select content and provide experiences that are consistent with such a philosophy. . . . Moreover, the Lutheran elementary school teacher will constantly search for materials that can be correlated with basic texts and that enable him to emphasize more fully a Christian point of view.

A very interesting comparison is the manner in which mathematics and religion are integrated by Catholic and Protestant textbooks. On the basis of the data which La-Noue provides, we saw that the extent to which Catholic textbooks integrated religion with mathematics was the use of sacral illustrations. In a text published for use in schools established under the auspices of the Christian Reformed Church there is a far more intimate integration of religion and mathematics. We excerpt from two pages:

> "Ideas of quantities and exact relationships have their source in God."
>
> "God apparently used what in our language is called higher mathematics to plan the course of the stars, etc."

Repeatedly in successive statements mathematics is said to be part of God's revelation, part of the pattern of truth, and the study of it will "instill in the student a sense of

318

wonder for the orderliness and beauty of God's creation as interpreted by mathematics."

Passages of the science textbooks used by the Seventh Day Adventists disclose a total integration to perhaps an even greater degree than other church schools. They integrate their natural and social sciences with theological tenets, relating all phenomenon, all human values and behavior to their literal biblical construction. While LaNoue is careful to advise us that most Protestants object to federal aid (without ever mentioning the Orthodox Jews who are in favor of it) he seems to overlook the profound significance of the religious permeation of Protestant parochial schools, namely, that these confessions consider the state schools not sufficiently adequate to prepare their faithful morally and spiritually in those obligations that should rule the conduct of their conscience in their private and communal lives. In other words, they feel that the tax-supported state schools do not—perhaps because of the enormous difficulties—provide an educational process which takes due regard for religious liberty in education. Further, while these Protestant parochial schools may oppose federal aid to church-related schools, they would not allow the criticism that they are not fulfilling the requirements set down by the state educational agencies or that they are preparing their students less competently for their civic duties or for further studies in other educational institutions. Nor would they allow that in teaching sciences and languages they are not achieving the secular aspects and functions of these studies even within the religious perspective of their textbooks.

It may be that the opposition of some Protestants to federal aid for parochial schools is reinforced by the fact that the economic demands upon the financial resources of their faithful for the support of their church schools is not, comparatively speaking, the great burden that the high percentage of Catholic parochial school children would impose upon the Catholic faithful. And it may also be that Catholics (together with some eminent non-Catholic constitutional jurists) hold not only that the extension of governmental subsidies to their school children is constitutionally permissible but also sound public policy. Undoubtedly an enormous federal aid program which excludes them would place them at a greater economic disadvantage. Whether or not, in the unreal hypothesis of a financial self-sufficiency that would meet all their educational needs and be on a parity with state schools in the national interest, Catholics would still ask for federal aid, is a choice they would surely make without disowning the constitutionality of such subvention. There should be nothing in constitutional law which places disabling consequences upon church-related schools, Catholic, Protestant or Jewish Orthodox, for insisting upon a religious integration of the school curriculum if it can be attested that the secular studies in these schools are proficiently taught. And in the minds of many educators, secular studies as distinguishable from theological studies are enhanced rather than obstructed by religious permeation, are suffused with divine purposes and designs, and offer a totality and coherence of moral and intellectual experience that can only offer safeguards to the manifold passions and volitional struggles that are the lot of everyone, and more so of the young. The young need not less but more religious motivation and inspiration. The national government should welcome any educational process that may further not only its program of national defense through education, but also the nation's cultural and spiritual life, upon whose vitality it must

320

ultimately rely for the efficiency of its laws. Aristotle has said that a stone obeys laws and man forms habits. Our governments, federal and state, expect the cultivation of civic virtues in the elementary and secondary schools. The law does not say upon which motives of conscience the obligations to society must be founded. Least of all may it prejudice the theistic or Christian or Judaic conscience in comparison with ethical culturism or humanism or some other ultimate commitment.

THE JUDGE AND THE SCHOOL MASTER

Unwittingly or not, LaNoue has stirred up more important questions for study than he has cared to answer. And for the issues which he has chosen for his immediate attention, he has not gotten to the roots of the problem. An extraordinary opportunity offered itself to him for a truly catholic study—the spiritual nature of the educational process, the degree to which various secular studies may entail religious considerations, the indefectibility of secular aspects and functions of the nontheological studies as taught in the parochial schools to the extent that the national interest requires, the common utility of these science and language studies, the equality of religious liberty in education, and the academic freedom about which so much is heard in higher rather than in lower education. Academic freedom is more glibly identified with the dissenter's freedom of choice than with the conformist's, who for some strange reason is thought to be less reputable intellectually for being in agreement. But above all he has failed in his catholicity to inquire into the spiritual content of textbooks used in tax-supported schools. There is one factor in the educational process and, at that, the principal one, which

321

LaNoue took no cognizance of—the school teacher. If a scissors and paste job could purge parochial school textbooks of all the religious referrals in order to qualify for federal aid, then how would LaNoue control the presentation, the moral and intellectual influence, of the school teacher in any classroom in state and private schools? Neutrality in education has never been more than a hypothesis from which constitutional reasoning can hang only too precariously.

Apart from LaNoue's failure to be truly catholic in his study, he has perhaps unwittingly initiated legal discourse, without setting down the ultimate grounds of relevance. The point is that the Court has neither the primary competence nor the jurisdiction to determine what should be constitutionally acceptable pedagogy. Apart from the incontrovertible right of local educational authorities to subject to examination the proficiency of teaching and learning in any publicly accredited school, the courts do not have primary competency in education; that is to say, except to review a possible legal challenge in the courts to cancel accreditation. What is or is not required in publicly accredited schools is the function and obligation of educators, not of jurists *qua* jurists. The Court may take cognizance of the legal challenge before the bench to review the action of state educational officials in withdrawing an accreditation and to adjudicate whether such action was arbitrary or not. The distracting factor in these considerations is the hypothesis of neutrality which is supposed to prevail in public schools. As we have repeatedly insisted, the neutrality in public schools is a necessitous course dictated by the conflicting claims of conscience; it is a negative retreat, not a positive affirmation of an ideal educational process. In its ultimate resultant it fails to satisfy the positive requirements of the religious conscience which finds itself a captive attendant by virtue of state compulsory school attendance laws and by an inability to afford a privately financed education in parochial schools. If public schools are striving earnestly for neutrality without hostility it cannot be said they have attained beyond question impartial neutrality.

But what of the Court's competence and jurisdiction to pass upon parochial schooling for the benefit of federal aid? Would it be constitutional to tell the secular facts of Columbus' voyage to the New World—the intrigues at the Spanish court, his difficulties with the crew, and so on—but constitutionally disabling to give at appreciable length excerpts from his writings so profuse with the religious confession of a sustaining spiritual force behind his perseverance against discouraging odds? When is emphasis without bias, silence without prejudice, omission without disparagement? The United States Supreme Court cannot be expected to review these questions as issues of law without being conferred the competence and jurisdiction of a national school board, which by law it does not have. Ethical culturists, secular humanists and educational neutralists are no less committed to a principle of integration of a school curriculum than the advocates of a religiously oriented educational process, nor do they deny that only value judgments and civic virtues be taught to students in public schools. The Court has neither the competence nor jurisdiction to choose between one spiritual principle of integration or another. It does have the competence and jurisdiction to ascertain whether the spiritual principle of integration is conducive to good civic livng. The law can inquire whether an educational process subserves a public good, fulfills a public function and contributes to the public

323

interest, and thereby merits official public approval and shares in its benefits. If the law knows no orthodoxy and no heresy, it is not unconcerned about orthodoxy and heresy. A number of federal and state court decisions attest to a public morality which no orthodoxy or heresy may violate. It is here that the educational neutralists engage in a pious deception. They insist on religious liberty in education, and they will even admit to much good in parochial schools. But they also insist on identifying sectarian schools as private interests unrelated to a public interest. The supposition that the constitutional distinction between private and public interests will allow the public interest to be served by a private agency, provided the primary public purpose is fulfilled even to consequent benefit to the private agency, is attested by many federal subsidies of industrial, commercial and agricultural enterprises for the national interest. So too, in Everson, Justice Black, in the opinion of the Court, admitted that "to help parents get their children to school, regardless of their religion, safely and expeditiously to and from accredited schools" undoubtedly brought some incidental benefit to the church school. And similarly in the earlier Cochran case: "Individual interests are aided only as the common interest is safeguarded." It seems that this compatibility-of-interest doctrine, while sufficient to sustain private performance of public services with the help of governmental funds, either in hospital work or social welfare work, or in state provision of textbooks for school children, or bus transportation of school children at public expense, ought not to suffer constitutional embarrassment because in the very employment of a religious agency the public interest is touched with a moral and religious quality. The supposition that a private interest—here a religiously oriented

324

education in an accredited school—is far less related to public needs because it is invested with a religious conception of life has been seriously challenged by one scholar who confesses to the nonrelevance of transcendental values to human purposes. In the aftermath of the McCollum decision banning sectarian religious instruction in public school classrooms, Dr. Alexander Meiklejohn reflected on the constitutional distinction between private and public interest on which Everson was based, arguing that private interest in a religious apostolate "to aid religious groups to spread their faith" ought not in McCollum have been considered without purpose to the public:

As one questions the distinction here made, one is not denying that parents have a private interest in religious teaching. But they have, likewise, a private interest in the physical safety of their children. In this respect the two cases are identical. But the presence of a private desire does not prove the absence of a public need. And the values to be gained by religious teaching are not merely private. To say that is to rob religious attitudes of all objective "spiritual" meaning. It is to reduce their significance to that of private personal idiosyncracies. As against such false sectarianism, surely the value of all our creeds, religious or nonreligious, lies in their common, though varied, attempt to interpret men and society and the world as to find, in those interpretations, bases for human behavior, for human association. In relation to that common purpose, credal differences are accidental. Our sects can live together in peace, not by ignoring each other as "private," but by recognizing and honoring one another as fellows in a common cause. Just as the teaching of "geography" is public, so is the teaching of religion or nonreligion. In whatever varied ways are available, the general welfare requires that our young people learn the lessons which we call "spiritual."

The argument just stated seems to require that the writer of these words indicate, if not explain, his own "private" conviction. My own beliefs are definitely on the side of nonreligion. So far as I can see, human purposes have no extra-human backing. Yet, so long as half our people, more or less, are interpreting and conducting their lives,

325

their family relationships, the upbringing of their children upon a basis of some religious belief, the Constitution requires of us that those beliefs shall be given not only equal status but also positive status in the public planning of education. The freedom of religion has the same basic justification as had the freedom of speech or of the press. In both sets of cases, a strong and passionate private desire is involved. But far deeper than this is a public necessity. When men are trying to be self-governing, no other single factor of their experience is more important to them than the freedom of their religion or of their nonreligion. The interpreting of our spiritual beliefs is a public enterprise of the highest order.

. . . .

The shift in the meaning of Jefferson's "wall of separation" is a striking illustration of the change from the organic to the mechanical interpretation of a figure of speech. As one reads the words of the Rector of the University of Virginia, it is clear that the beliefs and attitudes of religion are, for him, "separated" from the other factors in education and in much the same way as is the bloodstream of a living body from its other structures and functions. That bloodstream must be kept separate by the walls of the circulatory system. A break in them is disastrous. And yet the blood performs its living function only as it nourishes the whole body, giving health and vigor to all its activities. It is some such organic meaning as this which seeks expression in Jefferson's "wall of separation." But men who claim to follow him have transformed his figure into one of mechanical divisions and exclusions. They speak of his wall as if it were made of brick or stone or steel. By so doing they cut off our spiritual education from its proper field of influence. They make "private" a matter of supreme "public importance." And the effect of that operation corresponds closely to what would happen if we should substitute for the living tissues which enclose the cortex, or the nerves, or the blood, casings of impenetrable steel.[134]

These reasoned and enlightened thoughts of Dr. Meiklejohn were on formal sectarian religious instruction in public school classrooms. *A fortiori* they are pertinent to our present discussion and should encourage continuing reflections on the necessary immanence of spiritual values in the educational process, the equal rights of religion and nonreligion in education, and the significance of religion and nonreligion to the public interest. Most likely, no court test of federal aid to religious schools will be decided wholly within the context of past decisional law. We have been warned that a categorical affirmation (within these narrow confines) one way or another will work to self-deception and to the deception of others. The legal test, whether openly acknowledged or not, will be permeated—paradoxical as it may seem—by one or the other concepts of the educational process.

Plato in his *Republic* prescribed the educational training of the young auxiliaries who were to guard the Republic against the assaults of the enemy. Superior to the physical exercise of bravery upon the battlefield, he insisted, was an intellectual training that would resist the spiritual subversion of the civic values which the Athenians ought to hold dearer than life itself. Profession of loyalty alone will not long endure against the clever and cynical dialetic of the enemy or against the comforting blandishments that weaken loyalty to the City. There are many Americans who find that the high call of patriotism must be rooted deeply in a religious commitment to the civic duties of man to his country.

A study of American prisoners who succumbed to indoctrination by their Korean captors disclosed:

A really convinced religious person, be he a devout Catholic, or devout Orthodox Jew, or a member of a fundamentalist Protestant sect—whatever his religion, if it had been part of his whole life, if his family were organized along lines of religious training, such a man often was able to defend himself and his principles with this armament.

(From these things) it is tragically clear that the American educa-

327

tional system, fine as it is, is failing miserably in getting across the absolute fundamentals of survival in a tense and troubled international society.[135]

A neutral education, that is, one stripped of all theistic values, may not suffice to sustain a persevering loyalty to our country.

The question is sometimes asked why the churches have not been more effective in removing from their faithful racial bias and discrimination. But it requires no less than a complete spiritual effort to shatter the hardened prejudices of generations. Whatever prayerful hopes we all share for the social reconstruction of society will not be realized without the divine law of love and justice. Organizing peace on earth is a task too vast to rest, on the one hand, on a neutral educational process, and, on the other hand, on the expectation that church and home can fulfill these responsibilities without further assistance. To ask the parochial schools to immunize their students against any or all religious orientation in order to be eligible for federal assistance is to compound beyond all hope this moral problem that weighs heavily on us all.

For some time we have heard that religious formation is the task properly of the church and of the home. This is said so solemnly that it sounds at times as if that prerogative was in danger of violation. But the facts and requirements of law have so situated this law of human nature that both the natural right and duty of parents can no longer be viewed so exclusively. When the state compels parents by public law under pain of legal judgment to send their children for the greater part of the day, for five or six hours, away from their immediate control and influence to a publicly accredited school, then the duties of the parental prerogative are delegated and shared. And if

328

those teachers to whom the education of the children has been confided are approved by the duly constituted educational authorities of the state, then it is an affront to civilized thinking to withhold federal aid because the educational process is permeated with religious rather than with purely secular values. The religious clauses of the First Amendment are no less operative upon the federal government than they are upon the states, and the education of students in church-related schools is no less a governmental concern than the education of students in state schools. The education of any child in any school is part of national education and national interest. To deny any sort of federal aid to parochial school children and their parents because their schooling is infused with religious values and ideals is not governmental neutrality but penalty and ought to be acknowledged as such.

LAW, POLICY AND POLITICS

The constitutional permissiveness of federal aid for parochial schools has in the past decade increasingly received the reasoned support from some of the nation's most eminent jurists. And the categorical charge of illegality made in high places has not gone without critical and at times caustic commentary. Some jurists who have had second thoughts on the constitutional proscription of such aids have taken to a new position, now arguing that it would not be good policy to do so. At its best such an argument is not without serious appeal for the future of public schools to which no American should be insensible. However, grave concern for the future of independent schools should strike an equally responsive chord among our citizenry. But the interest for the future of public schools cloaks the

329

fear behind a truly democratic process, namely, the free choice of every parent if they were economically free to send their children to either a state or a religious school. Lately a remarkably novel approach to public policy has been enunciated. A non-Catholic spokesman bases his opposition to federal aid for parochial schools in the name of the freedom and in the best interest of the Catholic Church itself! This new approach augurs intriguing prospects for intercredal relations and dialogue. Perhaps similar non-Catholics might come to allow that what the Catholic Church teaches is good morality for public law will no longer be viewed as the arbitrary interference of Roman Catholicism with the liberty of conscience of non-Catholics.

Not infrequently we hear too the complaint that Protestants should not pay for the education of Catholics. One would suppose that taxes paid to the public treasury are not tagged with the religious affiliation of the taxpayer. But allowing for the moment such a specious reasoning, the obvious answer is that Catholics are simply asking for an equitable return of the taxes they pay into the public treasury. As one body of faithful they constitute a very large segment of taxpayers, just as they constitute one of the larger manpower resources for military service.

The only real public policy question before our national legislature is whether the church-related schools are in fact as well as *de jure* part of the American educational system and whether federal concern for educational needs and achievements should extend to them as well as to state schools. To date, no opponent of federal aid to parochial school children has dared deny that these church-related schools are truly educational institutions.

Lastly, we should not discount in these discussions of constitutionality and public policy the hard considerations

330

of politics as a motivation for much of the current thinking. It is not so much the religious orientation of church-related schools as the numerical preponderance of Catholic parochial schools which stirs in the opponents constitutional qualms of conscience.

THE CONSTITUTIONAL QUESTION

What may we find in Court decisions which shed any light on the constitutionality of federal aid to a religiously oriented education? At the outset we have to admit to the same limitations as any other polemicists on state, church and school studies. Discussants on both sides select statements favorable to their own cause and excerpted from the same Court opinions. There is no court ruling on this precise issue—federal aid to a religiously oriented education—so a review of cases customarily referred to in state, church and school controversies will be necessary. We will also ascertain the significance of a particular ruling and the implications of the Court opinions for our discussion.

In 1899, the Supreme Court upheld in a unanimous decision the constitutionality of federal appropriation of funds for the construction of a building and public recompense for services rendered to a hospital owned and administered by a Roman Catholic sisterhood. Presumably the Hill-Burton Hospital Survey and Construction Act, repeatedly renewed since its enactment is 1946, rests squarely upon the ruling in Bradfield that such federal subventions are not in violation of the no establishment clause. More than one billion dollars of federal money has been spent to improve and enlarge the facilities of public and privately owned hospitals under the provisions of this law. Of the total amount distributed to religiously affiliated hospitals about three-fourths has gone to Catholic hospitals. One could scarcely argue conclusively from Bradfield that what is upheld in the noneducational area—hospital services and facilities—would necessarily apply to the area of education.

Allowing for the obvious differences between educational and medical situations, nonetheless appropriations for an officially recognized public service (performed in an undoubtedly religious environment) might be favorably constructed into an analogous constitutional principle for gauging the public interest in an officially accredited schooling. Nor has any constitutional embarrassment come from acknowledging that some benefit does accrue to the private religious corporation and in certain instances the benefit to the fortunes of an affiliated educational institution of learning is almost incalculable.

In *Quick Bear v. Leupp,* 210 U.S. 50 (1908), the Supreme Court sustained the legality of a contract made at the request of the Indians to whom money was due as a matter of right, under treaty, for the payment of such money by the Commissioner of Indian Affairs for the support of Indian Catholic schools. Here is an arrangement somewhat similar to the Zorach case, which did not find the administrative cooperation between tax-salaried officials and the churches forbidden by the no establishment clause of the First Amendment.

The importance of *Meyer v. Nebraska,* 262 U.S. 390 (1923), is generally overshadowed by the momentous decision two years later of *Pierce v. Society of Sisters,* which in great part was prejudged by the former. In 1919 Nebraska passed a statute governing the curriculum of its primary schools which provided that:

332

1. No person, individually or as a teacher shall in any private, denominational, parochial or public school, teach any subject to any person in any language other than the English language.
2. Languages, other than the English language, may be taught as languages only after a pupil shall have attained and successfully passed the eighth grade as evidenced by a certificate of graduation issued by the county superintendent of the county in which the child resides.

Meyer, a teacher in a parochial school affiliated with the Zion Evangelical Lutheran Congregation, was convicted by the state for using as a text a German biblical history. The Supreme Court reversed the conviction which the Supreme Court of Nebraska had affirmed on appeal. The reasoning of the United States Supreme Court in reversing the conviction of Meyer and striking down the Nebraska statute casts light on the tangled issues of the secular subjects as taught in parochial schools. Summarily, it strikes down pedagogic dictation by the state in any school, public or private, without denying it its legitimate and proper supervisory role over school curriculum. The quotations from the decision of the Supreme Court of Nebraska which the United States Supreme Court reversed are remarkably illuminating on the very problem before us and give perspective to the Supreme Court's own reasoning:

On appeal to the Supreme Court of Nebraska, the conviction was affirmed, 107 Neb. 657, 187 N.W. 100. Parts of that opinion follow: ". . . it is clear that the reading from the textbook was not, at least, solely, a devotional exercise. It was no religious worship, nor was it, primarily, religious instruction in itself. The textbook contained biblical stories, but the subject-matter of the text, used for the purpose of studying a language, does not alone control, nor indicate the object of the study. The object was, as stated, 'to have the children learn so much German that they could be able to worship with their parents.' "

Defendant argues, then, that the teaching of the German language

333

from this book containing Bible stories served a double purpose, in that it both taught the children the German language and also familiarized them with the Bible stories, and that the teaching, so characterized, was religious instruction. It must be conceded, even under that argument, that two subjects were being taught—one the German language and one a religious text. If the law prohibited the teaching of the German language as a separate and distinct subject, then, certainly, the fact that such language was taught from a book containing religious matter could not act as a shield to the defendant. The teaching of the German language, as a subject, would come within the direct prohibition of the law, regardless of what text might be used in the book from which the language was taught. It does not appear that the German language is part of the religion of this church, nor that the services must, according to the particular faith, be rendered in German.

Though every individual is at liberty to adopt and follow with entire freedom whatsoever religious beliefs appeal to him that does not mean that he will be protected in every act which he does which is consistent with those beliefs, for when his acts either disturb the public peace, or corrupt the public morals, or otherwise become inimical to the public welfare of the state, the law may prohibit them, though they are done in pursuance of and in conformity with the religious scruples of the offending individual.[136]

The United States Supreme Court, speaking through Justice James McReynolds, ruled that the Nebraska statute as applied impaired the plaintiff's "right thus to teach and the right of parents to engage him so to instruct their children (which), we think, are within the liberty of the (Fourteenth) Amendment."

It is striking that the Court in speaking of the importance of education should also choose to quote the Ordinance of 1787, which conjoins knowledge with religion and morality for the benefit of government and society. The high tribunal apparently agrees with the analysis of the case by the Nebraska Supreme Court—that two distinct and separate purposes remain intact: the teaching and learning of the proscribed German language and the teaching of Bible stories. The two concurrent objectives are recognized as separable and separate and accordingly both the federal and state supreme courts see no constitutional right of religious liberty at issue before them. In a word, the German language is being taught even in the learning of Bible stories and it is on that precise issue that both court rulings are made. Apparently the intermingling of religious matter in the teaching of a secular subject—a modern language— does not diminish or impair the proficiency of teaching and learning the secular subject. In upholding the fundamental rights of teachers, parents and students, the high tribunal denies the state exclusive pedagogic regulation even under the guise of police power:

> Evidently the legislature has attempted materially to interfere with the calling of modern language teachers, with the opportunities of pupils to acquire knowledge, and with the power of parents to control the education of their own.[137]

The Court in forbidding pedagogic dictation does not deny the state its proper and legitimate supervisory role in education:

> The power of the State to compel attendance at some school and to make reasonable regulations for all schools, including a requirement that they shall give instructions in English, is not questioned. Nor has challenge been made of the State's power to prescribe a curriculum for institutions which it supports.[138]

Taking note of the laudable motive of promoting cultural assimilation in the schools the Court nonetheless expressed its aversion to the statute by reaching back to the Platonic and Spartan legal experiments that attempted to mold the minds of the young by removing them entirely from parental care and submitting the youngsters to an educational process entirely controlled by the state.

335

Pierce v. Society of Sisters, 268 U.S. 510 (1925)

It is not without reason then that constitutional lawyers see *Pierce v. Society of Sisters* prejudged in great part in the Meyer ruling. In the consideration of *Meyer v. Nebraska,* the Supreme Court was aided by a brief amicus by counsel representing various religious and educational institutions. The purpose was not to take sides in the cause before the Court but to bring to the Court's notice "certain contentions of the parties and the implications which they may be said to involve" in respect to the validity of another statute, the Oregon Compulsory Education Act. That statute was not then before the Court, but the brief pointed out that the controversy in regard to it was in danger of being prejudged in the principal case. In the course of the oral argument, Justice McReynolds asked about the "power of a State to require children to attend the public schools." Thereupon a considerable part of the discussion at the bar was devoted to that question, thus injecting the validity of the Oregon statute (the subject of the Pierce Case) into the argument on the Nebraska statute.

Though Pierce is generally cited for its celebrated pronouncements on the rights of parents, the issue before the Court was the proprietary right of private corporations to engage in schooling in fulfillment of state compulsory school attendance laws. Actually, Meyer and Pierce were decided on the bases of the rights of teachers and of parents:

> Corresponding to the right of control, it is the natural duty of the parent to give his children education suitable to their station in life; and nearly all the States, including Nebraska, enforce this obligation by compulsory laws.[139]

But in Pierce the proprietary right of private corporations, secular, military or religious, to engage in publicly accredited schooling requires as a corresponding term the parental right to choose schools other than those owned and controlled by the state. The basic reason for the existence of independent schools is that they are differentiated from state-owned schools by a principle of integration of school curriculum and by a system of discipline, while sharing in common with them a proficiency in required subjects and the inculcation of civic virtues. The effect of the Pierce ruling is to deny any priority or superiority before the law to the state to compel parents to choose their schools.

> The fundamental theory of liberty upon which all governments in this Union repose excludes any general power of the State to standardize its children by forcing them to accept instruction from public schools only. The child is not the mere creature of the State; those who nurture him and direct his destiny have the right, coupled with the high duty, to recognize and prepare him for additional obligations.[140]

While there is no explicit discussion of a principle of integration in the school curriculum the Court does not seem to be unmindful of it when it states that the reason parents may choose an accredited education in an independent school is that in the judgment of the parents such schooling is ordained to assist the student for "his destiny" and "additional obligation" to those presumably provided for in the state-owned schools. The profound significance of the Pierce ruling is that the proprietary right of independent schools to operate is related to the prime moral obligations of parents to regulate the moral-educational process of their children without denying the state a supervisory role and without removing from the independent schools their obligations to the public welfare. In a word, the Court is not merely saying that a division of labor is legitimate and that the state need not have an exclusive role in education and that other agencies besides the state may be equally competent to educate the young. Rather, it relates the proprietary right of independent schools and of the parents of the school children to choose an educational process which not only serves the public welfare but in addition teaches subjects besides those required for civic duties. It denies the state an exclusive role in education because it refuses to acknowledge that there is only one standard educational process.

While it is true that Pierce was decided a few days before the guarantees of the First Amendment were for the first time transferred to the states through the Fourteenth Amendment, its significance for federal legislation on national education is not without some meaning even after Everson. Surely if the Court upholds the right and the competence of a private corporation to establish independent schools worthy of official approval, it admits to the comprehensive perspective that education of the children of the nation depends on a variety of accredited schools. We shall not, however, encounter the real stumbling block until we come to the Everson case, when the Court construes no establishment to mean no aid from federal and state governments.

Cochran v. Board of Education, 281 U.S. 370 (1930)

In 1930 the use of public funds to furnish nonsectarian textbooks to pupils in Louisiana parochial schools was sustained. The Supreme Court noted that the Louisiana statute referred to "school children of the State" without any qualifying phrase narrowing the beneficiaries only to those attending state-owned schools. The Court rejected the contention of the appellant that under the Fourteenth

Amendment taxation for the purchase of schoolbooks constituted the use of public property for a private purpose. "The purpose is said to be to aid private, religious, sectarian, and other schools not embraced in the public educational system of the State by furnishing textbooks free to the children attending such private schools." To this objection the Court replied:

> What the statutes contemplate is that the same books that are furnished children attending public schools shall be furnished to children in private schools.
>
> Viewing the statute as having the effect thus attributed to it, we can not doubt that the taxing power of the State is exerted for a public purpose. The legislation does not segregate private schools, or their pupils, as its beneficiaries or attempt to interfere with any matters of exclusively private concern. Its interest is education, broadly; its method, comprehensive. Individual interests are aided only as the common interest is safeguarded.[141]

What light, if any, does Cochran cast upon the argument of permeability as championed by LaNoue? While it is true, as the Court noted, that the textbooks are not religious books, the obvious fact could not possibly escape the Court anymore than it did the appellant—the very fact which LaNoue himself lists among the factors of permeability in parochial schools—namely, the religious confessions of the schools, the religious garb of the teachers, the religious symbols and exercises held in these schools; in a word, the general religious orientation of life-values in the educational process of private church-schools. Despite or in welcome acknowledgement of this broad fact, the extension of an educational facility for the promotion of an objective sought by the statutory provision was upheld to be for a public purpose. True, the religious clauses of the First Amendment were not brought to bear upon the issue since the plaintiff's

339

challenge of constitutionality of state action did not require the Court to do so. But the broad fact and the reason for church-related schools, the religious integration of school curriculum, was not on that account ignored by the Court:

> It is also true that the sectarian schools, which some of the children attend, instruct their pupils in religion, and books are used for that purpose, but one may search diligently the acts, though without result, in an effort to find anything to the effect that it is the purpose of the state to furnish religious books for the use of such children . . . What the statutes contemplate is that the same books that are furnished children attending public schools shall be furnished to children attending private schools. This is the only practical way of interpreting and executing the statutes, and this is what the state board of education is doing. Among these books, naturally, none is to be inspected, adapted to religious instruction.

The Court upheld the extension of the same educational facility, textbooks, nonreligious in themselves, to state and independent schools without trying to insulate it constitutionally from the religious permeation of the school curriculum or, more improbably still, immunize it from the teachers' use of it. It seemed to be the Court's understanding that the Louisiana legislature's intent could equally be realized in all the state schools, public and church-related, regardless of the ethos permeating the general school curriculum. The use by religious minded teachers of a neutral educational facility would not transform that instrumentality into a religious object or the subject matter into a theological science. The Cochran opinion was not unaware that parochial schools are an integral part of the Catholic Church's intellectual and spiritual apostolate, the formation of a Christian way of life. It would not on that account hold with the plaintiff that a private interest rather than a public purpose was being served.

The purpose is said to be to aid private, religious, sectarian, and other schools not embraced in the public educational system of the State by furnishing textbooks free to the children attending private schools.

Reaffirming what Pierce had established *de jure*—the duality of national education—it concluded:

Viewing the statute as having the effect thus attributed to it, we cannot doubt that the taxing power of the State is exerted for a public purpose. The legislation does not segregate private schools, or their pupils, as its beneficiaries or attempt to interfere with any matters of exclusively private concern. Its interest is education broadly; its method, comprehensive. Individual interests are aided only as the common interest is safeguarded.

The Court in a word refused to act as a supreme national pedagogue that would define the educational process narrowly, and therefore set down neither methods of instruction nor the manner of the use of state provided facilities. It is the only practical posture of legal adjudication that the Court can take within its constitutionally defined competence and jurisdiction. State aid for a public interest is not nullified simply because the educational process is committed to religious orientation. Some state legislatures continue to provide textbooks to students schooled in an environment permeated by religious influence and values. And since the Cochran ruling seems fairly well entrenched in American constitutional law, perhaps a convincing analogy can be drawn between the two government-provided educational instrumentalities.

Everson v. Board of Education, 330 U.S. 1 (1947)

In Everson the Court, speaking through Justice Black, upheld the constitutionality of a New Jersey statute which provided at public cost free bus transportation to school children including, by explicit mention, children attending Catholic parochial schools. The Court took cognizance of the fact that in making available free bus transportation to parochial school children, the church-related school undoubtedly was assured of school children whose parents might otherwise send them to a public school.

It is undoubtedly true that by the New Jersey program children are helped to get to church schools. There is even the possibility that some of the children might not be sent to the church schools if the parents were compelled to pay their children's bus fares out of their own pockets when transportation to a public school would have been paid for by the State.[142]

The Court justified this child-benefit provision on the premise that the education provided by the church school included, besides formal religious instructions, the study of secular subjects.

It is much too late to argue that legislation intended to facilitate the opportunity of children to get a secular education serves no public purpose.[143]

And the Court insisted that the validity of such a presumption can rest on an empirical test.

This Court has said that parents may in the discharge of their duty under state compulsory education laws, send their children to a religious rather than a public school, if the school meets the secular educational requirements which the state has power to impose.[144]

In Everson, for the first time in American constitutional history, the Court chose to acknowledge beyond the strict requirements of the issue before the appellant's contention that the no establishment clause forbade any governmental aid to religion.

No tax in any amount, large or small, can be levied to support any religious activities or institutions, whatever they may be called, or whatever form they may adopt to teach or practice religion.[145]

342

Be that as it may, this absolute proscription of aid must not be isolated from the specific ruling of the Everson case which acknowledges some undoubted aid to the church school, or be read apart from the paragraph that follows it:

On the other hand, other language of the amendment commands that New Jersey cannot hamper its citizens in the free exercise of their own religion. Consequently, it cannot exclude individual Catholics, Lutherans, Mohammedans, Baptists, Jews, Methodists, Nonbelievers, Presbyterians, or the members of any other faith, *because of their faith, or lack of it* (italics by the Court) from receiving the benefits of public welfare legislation. While we do not mean to intimate that a state could not provide transportation only to children attending public schools, we must be careful, in protecting the citizens of New Jersey against state-established churches, to be sure that we do not inadvertently prohibit New Jersey from extending its general state law benefits to all its citizens without regard to their religious belief.[146]

We have elsewhere maintained that an exclusionary rule for governmental benefactions based on religious profession ought to raise substantive constitutional questions about the legal consequences attendant upon the exercise of religious liberty. And the only practical way of interpreting and executing legislative statutes reaching to a public interest and service without prejudice to religious liberty is the empirical test of ascertaining whether secular aspects and functions of nontheological studies which the government has a direct interest in promoting are in fact proficiently and competently realized to the public benefit. Such an empirical device or measurement can meet the impartial requirement of Justice Black's "because of faith, or lack of it."

One cannot minimize the difficulties engendered by the absolute no aid formula, especially in light of the very decisions in which the Court upheld an undeniable aid to

343

religion but also because of the great variety of governmental aids to religious life and institutions which the federal and state governments are still supporting with enormous financial outlay. Yet, despite the ambiguities which interpose between the affirmative decisions of the Pierce-Cochran-Everson and some absolutist pronouncements, friendly and unfriendly polemicists of the constitutionality of federal aid to parochial schools see a constructive development that would seem to favor it.

Leo Pfeffer, certainly a principal opponent of federal aid to church-related schools, has admitted:

> When the Everson decision is coupled with the Cochran decision they lead logically to the conclusion that the state may, notwithstanding the First Amendment, finance practically every aspect of parochial education, with the exception of such comparatively minor items as the proportionate salaries of teachers while they teach the catechism.[147]

Professor Paul Kauper, who has argued for the constitutional permissibility of federal aid to parochial schools, has established a reasonable coherence between court decisions and legislative practices.

> But to distinguish on principle from this type of benefit (auxiliary) and the more substantial benefits that would accrue from subsidies to pay teachers' salaries or to provide educational facilities presents difficulties, particularly when it is noted that in the Everson case the Court emphasized that the state imposed a duty on all parents to send their children to some school and that the parochial school in question met secular educational standards fixed by the state. By hypothesis the school building and the instruction in secular courses also meet the state's requirements. When we add to this that education is appropriately a function of both government and religion, the question may well be raised whether the same considerations that govern the problems of bus transportation costs and textbooks, as well as the question of public grants to hospitals under religious

344

auspices, do not point to the conclusion, whatever different conclusions may be reached under state constitutions, that the First Amendment, in conjunction with the Fourteenth, does not stand in the way of governmental assistance for parochial schools.[148]

If education required by state law may competently take place in church-related schools (Pierce), and if nontheological textbooks provided by state funds may be used in religious schools (Cochran), and if the state may constitutionally finance the bus transportation of parochial school children to these schools, would not a protest directed against the religious permeation of the educational process have its hidden roots in a broad opposition to all the foregoing provisions?

PUBLIC SCHOOLS AND RELIGIOUS INSTRUCTIONS

McCollum and Zorach

The McCollum ruling of 1948 struck down the Champaign religious instruction program on school premises during a school hour. The Court, which prides itself on quoting Jefferson and Madison, has not, however, placed these men in precise constitutional focus. Jefferson was one of the earliest advocates of formal religious worship and religious instruction at the State University of Virginia. What is not usually noted is that ex-President Madison was one of the commissioners who concurred with Jefferson's educational plan of 1822. Believers were invited to establish religious schools on the University confines. University facilities for religious worship and instruction were readily made available, and university regulations were modified to give easy access to regular students and divinity students benefits each might seek from other disciplines. "Such an arrangement would complete the circle of the useful sciences embraced by this institution, and would fill the chasm now existing, on principles which leave inviolate the constitutional freedom of religion, the most inalienable and sacred of all human rights . . ." As for the elementary schools Jefferson was opposed to religious instruction or exercises "inconsistent with the tenets of any religious sect or denomination" and no more.

Some educators have used this text to justify in the name of Jefferson the exorcism of every religious influence in state elementary schools. The distinction between the higher and lower levels relating to religious instruction and exercises was intended by Jefferson to stress the necessity of safeguarding inviolable the religious conscience of the minor against indoctrination to an alien confession. This was not a negative action of total abstention from all religious influence but a positive implementation, a contrivance of circumstances to ensure the free exercise of religious expression. The chasm in a totally nonreligious elementary education would be no less forbidding to Jefferson than it would be in the higher institutions of learning. The mutual accommodations would from the very nature of the case be decidedly different.

Only within the concept of an educational process necessarily related to the higher duties of conscience can the insistence of a dismissed-time and/or released-time program for religious instruction make any sense. Why must religious instruction in one's own creed take place during a school hour? Parents who send their children to state schools are faced with a dilemma. They do not, obviously, want a single sectarian faith taught in public schools to all. On the other hand, an education which is immunized against every

346

spiritual and religious grounding is defective and without any of the ultimate motivations so necessary to give direction and inspiration to the formation of responsible conduct. Whether or not dismissed-time or released-time religious programs effectively satisfy this moral expectation, many American communities insist on the official, that is, legal affirmation of the relevance of religious life to the educational process. It is also a frank if discouraging admission of the insufficiency of the home and church to adequately cope with this problem when children have to spend the greater part of the day away from both by requirement of state compulsory school attendance laws.

McCollum did not allow the use of public classrooms for religious instructions even though no additional public expenditures were thereby incurred. Zorach permitted tax-salaried public school officials to cooperate with the released-time program conducted away from school property. McCollum and Zorach did, however, suggest some favorable considerations to the permeation discussion. In released-time religious instruction programs a local community under permissive official ruling wants the public schooling—caught between conflicting claims of rights and conscience—to be related to religious training. It may be that, as we have already noted, this sort of relationship may prove to be very tenuous, but its symbolic significance is profound. It is rooted in an ancient tradition which first found official expression in Article III of the Northwest Ordinance of 1787. The conviction that religious instructions are part of an integral education is no less Jeffersonian than his metaphor of the wall of separation. This underlying significance of the released-time program was not lost upon Justice Felix Frankfurter, who in his dissenting opinion noted:

347

The Court tells us that in the maintenance of its public schools "(the State government) can close its doors or suspend its operations" so that its citizens may be free for religious devotions or instruction. If that were the issue, it would not rise to the dignity of a constitutional controversy. Of course, a State may provide that the classes in its schools shall be dismissed, for any reason, or no reason, on fixed days, or for special occasions. The essence of this case is that the school system did not "close its doors" and did not "suspend its operations." There is all the difference in the world between letting the children out of school and letting some of them out of school into religious classes. If everyone is free to make what use he will of time wholly unconnected from schooling required by law—those who wish sectarian instruction devoting it to that purpose, those who have ethical instruction at home, to that, those who study music, to that, then of course there is no conflict with the Fourteenth Amendment. The pith of the case is that formalized religious instruction is substituted for other school activity which those who do not participate in the released-time program are compelled to attend.[149]

Justice Douglas' opinion takes approving cognizance of the same issue but within a broader scope:

When the state encourages religious instruction or cooperates with religious authorities by adjusting the schedule of public events to sectarian needs, it follows the best of our traditions. For it then respects the religious nature of our people and accommodates the public service to their spiritual needs. To hold that it may not would be to find in the Constitution a requirement that the government show a callous indifference to religious groups.[150]

Strictly speaking, only Bradfield, Cochran and Everson are directly relevant to the question of governmental provision of financial aid to church-related schools. The safe assumption is that it should not be startling news to the Court or anyone else that the whole curriculum in a church school is permeated by religion. Evidently the Court is equally aware that the secular education which the public interest requires can be fulfilled in a religiously integrated educational process.

348

It is much too late to argue that legislation intended to facilitate the opportunity of children to get a secular education serves no public purpose (*Everson v. Board of Education,* 330 U.S. 7 1947).

The Sunday closing law cases, the Maryland public notary case, and the prayer case offer fruitful opportunities of further reflections which while not directly pertinent are broadly relevant to the question of benefit through governmental action to religion in education.

McGowan v. Maryland, 366 U.S. 420 (1961)

All of the Court opinions in this and other blue law cases admitted the religious origin of the Sunday day of rest. But in each instance the Court majority opinion, even while aware that some state blue laws still literally refer to the Lord's day, held to the valid secular purpose which was said to emerge from and to prevail apart from its religious origins: "The proponents of Sunday closing legislation are no longer exclusively representatives of religious interests." There is no denial of the obvious fact, on the part of the Court, that there is here an intermingling of secular objectives and religious advantages partial to Christians. But the Court opinion refuses to allow that such concurrence of benefits, secular and religious, nullifies the valid secular purpose which government has a right and duty to secure.

However, it is equally true that the 'Establishment Clause' does not bar federal or state regulation of conduct whose reason or effect merely happens to coincide or harmonize with the tenets of some or all religions. In many instances, the Congress or state legislatures conclude that the general welfare of society, wholly apart from any religious considerations, demands such regulation . . . (*McGowan v. Maryland,* 366 U.S. 420, 422 (1961)).

Sunday closing laws, like those before us, have become part and parcel of this great governmental concern wholly apart from their original purposes or connotations. The present purpose and effect of most of them is to provide a uniform day of rest for all citizens; the fact that this day is Sunday, a day of particular significance for the dominant Christian sects, does not bar the State from achieving its secular goals. To say that the States cannot prescribe Sunday as a day of rest for these purposes solely because centuries ago such laws had their genesis in religion would give constitutional interpretation of hostility to the public welfare rather than one of mere separation of church and state.

One may reflect in similar terms upon an analogous situation, the intermingling of secular functions and religious aspects of parochial school education, although this will depend for the most part on the recognition by the state educational authorities of a secular goal of education in the curriculum in which the state has a substantive interest.

Justice Frankfurter, who had dissented in Everson, significantly relates his concurring opinion in the Sunday law cases to the Everson ruling.

(T)his Court held in the Everson case that expenditures of public funds to assure that children attending every kind of school enjoy the relative security of buses, rather than being left to walk or hitch-hike, is not an unconstitutional "establishment," even though such an expenditure may cause some children to go to parochial schools who would not otherwise have gone. The close division of the Court in Everson serves to show what nice questions are involved in applying to particular governmental action the proposition, undeniable in the abstract, that not every regulation some of whose practical effects may facilitate the observance of a religion by its adherents affronts the requirement of church-state separation (336 U.S. 467).

Along with the issues raised by the appellants under the religious clauses of the First Amendment was the economic argument, namely, the economic disadvantage claimed by Sabbatarians for observing their day of rest from religious motives and having to close their business shops on Sunday

350

under compulsion of state blue laws. Both the Chief Justice and Justice Frankfurter, in the latter's separate concurring opinion, took full cognizance of the economic argument raised by the Sabbatarians and held that—in the absence of a reasonable alternative that is within the competency of the legislature in determining the economic disadvantage incurred in the personal observance of religious obligations which do not coincide with the valid secular goal—it does not thereby taint the constitutionality of the statute. As Chief Justice Warren expressed it:

> If the state regulates conduct by enacting a general law within its power, the purpose and effect of which is to advance the state's secular goals, the statute is valid despite its indirect burden on religious observance unless a state may accomplish its purpose by means which do not impose such a burden.

Justice Frankfurter, after repeatedly stressing that in some activities public and religious interests "overlap" and "interplay" and that the history of blue laws have made them "the vehicle of mixed and complicated aspirations," asks when a benefit to religion may be allowable when there is an intermingling of religion and civic objectives. It is permissible, he answers, only when there is no other alternative of realizing the secular goals:

> Or if the statute furthers both secular and religious ends unnecessary to the effectuation of the secular ends alone—where the same secular ends could equally be attained by means which do not have consequences for promotion of religion—the statute cannot stand . . . The close division of the Court in Everson serves to show what nice questions are involved in applying particular governmental action the proposition, undeniable in the abstract that not every regulation some of whose practical effects may facilitate the observance of a religion by its adherents affronts the requirement of church-state separation.

351

Considered either negatively as the indirect burden that may be suffered following a religious conscience, or positively as an indirect benefit that may accrue to religion because of a valid secular purpose, the benefit is constitutionally permissible if there is no alternate means of effectuating the civil objectives just as well.[151]

Proponents of federal aid to education on the lower levels have argued that the exclusion of the parochial schools from sharing in governmental aid would place them in such a disadvantage against the enormous resources of the federal government that the educational facilities of the parochial schools might in comparison be reduced to a level of inferiority that could prove detrimental to the education provided by these schools. Has the government no alternate means of avoiding this alleged damage to private schools? One may push the question further and ask whether it is in the national interest to bring about, however indirectly, this imbalance. The root question, however, one that must be asked of the government, is what precisely is the status of parochial schools, apart from their constitutional right to educate in fulfillment of state educational requirements, in the comprehensive national educational program? Can they and do they contribute to the national education of the nation and can the government rely upon them as well as upon state-owned schools for its educational programs?[152]

The underlying import of the economic aspect of the Sunday law cases is that the state is obligated to hold in check the free play of open market competition (even on the claim of religious conscience) if in effect it would obstruct or frustrate a valid secular goal. Whether or not the federal government may be economically unconcerned about the educational facilities of approximately six million

352

parochial school children is a question that ought not to be settled out of hand without first determining their place in the scheme of the national interest.

In coming to a decision, the Congress first ought to make this frank confrontation of the crucial issue. Apart from the vast economic consideration is the evaluation of the educational process itself. Permeation means intermingled objectives—value judgments, motives, religious and secular aspects of the science studies. May the national legislature any more than the Courts choose only one value—inculcation against the others? Or, may it allow any value integration which is not offensive to the communal welfare, perhaps even tributary as a spiritual force, and which preserves intact the secular aspects and functions of the educational process which the public interest requires? If the indefectability of the secular studies are assured, then governmental aid ought not to be interdicted because of a religious consequence. The exercise of religious liberty should be no less inviolable in education and free of governmental prejudices and civil disabilities than are other public endeavors and enterprises—even more so if its educational functions are officially accredited and in fulfillment of state law requirements.

The best that may be derived from the study of court decisions that can reasonably be brought to bear on the constitutionality of federal aid to a religiously oriented public service in education are suppositional premises and inferential conclusions that are somehow lodged in the specific ruling and at other times logically implied in general statements of the Court opinions. These are the opportunities and uncertainties with which both sides of the discussants are faced. There has been as yet no direct raising of the constitutional issue of federal aid to a religiously orientated education before the Supreme Court. The problem is not in any manner helped by the contrary rulings of state courts on textbooks and bus transportation and is even further complicated by the fact that the Supreme Court has refused to review, with apparent disregard of the specific Everson ruling, the state proscriptive decisions which were openly based on the Everson opinion. Reluctantly both sides will have to admit that the hope for clarity must in great part rely on intelligent reasoning about law and not, as might have been expected, on the firm and consistent direction which law should provide for a rational discussion of unresolved constitutional issues. And this uncertainty is further compounded by doubts as to the extent of a logical thrust which is motivated more by public policy than by the exigencies of law itself.

Of the cases customarily cited, only three are directly relevant to the precise use of some benefit accruing to the private religious institution through governmental financing. Of these, Bradfield sustained the constitutionality of governmental funds supporting a private service in fulfilling a public need in a noneducational area. Permeability, that is, the presence and therefore the potential influence of religion in a hospital service, is in the general environment of a hospital conducted by Catholic sisters and certainly controlling in the permissible surgeries. Cochran upheld the constitutionality of state provision of nonsectarian books. Here too the general religious environment, the religious factors of the pedagogy that one would expect to prevail in parochial schools, the answers to moral and religious questions that may at times arise in the teaching of secular subjects, are undeniable suppositions of the situation of the Cochran case. In fact, the contention of the appellants that a private purpose and not a public one was being aided was based in great part on the grounds that these schools were religious and sectarian. While it is true that the religious clauses of the First Amendment were not involved, the reasonable supposition of permeability did not deter the Court from acknowledging that a public purpose and not a purely private interest was being fulfilled. The appellant did argue, however, that under the Fourteenth Amendment "taxation for the purchase of school books constituted a taking of private property for a private purpose," with particular notice taken that the ownership was "religious, sectarian." In Everson the supposition of a religious permeation of the parochial school curriculum might reasonably be conjectured though it was certainly not the precise issue before the Court or even explicitly noted by the Court, although Justice Black acknowledged that undoubtedly some benefit accrued to the private interest of the religious school.

From the cases which do not deal with the appropriation of tax funds for public services rendered by religious agencies, some inferences may be drawn not unfavorable to the permeation issue. Meyer denied to a state the absolute power to prescribe the school curriculum and Pierce upheld the proprietary right and competency of private corporations to share in the responsibilities and objectives of public schooling, whether they are integrated around military disciplines or religious confessions. In McCollum and Zorach the correlation of religious instruction to the public school educational process during a school hour was not ruled out of hand but was made to turn in part on the direct involvement of governmental, that is, tax-supported officials and facilities with exclusively formal theological indoctrination. Now if it is in accordance with the best traditions of our country, as Zorach held, to accommodate public service to the spiritual needs of school children, why should it be constitutionally offensive to share in a national educational program if the church schools, besides teaching religious doctrine in their catechetical courses, also teach secular subjects with relevance to their creed without impairing the secular aspects and functions of the nontheological courses? The educational problematic is a stubborn one. Not every public service or secular objective can be rendered by legal fiat impervious to religious values or every academic query insulated against value judgments to which the human conscience bears correspondence. The ultimate question is whether we may rightly expect the Court to have the competence and jurisdiction *ex banco* to favor one set of principles of educational integration against another. The Court has on occasion disowned such a prerogative to any other branch of government and is not likely to claim it for itself.

If there is any fixed star in our constitutional constellation, it is that no official, high or petty, can prescribe what shall be orthodox in politics, nationalism, religion or other matters of opinion. . . . (*West Virginia State Board of Education v. Barnette*, 319 U.S. 624, 642 1943).

The prejudice which is engendered by the necessities of an apologia for the religious permeation in church schools would not suffer from its defensive stance if parents who are constrained by economic disabilities to send their children for moral and intellectual development to public schools were to raise similar questions of conscience (within the terms of the religious clauses of the First Amendment) about the presence or calculated absence of spiritual values in the classroom. In recent days voices have been raised about the ethnic and cultural imbalance of several public school textbooks. Parents might ask, for example, whether

356

the religious heritage of America as embodied in basic national documents is studied with an emphasis proportionate to their importance; or on what ultimate moral principles are civic duties and social responsibilities grounded—on a moral law or on prevailing mores, on general consensus or the Divine Commandments. What answers are given to questions about the legitimate functions of human sex life? Professional historians of England and the United States are presently engaged in a joint project financed by the Ford Foundation and Britain's Nuffield Trust to rewrite Anglo-American history with the intent of removing the nationalistic biases and misrepresentations upon which the good relations between the two countries rest with reserved mutual suspicions. Similar readjustments might be made about American colonial history. In Parkman's often-quoted phrase, "Not a bay was turned nor a river entered but a Jesuit led the way." The enormous civilizing work as well as the religious apostolate of the Franciscan missionaries is recorded but dimly in histories which focus almost exclusively on the Plymouth landing. As noted above, the Catholic contribution to religious liberty in America, beginning with the Catholic colony of Maryland and continuing to this day, receives scarcely more than a brief notice of Lord Baltimore's Act of Toleration. The conventional portrayal of the Negro as a dependent, servile creature must give way to the real contribution of the Negro to American culture. His struggle for freedom must be viewed as a human struggle of men and therefore a profound chapter in the American history of civil liberty. These and so many other questions on the spiritual formation of students in public schools may point to the impossibility of neutrality in the educational process of public schooling.

In *Torcaso v. Watkins*, 367 U.S. 982 (1963), the right

357

of a citizen to become a notary public without being required by law to make a public declaration of belief in God was upheld. It would have been more felicitous had the Court not subsumed in a footnote, in an exercise of logical positivism, nontheistic beliefs into the meaning of religion in the First Amendment. The Court could have adequately rested its ruling on the Anglo-American tradition of law that the right to belief is a right to an internal domain of absolute inviolability, into which inner sanctum neither the law may require nor the coercive power of government force its disclosures. However, what does emerge from Torcaso for the purpose of our discussion is that no matter what the faith or lack of faith (Everson), the public service of a public office (whether correspondent to the official's conscience or not) must be in accord with the requirements of the duties of that office. If the conscience, religious or not, is tributary to or at least in conformity with the civic virtues of public office, the law will not inquire further to ask from what theological grounds such conduct is based.

The particulars of Torcaso mark it off by some distance from questions of federal aid to religiously integrated education. But it does suggest further reflections on the public benefit that the government expects and empirically ascertains in an educational process permeated by ultimates. It also raises the correlative consideration of whether the equality of religious liberty, whether theistic or nontheistic, should not ensure an equality of treatment when confronted by governmental benefactions. The Maryland state courts in upholding the constitutional requirement had relied on the common law attitude toward atheists as the reasonable basis for excluding the appellant from the office of notary public. The state court determined that the distinction between believers and nonbelievers as a security for good conduct

358

in office had not become so devoid of meaning that to adopt it would be arbitrary. The common law equated the ungodly with the untrustworthy. It was supposed, as Professor John Henry Wigmore has suggested, that the sanction of divine retribution for false swearing might add a stimulus to truthfulness. While it may be cynical to suggest that many good men are not deterred from perjury because of moral dictates, it seems equally unreasonable to restrict a facility for veracity to the believer. The equation of honesty with belief must in our day give way to the more conclusive evidence of the actual performance of civic duties.

A line of reasoning on the permeation issue might be constructed from Torcaso in this fashion: whether the agent of a public requirement is motivated by theistic or nontheistic belief, whether he invests his work with moral or theological virtues, the services he renders must be judged on their own merits and by the canons properly applicable to a specific performance. Similarly, one may reason, whatever the spiritual permeation of an educational process—secular humanism, ethical culturism, military discipline, theism, Christianity—the educational objectives in which the state has a public interest must be measured and evaluated by tests proper to the various intellectual disciplines. Has a student learned to spell, read, multiply? Does he learn in biology and history what the state educational authorities require of every schooling? In this wise the religious permeation of an accredited school would not disqualify it from participating in a national program for the improvement of education.

When the Court said in *Watson v. Jones*, "The law knows no heresy, is committed to the establishment of no religion, the support of no dogma," it did not mean to say that public law is indifferent to heresy or dogma. The First Amendment embraces two concepts, "freedom to believe and freedom to act. The first is absolute but, in the nature of things, the second cannot be" (*Cantwell v. Connecticut*). ". . . In every case the power to regulate must be so exercised as not, in attaining a permissible end, unduly to infringe the protected liberty." Since from the very nature of things not every public service and benefit is impervious to spiritual and religious values, public law must direct itself to the realization of its own interest whether or not its objectives and motives are intertwined with the objectives and motives of private interest, and whether or not that private agency is religiously inspired. The public good is itself definable and its efficacy is not impaired, perhaps even enhanced, by being invested with religious insights. On this basis, a good start can be made for the substantive construction of a principle of neutrality, with no prejudice to the rights of any conscience. Public law, moreover, must be interested in the outward behavior of religious belief. It does not disdain to call upon the religious faiths for support of its own secular programs in times of peace and war. It has an interest in the ulterior motivation that religious life can provide for the conduct that is conducive to the harmonious peace and tranquil order of the commonwealth. In the crucial hour for the advancement of civil rights, public law looks to religious authorities and creeds to enlighten their faithful who are blinded by social prejudices which obstruct the free exercise of civil liberties and bring discord and violence to fellow citizens. If public law can turn to religious faiths for support of its own civic programs and for a resolution of many of its complex problems, then it ought not look askance upon an educational process which fuses the spiritual life of the student with his learning. Man can-

360

not be departmentalized by requirements of law and then be asked to conjoin, supposedly, his dual, concurrent lives of citizen and believer whenever the national benefit requires it. In a word, the law and government are not neutral and indifferent to the motivations provided in an accredited schooling.

When in Meyer and Pierce the Court determined that parents have the right and the high duty of nurturing and educating their children for additional obligations, and reaffirmed in *Prince v. Massachusetts* the primary right of parental control of education, it was not simply denying exclusive monopoly to the state but rather affirming that both government and the church (parents) have a dual role in the educational process. The state sets its own requirements relative to its own interest. This interest remains indefectible, although subject to an empirical verification if necessary, when inspired by religious beliefs. There are very many among us who hold that a religiously oriented education is highly beneficial to the common purpose and tributary to the spiritual resources of the American community. *Pro Deo et Patriae* is the proud calling of the parochial schools.

There have been circumstances wherein the state has interfered in order to see that children are not taught beliefs at variance with the temporal welfare of the community. The state, for instance, can remove children from the custody of parents who refuse to give them the medical care, on religious grounds, which is normally taken for granted in our country. True, this is not strictly an interference with the rights of parents to teach their children. It is more an interference with the supposed right of parents to deal with their child according to their religious faith. But the underlying truth cannot be stressed too strongly,

361

namely, that public law is far from indifferent to the public effects of religious belief. If an educational process conforms to officially prescribed standards, if students learn to read, spell or multiply to the proficiency required by state educational officials, then the public interest has been met. The profound significance of Torcaso is the insistence that the government look to the service performed and not to the religious confession or lack of it. The no aid formula should also be considered in the context of the particular situation of Torcaso; no preferential status of eligibility for sharing in a public service should be based on religious grounds. Thereby an equality of opportunity is provided without prejudice to rights of conscience.

Admittedly, there are substantial points of disparity between Torcaso and the constitutional question of federal aid to education. In the disbursement of public financial benefactions, a sound public policy may justifiably restrict its subsidies. Because privately owned public services in industry and commerce, such as agriculture and airlines and railroads, may require governmental subsidies to sustain the public service, it does not follow that every other privately owned and controlled public service must equally be a recipient of governmental subventions. The controlling consideration is the substantive national interest. And so the original question must again be asked: are parochial schools part of national education, and should they share in federal programs for the advancement and improvement of educational facilities because they are part of the national interest?

The correspondence of probity and godliness presupposed by the common law rule was neither denied nor affirmed in Torcaso. What the court implicitly affirmed was that the test of office should be actual performance, not a prior profession of a way of life. Torcaso seems to reinforce the impartiality which Everson insisted upon in a passage less frequently quoted than the preceding passage on "no aid to religion." An interpretation that would see in Torcaso a public law disengaged from the influence and consequents of religious life—now broadly defined as a conscientious commitment to ultimates—would ascribe to the Court a negative neutrality not borne out by the specifics of the case. What Torcaso seems to say is that public service must be validated on its own merits without prejudice to the rights of conscience.

Engel v. Vitale and the Schempp and Murray rulings deal with religious exercises, Bible reading and prayer in circumstances of conflicting claims of religious liberty, religious pluralism and the alleged state support of those who choose as against those who do not. These cases highlight the need for giving positive substantive meaning to that neutrality which the Court "in accordance with the best of our traditions" may develop more constructively by the impartial formula of equal treatment as dictated by public need.

REFLECTIONS AND CONSIDERATIONS

The discussion of value permeability in school curriculum must take place within the broader dimensions of national education. We must first ascertain what a schooling must provide to satisfy the national needs and expectations of education or, in other words, how education can be defined for the public interest so that the various schools, state, private, church-related, may be measured against those objectives. The Pierce ruling does not simply say that military and religious schools may also exist by sanction of the state.

Rather, its import is that public law legitimizes what the Courts acknowledge to be the prior and primary rights of parents to direct the education of their children, a right that inheres in the very nature and vocation of parenthood (*Prince v. Massachusetts*), although subject, of course, to the supervisory role of the state. The national Congress must squarely confront the question of the place and role of church schools in the national education. Are they an integral part of a dual system of education or not? It will not do to acknowledge only their legal status under the Pierce ruling—namely, their right to exist in fulfillment of state compulsory school attendance laws. The import and underlying significance of Pierce must be fully explored and weighed; that is, are all publicly accredited schools that comply with officially prescribed standards of teaching, curriculum and facilities fulfilling the educational needs of the nation? By virtue of the end result of their educational process are they all equally eligible to participate in some way in a federal program for the advance and promotion of the nation's educational facilities?

The second consideration which seems to obstruct rational thinking about federal aid to schools is how absolute is the no aid to religion formula in the light of Bradfield, Pierce, Cochran, and Everson. In each of these Court determinations the undeniable public service of a private religious institution was the controlling fact on which the ruling of law was based.

Thirdly, is the principle of compatibility of interests—which prevails unchallenged when undoubted economic advantages accrue to private commercial and industrial interests that the government subsidizes in the public interest—not equally applicable to private religious institutions fulfilling educational needs?

364

Fourthly, where public and private motives and objectives intermingle, as the Court found in the Sunday law cases, may not the secular aspects and secular functions of education be preserved indefectible whatever the infusion of value judgments, whatever the principle of spiritual and religious integration? A twofold test may be applied: the primary one whereby an empirical test ascertains the competence of the educational process; and secondly, whether the spiritual values taught are tributary to the public good or harmful. It is *ultra vires* to require that a public service be officially impervious to any spiritual permeation.

Fifthly, it would be helpful to bear in mind that educational responsibility is tripartite: the primary rights of parents with which the law of nature has endowed them to direct the education of their offspring; the supervisory role of government to require minimal standards of teaching, curriculum and facilities in its own public interest; and the high expectations of religion, whether institutionalized or dictated by individual consciences. All three not only acknowledge the moral and legal claims of religious liberty but also constitute an essential spiritual resource for the Republic. An exclusive control by one or other of these agencies would threaten not only academic freedom but also the very integrity of the educational process.

Sixthly, man does not live by bread alone. Civil society does not survive solely by its own political and legal determinations. It will not do to speak of civic virtues and the duties of patriotism without reference to the spiritual life of the citizen and the spiritual heritage of the nation. Values to be gained by religious teaching are not meant to be confined wholly to an inner sanctum of spiritual life, nor can they be. Religious pluralism will have an added significance and truly unique meaning for society if it means that all

365

faiths and churches are tributary to the good dispositions, the proper inclinations and the civil sensitivity to obedience to laws, and to that peace and concord among fellow citizens which is the distinguishing mark of the good republic. This spiritual interdependence of the political and moral order does not need to be prescribed by law, for it emerges from the very nature of things. The separation of church and state which the religious clauses of the First Amendment are intended to ensure bears no contrariety to a mutual accommodation of purposes and objectives for the vitality of both. Separation is not insulation. Neutrality must be understood in terms of independence and impartiality. Only on such firm foundations may the proper relationships between free institutions and free churches become possible of formulation. Within the correlative terms of discernible public service and freedom of religion in education no prejudice should operate to the disability of religion to fulfill a public interest merely because it is infused with religious values.

Seventhly, in the judicial interpretation of the religious clauses of the First Amendment no less emphasis should be given to religious liberty than to the establishment clauses. And the rights of consentients should not be any less inviolable than those of dissidents. Coercion has been one of the middle terms by which the establishment clause has been brought to bear upon a litigated issue. Even in those instances where the Court declared that violation of the establishment clause did not depend on the factor of coercion, it would nonetheless take notice of it in either or both forms, the embarrassment allegedly suffered by the plaintiff, or the prestige, power or influence of the government was said to be weighted to one side by its permissiveness of certain religious exercises in public schools. But when can an embarrassment be construed as so substantive a hurt as to warrant the elimination of a whole program of voluntary participation willed by the majority of the local community, or when does an accommodation in the best of traditions amount to proscribed establishment? The problematic of rights of conscience in education in both state and independent schools poses questions which are unique to each situation. The conformity of creed in a parochial school should not be legally viewed to its disadvantage without concretely infringing upon religious liberty. The tendency toward a neutrality of abstention which the peculiarities of religious pluralism in public schools forces upon the Court should not pertain to rulings on constitutional questions that are raised about federal aid to church-related schools. The controlling principle subject to empirical verification is whether learning in the prescribed studies of interest to the national congress is competently realized.

Eighthly, in his concurring opinion in McCollum, Justice Jackson forewarned about the legal presumptions which the Court might risk assuming if the complainant's petition for a complete separation of secular from the religious in public schools were acknowledged.

The task of separating the secular from the religious in education is one of magnitude, intricacy and delicacy. To lay down a sweeping constitutional doctrine as demanded by complainant and apparently approved by the Court, applicable alike to all school boards of the nation "to immediately adopt and enforce rules and regulations prohibiting all instruction in and teaching of religious education in all public schools," is to decree a uniform, rigid and, if we are consistent, an unchanging standard for countless school boards representing and serving highly localized groups which not only differ from each other but which themselves from time to time change attitudes. It seems to me that to do this is to allow zeal for our ideas of what

367

is good in public instruction to induce us to accept the role of super board of education for every school district in the nation . . .

A fortiori it would seem even less warranted to require purely secular subject studies in circumstances where religious liberty in education should be paramount.

CONCLUSION

LaNoue has initiated a study which if broadened into its full dimensions would be highly enlightening in approaching constitutional questions of the role of the state, education and religion in all schools. Unfortunately, he bases a constitutional argument on an assumption of the purely secular subject concept without inquiring into its validity. Nonetheless he could have turned a discussion of the purely secular subject concept into a very profitable opportunity for an analysis of the educational process that *de facto* or *ex professo* obtains in state, church-related and other independent schools and could have inquired whether the public requirements and interests were being served. He might have then proceeded further to show how each educational process imbued with a spiritual content might be tributary to the spiritual resources upon which the faithful performance of civic duties must depend. Instead of simplifying the problem by absolute insulations (for eligibility for federal aid) he might have enlightened the complexities of religious pluralism and the multi-school system of the nation that confronts our legislatures and courts. With light and understanding the approach to the constitutional questions of federal aid to education would be less burdened by partisan polemics of law, education and religion.

368

8

In Conclusion: This Nation Under God

Through the centuries, men and societies have admitted to two polities. One, old as ancient Greece, has always subordinated the civic duties between men to supernal standards of right order, the heavenly paradeigma of absolute justice and goodness, to first principles, to immutable verities, to the eternal law, and to the God of revelation and of the philosophers. The other polity, always a tragic aberration in Western civilization since the advent of Christianity, is the absolute state, completely self-sufficient, with the prerogatives of transcendence, the first and last claim to every human allegiance.

America by the providential course of its early history and by the deliberate intent of its Founding Fathers has been posited within the western Christian tradition. This is made incontestably clear from the first acts of the Continental Congress and from the proclamations of the early presidents. The founders were persuaded that the fortunes of civil governance are dependent upon Divine Providence. Reference is made here not to their personal conviction that a profound religious life will have great moral influence upon the exercise of civic duties but to their deeply felt conviction, expressed in official capacity and circumstances, of the sovereignty of God over nations and societies as well as over individuals. They speak of the duty of the Congress to acknowledge the superintending providence of God, of the need of divine interposition, as they expressed it, in the deliberations of public councils for the wise and effectual disposition of matters of state, for securing civil and religious rights and privileges for themselves and their posterity. As public representatives acting in official capacity and in concert they related good and just government to a Divine Providence that must be sought by intercessory prayer just as individuals would pray for their personal needs, spiritual and material. One of the most striking instances of this dependence of nations upon God is to be found in a speech made by Benjamin Franklin at the federal Convention, when he noted that the deliberations had gone on for some time without benefit of prayer.

Mr. President:

The small progress we have made after four or five weeks close attendance and continual reasonings with each other—our different sentiments on almost every question, several of the last producing as many noes as ays, is methinks a melancholy proof of the imperfection of the Human Understanding. We indeed seem to feel our own want of political wisdom, since we have been running about in search of it. We have gone back to ancient history for models of Government and examined the different forms of those Republics which have been formed with the seeds of their own dissolution and now no longer exist. And we have viewed Modern States all round Europe, but find none of their Constitutions suitable to our circumstances.

In this situation of this Assembly, groping as it were in the dark to find political truth, and scarce able to distinguish it when presented to us, how has it happened, Sir, that we have not hitherto once thought of humbly applying to the Father of lights to illuminate our understandings? In the beginning of the Contest with Great Britain, when we were sensible of danger we had daily prayer in this room for the divine protection. Our prayers, Sir, were heard, and they were graciously answered. All of us who were engaged in the struggle must have observed frequent instances of a superintending providence in our favor. To that kind providence we owe this happy opportunity of consulting in peace on the means of establishing our future national felicity. And have we now forgotten that powerful friend? or do we imagine that we no longer need his assistance? I have lived, Sir, a long time, and the longer I live, the more convincing proofs I see of this truth—that God governs in the affairs of men. And if a sparrow cannot fall to the ground without his notice, is it probable that an empire can rise without his aid? We have been assured, Sir, in the sacred writings, that "except the Lord build the House they labour in vain that build it." I firmly believe this; and I also believe that without his concurring aid we shall succeed in this political building no better than the Builders of Babel: We shall be divided by our little partial local interests; our projects will be confounded, and we ourselves shall become a reproach and bye word down to future ages. And what is worse, mankind may hereafter from this unfortunate instance, despair of establishing Governments by Human Wisdom and leave it to chance, war and conquest.

I therefore beg leave to move—that henceforth prayers imploring the assistance of Heaven, and its blessings on our deliberations, be held in this Assembly every morning before we proceed to business, and that one or more Clergy of this City be requested to officiate in that Service.[153]

(Though Franklin's motion for prayer at the federal convention was seconded, some present felt that it would have been more appropriate had the resolution been adopted at the beginning of the convention. They feared that to carry out the proposal now, in the midst of the proceedings, might have advertised to the public the impasse to which they had come. Others countered that it was never too late to redress an omission. Mr. Williamson seemed to settle the matter for the moment when he observed that "the true cause of omission could not be mistaken. The convention had no funds." Franklin's proposal had been for prayer

371

with "one or more Clergy of this City . . . to officiate in that Service." Nonetheless, Franklin's statement is remarkable from one who is more often than not reputed to have been a freethinker or at most a deist.)

The second polity proposes to be the embodiment of the cosmic or divine purpose or at least claims to be its authentic oracle and its most trusted vehicle of power. As such it recognizes no power superior to itself and no restrictions save self-imposed limitations. It may be cruel or benign. It is not always and necessarily without its own order of liberties and rights, but it insists that it is the sole and supreme regulator of all civil living among men and as such will brook no contrary claim. The rights of conscience in their social projection are to be exercised conditionally, subject only to human law whether that law is promulgated by a dictator or by the democratic process of majority vote, or by the Party in the interests of a Class. Under one form or another, *vox populi est vox Dei.*

Each of these two polities constitutes in its inner core a political faith expecting or demanding as the case may be patriotic obedience or subjection. The nature of the political order is no idle object of speculation. How it is related consciously or subconsciously to other orders which make claims upon the human conscience will work to outward effects. Truth, falsehood and ideals will have consequences which we shall have to accept or readjust or reject. In our own times we have had tragic political experiments with the destinies of men. We in America cannot rest all too confidently behind free institutions. Since the War many thoughtful people have wondered how a cultured and civilized nation of eminent scientists, artists and intellectual giants could have succumbed to an *ism* of human and racial perversion. It may be that a sterile intellectualism, uncommitted

372

to dogmas of the dignity of the human personality rooted in a divine transcendence and the awesome responsibility of power as a ministry dedicated to the pursuit of human happiness as God has willed it, provided that spiritual vacuum wherein an unchallenged earthly power could wax strong and brutal. This relevance of earthly power over men in abrogation of the higher law is the fundamental and crucial question for all thinking men. It may be that in our country, where free institutions flourish, some persons may settle for these legal and political institutions as sufficient intermediate barriers between the pretensions of authority and the people and still remain unconvinced of the further need of the spiritual wellsprings from which these free institutions were historically derived. But the raw fact remains whether or not we are fair to American history and take intellectual cognizance of the moral consensus which underlies our free way of life. For if there is no consensus with regard to what freedom consists in, if serious doubts exist as to its meaning not merely for the citizen of America but for man himself, then our mobilization of resources, strategy of containment and military alertness on a worldwide horizon is directed to an enemy of our own conjuring. There are those who try to demonstrate that our Founding Fathers were at best deists of the Enlightenment and that religious life in the formative years of the Republic was hardly what it is generally alleged to be. In a word the religious foundations of the Republic are exaggerated pretensions of religious enthusiasts. The alternate supposition is all the more remarkable then in that the language of the professions and propositions in our basic national documents are of unquestionable theism and not infrequently of traditional Christian orthodoxy. Some secularists entertain the hope that the moral consensus upon which our Republic depends for its stability and progress in freedom could be inspired and sustained by a fortuitous coincidence of good private lives that infuse the body politic with the overflow of virtuous living. But here again the intellectual nexus between the higher law and government must be affirmed explicitly as part of our political thinking, a necessity which our founders and our highest government officials have felt called to reaffirm solemnly through the decades to our times. It should be no small comfort for the dissenter to know that he lives in a society which holds that we are free and equal but originally not by title of human law, that there is a divine justice by which we measure legal justice, that the reach of temporal power is not to be validated solely by a majoritarian dictation.

This brings us to reflect on the uniqueness of the American experience. Other countries have been held together by culture, tradition or race. Our Republic has rested on a common will to live together through ethnic diversity, racial distinctions, even through the plurality of religious beliefs. Other countries have been held together by the bond of a faith. The uniqueness of the American experience has been that men of different faiths have confessed to a core of religious and moral truths which are an integral part of their own distinctive creeds. In effect, the concurrence has been on that substance of religious beliefs which are also part of the divine natural law doctrine wherein civic society is to be correctly collocated. This religious and moral consensus has emerged through deliberate effort as on the occasion of the drafting of the Declaration of Independence. It has been a deliberate arrival to a solemn affirmation and as such constitutes the most vital sort of national tradition. Our nation is consolidated by a unity descending from above, a unity superior to the legally and politically structured federalism of our government. In an address to the Republican Party on Sept. 22, 1953, President Eisenhower gave memorable expression to this superior and moral unifying bond that has drawn a nation of many and diverse interests together.

> We are one nation, gifted by God with the reason and the will to govern ourselves, and returning our thanks to Him by respecting His supreme creation—the free individual.
> Here we stand. Here, also—if you will—are the plain moral precepts, which define our course and govern our conduct.
> We are one nation and one people. We—this American society —are not the product of some tentative, calculating, self-interested social contract or alliance between conflicting classes and sections. We are not some perilously balanced equation of political convenience in which labor plus farm plus capital plus management equals America....
> We must even in our honest political fervor, fear neither partisan criticism nor self-criticism. For the pretense of perfection is not one of the marks of good public servants....
> We are many things. We are liberal—for we do believe that, in judging his own daily welfare, each citizen, however humble, has greater wisdom than any government, however great.
> We are progessive—for we are less impressed with the difficulties we observed yesterday than the opportunities we envision tomorrow.
> And we are conservative—for we can conceive of no higher commission that history could have conferred upon us than that which we humbly bear—the preservation, in this time of tempest and peril, of the spiritual values that alone give dignity and meaning to man's pilgrimage on this earth.[154]

This religious consensus on the existence of God and on his sovereignty over societies and men, and the repeated recourse in our national history to prayer for divine enlightenment and assistance in the government of our Republic, was in the earliest years of our history associated with education for the benefit both of man and government.

> Religion, morality, and knowledge, being necessary to good government and the happiness of mankind, schools and the means of education shall forever be encouraged.

375

This nexus of religion, government and education found classic expression in the Northwest Ordinance of 1787. There is no intimation of whose religion or what religion was meant. Such a question would probably not arise among men of diverse faiths who had concurred to a natural law doctrine of theism in the Declaration of Independence but, if one may judge from the prevailing religious faiths, it is not unlikely that they meant Christian theism. Of the schools, there can be no doubt that they were speaking of schools established and supported by the revenue from public land set aside for that purpose.

It is within this ancient tradition of the partnership of religion, morality and education that the American educational system finds its congenial place. Of the place of religion and morality in public schools there can be no doubt. The role and function of religion is obviously different in circumstance and definition in public schools and in church-related schools. The nexus between religion, morality and education will depend on the supposition that religion is pervasive of the whole man, that morality is its first fruition and beyond limit in its reach, and that education is a process from which neither one nor the other can be excluded. This is an old educational position. The last Congress of the Confederation, which enacted the Northwest Ordinance, held that this tripartite nexus is *necessary* to good government and to the happiness of mankind, thus somehow committing the government to a part in the educational enterprise and, it would seem, to a part in the very educational process which acknowledges that tripartite nexus.

Within the context of those suppositions, the place of religion in public and private schooling is undoubted, although the difficult problems which the diversity of claims of conscience would inevitably engender in a public school offer challenges to a constitutional balancing of rights wholly wanting in a school of one religious confession. Be that as it may, the question remains whether the referral of American good government to a theistic profession should be taught meaningfully, that is, at least, as meaningfully as the governmental authorities have said it is from the Declaration of Independence to the latest presidential Thanksgiving proclamation. As for any formal religious exercises in public schools, the approach and reasoning of the Court in *Engels v. Vitale* is far from persuasive. If civil and religious rights inhere in the individual they inhere no less inviolably when the consentients outnumber the dissidents. And if some discomfort is experienced by the dissenter in the exercise of his own choice in the midst of contrary free choices, then it is an experience that he will have to contend with all his life. Appropriate disciplinary action should cope with any instance of rudeness while at the same time extraordinary educational opportunity is provided for the development of sensitive civility for our neighbors. With such precautions and affirmative attitudes, a "hurt" could scarcely be of such magnitude as to proportionately outweigh the choice of a large number of individuals. It may well be that the history of the expansion of religious freedom has been for the most part measured by more effective legal protection for the dissenter. The time has now come when the dissident's right of conscience must take equal cognizance of the choice of consentients. A balancing of interests may suggest an adjustment of circumstances or of conditions ensuring freedom of individual choice in place of one position prevailing absolutely against the other. Beliefs about the basic relations of an individual to himself, to his community, to his country, to the world and to God are of primary importance for the cultivation of civic virtues.

377

It is not a question of inserting a good thing, religion, into education. To take this attitude is to misconstrue the question, to prejudice it and to provide answers which avoid the problem. The way we think of ourselves and our neighbors and the innermost motivations that inspire and promote these relations become the unifying or disintegrating forces of society. Religion is a spiritual process of union, the question being whether the unifying bond be God and his laws or some pragmatically established ethos. Freedom of belief means independence of beliefs, that is, the beliefs must be unhampered by political institutions and by private action. Official supervision and appropriate disciplinary action should be directed to ensuring free and independent choice, so that any discomfiture that a dissenter experiences is the incidence of his own choice. It is not that the others have chosen otherwise but rather that he has. The question here is not of conformity but of consensual agreement, a plurality of individuals who want to pray together for their neighbors, their teachers and their country. If this is divisive, if this is an unhealthy conformity, why this fervor of intercredal dialogue, mutual understanding and ecumenism?

It is a sort of paradox that those schools which allow for the full exercise of religious liberty in education, uncomplicated by a diverse claim of conscience, relieved of the problematics that plague a public school, should in their wonderful advantage suffer a disability for sharing equitably in governmental aid to education.

Our government has called upon the churches to assist it in providing the religious motivation for the effectual realization of equal civil rights for all. It will require profound spiritual convictions to dissolve deep-rooted bias and prejudice. Religious spokesmen have testified before congressional committees that racial discrimination is blasphemy

378

against God. The legislators did not rule their testimony out of order; rather it was inserted in the records as part of the consideration for congressional action on civil rights legislation. Our government cannot consistently seek religious support or consult religious authorities for reasons of faith touching on national legislation on the one hand, and then in a federal aid to education program look upon the religious orientation of an educational curriculum with doubts of constitutionality. Such action offends the common sense of the matter.

One last reflection. We have elsewhere considered that the particular choice of the spiritual integration of a schooling cannot be one of judicial determination—except to ascertain whether the state educational authorities have properly exercised their supervision within the bounds of their competence and jurisdiction. We have also noted that public law is not wholly indifferent to dogma and heresy. Public law would forbid whatever it considered effectively harmful to society and the observance of law. But at a time when our country is endeavoring to mobilize all its spiritual and material resources for the realization of a life of freedom at home and abroad, nothing could be more divisive than to exclude a significant section of our people from the benefits of a governmental program for the betterment of national education.

In 1942, Justice Jackson in his memorable opinion of the Court in *West Virginia State Board of Education v. Barnette* observed:

> Probably no deeper division of our people could proceed from any provocation than from finding it necessary to choose what doctrine and whose program public educational officials shall compel youth to unite in embracing.

379

True, there is no fear whatsoever of a legal compulsion against the religious orientation of parochial schools nor are state school authorities casting any doubt on the proficiency in learning the required subjects in these schools. But an exclusion from federal aid based on religious grounds would constitute a most effective act of divisiveness in our national education and among our citizens.

Footnotes to Part Two

[1] *Everson v. Board of Educ.*, 330 U.S. 1 (1947).

[2] *McCollum v. Board of Educ.*, 333 U.S. 203 (1948).

[3] *Everson v. Board of Educ.*, 330 U.S. 1, 15–16 (1947).

[4] 333 U.S. 203 (1948).

[5] 330 U.S. at 28–74.

[6] The Vermont Constitution is silent on this point.

[7] 343 U.S. 306 (1952).

[8] *Ibid.*, 312.

[9] 268 U.S. 510 (1925).

[9a] 330 U.S. 1, 16 (1947).

[10] 314 U.S. 252, 289 (1941).

[11] Six versions were proposed:

(1) "The civil rights of none shall be abridged on account of religious belief, nor shall any national religion be established, nor shall the full and equal rights of conscience in any manner or on any pretext be infringed." 1 *Annals of Cong.* 434 (1789).

(2) ". . . No religion shall be established by law, nor shall the equal rights of conscience be infringed." *Ibid.* at 729.

(3) ". . . Congress shall make no laws touching religion, or infringing the rights of conscience." *Ibid.* at 731

(4) ". . . Congress shall make no law establishing religion, or to prevent the free exercise thereof, or to infringe the rights of conscience." *Ibid.* at 766.

(5) "Congress shall make no laws establishing articles of faith or a mode of worship, or prohibiting the free exercise of religion." *Journal of the First Senate* 77 (Gates and Seaton ed. 1820).

(6) "Congress shall make no laws respecting an establishment of religion, or prohibiting the free exercise thereof . . ." 1 *Annals of Cong.* 913 (1789). After the House approved of the sixth version

on the 24th of September and the Senate the following day, it was sent to President Washington for submission to the states. See 1 *Annals of Cong.* 913–14 (1789). The first four versions were either proposed, altered or adopted by the House alone, and rejected by the Senate. In response to the House's fourth version which was forwarded to the Senate for its concurrence, the Senate adopted its own formula, the fifth version, which the House in turn rejected. A committee of three from each House of Congress settled upon the final text, our present First Amendment.

[12] 1 *Annals of Cong.* 434 (1789).

[13] *Ibid.,* 729.

[14] *Ibid.,* 730.

[15] To point out more sharply the unique Madisonian meaning for the federal religious guarantees, namely, the instrumental subordination of no establishment to the free exercise thereof we may recall that Madison's original fifth amendment guaranteed religious freedom against encroachment by the states without at the same time requiring state disestablishment. See 1 *Annals of Cong.* 435 (1789).

[16] 1 *Annals of Cong.* 730 (1789).

[17] *Ibid.,* 730–31.

[18] *Ibid.,* 731. Despite Madison's repeated reassurances that the federal amendment left untouched state dispositions of religious life we find today the converse attributed to him, that his mind on the disposition of religious matters in his own state of Virginia, expressed in his *Memorial and Remonstrance* of 1785, six years before the final ratification of the ten amendments, as interpretative of the intent of the federal First Amendment!

[19] *Journal of the Virginia Senate* (1789), 63 (1828 edition).

[20] We remonstrate against the said Bill, because we hold for a fundamental and undeniable truth, "that Religion or the duty which we owe to our Creator and the Manner of discharging it, can be directed only by reason and conviction, not by force or violence." . . . We maintain therefore in matters of Religion, no man's right is abridged by the institution of Civil Society . . . that the majority may (not) trespass on the rights of the minority . . . if religion be exempt from the authority of the Society at large, still less can it be subject to that of the Legislative Body. . . . Who does not see that the same authority which can establish Christianity, in exclusion of all other Religions, may establish with the same ease any particular

sect of Christians, in exclusion of all other Sects? That the same authority which can force a citizen to contribute three pence only of his property for the support of any one establishment, may force him to conform to any other establishment in all cases whatsoever? . . . the bill violates that equality which ought to be the basis of every law . . . all men are to be considered as entering into Society on equal conditions; as relinquishing no more, and therefore retaining no less, one than another, of their natural rights. Above all are they to be considered as retaining an equal title to the free exercise of Religion according to the dictates of conscience. . . . As the Bill violates equality by subjecting some to peculiar burdens; so it violates the same principle, by granting to others pecuniary exemptions . . . the bill implies either that the Civil Magistrate is a competent Judge of Religious truth; or that he may employ religion as an engine of Civil policy. . . . It (the Bill) degrades from the equal rank of Citizens all those whose opinions in Religion do not bend to those of the Legislative Authority. 2 *The Writings of James Madison,* 184–88 (Hunt edition, 1901).

[21] Corwin, "The Supreme Court as National School Board," 14 *Law & Contemporary Problems,* 3, 16 (1949).

[22] After the Preamble of Section I which set forth in fourteen statements the incidents usual in an establishment, the inequities and injustices visited upon dissenters and nonconformists as well as the hypocrisy it may engender, Section II reads:

> We the General Assembly of Virginia do enact (1) that no man shall be compelled to frequent or support any religious worship, place, or ministry whatsoever, (2) nor shall be enforced, restrained, molested, or burthened in his body or goods, or shall otherwise suffer, on account of his religious opinions or belief; but (3) that all men shall be free to profess, and by argument to maintain, their opinions in matters of religion, and (4) that the same shall in no wise diminish, enlarge, or affect their civil capacities.

See Padover, *The Complete Jefferson,* 947 (1943). Like Madison, Jefferson's opposition to "establishment" in Virginia was inspired by the dominating idea of religious freedom "I am for freedom of religion, and against all maneuvers to bring about the legal ascendency of one sect over another. . . ." Letter to Elbridge Gerry, 1700, 7 *The Writings of Thomas Jefferson,* 328.

[23] Padover, *The Complete Jefferson*, 1064–69 (1943).

[24] *Ibid.*, 1076.

[25] *Ibid.*, 1104.

[26] *Ibid.*, 957–58.

[27] *Ibid.*, 958.

[28] 10, *The Writings of Thomas Jefferson*, 242.

[29] *Ibid.*, 243.

[30] In our annual report to the legislature, . . . we suggest the expediency of encouraging the different sects to establish, each for itself, a professorship of their own tenets, on the confines of the university, so near as that their students may attend the lectures there, and have the free use of our library, and every other accommodation we can give them; preserving, however, their independence of us and of each other. This fills the chasm objected to in ours, as a defect in all institutions professing to give instruction in all useful sciences. *Ibid.*

[31] Padover, *op. cit. supra* note 24, 1106–11.

[32] *Ibid.*, 1110.

[33] *Ibid.*, 518–19.

[34] See 1, Stokes, *Church and State in the United States*, 480 (1950).

[35] *Ibid.*, 481.

[36] 4, *Am. State Papers*, Class 2, Indian Affairs 54 (Cong. 1832).

[37] 1, *Am. State Papers*, Class 2, Indian Affairs 687 (Cong. 1803).

[38] 25 U.S.C. § 278 (1928).

[39] Exec. Order 7086 (June 26, 1935).

[40] 10 U.S.C. § 381 (1927).

[41] 42 U.S.C. §§ 1751–60 (1952).

[42] Servicemen's Readjustment Act, 58 Stat. 284, 290 (1944).

[43] 60 Stat. 812 (1946).

[44] 42 U.S.C. § 291 (1952).

[45] 93 Cong. Rec. 4459 (1947).

[46] 62 Stat. 172 (1948).

[47] Dept. of Army Pam. 16–8 (1950):

". . . the character development programs stress . . . the moral principles that sustain the philosophy of American freedom, particularly as it is set forth in the opening paragraph of the Declaration of Independence. That philosophy regards man as a creature of God."

384

Air Force 50–21, Living for Leadership (1955):
"There is an objective truth which we can discover with
our own intellects concerning the nature of man, and of
society, and of the purpose of life. There is a natural law
and order. . . . There is a God who has created man with
rights and duties and a purpose in life."

[48] The courts have on numerous occasions insisted that the determining factor whether the school was parochial or public was *who
controlled it*. Control must be distinguished from supervision and
inspection which ascertains the conformity to state prescribed standards in order to be a publicly accredited school, attendance at which
satisfies the requirements of the state compulsory school attendance
laws. Control is a concomitant right of a proprietary title. Though
the courses of study are prescribed and supervised by the state, and
their pupils' attendance at church-affiliated schools is a compliance
with state compulsory attendance laws, this does not constitute control (*Cochran v. Louisiana State Board of Educ.*, 281 U.S. 370,
1930).

Viewing the statute as having the effect thus attributed to
it, we cannot doubt that the taxing power of the state is
exerted for a public purpose. The legislation does not segregate private schools, or their pupils, as its beneficiaries or
attempt to interfere with any matters of exclusively private
concern. Its interest is education, broadly; its method,
comprehensive. Individual interests are aided only as the
common interest is safeguarded (*Ibid.*, 375).

[49] See National Citizens Committee for Public Schools, Financing
Public Education in the Decade Ahead (1954); Freeman, Federal
Aid to Education—Boon or Bane? (American Enterprise Ass'n Inc.,
Washington, D.C., 1955); National Citizens Comm'n for Public
Schools, How Do We Pay for Our Schools? (1954); Comm'n on
Intergovernmental Relations, Federal Responsibility in the Field of
Education (1955); A Report Prepared in the Legislative Reference
Service of The Library of Congress for the Subcommittee on Educa-
tion of the Senate Committee on Labor and Public Welfare, Action
by the 83rd Congress Affecting Education and Educators (U.S.
Govt. Printing Office, 1955); A Report Prepared in the Legislative
Reference Service of the Library of Congress by Charles A. Quattle-
baum, Specialist in Education, Federal Aid for School Construction

385

(U.S. Govt. Printing Office, 1955); A Report Prepared in the Legislative Reference Service of the Library of Congress by Charles A. Quattlebaum, Educational Issues of Concern to the 84th Congress (U.S. Govt. Printing Office); A Report Prepared in the Legislative Reference Service of the Library of Congress at the Request of Senator John Sherman Cooper, Chairman, Subcommittee on Education of the Committee on Labor and Public Welfare, Federal Aid to States and Local School Districts for Elementary and Secondary Education (U.S. Govt. Printing Office, 1954).

[50] 281 U.S. 370 (1930).

[51] In 1854 the Maine Supreme Judicial Court upheld the expulsion of a Catholic child from school for refusing to read the Protestant Bible. *Donahue v. Richards*, 38 Me. 379 (1854).

[52] See BILLINGTON, *The Protestant Crusade* 1800–1860 (1938); MYERS, *History of Bigotry in the United States* (1943).

[53] 2, *Complete Works of Abraham Lincoln* 287 (1905). See also Bates, *Religious Liberty*, 363 (1945).

[54] BEALE, *A History of Freedom of Teaching in American Schools*, 95 (1941).

[55] *Ibid.*, 97.

[56] *Ibid.*, 98–99.

[57] *Ibid.*, 104–05.

[58] 310 U.S. 296 (1940).

[59] 7 U.S.C. § 301 (1946).

[60] 42 U.S.C. § 291 (1952). In Kentucky the Court of Appeals upheld the federal statute against the contention that the federal-state grant to church-affiliated hospitals violated both federal and state constitutions.

> . . . (4) private agency may be utilized as the pipe-line through which a public expenditure is made, the test being not who receives the money but the character of the use for which it is expended. . . . The fact that members of the governing board of these hospitals, which perform a recognized public service to all people regardless of faith or creed, are all of one religious faith does not signify that the money allotted the hospitals is to aid their particular denominations. . . . Courts will look to the use to which these funds are put rather than the conduits through which they run. If that use is a public one . . .

386

it will not be held in contravention of sec. 5 merely because the hospitals carry the name or are governed by the members of a particular faith.

Kentucky Bldg. Comm'n v. Effron, 310 Ky. 355, 358–59, 220 S.W. 2d 836, 837–38 (1949). In Mississippi, the State Supreme Court also upheld the federal-state interlocking subsidization of a church-affiliated hospital on the same constitutional grounds of public service. *Craig v. Mercy Hospital,* 209 Miss. 427, 45 So. 2d 427 (1950).

[61] The education of its citizens is no less a concern and responsibility of the federal government as it is for the states. An illiterate and politically irresponsible citizen may be a liability to the federal as well as to the state governments.

[62] Cf. Harrison-Thomas Bill, S. 1305, 76th Cong., 1st Sess. (1939); Harrison-Thomas Bill, S. 1313, 77th Cong., 1st Sess. (1941); Hill-Thomas Bill, S. 637, 78th Cong., 1st Sess. (1943); Thomas-Hill-Ramspeck Bill, S. 181, 79th Cong., 1st Sess. (1945); Taft-Hill-Thomas Bill, S. 472, 80th Cong., 1st Sess. (1947).

[63] S. 717, 79th Cong., 1st Sess. (1945).

[64] H.R. 7160, 81st Cong., 2d Sess. (1950).

Expenditures of Funds and Judicial Review Sec. 5. Amounts paid to any State under this Act shall be expended only for current expenditures for public elementary and secondary schools within such State. . . .

(2) . . . Whenever in the judgment of any member of the board or commission of education or equivalent agency of such State, or of any member of any local school board or equivalent agency of such State, any person has engaged, or is about to engage, in any acts or practices which constitute or will constitute a violation of any provision of the first four sentences of this section, such member may make application to the appropriate United States district court . . . for an order enjoining such acts and practices, or for an order enjoining compliance with the provisions of the first four sentences of this section. Upon a showing that such person has engaged, or is about to engage, in any such acts or practices, a permanent or temporary injunction, restraining order, or other order may be granted.

Definitions. Sec. 7. For the Purpose of this Act—

. . . .

(2) The term 'current expenditures' includes only expenditures for salaries of teachers and of school supervisory, administrative and maintenance personnel, expenditures for school supplies, and expenditures for the maintenance of school buildings.

(3) The term 'public elementary and secondary schools' means tax-supported grade schools and high schools which are under public supervision and control.

(4) The term 'number of children of school age in such State' means the number of children from five to seventeen years of age, inclusive, in such State . . .

[65] S. 1411, 81st Cong., 1st Sess. (1949).

[66] The preeminence of the religious guarantees as the First Amendment is a historical accident. To begin with, only in the closing days and under much persevering prodding from Madison did the First Congress finally attend to the formulation of a bill of rights. Cf. Rutland, *The Birth Of The Bill Of Rights* 1776–1791 (1955). When Madison first introduced his amendments, the two which dealt expressly with the subject of religion were fourth and fifth. The fifth amendment which restricted state action on religious conscience was dropped by the Senate and the fourth which regulated federal activity was altered by the House and was submitted to the states as the third of all the amendments actually proposed for ratification. Because the first two failed of ratification the third proposed amendment became our present First Amendment. Justice Jackson was not historically accurate when in his dissenting opinion in the Everson case he observed: "This freedom was first in the Bill of Rights because it was first in the forefathers' minds. . . ." *Everson v. United States,* 330 U.S. 1, 26 (1947).

[67] *Pierce v. Society of Sisters,* 268 U.S. 510 (1925).

[68] *Cantwell v. Connecticut,* 310 U.S. 296 (1940).

[69] No little confusion is engendered by the reference to "church and state." Neither in the First Amendment nor elsewhere in the Constitution is there any mention of "church" or of "state" in the generic sense. Both the debates in the First Amendment and in the states at the time of the adoption of the First Amendment clearly show that the explicit intent of the Amendment was to effectuate a separation between the federal and state jurisdictions respecting religion and hardly at all raised the continental questions of union

or separation of church and state. There was no dominant church vis-a-vis the federal government. The variety of state establishments at the time of the First Amendment, as well as the privileged position which the disestablished churches in the other states still retained and the prevailing numbers of a denomination in the three states which never had an established church made it practically impossible for the federal government to favor any one church by national establishment. Indeed, it is clear from Madison's rejoinders to objections raised at the First Congress, the amendment was not directed to interfere with state settlements on the subject of religion. Very often the amendment is quoted to read "respecting *the* establishment of religion" as if it prohibited the federal government to favor religious life whereas the literal meaning is "respecting *an* establishment of religion"—an accurate denial of legal preference for any one belief. A serious and very facile misconception is to identify government relation with religious education with church and state relationship. The state has no jurisdictional rights in matters of creed, worship and their free exercise, except to cooperate and encourage the freedom of the churches and of the individual believers. But the state has a jurisdictional right—though not an absolute and exclusive one—in education; a right which it has together with the parents and the churches. The separation of church and state which secures to each its own proper jurisdiction from encroachment by the other is consequently not applicable to education which fulfills authorized requirements and provides, besides, religious instruction. This is not therefore a theological question but a political one which the First Amendment fixes in constitutional, i.e., legal terms. The proper approach to a discussion of federal aid to education is to consider the responsibilities of the state for the education of its citizens in a manner consonant with civic and religious duties and liberties.

In such a sound perspective, civil and religious empowerments are kept by law inviolably separate. The distinct and correspondingly proportionate responsibilities of parents, church, and state in education upon one and the same subject, citizen-believer, unavoidably requires moral and material cooperation.

[70] *Pierce v. Society of Sisters,* 268 U.S. 510, 535 (1925).

[71] 60 Stat. 812 (1946).

[72] The Court of Appeals in *Zorach v. Clauson* struck at the heart

of the matter when it warned against exalting no establishment to the detriment of the free exercise clause: "We must not destroy one in an effort to preserve the other." 303 N.Y. 161, 172, 100 N.E. 2d 463, 468 (1951). And Judge Desmond in his concurring opinion:

> The basic fundamental here at hazard is not, it should be made clear, any so-called . . . principle of complete separation of religion from government. Such a total separation has never existed in America, and none was ever planned or considered by the founders. The true and real principle that calls for assertion here is that of the right of parents to control the education of their children, so long as they provide them with the State-mandated minimum of secular learning, and the right of parents to raise and instruct their children in any religion chosen by the parents. *Pierce v. Society of Sisters of the Holy Names of Jesus and Mary,* 268 U.S. 510; *Meyer v. State of Nebraska,* 262 U.S. 390. . . . *Packer Collegiate Inst. v. University of State of New York,* 298 N.Y. 184, 192. . . . These are true and absolute rights under natural law, antedating, and superior to, any human constitution or statute.

> I cannot believe that the Chief Justice of the United States, in his opinion for the Supreme Court majority in *Dennis v. United States,* 341 U.S. 494, 508 . . . meant literally, what he wrote: that there are no absolutes and that all concepts are relative. Of course, even the constitutional rights of freedom of speech and freedom of religion are, to a degree, nonabsolute, since their disorderly or dangerous exercise may be forbidden by law. But embodied within 'freedom of religion' is a right which is absolute and not subject to any governmental interference whatever. Absolute, I insist, is the right to practice one's religion without hindrance, and that necessarily comprehends the right to teach that religion, or have it taught, to one's children. 303 N.Y. at 178, 100 N.E.2d at 471.

[73] *Everson v. Board of Education,* 330 U.S. 1, 16 (1947).

[74] H.R. 7535, 84th Cong., 2d Sess. (1956).

[75] Katz, "Freedom of Religion and State Neutrality," 20 *U. Chi. L. Rev.* 426 (1953).

[76] Madison's preoccupation for religious liberty carried him years

later to a narrow logic. We find him noting in his Detached Memoranda constitutional doubts about the practice of governmental support of congressional chaplains which he as President had approved.

The establishment of the chaplainship to Congs, is a palpable violation of equal rights, as well as of Constitutional principles: The tenets of the chaplain elected . . . shut the door of worship against the members whose creeds and consciences forbid a participation in that of the majority. To say nothing of other sects, this is the case with that of Roman Catholics and Quakers who have always had members in one or both of the Legislative branches. Could a Catholic clergyman ever hope to be appointed Chaplain? To say that his religious principles are obnoxious or that his sect is small, is to lift the evil at once and exhibit in its naked deformity the doctrine that religious truth is to be tested by numbers, or that the major sects have a right to govern the minor."

Fleet, "Detached Memoranda," *The William and Mary Quarterly,* October, 1946, 588. Madison's fears of the majority's dictation to a minority deserves universal concurrence but his fears were in great part inspired by an overexaggerated notion of the relation of the congressional chaplain to the congressmen. These owe him no obedience. He is neither their ecclesiastical authority nor their teacher of sectarian dogma. He exercises neither a magisterium, properly speaking, nor a jurisdiction in matters of religious belief. Indeed the religious functions of the congressional chaplain whatever his denomination are characteristically, as discretion dictates, nonsectarian. The underlying significance of his office is the testimony it bears to one of the many traditional expressions of the official and authoritative protestations of the American Government of the religious foundations of our republic and the continuing spiritual need for invoking divine guidance in the governance of men.

[77] *Prince v. Massachusetts,* 321 U.S. 158, 166 (1944).

[78] 210 U.S. 50 (1908).

[79] This present study follows the divisions of the Memorandum beginning on p. 4. It passes over, for obvious reasons, the Summary of Conclusions With Respect to Elementary and Secondary Schools (pp. i-iii) and the Introduction (pp. 1-3) which explains the paucity of Supreme Court rulings on governmental aid to religious schools.

[80] "The (lower) court ruled that the Fourteenth Amendment guaranteed appellees against the deprivation of their property without the due process of law consequent upon the unlawful interference of appellants with the free choice of patrons, present and prospective. It declared the right to conduct schools was proper and that parents and guardians, as a part of their liberty, might direct the education of children by selecting reputable teachers and places. Also that these schools were not unfit or harmful to the public, and that enforcement of the challenged state would unlawfully deprive them of patronage and thereby destroy their owners' business and property." 268 U.S. 510.

[81] "The fundamental theory of liberty upon which all governments in this Union repose excludes any general power of the State to standardize its children by forcing them to accept instruction from public teachers only. The child is not the mere creature of the State; those who nurture him and direct his destiny have the right coupled with the high duty, to recognize and prepare him for additional duties." *Ibid.,* 534-535.

[82] *Meyer v. Nebraska,* 262 U. S. 390 (1923).

[83] "The capacity to impart instruction to others is given by the Almighty for beneficent purposes and its use may not be forbidden or interferred with by Government—certainly not, unless such instruction is, in its nature, harmful to public morals or imperils the public safety. The right to impart instruction, harmless in itself or beneficial to those who receive it, is a substantial right of property—especially, where the services are rendered for compensation. But even if such right be not strictly a property right, it is, beyond question, part of one's liberty as guaranteed against hostile state action by the Constitution of the United States. . . . The right to enjoy one's religious belief, unmolested by any human power is no more sacred nor more fully or distinctly recognized than is the right to impart and receive instruction not harmful to the public. The denial of either right would be an infringement of the liberty inherent in the freedom secured by the fundamental law." Harlan, J., dissenting in *Berea College v. Kentucky,* 211 U.S. 45, 47, (1908).

[84] 1 *Annals of Congress,* 730 (1789).

[85] *Ibid.,* 730-731.

[86] *Ibid.,* 755.

[87] *Ibid.*

[88] "The establishment of religion clause of the First Amendment means at least this: Neither a state nor the Federal Government can set up a church. Neither can pass laws which aid religion, aid all religions, or prefer one religion over another. Neither can force nor influence a person to go to or remain away from church against his will or force him to profess a belief or disbelief in any religion. No person can be punished for entertaining or professing religious beliefs or disbeliefs, for church attendance or nonattendance. No tax in any amount, large or small, can be levied to support any religious activities or institutions, whatever they may be called, or whatever form they may adopt to teach or practice religion. Neither a state nor the Federal Government can, openly or secretly, participate in the affairs of any religious organizations or groups and vice versa. In the words of Jefferson, the clause against establishment of religion by law was intended to erect 'a wall of separation' between Church and State." 330 U.S., 15-16.

[89] In 1789 the First Congress appropriated funds for the support of Christian missionaries among the Indians in implementation of a recommendation made by General Knox, Secretary of War, and approved by President Washington. "The object of this establishment would be the happiness of Indians, teaching them the great duties of religion and morality, and to inculcate a friendship and attachment to the United States." 4 Am. State Papers, Class 2, Indian Affairs 687 (Cong. 1832). This government policy of supporting with public funds religion and religious education continued under Jefferson's administration. In 1897 Congress abandoned this century-old policy and by the Act of June 7th decided no longer to make appropriations for sectarian education with a proviso, however, that such financial assistance continue in diminishing sums until 1900. The change was one of policy unless we are to suppose that Congress can declare a three-year moratorium on constitutionality.

[90] For example, the National Youth Administration Act of 1935, the Reserve Officers Training Corps program, disposal of war-surplus material, construction of "temporary" buildings on university campuses during the war.

[91] The Champaign plan had the singular virtue of protecting the public schools from the charge of being a-religious.

[92] "We are a religious people whose institutions presuppose a Su-

preme Being. We guarantee the freedom to worship as one chooses. We make room for as wide a variety of beliefs and creeds as the spiritual needs of man deem necessary. We sponsor an attitude on the part of government that shows no partiality to any one group and that lets each flourish according to the zeal of its adherents and the appeal of its dogma. When the state encourages religious instruction or cooperates with religious authorities by adjusting the schedule of public events to sectarian needs, it follows the best of our traditions. For it then respects the religious nature of our people and accommodates the public services to their spiritual needs. To hold that it may not would be to find in the Constitution a requirement that the government show a callous indifference to religion over those who do believe. Government may not finance religious groups nor undertake religious instructions to force one or some religion on any person. But we find no constitutional requirement which makes it necessary for government to be hostile to religion and to throw its weight against efforts to widen the effective scope of religious influence. The government must be neutral when it comes to competition between sects. It may not thrust any sect on any person. It may not make a religious observance compulsory. It may not coerce anyone to attend church, to observe a religious holiday, or to take religious instruction.

[93] 197 Va. 419, 89 S.E. 2d 851 (1955). ". . . public funds to support religious instructions contrary to the principles laid down in Everson . . . It affords sectarian groups an invaluable aid in that it helps to provide pupils for their religious classes through use of the state's compulsory school machinery . . . It compels taxpayers to contribute money for the propagation of religious opinions which they may not believe" (89 S.E. 2d, 858).

[94] Veterans' Benefits, P.L. 85-857, Chap. 35, secs. 1701 f.

[95] Vermont Statutes Annotated, title 16, no. 739 (1958):

    (a) "Each town district shall maintain a high school or furnish secondary instruction, as hereinafter provided, for its advanced pupils at a high school or academy, to be selected by the parents or guardian of the pupil, within or without the state. The board of school directors may both maintain a high school and furnish secondary instruction elsewhere as herein provided as in the judgment of the board may best serve the interests of the pupils.

(b) Each . . . district shall pay tuition per pupil per school year . . . but not in excess of $325. . . ."

[96] "Government may not finance religious groups nor undertake religious instruction nor blend secular and sectarian education nor use secular instruction to force one or some religion on any person."

[97] *Swart v. South Burlington Town School District,* 167 A. 2d 514, 520 (1961). Petition for writ of certiorari filed in United States Supreme Court, docket no. 856, Court denied review on May 15, 1961. This was the first time that the issue of tuition payments for church schools had been taken to the Supreme Court.

[98] It will be noted that the law provided that parents might sometimes select a high school for their children even when the town furnished a public high school.

[99] "New Jersey cannot consistently with the 'establishment of religion' clause of the First Amendment contribute tax-raised funds to the support of an institution which teaches the tenets and faith of any church. On the other hand, other language of the amendment commands that New Jersey cannot hamper its citizens in the free exercise of their own religion. Consequently, it cannot exclude individual Catholics, Lutherans, Mohammedans, Baptists, Jews, Methodists, non-believers, Presbyterians, or members of any other faith, *because of their faith or lack of it,* from receiving the benefits of public welfare legislation. While we do not mean to intimate that a state could not provide transportation only to children attending public schools, we must be careful, in protecting the citizens of New Jersey against state-established churches, to be sure, that we do not inadvertently prohibit New Jersey from extending its general state law benefits to all its citizens without regard to their religious belief."

[100] *Chance v. Mississippi Text Book Rating Bd.,* 190 Miss. 453, 467-68, 200 So. 706, 710 (1941).

[101] Opinion of the Justices, 99 N.H. 519, 113 A. 2d 114, 116 (1955).

[102] *Kentucky Building Commission v. Effron,* 220 S.W. 2d 836 (1949). See too *Bradfield v. Roberts* 175 U.S. 291 (1899).

[103] Here too logistics may give direction to thought. About 90 per cent of the school children attend public schools and about 90 per cent of those who attend religious schools are Catholics. Non-Catholics have a larger share of private hospitals as they do of

395

higher institutions of learning compared with Catholic hospitals, colleges and universities.

[103] 45 So. 2d 809 (1950).

[104] 319 U.S. 624 (1943).

[105] In 1915 the Rabbi Isaac Elchanan Theological Seminary and Yeshiva Etz Chaim, both of which were devoted exclusively to religious studies, merged under the direction of Dr. Bernard Revel to become the second largest Jewish-sponsored university in the world, the Hebrew University in Jerusalem being the largest. Since its founding, a cluster of secular schools of higher learning grew around the orthodox rabbinical seminary. University status was achieved in 1945. A state charter authorizing the opening of medical and dentistry schools was granted in 1950. On its main campus, known as the Main Academic Center—extending from 184th Street to 187th Street on Amsterdam Avenue in the Washington Heights section of Manhattan—there are nine schools: Yeshiva College for Men, Rabbi Isaac Elchanan Theological Seminary, the Graduate School of Mathematical Sciences, the Bernard Revel Graduate School, the Harry Fischel School for Higher Jewish Studies, the Teachers Institute for Men, the Israel Institute, the Cantorial Training Institute and the Yeshiva University High School for Boys. Nine more schools, including the Albert Einstein College for Medicine, are spread over six teaching centers in three boroughs. Cf. Myron Kolatch, "The Yeshiva and the Medical School" in *Commentary,* May, 1960, 387-398.

[106] The Bronx Municipal Hospital Center is situated in the Westchester Heights section of the Bronx, adjacent to the Albert Einstein Medical School campus, and consists of the Abraham Jacobi Hospital, the Nathan B. Van Etten Hospital and a staff residence building.

[107] Signed Oct. 15, 1953. Citations are from a photostatic copy of the record, Cal. no. 542.

[108] New York State Constitution. Article XI, Sec. 1, Par. 4 (1895): "Neither the state nor any subdivision thereof, shall use its property or credit or any public money, or authorize or permit either to be used, directly or indirectly, in aid or maintenance, other than for examination or inspection, of any school or institution of learning wholly or in part under the control or direction of any re-

ligious denomination, or in which any denominational tenet or doctrine is taught."

[109] *Commentary, art. cit.,* 396–7: "Why doesn't Yeshiva demand certain minimum religious observances, e.g., wearing a skullcap, at the College of Medicine and at its other secular graduate divisions?"

"Once our young men or young women have completed college," Dr. Belkin replied, "they have made their decision about religion. The molding period is over. On the undergraduate level, in high school, and college, the molding process is at a critical stage. There we are interested in the yeshiva-type student; we require strict adherence to traditional Judaism and will not countenance any violation of that tradition. On the graduate level, our objective is twofold: to provide the Orthodox student with professional schools where he can maintain his religion to the maximum, and to contribute to the general welfare of the nation."

[110] In *Marbury v. Madison* (1803) Chief Justice Marshall ruled "Questions in their nature political" not subject to court determination. Subsequent court rulings have elaborated upon the concept of political question to subsume these specific instances under that classification: the issue of what proof is required that a statute has been enacted; questions arising out of the conduct of foreign relations; the termination of wars, or rebellions; the questions of what constitutes a republican form of government; when is a constitutional amendment ratified; questions arising from the manner of choosing presidential electors, state officials, etc. The ultimate determination rests either with Congress or the President, and in local matters, with state officials. The alternate recourse is to the electorate.

[111] 219 U.S. 346 (1911).

[112] *Massachusetts v. Mellon,* 262 U.S. at 486–487 (1923).

[113] 41.

[113a] "Parochial Texts Called Bar To Aid" in *New York Times,* May 11, 1962, 1, 38. The survey study was made by George R. LaNoue, at that time a doctoral candidate at Yale University, department of political science, at the request of the department of religious liberty, division of Christian Life and Work, of the National Council of the Churches of Christ in the U.S.A. On May 18, 1962, the department of religious liberty made available photo-offset copies of an abbreviation of the original lengthy report. A substantial exposition with more detailed documentation and examples appeared in

the June issue of the *Phi Delta Kappan* titled "The National Defense Education Act And 'Secular' Subjects." A lengthier version appeared in the *Harvard Educational Review,* vol. 32, no. 3, Summer 1962, titled "Religious Schools and 'Secular' Subjects," 255–291. All references will be to this last publication.

114 National Defense Education Act, P. L. 85–864, sec. 305; 20 U.S.C. 445.

115 Joint Subcommittee on Education of the House Committee on Education and Labor, *Hearing,* on H.R. 6774, H.R. 4253, H.R. 7378, 1961, Part 1, 121–122.

116 *Ibid.,* Part 1, 280.

117 *Ibid.,* Part 2, 471.

118 *Ibid.,* Part 2, 471–472.

119 LaNoue, *Op. cit.,* 259 n. 11.

120 *The Supreme Court on Church and State,* edited by Joseph Tussman (Cambridge: 1962), XXIV.

121 *Teacher Education and Religion,* by A. L. Sebaly, E. R. Collins, K. S. Cooper, E. E. Dawson, K. C. Hill, E. J. Kircher, H. K. Schilling (1959), 95–96, (by E. J. Kircher).

122 *American Education and Religion:* "The Problem of Religion in the Schools," edited by F. Ernest Johnson (New York: 1952). Secularism is "a faith that conflicts with the tenets of traditional religion . . . we should recognize it for what it is: an affirmation of faith, a religion, if you will, which entitles it to the right of competition in the marketplace, with all the privileges and limitations that apply to the propagation of other religions." Vivian Thayer, 30.

123 *McCollum v. Board of Education,* 333 U.S. 203, 235–236 (1948).

124 LaNoue, *Op. cit.,* 262.

125 *Ibid.,* 236.

126 *Ibid.,* 263.

127 *The Supreme Court As National School Board,* by Edward S. Corwin in *Law and Contemporary Problems,* Winter, 1949, vol. 14, no. 1, 21.

128 LaNoue, *Op. cit.,* 264–265.

129 *Ibid.,* 271, 273–280.

130 *Ibid.,* 271–273.

131 *Ibid.,* 273–276.

132 *Ibid.,* 276–280.

[133] *Ibid.,* 280–288.

[134] *Educational Cooperation Between Church and State* by Alexander Meiklejohn in *Law and Contemporary Problems,* vol. 14, no. 1, Winter, 1949, 66–67, 69.

[135] Confer "Why Did Many G.I. Captives Cave In?" Interview with U.S. Army psychiatrist, Maj. William E. Mayer, in *United States News and World Report,* Feb. 24, 1956, 56–72.

[136] Quoted in Dowling, *Cases on Constitutional Law,* 5th edition, Foundation Press, 1954, 1060–1062.

[137] *Meyer v. Nebraska,* 262 U.S. 390, 401 (1908).

[138] *Ibid.,* 402.

[139] *Ibid.,* 400.

[140] *Pierce v. Society of Sisters,* 268 U.S. 510, 534 (1925).

[141] *Cochran v. Board of Education,* 281 U.S. 370, 375 (1930).

[142] *Everson v. Board of Education,* 330 U.S. 1, 17 (1947).

[143] *Ibid.,* 7.

[144] *Ibid.,* 18.

[145] *Ibid.,* 15–16.

[146] *Ibid.,* 16.

[147] *Church, State and Freedom,* 476.

[148] Paul G. Kauper, *Frontiers of Constitutional Liberty* (Detroit: 1956), 136.

[149] *Zorach v. Clauson,* 343 U.S. 306, 320 (1952).

[150] *Ibid.,* 312.

[151] However, compare with the Court ruling in *Sherbert v. Verner,* 373 U.S. 83 (1963) the South Carolina case decided the same day as Schempp and Murray. This was an unemployment benefits case. A Seventh Day Adventist was out of work because she would not work on Saturdays. The Court held that she must be given unemployment benefits on the grounds "that South Carolina may not constitutionally apply the eligibility provisions so as to constrain a worker to abandon his religious convictions." Although this case does not overrule the decision in the Sunday Closing Law cases as the dissenting opinion of Justice Harlan, whom Justice White joined, insisted it did, it is an important qualification of that decision. Justice Stewart agreed with the result but disagreed with the Court's opinion. He rightly, it seems to me, pointed to the "dilemma posed by the conflict between the Free Exercise Clause of the Constitution and the Establishment Clause as interpreted by

the Court" for the disjunctive and at times contrary considerations of religious liberty and secular public law purpose, when the two are inextricably bound together in the concrete.

[152] The public service performed by the parochial schools is presently acknowledged indirectly by its tax preferment benefits. The time has come to make this acknowledgment more directly. The only justification for the exemption of private, nonprofit schools from taxation is that they are essentially public institutions in the sense that their functions of teaching and learning are performed in the public interest and to the satisfaction of public expectations. Parochial schools are tax exempt not primarily because they are church–related and their educational process is religiously oriented such as are rabbinical and divinity schools. Rather, they are tax exempt because the teaching and learning that obtains in these schools, permeated with religious values and beliefs, perform a public service by fulfilling the educational requirements set down by the state authorities. While it is undoubtedly true that the denial of tax exemption would make less feasible the efficient functioning of these schools, the primary incidence of public benefit should not be misconstrued. These schools help subsidize the educational needs of the local community. When then the government gives financial assistance to these schools in one way or another, it is acting in its own interest.

[153] *Documents, Illustrative of the Formation of the Union of the American States,* selected, arranged and indexed by Charles Callan Tansill, GPO Washington 1927, 295–96.

[154] *New York Times,* Sept. 22, 1953.

APPENDIXES

NOTE

A discourse on federal aid to church-related schools begins with a discussion of constitutionality but almost always brings in its train an array of suppositions and presuppositions. If a discussant is brought to acknowledge—if not agree with—the position of a number of eminent constitutional jurists that such aid would be legally permissive, he will most likely fall back upon considerations of public policy. It has yet to be proved that the exclusion of approximately six million students, one-fifth of America's school children, attending about 10,400 grade schools and 2,500 high schools (not counting the Hebrew and Protestant parochial school children and schools) is required by good public policy in a federally financed program whose twin goals John F. Kennedy set down as "a new standard of excellence in education—and the availability of such excellence to all who are willing and able to pursue it." Then this supposition gives way to a presupposition. What of the danger that a flourishing system of independent schools would pose to the survival of the public school system? The reasonable rejoinder is that if such a danger were a real prospect it would not be forthcoming from the parochial schools, but from the public schools. What choice would parents of students attending public schools make if they were economically free to send their children to the school of their preference? If parents still wished to send their children to public schools there is nothing to stop them from doing so. It is rather the very real prospect of an economically free choice that stirs these disturbing apprehensions about the future of public schools. It is well to bear constantly in mind that the legal existence of church-related schools is an immediate corollary of the constitutional recognition of the parents' natural right to guide the education of their children and, therefore, supplementary to this original right, of the proprietary right of independent schools to fulfill the requirement of state compulsory school attendance laws. Strictly speaking, the legal right of parochial schools to exist does not derive directly from the right of churches to have schools. Rather, the right of churches in American law to participate in public law schooling is an exercise of the proprietary right of corporations to engage in education that meets the secular educational requirements which the state has the power to impose.

Then the argument falls back upon an ulterior supposition which all along has lurked in the background and given direction to much of the prior argument. It is contended that the public schools are the principal and better instrumentalities for preparing school children for responsible and active citizen participation in American democracy. Or, in other words, the Catholic schools—here the argument rests heavily on the one particular religious confession—do not serve the public purpose as well. This is the diehard objection, impervious to enlightenment. Granting the great strides made by parochial schools, the countless degrees from secular universities which many of their teachers have, the good proportion of academic prizes and scholarships awarded them by public and private institutions of no religious affiliation, their competence and successes in the various professions and in public service, the undoubted personal sacrifices and dedications of the priests, nuns and brothers—still the product of Catholic education is a type of mind authoritarian in its sympathies and attitudes.

The hard core argument of last resort—implicitly present in most discussions and sometimes explicitly stated—is that the educational process of Catholic schools on all levels is attuned to the philosophical and theological dogmas of the Catholic Church and that the teaching of secular branches of learning, not excluding the natural sciences, must be in conformity with them. The reach of papal authority over the faithful in matters of faith, morals and church discipline, according to the argument, results in an inner finalism directed to the formation of an authoritarian bent of mind less congenial to political democracy than, say, membership in the Congregationalist Church.

While there is nothing in the conduct of Catholics and in the official pronouncements of the Catholic hierarchy in America since early colonial times to give substance to these notions, there is the "outside" evidence that is adduced to give it credence: the preferred status in public law accorded to the Catholic Church and the existence of authoritarian governments in some predominantly Catholic countries. History is brought to bear with a heavy handed imbalance to construct a credal-political formula for the Catholic faithful. The broad fact that identical and similar church-state arrangements have obtained in predominantly Protestant and non-Christian countries, past and present, on the continent and on our own shores, and that they too have engaged in religious persecution of dissenters and nonconformists in the name of the "true" religion, does not seem to stir similar apprehension in the popular mind. These are all very complex and intricate questions and the most con-

scientious scholar would have to exercise the greatest caution in sorting out facts, avowed purposes and ulterior
motivations, the confluence of religious, political, economic
and social factors, and their significance at a fixed time and
at fixed places. But the popular mind is so accustomed to
the speed of efficiency and ready answers that it has grown
impatient and perhaps too weary of necessary distinctions
and critical analysis.

The whole discourse constitutes a remarkable *argumen-
tatio elenchi,* a concatenation with no first or last link. The
advocate of federal aid for church-related schools who is
a Catholic must have to encounter an array of seemingly
endless suppositions and presuppositions. While the objections are specious and misleading, they have their roots in
profound philosophical problematics: the distinction between natural theology as a philosophical inquiry and
revelational theology, the meaning of freedom in the pursuit of truth, the significance of truth to political freedom,
the proper and correct relation of ends and values of diverse orders, intellectual realism, the meaning of human
existence, and so on.

In the 1950's there was astir public debate on the meaning and prerogatives of academic freedom in institutions of
higher learning, and the Catholic intellectual, because of
his publicly avowed commitment to dogmas, was obviously
very much a part of the discourse. Before the 1960 presidential election many honest doubts were expressed even by
men of cultivated intelligence about the independence of
judgment and faithful allegiance to the Constitution by a
Catholic aspirant to the presidency. The election of a Catholic to the White House has undoubtedly done much to
dispel many of these misgivings. However, the hard core
argument of last resort on Catholic education is still exer-

cising its influence on the thinking of a number of people. In a discussion of federal aid to education it will not unlikely reappear under the form of a protestation beyond challenge that the public school is the principal and better schooling for the development of mental attitudes favorable to democratic living.

1
ACADEMIC FREEDOM AND THE CATHOLIC INTELLECTUAL

Discussions of the past decade on academic freedom have brought to the surface not only the many issues therein involved but also the divergent vantage points from which they may be considered and, supposedly, resolved. Prevailing through most of these discussions is a persistent, ever-recurring charge that Catholics, whose religious convictions are allied to a teaching authority outside and above the individual, can scarcely pretend to intellectual liberty. Surely, it is said, a unity of faith through obedience to authority will not allow the Catholic scholar the same degree of uninhibited intellectual freedom as the scholar who is not subject to papal teaching on faith and morals. Such a prior commitment in conscience, it is alleged, is bound to restrict intellectual inquiry, scientific research and experimentation. And in light of all the incidences of adherence to Catholic orthodoxy, such as ecclesiastical review, imprimaturs, censorship and the Index, the submission to papal teaching amounts almost to intellectual servitude. The act of obedience to the Church's magisterium is considered objectionable because the faithful thereby give intellectual assent to certain propositions as dogmatically unerring. Instead of the truth making us free, we are told that we are made captive

407

by it. In a word, religious dogma and academic freedom are considered mutually opposed.

A frontal approach should be made to the innuendo lodged in the proposition that the Catholic intellectual cannot be academically free—an innuendo which says that as a sociological fact academic freedom in a community will be in inverse proportion to the Catholic population. Where Catholicism prevails, academic freedom will be extremely narrow if not extinct.

Obviously, Catholics cannot be indifferent to these imputations. Surely we should examine them because they are sometimes made by intellectuals who bear us good will. These suppositions rest on a misconception and on a controverted question, however. The misconception is that dogmas are only religious. On the contrary, dogmas are unconditional truths—as distinguished from conjectures, opinions, theories and hypotheses. They are declarative of a truth to which the mind adheres with a degree of certainty that precludes all reasonable doubt. Every science has its dogmas, including the natural sciences. Dogmas are not only the ultimate answers to some questions, they also prompt further questioning and research. Since science is the cumulated knowledge of the necessary and the universal —of what is not accidental and merely transient—the scientist is not at all embarrassed in admitting to scientific axioms.

The controverted question is how the libertarian end should be defined. It is not sufficient to inquire simply what is freedom or to engage in the endless debate of whether freedom is to be defined absolutely in a negative or positive way. The prior question is freedom of whom—only in this wise shall we begin to distinguish instinctual freedom and

408

freedom of physical movement from specifically human freedom.

Academic freedom derives from the rationality of man, who is uniquely set above and apart from the rest of the universe. Its meaning is correspondent to the nature and purpose of the intellectual activity of man, to whom God has entrusted the dominion and stewardship of this earth. Either we hold with the Greeks and the Schoolmen that the actual is real and the real intelligible and that man can know phenomenon and being with his senses and his intelligence, or we are forced to suppose that we must conduct ourselves as if these truths are so even if they are not. This philosophical make-believe helps us find our way conjecturally and pragmatically like the blind man who gropes his way by tentative touch and reaction.

But history is a stubborn witness against the protestations of libertarian rationalism. At a time when western Christendom was united by the bond of the Catholic faith, the Middle Ages produced its most unique and original achievement, the universities. Antiquity knew the schools of Athens and Alexandria, the Academy and the Lyceum of the Peripetetics, and the Porch of the Stoics. But the institutional embodiment of an educational ideal, the organization of the various faculties of arts and sciences, the interdependence of all the sciences to the full complement of learning and wisdom was a distinctly medieval creation of which our own universities are the modern heirs. What glowing memories are brought to mind when we recall the universities of Paris, Oxford and Cambridge, of Padua, Naples and Bologna, of Valencia, Salamanca and Valladolid. Though the medievalists considered theology the central and supreme science, it was far from being dominating and exclusive. The medieval universities singly distinguished themselves for their faculties of law, medicine and liberal arts as well as for philosophy and theology. Bologna was pre-eminent for its faculty of law, Paris was renowned for philosophy and theology, Salerno was the great center of medicine. Before the revolt of Luther, eighty-one universities were dispersed throughout Christendom and the majority of them were founded by papal charters. The major universities numbered from five to twenty thousand students, lay and ecclesiastic. Under the presidency of the theology of a universal faith, sciences flourished in medieval universities and thousands of students crowded to its lecture halls.

THE MEDIEVAL UNIVERSITIES

What does history record of academic freedom in the universities when the Catholic faith was all-prevailing? What effect did religious dogma and obedience to the magisterium of the Church have upon the intellectual life as exemplified in the medieval universities? Unlike the mysteries of pre-Christian pagan religions that were occult, not open to rational inquiry, scarcely cognoscible even to their custodians, the dogmas of Christian revelation broke upon new visions of truth heretofore unknown to man. St. Augustine, taking up St. Peter's exhortation to the early Christians "to give reason for their faith," gave added impetus to intellectual inquiry by his dictum, *"fides quaerens intellectum,"* which St. Anselm in turn enlarged to mean *"credo ut intelligam."* For the first time in the history of religions, Christian revelational dogma initiated the intellectual inquiry by human reason left to its own connatural powers into the existence, nature and attributes of God and his creation. The Christian conception of divine mysteries was far from an inhibiting one. Paradoxical as it may seem,

410

medieval theologians considered the greatest of all divine mysteries, the Trinity, as the most fruitful for speculation.

One can very easily enlarge upon the increased and broadening opportunities for intellectual inquiry into the nature and purpose of human existence which were provided by the Christian dogmas of supernatural elevation, original sin, the redemption or salvation through faith and charity. We have come to know about man through Christian revelation what we would otherwise not have guessed. Only the myopic mind of a libertarian rationalist can insist that a wholly secular education is necessary for academic freedom. The medieval universities give lasting testimony to the exuberance, originality and resourcefulness of intellectual activity which revelational theology animated and inspired. In Dante's *Divine Comedy,* divine wisdom is compared to "light intervening between truth and intellect"— *"che lume fia tra il vero e l'intelletto."* This was but the Psalmist's poetic exultation, *"Dominus illuminatio mea et salus mea"*—an illumination which burst upon us with the advent of the Light of the World.

The age of faith was the age of reason. Christian revelational dogma, far from being repressive of intellectual inquiry under the magisterial authority of the Church, unleashed a vigorous, intensely curious and penetrating intellectual activity. Between faith in this life and the beatific vision in the next there is an intermediary which is the understanding of faith. In this striving, the medievalist could scale heights which the pagan philosophers had dimly glimpsed. The medieval intellectual did not confuse credibility with credulity, and though many articles of faith are transrational, yet reason was impelled by the innermost dynamism of faith to strive to comprehend according to its capacities what it would otherwise never know. St. Augus-

411

tine expressed the thought of all Christian philosophers and theologians when in a letter to Consentius he wrote: "Far be it from us to suppose that God abhors in us that by virtue of which he has made us superior to other animals. Far be it, I say, that we should believe in such a way as to exclude the necessity either of accepting or requiring reason since we could not even believe unless we possessed rational souls" (Ep. 120.3: *ad Consentium*). Like Jacob, it was given to them to wrestle with God. The religious unity of the Catholic faith did not then, nor should it at any time, put a quietus on intellectual inquiry. To the medieval mind faith presupposed reason, grace presupposed nature, and revelation presupposed that God can be known to reason.

Some critics would allow that if only Catholic intellectuals would keep their religious dogmas somehow departmentalized and isolated within their minds they might still enjoy some measure of academic freedom. But unfortunately, the objection continues, they admit to philosophical doctrines. Here, too, misconception gives direction to the criticism.

Philosophical doctrines are, like religious dogmas, unconditional truths, such as, man has an immortal soul, man is a moral agent subject in conscience to the moral law of a personal God according to which he must regulate his life and which holds him accountable for all eternity. But unlike religious dogmas which are characteristically authoritarian—that is, intellectual assent to a proposition is required because of the veracity and infallibility of the divine disclosures—philosophical doctrines are held through the compelling force of rational conviction motivated solely by the evidence of the truth affirmed.

Scholastic philosophy is the most conspicuous example

412

of a philosophy animated and inspired by religion. Yet it maintained its intellectual independence. Whatever the role of authority in matters of revelational theology, in philosophy, according to the medieval maxim, authority was as good as its reason. Far more than were the seventeenth and eighteenth centuries, the age of faith was the age of reason. Abelard's method of inquiry, the *Sic et Non,* the Thomistic *videtur quod non,* and the *ego autem contra* of the Schoolmen were more characteristic of skepticism than of credulity, and it was by these critical, probing methods that the most important systems of knowledge, the medieval *summas,* were constructed. It was a time of *controversiae, disputationes, quaestiones, argumenta,* distinctions and contradistinctions. It was of the medieval universities that John Henry Newman wrote: "If ever there was a time when the intellect went wild and had a licentious revel, it was at the date I speak of." But the most remarkable phenomena of the medieval universities which flourished under the unity of the Catholic faith were the divergent schools of philosophy, Augustinianism, Scotism, Thomism and, later on, Suarezianism, plus the variations within each school. We are not making an appeal for a return to medieval intellectual life. In the ensuing centuries giant strides in the various branches of learning, if not always in wisdom, were made. Knowledge and mastery of the forces of nature and their utilization have given us amazing inventions and discoveries undreamed of in the Middle Ages.

Perhaps the principal difference between medieval intellectual life and that of modern times is that in the former the desire for knowledge was motivated by the rational conviction that human reason could know the intelligible universe and read therein the natural revelation of the divine intentions imprinted in all creation. Our

413

quest for wisdom may not be as relentless. In contrast to the modern world, the medievalists were fully convinced that there was an order of absolute religious truths, of absolute ethical goodness, of absolute political and social justice, to which all differences of opinion had to submit and by which they had to be judged. And in this quest for wisdom they did not disdain to turn to Greek and Roman pagan philosophers for assistance and enlightenment. Might not the pagan mind of today emulate this desire to know by seeking whatever assistance and enlightenment it might obtain from Christianity? We have resorted to history to bear witness against the charge that the Catholic intellectual is restrained in academic freedom to the measure of his Catholicism and the concomitant innuendo that academic freedom in the community at large is in inverse proportion to the prevalence of Catholicism.

In all fairness we must admit that the allegations are not personal, they are not directed against individual Catholics. Rather, they are an assault upon intellectual realism. They have their roots in religious agnosticism and philosophical skepticism and relativism even though, paradoxically, they are often made by intellectuals who are church-affiliated or who profess a religious belief, and who live their daily lives with many presumptions of dogmatic certitude. There are also those intellectuals who would admit to intellectual realism save for some unresolved doubts and lingering fears about the consequences that philosophical dogmatism might entail.

These fears rationally formulated are basically three: first, that a mind which admits to religious dogmas and philosophical doctrines is no longer an "open" mind; secondly, that dogmatic convictions preclude or impede pro-

414

gressive inquiry; and thirdly, that a dogmatist is prone to be intolerant with those who disagree with him.

Let us acknowledge at the outset what is undeniably true and partly the basis for the popularity of these suspicions. Who has not met those persons who claim they know the truth and are antagonistic toward those who supposedly do not; whose minds are too positive to be cautiously critical, too combative to be understanding and fair, too confident to be persuasive? They unfortunately bring disfavour upon their beliefs rather than upon themselves. But we must also allow that these mental distempers are subjective: they not infrequently stem from personal incompetence and from inexperience in the rational exchanges of the dialogue. There is, too, the limitation common to so many of us—the inability to appreciate another mind's genuine difficulties. But we can dispense with these distempers and incompetencies in our consideration because we are concerned with the virtues that ought to obtain among the enlightened, not with the failures to which all flesh is heir.

When we speak of an open mind, we generally mean a mind willing to be informed, to be corrected, eager to learn more, willing to submit acquired judgments to criticial re-examination. Greek philosophy began with a sense of wonder about reality and the intellectual curiosity to know all that could be known. It was not satisfied with sense knowledge or with a manner of living based on such knowledge. For the Greeks the actual was real and the real was intelligible and human intelligence was self-transcendent. Greek speculation—*spokeo*—was the affirmation of intellectual insight into the transempirical, the eternal verties, first causes and ultimate principles, into absolutes, natures, essences, substances and forms. The excellence of intelligence—its *arete*—consisted in the mind finding its complement in valid knowledge. For the Greek the mind was open to knowledge of reality, and found its fulfillment and perfection therein.

An open mind is one that is open to whatever is humanly cognoscible that it might adhere to truth when acquired. An open mind admits to ignorance, to insufficiency and perhaps even to dissatisfaction about knowledge already possessed; but its pursuit of learning starts with the rational conviction in the capacity of human intelligence to know. When reason affirms categorically that this is true, it does not claim it knows the whole truth or all about that particular partial truth but simply that the direct and specific contradictory is not true. And open mind that claims not only that it is ignorant but further that it cannot even know is not open at all to anything. Intellectual impotence can scarcely be the virtue of the academic and hardly the basis for any right to freedom. When human reason is confronted unmistakably with objective evidence, it cannot but register the dictates of reality. Such a judgment is dogmatic if the truth it affirms is unconditional. It does not mean that it is unquestionable and above controversy. Rather, through reflection, the prior judgment is reviewed, validated, corrected or abandoned. A mind incapable of knowing with certitude is not open—it is empty, save for the one exempt dogma of agnosticism and skepticism about the nature of the mind itself.

The justification of the academic life is to search out truths in order to discover truths. It is not the quest for truths that is important so much as is the discovery and transmission of truths. The educational experience of recorded civilization has yielded a vast store of verities in all branches of learning, including the study of man. It was one of the many profound achievements of the Greek genius

416

to have admitted to the possibility of man studying himself. The subject thus became the object and thus there became possible an intellectual realism about human values whose ultimate truthfulness transcended the historic conditions of time, place and environment. Because of this reasonable conviction, we can in our own time probe beyond the political, economic, diplomatic and military challenges of the Soviet Union and affirm that we are as certain that Communism errs in its concept of man and the meaning of human existence as we are that the whole is equal to the sum of its parts. Man is a rational being not merely because he can think but because he can know realities not of his own conjuring. And we wonder at the anti-intellectualism of those who, in the name of intellectual freedom, show so little respect for the human mind that they cannot credit it with the power to encounter and accept the natural revelations of the endless realities that have from the beginning of time waited in attendance upon it.

The second allegation, the dogmatic mind is a closed mind, does not allow for progress in learning. Certitude is somehow opposed to it. But if progress in learning means an increase of knowledge quantitatively and qualitatively, there is not only so much more to know but also the constant need to deepen and broaden our knowledge, to re-examine and explore anew many more realities in the universe. Only in this wise do our insights deepen and multiple interrelations of the order of different natures become increasingly apparent. When, therefore, human reason affirms that it knows, it does not pretend to know all reality or all about one reality but only partial reality. Nature does not leap, and neither does knowledge. The progress is not from the known into the unknown but,

417

apart from accidental discoveries, always from the less known toward the more. As long as dogmatism is correspondent with realism, it will not be stationary, fixed, self-satisfied. There is a congenital impulse of thought that will not rest satisfied with any but the whole truth. There is an ever-recurring disquiet characteristic of intellectual finalism, an essential discontent which prevents man not only from clinging to any stable form but also from being satisfied—to progress always in the direction of more truth and more of truth. Knowledge already possessed is the point of departure for the further enterprises of the intellect and an enlightened exploration of the less known. Our sciences are but an accumulation of acquired knowledge and, apart from theories, hypotheses and experiments, each science has its own deposit of firmly established facts and laws. There can be no advance in any branch of learning without continuity of knowledge. Doctrinal certainty is inherently progressive because it is correspondent with reality, whose many splendored truths are inexhaustible. To affirm or to deny is to say that we know. How can knowledge, the complement of intelligence, be its own frustration? There is a subtle sort of intellectual escapism in the skeptics' "open" mind. They fail to see that disagreement is impossible if agreement is improbable. Both in disagreement and agreement the appeal is to the evidence of reason; both in certitude and probability the evaluating judgment addresses itself to the presence or absence of conclusive evidence.

The third allegation contends that the dogmatic mind is intolerant. Perhaps the best way to discuss intellectual tolerance and intolerance is to turn to the world of science. It is difficult to imagine any university employing a professor of science who refused to admit to certain undenia-

418

ble truths about the very science he professes to teach. A medical board will not pass a student who did not recognize some uncontroverted facts and laws about the health of the human body. And yet no one would think of calling the universities or the state medical boards intolerant. The fact is that valid knowledge is intolerant of error and falsehood.

Our charity for our fellowmen does not blind us to falsehood. We do not tolerate what is false nor are we free to tolerate what is true—tolerance is not an intellectual virtue. We are not expected to accept falsehood but to denounce it; we are expected to accept truth and communicate it. We are morally obligated to seek and speak the truth. Tolerance is a moral virtue whereby we tolerate men whom we know to be in error because they too are sincerely striving for the truth. No one respects the man who deliberately intends falsehood for himself, and by communicating it intends the deception of others. Properly speaking, only he who knows the truth is capable of tolerating the person who is in error. More specifically, tolerance is an exercise of the virtue of charity which is directed to our fellowmen, not to ideas.

No scientist is wantonly free to disregard the terms of his science. Scientists distinguish quite rightly between opinions, conjectures, theories and hypotheses and axioms —the dogmas of the world of science. Why should the scientists' intolerance of error and falsehood and their insistence on the knowledge of scientific dogmas become so unwelcome and obnoxious in the philosopher? The dogmatic scientist does not claim to know everything, or even everything he is certain of; neither does the dogmatic philosopher. Investigation and research simply imply an earnest intention to attain the truth, to which all the natural sciences

419

are committed. They are bound by the methods of demonstrations and objectives settled upon by the consensual agreement of the community of scientists in each field of learning. An invasion of an alien field is allowable only by complying with the terms set by that community of scientists. But this is true of all branches of learning. The theologian who is not an astronomer is not equipped to speak for astronomy. The eminent lawyer may not speak for the philosopher or the latter for the chemist. And in all sciences the objective in general is the "find," the discovery of a fact of reality, its laws of operation and reaction. When consequent to the findings of scientists the community at large wishes to utilize the benefits of human mastery over natural energies, both the scientists and the community must come to terms with the dictates of nature. It may be more appropriate to say we must first accommodate ourselves to nature and cooperate with it before it responds to our needs and desires. The natural sciences are not embarrassed by nature's categorical "it is" or "it is not."

Academic freedom at the very least means unimpeded access to evidence. Every science reaches out to an alterity in order that it may know it and thereby come to terms with it. The moral right to academic freedom arises from the inviolability of proper action necessary to scientific employment as well as from its original source, the connatural inner dynamism of human intelligence. Implied in this moral right to immunity of action is the freedom to err: not that an individual may deliberately intend to err but that the moral right to seek out truth does not always proceed successfully and infallibly.

One might add that the right to err is an incidental of the various forms of experimentation, of trial and error,

420

so that by a process of exclusion multiple hypotheses and alternatives are narrowed and reduced to the more probable. Right to err is wholly medial; it is a necessary incidence of that freedom understood as accessibility to evidence. Strictly speaking, neither truth nor error have rights; only persons do. Things, on the other hand, may be said to be truthful but they are incapable of error and cannot deceive. Their realism and fixity of purpose and operation provide the conditions for safe living and the means of prospering. When thoroughly understood mechanism, for example, instead of shutting us in on every hand, constitutes the means at our disposal for acting upon things and obtaining power over them. Realism and intelligence are the prerequisites of free living in the midst of cosmological necessitarianism. But there is a higher world of which we humans are a part and on earth its most significant part is the life of the human spirit. What is man himself and all the social, cultural and political associations which he projects but the embodied enlargements of his spiritual capabilities? Above all else these are areas for profound inquiries among men of learning.

The philosopher who claims he has the correct philosophy of life has the burden to convince others of the same truth by appealing to the reason of his auditors and by manifesting to their intelligences the evidence that confronted his own reason. The appeal to reason is the only avenue of persuasion, and evidence is the whole force of truth. The only authentic witness to intellectual conviction is personal conscience. The philosopher's approach presupposes that all men are connaturally endowed with reason, and though his facility and experience as a thinker is superior to theirs, he nonetheless holds fast to the truth that each intelligence must see the evidence in the light of

421

its own reason before it will acknowledge that same truth. Intellectual freedom is simply concurrence of different minds on the same evidence and in the light of each one's reason, and assented to free of any compulsion save the compelling force of evidence. Needless to say, any other compulsion may exact at most a lip service judgment but it cannot bring a personal intellectual assent. Failing persuasion, there is no free disagreement or no general agreement.

To say then that philosophical dogmatism engenders political intolerance is to ignore the history of politics and to misconstrue the meaning of philosophy. Persons who deny the possibility of certitude are entitled to their point of view, but they are definitely not entitled to the privilege of feeling moral indignation at the evil which they cannot be sure ever took place, or which, if it did take place, cannot be called either right or wrong. Totalitarianism breeds on intellectual insecurity and fattens on the philosophical agnosticism and skepticism of the academy. If the philosophers cannot be validly sure of the meaning of human intelligence, then how can anyone be sure of the error of Marxism? And what would be the sense of fighting it at the cost of life and possessions? Philosophical dogma is not only the prize achievement of the free academy: it is also the condition for a free society.

The moral law is the law of human nature, not the law of men. It is no more the invention of men than fire, and justice among men is but the conformity of human choice to the principles of moral justice. Human laws do not constitute justice; they have no other purpose save to embody it. And human laws may command man's obedience only to the extent that they express a right inherent in nature, that is, the end which has been appointed to man, and over which man has no control. This is what the ancients and medievalists meant by the necessary, universal, immutable verities which invested man with a unique meaning in the universe. This too is the message of Christianity, the absolute and imperishable value of the individual: that every individual by virtue of his eternal destiny and divine vocation is at the core holy and indestructible even in relation to the highest power on earth; that the least among men have an undiminished value of their own, and not merely because they are a part of the whole; that every man is to be equally regarded by every community never as a mere instrument but as an end. And history records the relentless human struggles to surround this sacredness with legal guarantees variously denominated as franchises, liberties, privileges and immunities until finally the *homo legalis* became consonant with the *homo liber*.

It is neither fair nor correct to hold that the libertarian desires the rise of totalitarian government. The fact is that the libertarian and the totalitarian Communist are at opposite poles in their basic philosophy. The former defines academic freedom as wholly procedural, as the open market and free and peaceful competition of ideas, with cavalier unconcern for substantive truths, and representing unrestrained freedom, moral and intellectual. The latter is the most rigid thought-behaviour control ever contrived by man. But the libertarian prepares the intellectual and moral vacuum into which the heavy-booted dogmatizing state will step unchallenged. The libertarian fails the free society at the very time when the free society needs him most. He is not only by his own avowal intellectually impotent to unmask the arrogant usurpations of the dogmatizing state; he is also helpless to assert any valid and authentic rights for the academy and society. He can only confront the situation with Delphic ambiguity: correct either way. If the positive guarantees of liberty are to be claimed on the grounds of consent then its exercise must conduce to the principled direction of that consent which originates and perpetuates the free society.

A discussion which touches upon any expression of human freedom must be radical in order to authenticate its position. We can get to the roots of the problem only by asking the original questions of whether man can be free in any capacity and association, as a member of the academy and a subject of the city, within the terms of a philosophy of freedom which rejects or ignores the existence of God and his universal moral order; or of whether in such a philosophy of negation man risks the hazards of greater numbers and predominant force, of the pragmatic test of consequences, of man-made values, of a new morality of efficiency.

We are of the dogmatic mind that only by sharing the divine transcendence will man be truly free. By adhering to absolute truths he is superior to the transient and relative. By acknowledging and submitting to absolute good and divine moral law, by recognizing objective standards of social and political truths, man is able to live freely in an order that makes freedom possible.

We must consider again, then, the original question: what is intellectual freedom?

Intellectual freedom is the ability of reason to see freely for itself—even though assisted by other means—the conclusive evidence necessitating a categorical judgment. It is the freedom which human reason must have in order that it may see objective evidence for itself.

Intellectual freedom is freedom from any compulsion which either tries to impose a dogma or attempts to interfere with the full avenue to truth. To see in dogma a stoppage to intellectual inquiry or an inhibition and restraint upon academic freedom is to misconstrue the question of whether the human reason can know reality.

If the human intelligence is meant to know truths about God, the universe and human society, then the knowledge of these truths is possible because the human mind is open to them, because the increase of knowledge is ensured by certitude, and because truth, far from being divisive, is meant to be the spiritual source of agreement among men.

2

THE DIVIDED ALLEGIANCE OF THE CATHOLIC

It is an unpleasant experience in American politics that the Catholic faith of an American citizen becomes a stirring issue almost solely when he runs for the highest magistracy of the land, the office of the president of the United States. The national debates of 1924, 1928 and 1960 have made this incontestably clear. There seems to be no insurmountable problem about any other office of public trust, military or civil, federal, state or foreign service, legislative, judicial, executive. But let an American Catholic aspire to the presidency and the air is filled with refined insinuations and raucous warnings. At its worst anti-Catholicism is a witches' brew of blinding bias, inherited prejudices and stubborn prepossessions. On a much higher plane it seems possible to disengage anti-Catholicism from crude forms of bigotry and from the clutter of irrational motivations which inspired and characterized the nativist and Know-Nothing movements of the pre-Civil War period, from the American Protective Association movement after the Civil War and the repellent vulgarities of the Ku Klux Klan after World War I. Many non-Catholics of deep piety and great learning who are respectful friends of the Catholic Church have unresolved doubts and anxieties about a Catholic in the White House. We owe it to them in charity to explain our-

426

selves just as we ought to acknowledge that they are honest in their criticisms and fears.

Anti-Catholicism in its rational core is a composite of three apprehensions: a Catholic, it is said, by reason of his spiritual allegiance to the papacy, as his faith prescribes, is subject to the foreign jurisdiction of the pope, who is also a temporal sovereign. This obedience to the papacy in faith and morals, it is alleged, can and may operate in conflict with the American citizen's oath to uphold and obey the laws of his country. Secondly, the religious dogmatism of Catholicism is dialectically incompatible with political democracy. Doctrinal dogmatism and intolerance conduce to political dogmatism, civil intolerance and absolutism while, on the contrary, religious and philosophical relativism promotes civil tolerance and political democracy. Thirdly, the growth of Catholicism poses a grave threat to the existence of Protestantism. A numerically superior Catholic electorate might be tempted to change the Constitution in order to restrict the exercise of religious freedom for non-Catholics.

None of these suppositions is flimsy, nor will a satisfactory explanation dispel all lingering doubts and suspicions. The Catholic and non-Catholic worlds (and they are distinct worlds) have too long been divided by diverse histories which have engendered adverse habits of biased appraisals of one another.

First, then, let us consider the divided allegiance of the Catholic. In its most acute form this is a relatively modern problem that arose with the emergence of the national secular state and deepened with the Reformation. Historically the early Christians were the first to protest against the overweening pretensions of a pagan omnicompetent state, that "we ought to obey God rather than men," without denying Caesar's due. For centuries thereafter, long before

427

legal positivism hammered its shattering blows, all men held fast to the universal supremacy of the moral law, to the primacy of the spiritual over the temporal, to the moral and practical necessity of a plurality of allegiances complementary to one another. No one questioned the moral–legal continuum.

In the fifth century Pope Gelasius distinguished the separate spheres of jurisdiction for the spiritual and temporal empowerments. Both authorities are from God, each superior to and independent of the other in the legitimate exercise of power over the proper objects of its competence. Unfortunately a turbulent history, the unsettling of legal and political institutions by the barbarian invasions and the blending of the two powers in the same hands, now secular, now ecclesiastic, did not provide the tranquil conditions for the evolution of church–state relations envisioned by the Gelasian formula. The enormous religious and political problems that followed upon the breakup of the unity of medieval Christendom were complicated almost beyond hope by the generally prevailing consensus on all sides that political allegiance depended on and demanded religious uniformity. The Peace of Westphalia in 1648 simply froze the question without solving it by the expedient arrangement of *cuius regio eius religio*.

Our American colonists were heirs of these religious–political tensions. Many of them came to the new world to escape religious persecution and civil disabilities inflicted by the state–church establishments of the old world and then, with a remarkable loss of memory, proceeded to set up their own church establishments, often with intolerable restrictions for dissenters in their midst.

The fear of foreign domination through an ecclesiastical agency was widely evident during most of the colonial

428

period and became increasingly acute as the movement for political independence gained momentum. It was in no way exclusively or even mainly an anti-Catholic bias. Seven of the ten established churches were of the Church of England. For a complex of reasons these were without bishops during the entire colonial period despite the genuine need for their spiritual ministrations. It was feared that English bishops, being sworn supporters of the crown and members of the House of Lords, would be unlikely to support the colonies in political issues. Besides, the defection of a number of their leaders who sympathized with the British government to loyal British colonies in Nova Scotia and other parts of Canada did not endear them to the rank and file of the people as the revolutionary cause became more clearly defined. There was too much opposition from those disaffected with the course of the Reformation in the Church of England. Presbyterians, Congregationalists and Baptists viewed with alarm the prospects of an Anglican prelacy in their midst with all its historic ties with the crown and reminiscent of the persecutions they had fled from in the homeland. It is within the context of this all-pervading opposition to the presence of a foreign prelacy in the colonies that we must view the Laity Remonstrance of 1765 in which two hundred and fifty Catholic laymen of Maryland protested against the appointment of the bishop of Quebec as their apostolic vicar. Charles Carroll of Annapolis, father of Charles Carroll of Carrolton, wrote at the time to Bishop Challoner:

Your Lordship must know, yet for many years past attempts have been made to establish a Protestant bishop on this continent, and yet such attempts have been as constantly opposed through the fixed aversion the people of America in general have to a person of such character. If such is the aversion of Protestants to a Prot-

429

estant bishop, with what an eye will they look upon an Apostolic Vicar?

In 1784 the Maryland clergy addressed a memorial to Pope Pius VI in which they advised against the designation of a bishop, reporting that a superior *in spiritualibus* would suffice for the spiritual needs of the faithful. Father John Carroll, in a letter to Cardinal Antonelli (dated Feb. 27, 1785), perhaps gave the most acute expression to the colonial aversion to a foreign bishop when he urged that Rome permit the Catholic clergy to select its own native ecclesiastical superior. He called attention to the sixth of the Articles of Confederation that "no one who holds office under the United States shall be allowed to receive any gift, office or title of any kind whatsoever from any king, prince or foreign government."

Carroll was of the opinion that this prohibition extended only to those appointed to public office in the republic but added significantly, "it will perhaps be wrested by our opponents to apply also to ecclesiastical offices."

Though the construction which was rightly placed upon the Anglican bishop's tie to the British Crown should not have applied to the Catholics' religious allegiance to the papacy, nevertheless the Catholic colonials were eager not to give any grounds to this misconception. With political independence, the Protestant Episcopalian Church in the United States was freed from its oath of fealty to the Crown and gradually became entirely self-governing in its ecclesiastical jurisdiction, though it continued in regular communion with all branches of the Anglican Church. While Catholics on their part developed a native American hierarchy, the fear of popery continued to linger in American minds and at different times and for varying reasons would

430

come to the surface and even erupt into open violence. Such occasions were the rising rate of Catholic immigration, disputes about Bible reading and sectarian religious indoctrination in public schools, episcopal requests for tax support of Catholic parochial schools, and legislation about divorce, birth control and sterilization.

What shall we say about the implications of foreign jurisdiction in the Catholics' allegiance to the pope, who is also a temporal sovereign? Does this imply that the Catholic's patriotism is not entire but divided? Apart from the official doctrinal response to this charge by ecclesiastical authorities, there is an objective approach, that is to say, a consideration which transcends or cuts across religious lines, namely, the status accorded to the Holy See in international law by the practice of states.

States which in their public laws grant preferential status to different faiths—Protestant, Catholic, Islamic, Oriental —and states which profess religious neutrality have for decades recognized the Holy See to be a general, permanent and perfect subject of international law. As such the Holy See has *in its own capacity* always enjoyed the rights of active and passive legation and concluded agreements (concordats) with states. In addition the Holy See can conclude normal international treaties on behalf of her temporalities, before 1870 for the Papal State, and since 1929 for the City of the Vatican. The unique status of the Holy See in general international law consists in the fact that it is precisely as a spiritual sovereign that she enjoys the rights of sovereignty ordinarily accorded to national political sovereignty and that no other Church or religion has known the same status in the world community of states.

Sovereignty and international personality is vested with the Holy See precisely as a spiritual authority, independ-

431

ently of the existence of a papal state. From 1870 to 1929 when she was without territories her unique status remained unchanged and she continued to exercise her customary rights in international law. The reason for the existence of the State of Vatican City is wholly derivative and contingent upon the presupposition that the free exercise of a supra-national spiritual sovereignty by the Holy See is better en-sured by an independent territorial jurisdiction of its own. Prior to 1870 and subsequent to 1929 there have been two subjects of international law, the Papal States, or the State of Vatican City, and the Holy See. The pope united in his own person these two distinct subjects of international law, and of the two obviously the more important and primary is that of the Holy See. Papal nuncios and apostolic dele-gates are accredited by the Holy See, not by the papal state. Diplomatic relations by the states of England, The Nether-lands, Finland, Japan, Egypt, India, Indonesia and others are established with the Holy See and not, as is popularly supposed, with the Papal State. Their diplomatic repre-sentatives are accredited to the spiritual sovereignty and not to the temporal jurisdiction. None of these states suffers any qualms about divided allegiance or contrary allegiances and it is patently absurd to suppose that their diplomatic rela-tions with the Holy See import a confessional bias.

What then is the significance of the State of Vatican City? A study comparing it with the Holy See may make this clear. Both are subjects of general international law. The Holy See is a nonterritorial international personality; Vati-can City is a territorial international personality. The Holy See is not a state but it exercises sovereign prerogatives, including sovereignty over the Vatican State. Some writers on international law call Vatican City a "vassal" state. It is not autonomous, its existence is wholly derivative and it is subordinate to and subserves the purposes of the Holy See. Even as a territorial personality Vatican City is wanting as a state, for it does not meet the Greek requirement of self-sufficiency. There are no industrial, agricultural or commercial enterprises that could sustain an economy. Actually the state of the Vatican City, and for that matter of the Holy See, is almost wholly dependent for its financial resources on worldwide contributions of its faithful for maintenance and administration. Furthermore it barely fulfills the Roman law requirement of territorial definition and a coterminous jurisdiction. Because of its small size and because its activities and purposes are totally different from those of national political states, it does not enjoy membership as a state in the United Nations. Its constitution derives wholly from the necessity of the Holy See to be independent and free from any political domination. The spiritual office of all papal representatives is symbolically attested by the honorary precedence that they enjoy in the diplomatic corp over all political diplomats.

International law does not, of course, commit itself to any theological position. Its recognition of the nonterritorial international personality of the Holy See precisely as a spiritual sovereign cannot be construed as having any confessional implication whatever. That being so, we may add that Catholic ecclesiology, which understandably is not acceptable to non-Catholics, should be reassuring to them on this matter. The pope or bishop of Rome is acknowledged by Catholics to be the Vicar of Christ on earth. In virtue of the apostolic succession the Roman pontiff exercises a primacy of jurisdiction over all the bishops and over all the faithful. His jurisdiction extends not only to faith and morals but also to those matters which pertain to the discipline and law of the Church throughout the world. It is

433

clearly necessary that the Holy See enjoy complete immunity from the influence, dictation or interference of any national political sovereignty in the exercise of its spiritual authority over its faithful who are citizens of different national governments throughout the world. In matters touching on faith and morals the pope is never a foreigner. Wherever the Catholic faithful are, there too is the pope as Vicar of Christ, present by the universal extension of his divinely invested spiritual office.

There are also non-Catholics who readily admit to the purely spiritual allegiance of Catholics to the Holy See but who fear that this may be the very vehicle through which papal or hierarchal influence or "pressure" may be exerted upon the religious conscience of a Catholic in the exercise of his presidential duties. This fear is emphasized by the difference between the dominance that Protestant theology gives to private judgment as the ordinary guide of conscience and the deference which Catholics ordinarily and normally show to the authoritative direction of the Church. The difficulty is further confounded by the misconception about the extent of papal authority, which is considered to be so absolute and complete that a Catholic president would be inhibited in making any independent political judgments by an apparent conflict of the two allegiances. One would think that John Henry Newman had disposed of this lingering ghost by his reply to the identical allegations of Mr. Gladstone:

> When, then, Mr. Gladstone asks Catholics how they can obey the Queen and yet obey the Pope, since it may happen that the commands of the two authorities may clash, I answer that it is my *rule*, both to obey the one and to obey the other, but that there is no rule in this world without exceptions, and if either the Pope or the Queen demanded of men an "absolute obedience" he or she would

434

be transgressing the laws of human nature and human society. I give an absolute obedience to neither. Further, if ever this double allegiance pulled me in contrary ways, which in this age of the world I think it never will, then I should decide according to the particular case, which is beyond all rule, and must be decided on its merits. I should look to see what theologians could do for me, what the bishops and clergy around me; what my confessor; what my friends whom I revered; and if, after all, I could not take their view of the matter, then I must rule myself by my own judgment and my own conscience.

And in the same letter:

The Pope's infallibility indeed and his supreme authority have in the Vatican *capita* been declared matters of faith; but his prerogative of infallibility lies in matters speculative, and his prerogative of authority is no infallibility, in laws, commands, or measures. His infallibility bears upon the domain of thought, not directly of action, and while it may fairly exercise the theologian, philosopher, or man of science, it scarcely concerns the politician.

All moral obligations descend from God. A reasonable person will generally in difficult cases consult those invested with the proper authority and competence to ascertain the correct course of action. To be bound in conscience is to be bound by one's own conscience. That is not to say that it is a self-imposed obligation. Rather it is the free personal acknowledgment of what ought to be done.

Almost all theologians and political philosophers hold that the province of faith is that of the church and that politics is the proper domain of the state. Almost all agree that morality is the common concern of both jurisdictions because man as citizen and believer acts as a moral agent. This provides the potential source of conflict and friction between the two authorities, religious and secular, and it may be attributed not so much to the mutual denial of jurisdiction as to the priority and extent of its exercise.

435

The objectives of civil society are eminently moral: social justice, public order, security, peace, the legal protection of natural rights which it is not in the power of the state to deny or abrogate, such as the right to religious freedom. The distinction between positive law and morality is that of a part to the whole. The performance of a human act is always under the jurisdiction of the universal moral law. The problem arises in the pluralist interpretation and opposing application of the moral law to an action of public law. Political authority may not shirk its responsibilities in assisting the moral life of its subjects and yet on the other hand should not arbitrarily impose one moral philosophy rather than another upon its citizens. Reason would require that the political authorities should expect and welcome the efforts of all duly constituted religious authorities such as the Board of Rabbis, the Protestant Council of Churches, and the Catholic bishops, as well as private citizens to express themselves on grave moral questions affecting the public order as becomes their duty. In turn the public at large has the right to weigh the justice and reasonableness of these authoritative pronouncements, with sensitive regard for the rights of all consciences and the exigencies of public order. Where contrary and conflicting positions are affirmed then public discussion and debate should proceed on the basis of reason and with an appeal to reason. The natural law, which is the law of human nature and not the law of men, offers the most optimistic possibility for civilized men to discourse their way to agreement. The natural law remains unalterably the unitive bond of all men of different faiths, and at the same time the proper context in which to view the legitimate role of public power. This author believes the source of the difficult is generally a flight from reason, the fear that an agreement might be

436

reached which the absolutist dissenter might be required to respect.

On the American scene three specific issues are usually raised about a Catholic in the White House: provisions for a birth control program in a foreign aid bill, diplomatic relations with the Holy See and federal aid to all publicly accredited schools, including religious schools.

It is the unique genius of the American Constitution that it guarantees the exercise of religious freedom for the president of the United States without thereby impairing the operations of the political process or imposing forcibly by virtue of presidential authority his moral conscience upon others. Should a Catholic president then, in response to his moral convictions on birth control, refuse to approve it, the congressional bill might still become law automatically without his signature after the passage of the constitutionally prescribed time or by congressional action overriding the veto. Every presidential action must always be viewed within the context of the political process. One might add, too, a *sotto voce* reflection that obedience to one's own personal conscience is not always and necessarily in conformity with the publicly avowed dictates of its religious profession. Not every Quaker public officer subscribes to pacifism.

Federal aid to religious schools and formal diplomatic relations with the Holy See are nonreligious questions. They are political decisions dependent upon congressional action which is sensitively respondent to the public and ultimately subject to judicial review. No one may reasonably insist that there *must* be formal diplomatic relations with the Holy See. But to insist that they must never be established at any event for any reason may well conceal a symbolic affront to Catholics not unlike that shown to

437

past Catholic presidential aspirants. The practice of Protestant, Buddhist, Hindu, Moslem states with legally established religions and of states with separation of church and state contradicts the misconception that formal diplomatic relations with the Holy See imply a preferential status for one church or discrimination against other churches.

Our second consideration is on the alleged incompatibility of the philosophical and religious dogmatism of Catholicism and political democracy. The common Protestant assumption is that Luther and the Reformation brought freedom into the world, that American liberty is a late product of the Reformation of the same type as those liberties so loudly advertised on the European continent by anti-Catholic liberals throughout the nineteenth century. Hence it can be an occasion of sincere and agreeable surprise to discover that the American Catholic can be loyal to his country. This assumption is uncritical and wholly gratuitous because it is invalid both historically and sociologically. The freedoms proclaimed by Luther and spread by the Reformation may not be isolated from the theological and political syntheses of the various Protestant theories: justification by faith, the servile will, the debased value of human reason, the concentration in the sovereign of all external powers even where ecclesiastical matters were concerned imply rather politico–religious intolerance and a rigid religious–political structure of communities. Luther and Calvin were logical when they maintained the right of banishing or burning heretics, sectarians and all those who by denying one of the dogmas resulting from the common interpretation of the Bible denied at the same time the new Christian society and the basis of social power. As for the American experience we should not blithely forget that many of our colonial immigrants fled from persecution in

438

Protestant state–church establishments of the old world and that they in turn persecuted religious dissenters in the new world. The historical process leading to religious toleration has other theoretical and historical roots than Protestantism.

The rational misconception derives from the false juxtaposition of two different levels of human experience as though the relation between the two—and related they are—was of an arithmetic or geometric proportion. It is argued that philosophical and religious dogmatism engenders habits of intolerance for what is believed to be false, and is therefore conducive to political absolutism and civil intolerance. Such an equation misconstrues as equivalent the ends and purposes of religious and civil life. Man is determined as to his end and indeterminate as to the means for realizing his end. It is the rightful province of theologians and philosophers to ascertain the meaning of human existence and to yield intellectual assent to conclusive evidence. They are free to inquire but not free to fashion man's destiny. It is the proper domain of statesmen to contrive apt means and multiple courses of action from which a choice may be made for the governance of the civil order, ever mindful and respectful of the religious conscience of its subjects. Dogmatism in any science is an intellectual achievement; it is the goal toward which all learning strives and upon whose certainties rest the possibilities of a life of convenience without fear. For example, dogmatism in the natural sciences, instead of shutting us in on every hand, constitutes the means at our disposal for acting upon things and for obtaining power over them. A knowledge of the laws of things enables us to control them; consequently instead of checking our freedom natural physical laws make it efficacious. Religious dogmatism frees us from the phantom world of blind fate and the mythical world of demons by assuring us that we are children of God, for whose sake the world of forces and life has been created. Philosophical dogmatism tells us that men have been created equal by God and that therefore no one has by nature a right to govern another, save by his consent. Historically revolutions for political freedom have been fought by men who were willing to sacrifice their possessions and their lives for their beliefs. Conversely, theological and philosophical skepticism and relativism deprive a people of the spiritual and intellectual resources with which to withstand the pretensions of the omnicompetent state. As modern history only too patently proves, the totalitarian state steps into this intellectual vacuum and makes the arrogant claim to dogmatize (with force if necessary) not only politically but theologically and philosophically as well. If the theologians and philosophers cannot be validly sure of the meaning of human existence then how can anyone be sure that Marxism is an error? What would be the sense of fighting it at so great a sacrifice? Dogma is not only the prize achievement of human intelligence; it is also the condition for a free society.

The third consideration focuses on the fears that many Protestants have about a numerically superior Catholic electorate. Might it not be tempted to change the Constitution to restrict the religious freedom of non-Catholics? The source of these fears, European history, past and present, and our own colonial period, is creditable to neither side. Broadly speaking there have been in both religious camps two traditions on church–state relations. The major tradition would have public law confer a preferential status to the "true" religion and civil restrictions upon or civil tolerance for the dissenters. The minor tradition affirms that

440

civil society is an exigency of the divine natural law and that it prescinds from the prerogatives of revelational theology. It maintains that both religious and secular empowerments are each independent of the other and superior in their own proper domain. It is forced to recognize that there are certain common areas of morality wherein both jurisdictions converge, which provide the potential source of conflict as well as the occasion of harmonious cooperation. In America the minor tradition has gradually emerged as the major one, for Catholics and Protestants alike, in the post-Civil War period.

The Catholic record in American history beginning with Lord Baltimore's Act of Toleration of 1649 and continuing to this day is remarkably reassuring. The Catholic hierarchy, since the days of Bishop John Carroll, has without exception repeatedly professed great devotion to and grateful appreciation of the American Constitution, particularly the religious clauses of the First Amendment. Catholics as private citizens and in public office have given no cause for us to doubt their patriotism. In matters political, there is no instance of an ecclesiastical call for Catholic political solidarity. Catholics in both houses of Congress do not vote *en bloc*. And in surveys of state and municipal elections there is no consistent pattern that large concentrations of Catholic voters are committed to Catholic candidates. Catholic political solidarity is a myth.

But what of a Catholic bloc vote understood as a conscientious response to a religious position on a public law issue such as birth control and sterilization? Such controversies are inevitable wherever there is religious pluralism and the possibility of a bloc vote involves Protestant and Jew no less than Catholic. Now the political process of democratic society settles public issues through the pre-

441

sumably reasonable procedure of majority decision. In the rational and tentative expectation that the formal unit for the numerical majority be outside itself—in reason—this procedure, subject to review and reversal, allows for peaceful change and progress while at the same time it serves to express corporate capacity and responsibility. If then a group, religious or not, should express the solidarity of its convictions through the voting process, this is the expectation or hazard, if you will, inherent in the process of arriving at majority decision. The problem incumbent upon all is so to condition this democratic process that there does not ensue an arbitrary majority rule over a minority. The only possible way of resolving this dilemma in a rational manner is by recourse, through reason, to the unitive bond of the divine natural law which is the law of man and not of men. Doctrinal positions are generally affirmed authoritatively from opposing camps. Despite the agreement about the necessity and desirability of intercredal dialogue there is not in evidence as much collective and cooperative discussion as is needed. Roundtable discussions by theologians, philosophers, statesmen, which prescind without disavowing religious dogmas, might inquire into the moral laws of human nature and ascertain what, in the political order, would be in accord with them. Such collective thinking might reveal that there is much more substance than shadow in the natural law and, further, might provide the political authorities with that general consensus which legislation should recognize. What of the obdurate and exceptional dissenter? It is a strange pathology of modern politics that it abhors the absolute dictator, totalitarian democracy, majoritarian rule but cannot place in proper perspective the absolutist dissenter.

In conclusion it is suggested that a Catholic candidate for the presidency might choose, even at the cost of votes,

442

not to confine himself to a series of disclaimers on hypothetical issues. He might take a more positive approach and explain how his Catholic faith would enrich his subjective dispositions in the performance of public duties. He might, without embarrassment, point to papal teaching on social justice, on the social responsibilities of labor and capital not only to one another but also to the community at large, on the principle of subsidiarity which Pope Pius XI opposed to the monolithic state. He might call attention to the contributions of Pope Pius XII on international relations and institutions. He might explain how his faith encourages foreign aid for deeper reasons than expediency. He might explain that the opposition between Catholicism and Communism is profoundly theological and humanist; he might point out papal teaching on the necessity of never acknowledging as final the captivity of certain peoples. He might point to the remarkable agreement of certain central Catholic dogmas with the American Declaration of Independence, how the Church insists on the moral basis for education, patriotism, the fulfillment of all civic duties. The Catholic conception of the social order supports and promotes legislation for the betterment of labor conditions, of housing facilities, for economic provisions for the aged and the needy. All of these and many others are not exclusively Catholic doctrines but nonetheless Catholic they are and they should inspire the faithful in the promotion of a better and a more expansive life for the whole community. If a Catholic candidate for president is challenged on matters of his faith then he might welcome the opportunity to make it better known and perhaps better understood. Surely one would suppose that the historical record of over two centuries would disclose convincing and conclusive evidence of the patriotism of the Catholic, his devotion to the laws of his country and his full share of sacrifice in her behalf.

443

The author wishes to thank the editors of *Thought, University of Detroit Law Journal*, the *Journal of Public Law* of Emory University School of Law, *Continuum* and the Newman Press for the kind permission to use in a revised form studies which first appeared in their publications. The author is also very grateful to Mr. Justus George Lawler, the gracious editor of HERDER AND HERDER, at whose gentle and encouraging insistence he has prepared this work.

TABLE OF LEGAL CASES

Almond v. Day, 197 Va. 419, 89 S.E. 2d 851 (1955), 248

Berea College v. Kentucky, 211 U.S. 45 (1908), 392 n. 83

Bradfield v. Roberts, 175 U.S. 291 (1899), 331

Bridges v. California, 314 U.S. 252 (1941), 164

Cantwell v. Connecticut, 310 U.S. 296 (1940), 189, 204, 222, 360

Carmichael v. Southern Coal and Coke Co., 301 U.S. 495 (1937), 234

Chance v. Mississippi State Textbook Board, 190 Miss. 453, 200 So. 706 (1941), 252

Church of the Holy Trinity v. United States, 143 U.S. 457 (1892), 141, n. 15

Cochran v. Louisiana State Board of Education, 281 U.S. 370 (1930), 183, 228, 229, 233, 338–341

Craig v. Mercy Hospital, 45 So. 2d 809 (1950), 254

Engel v. Vitale, 370 U.S. 421 (1962), 117, 135, 363, 377

Everson v. Board of Education, 330 U.S. 1 (1947), 69, 160, 163, 212, 217, 234–236, 245, 341–344

Kentucky Building Commission v. Effron, 220 S.W. 2d 836 (1949), 253

Massachusetts v. Mellon, 262 U.S. 447 (1923), 271

Meyer v. Nebraska, 262 U.S. 390 (1923), 332–335

McCollum v. Board of Education, 333 U.S. 203 (1948), 45, 160, 161, 163, 181, 206, 245, 251, 275, 300, 345–348, 367

McCulloch v. Maryland, 4 Wheat. 316 (1819), 38

McGowan v. Maryland, 366 U.S. 420 (1961), 349–353

Muskrat v. United States, 219 U.S. 346 (1911), 270

Opinion of the Justices, 99 N.H. 519, 113 A. 2d 114 (1955), 252

Palko v. Connecticut, 302 U.S. 319 (1937), 141 n. 21

People v. Ruggles, 8 Johns (N.Y.) 290 (1811), 140 n. 14

Pierce v. Society of Sisters, 268 U.S. 510 (1925), 229–233, 245, 336–338

Prince v. Massachusetts, 321 U.S. 158 (1944), 361, 364

Quick Bear v. Leupp, 210 U.S. 50 (1908), 221, 332

School District of Abington Township, Pennsylvania v. Schempp, Murray, Murray v. Curlett, 374 U.S. 203 (1963), 363

445

Sherbert v. Werner, 373 U.S. 398 (1963), 399 n. 151

Swart v. South Burlington Town School District, 167 A. 2d 514 Vt., (1961), 249, 272

Torcaso v. Watkins, 367 U.S. 982 (1963), 293, 357–358

Watson v. Jones, 13 Wall. 679 (1872), 359

West Virginia State Board of Education v. Barnette, 319 U.S. 624 (1943), 204, 254, 356, 379

Zorach v. Clauson, 303 N.Y. 161, 100 N.E. 2d 463 (1951), 45

Zorach v. Clauson, 343 U.S. 306 (1952), 45, 49, 105, 134, 137, 162, 163, 210, 246, 275

Adams, John, 35–36, 53, 61
Aiken Mead Bill, 198
Aristotle, 24, 41
Army Character Guidance Program, 112, 181
Augustine, 25

Barden Bill, 199, 387 n. 64
Beale, Howard K., 186–188
Black, Hugo L., 239
Blaine, James G., 159, 180
Brownson, Orestes, 153 n. 131
Bryson, Joseph K., 180
Burke, Edmund, 33, 42
Butler, Nicholas Murray, 94, 149 n. 110

Calvin, John, 62, 438
Carlyle, A. J., 26
Carr, Peter, 75
Carroll, Charles, 429–430
Common Prayer Book, 124
Continental Congress, 33–34
Cooper, Thomas, 81, 84, 175
Corwin, Edward S., 45, 99, 170, 308

Danbury Baptists, 70, 176
Declaration of Independence, 29–31, 33, 47, 83
Dickinson, John, 28, 30
Donegan, Rt. Rev. Horace W. B., 114–115
Douglas, William O., 10, 49, 118, 121

Eisenhower, Dwight D., 37, 47, 375

Federalist Papers, 28, 44
Federal School Lunch Program, 11, 180, 200, 202
Frankfurter, Felix, 350–351
Franklin, Benjamin, 370–371

Gierke, Otto von, 139 n. 1
G.I. Bill of Rights, 180, 182, 202, 281
Gladstone, William, 434
Grant, Ulysses S., 180

Hamilton, Alexander, 88
Henry, Patrick, 169
Hill-Burton Survey and Construction Act, 180, 182, 193, 200, 215, 244
Holy See, 431–432
Huntington, Benjamin, 168, 238

Indians, Kaskaskia, 72, 179

Jackson, Robert H., 300, 367, 379
Jefferson, Thomas, 20, 49–87, 99, 126, 171–177, 208, 238
Johnson, Ernest, 151 n. 114

Katz, Wilbur G., 150 n. 113, 216
Kauper, Paul, 344

Kennedy, John F., 223–224, 402
Know-Nothings, 186, 426
Ku Klux Klan, 426

Laity Remonstrance of 1765, 429–430
LaNoue, George, 287f
Lee, Henry, 31
Legislative Reorganization Act of 1946, 180, 206, 249
Lincoln, Abraham, 36, 186, 240
Lincoln, Levi, 70

Madison, James, 30, 68, 80, 88, 166–169, 238
Mann, Horace, 102
Marshall, John, 38
Meiklejohn, Alexander, 325–326
Memorial and Remonstrance, 68, 127–128, 170
Monroe, James, 30
Morrill Act of 1862, 190

National Defense Education Act, 225, 260, 262, 273, 285
Newman, John Henry, 413, 434–435
Northwest Ordinance, 34, 153 n. 123, 177–178, 192, 205, 264
Notes On the State of Virginia, 64, 69

Otis, James, 28

Polk, James, 240
Protestant Council of the City of New York, 115, 436
Pucinski, Roman C., 289–291

Rabbis, New York Board of, 94, 436
Regents, New York Board of, 47, 89, 90, 111, 119, 123
Reserve Officers Training Corps, 180, 182, 202
Ribicoff, Abraham, 224, 275
Roosevelt, Franklin Delano, 36–37
Rossiter, Clinton, 28
Rousseau, J. J., 39
Rutledge, Wiley B., 122, 159, 170, 212, 237, 239

Smith, Mrs. Samuel Harrison, 50
Speed, Joshua, 186
Storey, Joseph, 44
Sylvester, Peter, 167, 238

Taft-Thomas Bill, 198–200
Thayer, Vivian, 151 n. 121, 295
Truman, Harry S., 36, 181, 206
Tucker, Thomas, T., 238
Tussman, Joseph, 295

United States Air Force Training Manual, 181

Vatican City, 432–433

Washington, George, 91, 120, 147 n. 76, 178, 239
Weigle, Luther A., 150 n. 113
Wilson, James, 29–30
Wright, Frances, 295
Wyckoff, D. Campbell, 151 n. 118

Yeshiva University, 257–259